THE PLO

Also by Jillian Becker

*Hitler's Children: The Story of the
Baader-Meinhof Terrorist Gang*

THE
PLO

The Rise and Fall of the
Palestine Liberation Organization

Jillian Becker

ST. MARTIN'S PRESS   NEW YORK

Library of Congress Cataloging in Publication Data

Becker, Jillian, 1932–
    The PLO: the rise and fall of the Palestine Liberation
Organization.
    Bibliography: p.
    Includes index.
    1. Munazzamat al-Tahrir al-Filastiniyah. 2. Jewish-
Arab relations—1917– I. Title.
DS 119.7.B36   1984   956'.0049275694   84-40120
ISBN 0-312-59380-5

Contents

Illustrations

Notes on Translation and Transliteration

Translations from the Arabic are by Hanita Brand, except where otherwise stipulated in the reference notes.

In general, transliteration from the Arabic is according to sound, so that the pronunciation of the original is approximated with the English spelling. However, even this principle has not been strictly observed. Some names are spelt in the way they commonly appear in English-language publications because they are familiar to many readers in these forms, and others are spelt as their owners spell them. The 'ch' form has been used for spelling Lebanese names with Roman letters, which follows the French convention used in Lebanon.

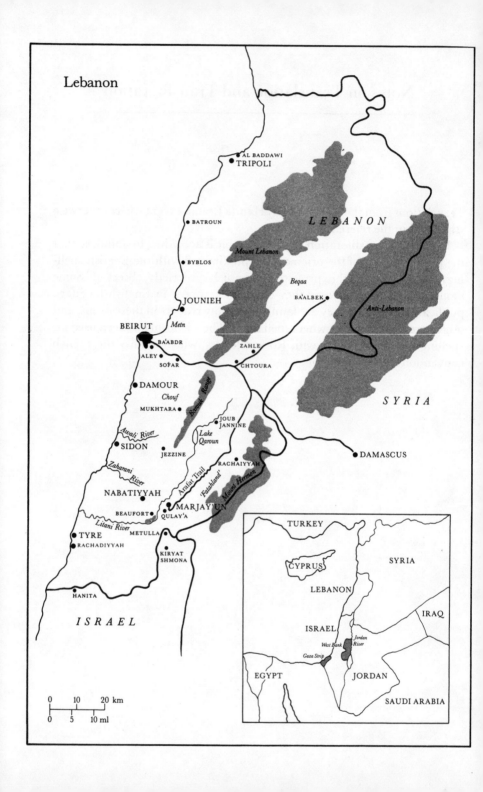

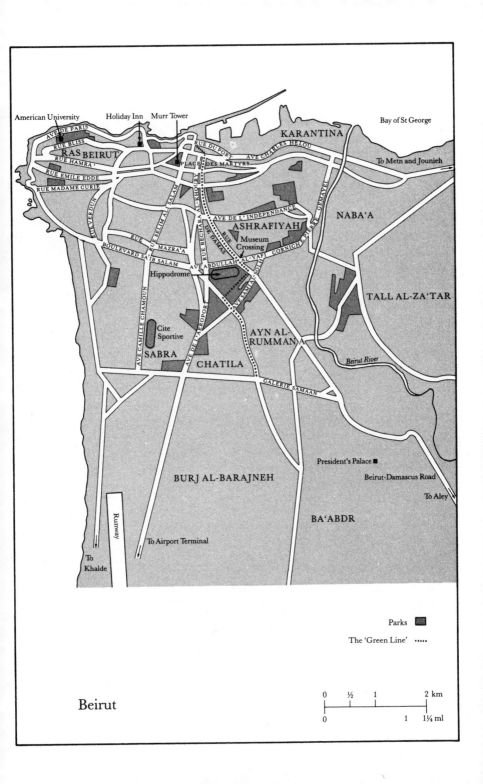

Beirut

Introduction
Wars of the Worlds

The Arab-Israel conflict has become a central issue in world politics. It affects, and is profoundly affected by, relations between the United States and the Soviet Union. The Arab states placed responsibility for their policies in regard to Israel in the hands of the Palestine Liberation Organization, a conglomerate of armed bands which the Arabs and the Soviet Union invested with enough power seriously to threaten the peace of the world. For a while this organization attained global significance, then it disintegrated. Its rise and fall is the subject of this book.

To explore the history of the PLO, I spent much of 1982 in the Middle East, mostly in Lebanon, and was there in August when the Israelis expelled the PLO from Beirut. There were wide differences between what I saw happen in Lebanon at that time, and what I read and heard about the war in Western news reports. While I read in English newspapers that Beirut had been flattened by Israeli bombing into a condition of devastation 'worse than Hiroshima, worse than Dresden', the city was standing about me. It was badly damaged in parts, with some entire streets in ruins, almost all of which had been in that state since the 'civil war' of 1975 and 1976. Local residents could remember exactly which militia or army had destroyed what. 'That was done by the Mourabitoun,' they would say, 'and that [by far the most] by the Syrians, and this, last night, by an Israeli bomb.' But it is not my intention to relate in any detail the history of the 1982 war in Lebanon, only to draw readers' attention to the fact that they have been given a distorted view of it. Plain misrepresentation in the world press of the actual events of that time did harm enough to the truth, but the gross degree of the distortion resulted from disregard of historical fact. What the world was not told was that Lebanon was destroyed by, and because of, the PLO. Whatever blame must be borne by some of the press corps for the deception, its causes are deeper than error or prejudice: the gauge of values by which events were measured had been falsified by powers and governments. Most journalists, editors and commentators could not place blame where it belonged, because those who were really the culprits had long been misrepresented as the victims. How this could happen is a question that this history may serve to answer.

Many misapprehensions about the Palestine issue have become entrenched in the popular view. Two are most prevalent and serious: one, the belief that there was a state of Palestine which was usurped by Jews, who drove out its nationals, the Palestinians; and the other, that the Palestinians have a body of chosen representatives, the PLO, to speak, act and fight for them in accordance with their wishes.

There has never been a state of Palestine. There could have been, but extremist Arab leaders made an impossible condition: that a state of Palestine must exist *instead* of the State of Israel.

The existence of Israel was intolerable to the Arab policy-makers because its territory was, in their belief, 'Arab land'. Arabs sold land to Jewish buyers, and most of the land which the Jews bought in the Palestine region was uncultivated and very sparsely populated. It was only as the State of Israel that much of it has become fertile, productive, and well peopled. (Readers who doubt that the land was for the most part barren and empty in the last century might consult the testimony of a wholly objective observer who had no admiration for either the Jews or the Arabs of the Holy Land – Mark Twain, who travelled through it in 1867, and recorded his impressions in his book *The Innocents Abroad*.)

It is interesting to compare the size of Arab territory with the size of Israel: the land area of Israel is less than a quarter of a per cent of the most conservative estimate of Arab land. Much of the latter is natural desert and so is much of Israel. There are about fifty Arabs to every one Israeli, but Israel's population is ten times as dense.

The Arabs regard this comparison as irrelevant. Contrary to widespread belief among politicians and would-be peacemakers of the Western world, it is not the size of Israel that the Arab leaders object to, but that it should exist at all. The Arab case is that Israel has no 'right' whatsoever to its existence.

After the First World War, the League of Nations allowed more than three-quarters of the region it called Palestine to become an exclusively Arab state,[1] which its ruler chose to call 'Transjordan' rather than 'Palestine', and in which no Jews have ever been allowed to live. The rest, in which both Jewish and Arab 'Palestinians' lived, was put under a British mandate until a part of it became Israel in 1948. When that happened, the Arab powers launched a war against the new state, and some 700,000 Arabs fled from their homes. However, most of the refugees remained within the borders of 'Palestine'. Some hundreds of thousands of them were deliberately kept by their fellow Arabs in a condition of homelessness. Arab leaders would not allow them a country of their own on that part of the territory which had been allocated to them by the League of Nations. Nor would they allow them to become integrated citizens of the Arab states.

It was this homelessness and enforced separateness from other Arabs which turned the Palestinian Arabs into a nation. It can therefore be said that Zionism evoked 'Palestinism'; that Israel cast a shadow – Palestine.

An almost equal number of Middle Eastern Jews were also uprooted from their homes by the events of 1948. They were very old communities. Jews had been in Mesopotamia continuously since the Babylonian captivity in the sixth century BC, and at the time of the 1948 Arab-Israeli War they composed more than a third of the population of the city of Baghdad. About 900,000 Jews had their property confiscated by Arab governments and were driven out of Arab countries. Of these, some 750,000 went to Israel. Israel gave full rights of citizenship to all immigrant Jews and to those Palestinian Arabs who remained within her borders. There, for the first time since the birth of Islam, the Jews native to Islamic countries, where they had always been discriminated against and often cruelly maltreated, had equal rights with Muslims in one corner of Asia Minor.

So there was an exchange of population between the Arab states and Israel. But the Arab case against Israel recognizes only the immigration of Jews from Europe. The argument is that European Jews came, as Europeans had come to many parts of the undeveloped world in the nineteenth century, and 'colonized' the Palestine region; that European powers planted a new population of European origin into soil belonging, by right of long occupation, to Arabs. This they see as an invasion, a conquest by aggressive, expanding powers, and they liken it to the Crusades. The Jewish claim to the Holy Land on the grounds of ancient possession and continuous presence (which, at times, was in very small numbers) is wholly swept aside.

Even if this version of the facts were true, to argue that the State of Israel should therefore not exist is to assert a principle with startling implications. If a state created by newcomers on territory where there is already a long-settled population is illegitimate, then most nation-states in the world are illegitimate, since that is exactly how most of them have been created. One obvious example is the United States of America.

What is undeniable is that Israel sticks in the Arab throat. Israel obstructs the realization of a dream which came into existence after the First World War, the dream of a unified Arab nation. At the time, nationalism was alien to the Arab world, and was fostered by the European powers, chiefly the British. It was the dream of a minority, but no less beautiful for being new and esoteric.

In time Israel, ostensibly the obstacle to Arab unity, in fact provided the Arab states with their only unifying cause. At the same time, the need for concerted action to eliminate the new nation gave rise to one of the most divisive disputes among them: which of the powerful Arab leaders should lead the *jihad*, the holy war, against Israel, and so dominate the hypothetically united Arab world.

It was in pursuit of this ambition that President Nasser of Egypt invented the idea of the PLO and persuaded the Arab League to bring it into existence by means of a resolution in 1964. He appointed its president who, in turn, gathered its membership. The PLO's purpose was to serve Nasser's own political plans. He used it not to fight Israel, but to undermine the Hashemite Kingdom of Jordan. While not renouncing the holy war, he deferred the conquest of Israel until Arab unity under Egypt should be achieved.

Syria would not allow Egypt to dominate the holy cause of Palestine. Syria regarded Palestine as Syrian territory and wanted a war to eliminate Israel first, after which unification of the Arab states could be affected with no piece of Arab land missing from the grand scheme. So Syria created units of *feda-yeen* – fighters willing to sacrifice themselves for the cause – and launched Palestinian raids into Israel, to provoke Israeli aggression and force Egypt into a belligerence which resulted in the Six Day War of 1967. Far from destroying Israel, the war left more Arab territory in Israeli hands.

Nasser and the Arab armies were discredited by their defeat. By contrast, in March 1968 the *fedayeen* achieved a 'victory' – in fact, it was a defeat, but one which cost the Israelis twenty-eight lives – in a skirmish at a Jordanian village called Karameh. This 'victory' raised morale throughout the Arab world, and lifted the *fedayeen* to such prestige that they were able to take over the impotent and moribund PLO and turn it into their own instrument.

Three of the groups which now took control of the PLO were Marxist. The Soviet Union became its most powerful patron. Syria, Iraq and Libya kept their own left-wing groups, not exclusively composed of Palestinians, within the Organization. Its general assemblies were held in Cairo, under the Egyptian government's patronage. Its funds came largely from the Gulf states. The largest faction was Fatah, whose members were Palestinian. The chief problem of Fatah's leadership was how to maintain independence of decision and action while yet being sure of all the help the Organization needed from the Arab states. The various groups used the rivalries between the states by playing off one jealous Arab government against another. But the states manipulated the Organization too.

Syria would not let it operate against Israel from her own soil, but insisted that it do so from Jordan and Lebanon. Within these two countries, the PLO proved so disruptive a force that it very nearly destroyed the Kingdom of Jordan, and it succeeded in bringing about a bloodbath in Lebanon and the disintegration of the Lebanese state.

Yet the Arab governments loaded it with ever greater powers. After the

1973 Arab-Israeli War, the PLO, in itself a weak grouping of 'splintered organizations partly ruled by criminals' (as King Hussein of Jordan has called them[2]), was given a blank cheque by all the Arab states (including Jordan) to determine Arab policy over the all-important issue of Palestine. The Arab states, in other words, put themselves at the mercy of those 'criminals'. They went further to help the PLO gain international acceptance. They backed its demands for recognition by foreign governments with the threat of cutting off oil supplies. Many Western governments capitulated to the threat. PLO envoys then sat in the capitals of countries whose aircraft the Organization blew up, and whose citizens it kidnapped and murdered. By giving all manner of aid to subversive groups of many nationalities, it spread terror on every continent. Some of those Western governments which, of necessity, had respected oil more than morals, sought moral justification for the activities of the PLO. In the light of this history, it may seem sadly ironic that they found it in the plight of the homeless Palestinian refugees, because the PLO itself became their chief oppressor.

For the Palestinians, the PLO gained no territory and no statehood. Nor did it destroy Israel. Instead, its policies and methods strengthened its enemies.

The history of the PLO is a chronicle of wrong judgements, of repeated mistakes, of lessons never learnt, of faith in wishes. It is full of cruelty, wretchedness, atrocity, violent death and the destruction of a country, all proceeding from the follies of fanaticism and self-deception. It demonstrates how some of those wars which might be called 'Wars of the Worlds' have come about, erupting where dynamic 'First World' cultures come up against and clash with stagnant 'Third World' cultures – wars which have uses and dangers in the East-West conflict, in which tyranny threatens everyone, and freedom only threatens tyranny.

Part One

1915 to 1948

While stoking the flames of Arab nationalism, the British grant the Jews a national home in Palestine. An extremist Arab leadership wants all or nothing. It gets nothing. The Palestinian refugee problem is created.

I
Promises and Dreams

The Arabs were loyal to their Ottoman overlords in the First World War, but the British incited sedition among them, bribing a man in high religious office to head a rebellion. The inducement they offered him was power and glory, rule of an Arab independency of undefined dimensions.

The man was Hussein Ibn Ali, of the clan of the Hashemites and the tribe of the Quraish, Sharif of the Holy City of Mecca, a descendant of the Prophet. The British gave him arms, supplies, subsidies and advisers. When asked also for a firm definition of his dream-kingdom, the British High Commissioner in Cairo, Sir Henry McMahon, sent him a 'clarification' in a letter of 24 October 1915, which made it clear that the British could not promise to give the Arabs territory which the French might claim; but as they did not know what the French might claim, the promises remained unclear.[1] Ever since, the Arabs have interpreted the letter one way – that the Palestine region was included in the promised Arab state – and the British another way – that it was not. The vagueness was useful. Britain's immediate need was to gain an alliance with the Sharif without promising anything that could not be denied if a different need arose later. Britain was pursuing, as states must, the politics of interest. The Suez Canal route to India was her essential interest. If she conquered the Middle East, she would try to retain control of the region and keep out the French and Russians.

Two years later, on 2 November 1917, the British government issued the Balfour Declaration, which promised the Jews 'a national home' in Palestine, provided that 'nothing shall be done which may prejudice the civil and religious rights of the non-Jewish communities in Palestine'.[2] There were several motives behind it. One was compassion for the Jewish people who had suffered persecution for centuries; another was gratitude for their contribution to mankind in general and the British in particular. Lord Balfour felt that Britain had special reason to be grateful to Chaim Weizmann, the famous Zionist and scientist, for inventing a method of synthesizing acetone which was badly needed during the First World War. But there were two more compelling purposes. One was to induce American Jews to help persuade the United States government to enter the war; another to provide a pretext for keeping that part of the Middle East from France, a keen rival for power and influence there.

In 1916 the British and French had agreed, in a secret document known as the Sykes-Picot Agreement,[3] on how they would divide up the territory between them once they had conquered it from the Turks. It was against the spirit of the times, when high principles were asserted against the old ideas of empire, principles which President Wilson of the United States soon afterwards set out in fourteen points which were later enshrined in the Covenant of the League of Nations. By the new ideal, never again would the great powers impose their will on little nations.

The Sykes-Picot Agreement fell into the hands of the Bolsheviks when they seized power, and they published it, to the embarrassment of the British and French. It was never implemented, but it is important because it shows what the Powers intended, irrespective of any promises they made.

The British made another 'promise' to the Arabs in 1918. It is known as the Declaration to the Seven. The 'Seven' were Syrians, who came to Cairo to ask the British what their intentions were in the Middle East; they were given a pledge that Britain would recognize 'the complete and sovereign independence of any Arab area emancipated from Turkish control by the Arabs themselves'. It was a rash undertaking. It may have helped to prompt a deception that was to give the Arabs a false understanding of their own military power and achievements.

In order to provide Sharif Hussein and his sons, Ali, Abdullah and Faisal, with territory to claim on these conditions, T. E. Lawrence arranged a ruse whereby the Arab rebels seemed to 'liberate' Damascus. In fact, Damascus was taken from the Turks by the Australian Light Horse Brigade, and only after that did Lawrence and the Arab forces enter the city.[4] But the British allowed the fiction of a conquest by the Arabs to be treated as true.

After the British and French won the war, kingdoms were created for the Sharifians. Sharif Hussein was made King of the Hejaz, although he did not keep his crown for long. In 1924 Ibn Sa'ud, ruler of the neighbouring Nejd, deposed him, and joined the Hejaz and the Nejd into a new kingdom which he named Saudi Arabia after himself.

Ali, the Sharif's eldest son, was heir to the fleeting kingdom of the Hejaz, so the British did not have to provide him with a throne. Iraq was proposed for Abdullah, but meanwhile, Faisal, who had become King of Syria (but only from March to July 1920), was thrown out by the French. He was then given Iraq, and the British had to find something else for Abdullah. What remained in their power to give away, or so they made out, was Palestine, over which they had been granted a mandate. So, in September 1922, they presented three-quarters of it, stretching eastward from the River Jordan to a chosen line in the desert, to Abdullah, who named it Transjordan. They also paid him a handsome annual stipend from the pocket of the British taxpayer for ruling over it.

Transjordan immediately became one part of Palestine in which the Jewish national home policy 'promised' by the Balfour Declaration was not to be implemented; although it was because of the Declaration and the duty it imposed on the British to make Palestine a homeland for the Jews that they had been granted the Mandate at the San Remo peace conference in 1920 and by the League of Nations in July 1922.

What was left for a national home for the Jews was kept from Arab control, causing discontent among the Arabs. All the newly created Arab states fell far short of Arab dreams; but in Palestine the dignitaries, the men who had had a certain degree of power under the Turks, did not gain even a less-than-satisfactory piece of reality in the new dispensation.

2
The Slaughter by the Innocents

The *sanjaq*, the administrative area, of Jerusalem had grown in importance under Turkish overlordship in the fifty years or so before the war. Although the Jews were a majority in the city, it had been the prominent Muslim families who, under the Turks, divided the chief public offices between them, not amicably but in a rivalry which created its own balance of power. Under Muslim rule the Jews were second-class citizens, known as the peoples of the *dhimma* (non-Muslim subject peoples; literally the peoples of the covenant or obligation). They suffered from numerous disabilities designed to keep them humble: they were forbidden, on pain of death, to marry Muslim women; they were not allowed to build their houses higher than those of Muslims, or to ride horses, or to drink wine in public, or to pray or mourn with loud voices, and they had to wear distinctive clothing. While it is true that some Jews rose to high rank in Islam, to honours, riches and even to power, most lived poor and insecure lives. From time to time, at the whim of individual Muslim rulers, they were massacred,[1] stripped of all they possessed, reduced to virtual slavery. The Balfour Declaration ignored these customs.

Christians too were a *dhimmi* people, but they joined with the Muslims in opposing Zionism. The Jerusalem notables formed a Muslim-Christian Association for that very purpose, while similar organizations sprang up in Jaffa and other centres.[2] There were two Muslim Jerusalemite families prominent among those who took the lead: the Husseinis and the Nashashibis. In spite of longstanding mutual antagonism between them, they joined to oppose the Jewish national home policy.

At first, the movement against Zionism among the region's traditional Arab leadership did not aim for an independent Palestinian state. The idea of Arab independence had grown along with the new idea of Arab nationalism, but in 1918 there was no Palestinian nationalism. The Arab leaders in Palestine wanted union with Syria, which was to be granted independence. The British were determined not to let this happen. The French, however, encouraged the idea, so they could include Palestine in their own sphere of influence.

The British were happy to inform the League of Nations that they intended to implement the Jewish national home policy because it helped them to gain the Mandate over Palestine, but they shirked making their intention clear to the Arabs. They delayed publishing the Balfour Declaration in Palestine for two years; so the Arabs believed that if they demonstrated their hatred of the policy violently enough, Britain would give it up. Some of the British officials on the spot in Jerusalem seeded these hopes in Arab breasts, because they flowered in their own.

The late publication of the Balfour Declaration coincided with Arab excitement over the approaching coronation of Faisal in Damascus, and resulted in an outbreak of mass anti-Zionist protests in Palestine in early 1920. The slogans were aggressive: 'Palestine is our Land; The Jews are our Dogs.'[3]

The British military authorities banned demonstrations, but there was nothing they could do about religious gatherings, even if they wanted to. An important Muslim festival fell on 4 April – Nabi Musa, associated with the 'grave of Moses' between Jericho and Jerusalem – and the celebrations, with processions, reached their climax in Jerusalem. The authorities knew that these religious festivities were to serve as a demonstration in favour of Faisal becoming king of a united Syria and Palestine. One of the British officials, quietly intent on sabotaging his government's policy, actually urged the organizers to turn the celebration into a riot.[4]

The British helped them by arranging to have the army sent out of Jerusalem, although for the past two months there had been violence in the streets and repeated attacks on Jews, which should have provided reason enough for keeping the army there now of all times. Jewish policemen too were kept off duty in the city, and so it came about that the indigenous Jewish community in their Old City quarter was left without protection.

The organizers made full use of their opportunity, delivering inflammatory speeches when the procession halted on the way to the shrines in the Old City. Most fiery among them was Amin al-Husseini. Then the small police force which had been allowed to remain, consisting of Arabs only, diverted the crowd from the usual route through the Jewish quarter. What followed was a massacre. It went on for two days. Jews old and young were beaten to death, burnt alive, stoned. Their houses and shops were looted so thoroughly that even the frames of doors and windows were torn away when everything else was gone.

When order had been restored, the authorities set about finding and punishing the culprits. Two Arabs, who had fled the country as soon as the massacre was done, were found guilty of inciting a riot and were sentenced, in absentia, to ten years' imprisonment: one was Amin al-Husseini. For good measure, a Jew, Ze'ev Jabotinsky, an ex-officer of the British army, was also convicted. He had tried to get through to the Old City with a small

Jewish self-defence unit, but had been held back by the police. For attempting to come to the rescue of the victims with armed men, he was sentenced to fifteen years' imprisonment.

A court of inquiry found[5] that the attacks on the Jews were made 'in customary mob fashion with sticks, stones and knives', and were 'of a cowardly and treacherous description, mostly against old men, women and children, and frequently in the back'.

Yet the court concluded that the blame for the massacre lay with Jews and not Arabs. Zionist 'impatience' and 'attempts to force the hands of the Administration' were 'largely responsible'. How the riot had been caused by Zionist impatience was not explained. A small amount of blame was attributed to the Military Governorate for failing to prevent the inflammatory speeches and for withdrawing troops from the city. All allegations of bias on the part of the Administration were insistently dismissed as 'unfounded'. And the British government at home was rebuked for 'interfering' with its unbiassed administrators.

The Arabs who had carried out the massacre were excused and exonerated from all culpability, on the grounds that they had felt alienated and exasperated by 'non-fulfilment of promises made to them by British propaganda' and a 'sense of betrayal' caused by the Balfour Declaration. They feared Jewish competition and domination; the court sympathized. It was the Arabs who had been victimized, subjected to 'Zionist aggression'. The findings in its own report, that the Arab leaders had inflamed the mob with 'anti-British and anti-Zionist propaganda', did not persuade the court to attach any blame whatsoever to the Palestinian Arab leadership in general.

The court did, however, quash Jabotinsky's conviction, and not the sentences on the two young Arabs.

3
The Mufti

The massacre in Jerusalem did not prevent the granting of the Mandate to Britain at the San Remo peace conference later that same month, April 1920.[1] Arab leaders resented the terms of the Mandate because they incorporated the Balfour Declaration. The Jews did not complain. Now they could surely depend on the national home policy being carried out, especially as the first High Commissioner appointed to head the new civil administration on 1 July 1920 was himself a Jew and a believer in Zionism, Sir Herbert Samuel.

Almost immediately, however, Sir Herbert gave them cause to wonder if they could rely on better protection from the new administration than from the old. One of the first things he did was grant an amnesty to Amin al-Husseini: so five months after the massacre their arch-enemy was back in Jerusalem, a free man.

Amin's older half-brother, Kamil al-Husseini, held the highest religious office in Palestine as Mufti of Jerusalem. He was friendly to the Jews and smoothed the way for a Christian power to be accepted by the Muslims. The British rewarded him well. They even gave him a promotion not really in their power to give by bestowing on him the title of the 'Grand Mufti', never before used in Palestine. After his death, on 21 March 1921, his family received a pension much larger than Ottoman law prescribed.

The election of a new Mufti had to be in accordance with Ottoman law. The Husseinis put forward Amin's name, the Nashashibis put forward a name from another family, and two other candidates were proposed by other factions.

When the election results reached the High Commissioner, Amin al-Husseini's name stood at the bottom of the list. That should have meant that he was not considered for the appointment.

He was not even properly qualified for it. The Mufti was supposed to be a man of exemplary character, and Amin had been convicted for inciting a riot. He should be learned in religion, and Amin, although he had entered al-Azhar University in Cairo, had not graduated and was not a learned man of religion. Only, in 1913, he had made the pilgrimage to Mecca and was therefore entitled to call himself 'Haj', meaning pilgrim.

Haj Amin was so certain that he would be the next Mufti that he anticipated his appointment by growing the beard and putting on the turban traditionally worn by the holder of the office.

What he was relying on was the support of highly influential British friends in the Administration, including Sir Herbert's political adviser.[2] Their own anti-Zionism, and probably anti-Semitism too, made them urge Sir Herbert to appoint Haj Amin, despite his failure in the election, his criminal record and his lack of sufficient qualification. They also made out a case for appointing an Husseini on the grounds that several members of the family had previously been Mufti of Jerusalem, so a claim had been established by custom; and one of the family should again be Mufti in the present distribution of high offices.

Finally Haj Amin owed his appointment to his extreme hostility towards the Jews, which should have been the best reason for keeping him out. Sir Herbert, it seems, was determined not to make decisions which showed any bias towards his co-religionists. He could not be accused of that if he appointed Haj Amin. And he thought that Haj Amin should be brought in to work with the administration in an official capacity, because, if he had the power to cause massacres, he must also have the power to prevent them. Haj Amin assured him that he would devote himself to keeping the peace, and, in fact, he demonstrated that he had the power to do so when the 1921 Nabi Musa celebrations passed off without violence.

So Sir Herbert Samuel made him the 'Grand Mufti'. It was the decision of a man honourable in himself and faithful to a tradition of honour, who would never betray public trust and was not sufficiently suspicious of others to believe that they might do so. But no sooner was Haj Amin appointed, than he took advantage of his position covertly to unleash more violence against the Jews. Riots broke out in Jaffa, Hadera and Tulkarm, organized and led by a terrorist group called the Black Hand. Its members swore sacred oaths to die for Haj Amin.[3]

More anti-Jewish outbreaks towards the end of 1921 at last forced the government to act with determination. Culprits were arrested and tried, and such heavy penalties were imposed that there were no more violent outbreaks for nearly eight years. The Mufti himself, however, the moving spirit of the attacks, was not punished, nor officially blamed or accused; his victims, however, were penalized by the government restricting Jewish immigration. This measure was unfaithful to the solemn duty imposed on the British by the League of Nations and it did not appease the Arab leaders.

Haj Amin proceeded to amass even more power. He gained control of the religious courts and the management of the religious trusts and foundations by bringing them under an institution called the Supreme Muslim

Council. The Nashashibis tried to prevent his election to its presidency, but failed. The Council, with its wide powers and large sums of money which he was never called upon to account for, was turned into his personal political instrument.

With shrewd imagination, Haj Amin took advantage of the religious identification of Muslims as a means to gain support for the Palestinian Arab cause throughout Islam. His Supreme Muslim Council suddenly discovered an urgent need to carry out maintenance work on the two great mosques in the Old City of Jerusalem, al-Aqsa and the Dome of the Rock, and the work had to extend into that part of the sanctuary area which joined the Wailing Wall, the holiest of holy sites to the Jews. As Haj Amin had expected, the Jews saw the 'repairs' as desecration. They offered to buy the Wailing Wall and the area in front of it to save it, but the Supreme Muslim Council refused to let it go.

Next the Council complained about the Jews bringing chairs to the area. What with their attempt to buy the space near the Wall, and their bringing chairs to it, it was evident in the opinion of the Council that the Jews intended to take over the Muslim shrines in the sanctuary. Haj Amin tried to fabricate these designs on the part of the Jews into a scandal of global dimensions. Notification of this threat to the Muslims was sent to the pilgrims at Mecca, to Syria, Egypt, the Yemen, and as far afield as India. Money was raised in all Muslim countries to restore the shrines: Haj Amin received so much that he was able to have the Dome of the Rock covered with gold. As Islam became more aware of Jerusalem than ever before, the Mufti rose in importance, and his cause became a matter of increasing concern far beyond the borders of Palestine.

But still the Jews continued to bring their offensive furniture to the space in front of the Wailing Wall, so the Council made a place for loud Sufi ceremonies beside the Wall, and a new path for crowds to walk directly in front of it.

There was nothing the Jews could do. The British authorities ruled in favour of the Mufti: the Jews should not offend Muslim religious suscep-tibilities by bringing chairs and things to the Wall. Much encouraged, the Mufti decided that the next step must be an outburst of uncontrollable righteous indignation.

In August 1929 his followers fell upon the Jews. It was nothing less than a pogrom, the worst massacre of the Mandate period. A hundred or more Jews were killed in Jerusalem, Hebron and Safed. Again a British commission of inquiry blamed not the Arabs, but the Jews. Zionist activity in the country, the commission said, had provoked the violence all of a sudden, it had not been premeditated.[4]

The Supreme Muslim Council, the committee members of the Muslim-Christian Associations and the Arab newspapers all insisted that there had been an organized attack by the Jews on the Arabs. But then some of the Arab leaders changed their minds: four years later a Palestinian leader, Emil al-Ghuri, writing about the 'August revolt' on its anniversary, claimed it as a deliberate and noble act undertaken by the Arabs on their own initiative. He called it a day of 'brilliance and glory', of 'honour, splendour and sacrifice'. It was, he said, an attack on 'Western conquest, on the Mandate and the Zionists in our land'. The provocation came from the Jews' 'yearning to take over the Muslim holy places'. The Muslims had borne with this yearning in silence, but the Jews had read this as 'a sign of weakness', which was too much to bear. 'There was no more room in our hearts for patience or peace; no sooner had the Jews begun marching along this shameful road than the Arabs rose, stopped the oppression, and sacrificed their pure and noble souls on the altar of nationalism.'[5]

The sacrifice of Arab souls and Jewish lives brought the Arabs their reward. The British Colonial Secretary, Lord Passfield (Sidney Webb), issued a White Paper in October 1930 which tightly restricted Jewish immigration and land purchase. The condition of the Mandate that Jews were to be closely settled on the land was proving an annoyance and inconvenience to the mandatory power, thanks to the efforts of the Mufti. His reputation as the most important Palestinian Arab leader was greatly enhanced when his 'revolt' elicited the concessions from Lord Passfield.

However, there were still influential members of the British establishment who did not believe the Jews should be punished for the violence of the Arabs. The White Paper was repudiated, and the Prime Minister, Ramsay MacDonald, reassured the Zionists that the new restrictions were not, after all, to be imposed. The letter carrying the news was called the 'Black Letter' by the Arabs. They saw it as the breaking of yet another 'promise'. Their resentment was stoked up by the Mufti, and the spirit of militancy grew. Haj Amin's appeal to religious feeling was bringing gratifying results and he pressed on with it. In 1931 he convened a world Islamic conference 'in defence of the Holy Places' in Jerusalem, under his own presidency, to keep up the agitation among Muslims everywhere against alleged Jewish encroachments.

He fought on the political front as well. Other factions among the traditional leadership tried, by means of deputations and petitions, and sometimes strikes, to influence British policy. But the Mufti would not tolerate the more peaceful methods of his rivals and set out to destroy such influence as they still exerted by using armed gangs.

Between 1932 and 1935, political parties were formed among men of education, such as mayors, teachers, businessmen and lawyers. In December 1934 the Nashashibi faction formed the National Defence

Party, which was opposed to Zionism but sought accommodation with the Jews and co-operation with the British.

In March 1935 the Husseinis also formed a party, called the Palestinian Arab Party. It was, as its president Jamal Husseini freely boasted, inspired by German Nazism. It included a 'youth troop', modelled on the Hitler Youth, for a while actually called the 'Nazi Scouts'. The Mufti was on friendly terms with the German consul in Jerusalem and told him that the Muslims of the world, for whom he apparently felt he was spokesman, hoped for the spread of fascism to other countries and would assist a worldwide anti-Jewish boycott.[6]

Throughout the Mandate period, all the anti-Zionist factions continued to protest to the British government against the Jews being permitted to buy land. If nobody had been willing to sell, the Jews obviously could not have bought, but Arab owners eagerly took advantage of a booming market, even acquiring new properties in order to sell them.[7] But small and medium landowners sold to Jews at their peril. The transactions were often made in secret through impersonal agencies.[8]

Large landowners had acquired great estates in Turkish times by taking over the fields of the peasant-farmers who were deeply in debt to them. Often peasant owners would ask a rich and powerful landlord to let them register their land in his name to avoid being taxed into even deeper debt. Great landowners were themselves the tax-farmers, so in the one capacity or the other they took from the peasants the little that they had.[9]

These great landowning families were the ones who sold most land to the Zionists. Some lived in neighbouring Arab countries, but some in Palestine. They could not be stopped because they were the same families, and often the very same individuals, who led the anti-Zionist movement and worked hardest at preventing lesser men from selling Palestinian land to the Jews.[10]

A number of the Husseinis sold land to the Jews,[11] though not Haj Amin himself. It was a practice that particularly infuriated the Mufti. He preached that it was a crime against God. Heavy punishment was meted out to smaller landowners who dared to sell. They were beaten, their property was destroyed, and some were killed by armed bands under the Mufti's direction.

Under his patronage, terrorist groups proliferated in the 1930s. The most important was founded by another extraordinary fanatic, a Syrian named Izz e-Din al-Qassam. He was a religious sheikh of al-Azhar University, a teacher and preacher by profession, and was over fifty years old when he formed his organization to kill Jews in the cause of Arab nationalism. Al-Qassam had had experience of guerrilla warfare in Syria, where he had fought against the French when King Faisal was driven off his throne. Sentenced to death by a French military court, he had fled to Palestine, where he taught at an Islamic school in Haifa. He was an outspoken supporter of Haj Amin. He preached an austere, puritanical creed, of the Hanbali school of Islam, to which Haj Amin was also partial, and in which Ibn Sa'ud, the Wahhabi King of Saudi Arabia, was a believer. It forbade fornication, gambling and drinking; but to kill, to wield the avenger's sword, was a proof of purity of faith. Self-sacrifice was the noblest of all ideals. Those who embraced it were the *fedayeen*. An old idea in Arab history, the holy assassin, was being given new life in the twentieth century.[12]

In 1925 Qassamite cells began to be formed, but became active only in 1931. Then Qassamites began to attack the guards of Jewish settlements and to ambush travellers on the northern roads. In 1932 they killed four men. The murderers were caught and one of them was hanged,[13] but the Qassamites were not discouraged. Their most active years were yet to come.

In November 1935 a cargo of cement was being unloaded from a ship in Jaffa port. One of the crates burst open to reveal guns embedded in the cement. More guns were found in the cargo and were confiscated by the British authorities. They believed that the guns were intended for the Jews.

Izz e-Din al-Qassam saw this as his moment of destiny. If the Jews were arming themselves, the time had come for guerrilla war. On 6 November 1935 he took to the hills of Samaria. One of his followers was instructed to sell all his belongings and give the money to the resistance organizations. In the hills he and his armed band prayed five times a day, read the Qur'an, listened to the teaching of their leader and set out with their guns.

On 7 November they shot and killed a Jewish policeman in the mountains of Gilboa. Twelve days later the police caught them. Five were captured, two escaped and three were killed in the skirmish. One of the three was Izz e-Din himself.[14]

At once he became a legend and an inspiration to the cause of Palestinian nationalism, one of the supreme martyrs of the resistance. He has remained so ever since.[15]

His band did not break up after his death. It was unique in that its members were from among the common people. Some say they were peasants and workers, others that they were ruffians and indigents.[16] Whatever they were, they were not from the wealthy and powerful class – which is worth noting, because a popular anti-Zionist movement had not emerged in any other shape, for all the Mufti's efforts to create one.

Most Arabs reacted with sound commercial sense to the changes that Jewish immigration had brought. They shared in the benefits of growth. As swamps were drained, the land began to flower as never before, old cities revived and new towns were built. More and more Arabs came from all over the Middle East to share in the work and the profit (a fact which is frequently omitted from discussion of the history of Palestine in the Mandate period). Jewish immigrants needed permits to enter the country, so the Jews already there worked hard to create new jobs to justify applications for them. The system was intended to protect Arab labour, but instead any job a Jewish employer had to offer would necessarily be reserved for a Jew. On the other hand, the country's economy expanded, and there was more for everybody, Arab and Jew alike.

Then came the Great Revolt of 1936 to 1939, and the new comparative prosperity of the Arabs was seriously harmed.

4
The Great Revolt

In the middle of April 1936 Qassamites forced two Jews off a bus near Nablus and murdered them. Two days later a Jewish group, which was soon to give birth to the Irgun Zvei Leumi, killed two Arabs in retaliation.[1]

As the month went on Jews attacked Arabs and Arabs attacked Jews, and the police clashed with both. The government imposed a curfew and declared a state of emergency throughout the country.

The Mufti organized a strike in Jerusalem. Husseinis and Nashashibis came together to deal with the crisis, and they formed a committee with the heads of all the political parties called the Arab Higher Committee. The Mufti was its president. It kept the strike going. The intention was to bring the country to its knees and compel the British to stop all Jewish immigration, prohibit the sale of land to Jews, and to permit a national government.

Arabs had little enthusiasm for the strike. The peasants did not join in, and the fruit farmers, faced with the prospect of huge losses, soon gave up. In general, it affected the Arabs adversely and benefited the Jews. Jewish labourers took over the unloading of ships; Jewish wholesalers and retailers sold more goods. And as most of the main industries had been created and were owned by Jews, the strike could not in any case bite deeply. The main sufferers were the poorer Arabs; the main effect was a change for the worse in relations between Arabs and Jews.

The leaders had to resort to intimidation. Scouts and other youth organizations acting as spies tried to prevent Arab shopkeepers opening their businesses. The obstinate were made to suffer. Garbage was thrown into their shops and many of them were beaten. Some officials, such as mayors and police officers, were murdered by armed bands.[2] A bomb was thrown at Hasan Shukri, the Arab Mayor of Haifa, who was friendly to the Jews.[3] That such drastic measures had to be resorted to could be taken as a sign that the Arabs generally had no strong wish to fight against Zionism.

The violence escalated. Jewish factories and shops were looted and burnt, orchards were cut down. Haj Amin's nephew, Abd al-Qader al-Husseini, and the Qassamites openly rebelled against the British authorities with arms and explosives. The Qassamites became the organizers and commanders of other bands. Many of them died in battle or on the gallows.

The Arab states reinforced the rebels by sending in volunteers under a former Ottoman officer, Fawzi al-Qawuqji who titled himself 'the Commander of the Arab Revolt in Southern Syria (Palestine)'. They demanded their supplies from the villages with menaces. At his headquarters in the mountains, al-Qawuqji tried 'traitors' in a kangaroo court and ordered cruel punishments and executions.

'Relief' funds raised in the Arab states and India for the Arab population were channelled through the Mufti and the Arab Higher Committee to the armed bands.[4] Secretly, since neither the Nashashibi representatives on the Committee nor the government should know it, the Mufti directed the revolt through the agency of his kinsman Abd al-Qader al-Husseini.

It took about five months from the start of the strike and revolt for the British army to quell the rebels. When the Arab Higher Committee realized that the strike, such as it was, could not be kept going, they tried to find a face-saving formula. They suggested that the British government should request the kings of Iraq and Saudi Arabia to ask them, the Arab Higher Committee, to call off the strike. The British refused, but suggested the Committee do it themselves. King Ghazi of Iraq and King Ibn Sa'ud of Saudi Arabia were asked to make the request, they did so, and the Committee complied by calling off the strike.[5]

The government gave the armed bands one week to disperse. All did except for Fawzi al-Qawuqji's volunteers. When the army surrounded their base in the Samarian hills, the Arab Higher Committee hurriedly requested that they should be given free passage out of the country. This was agreed, and they returned to Iraq from where they had come. The Arab Higher Committee had to pay them to stay there; and the British government, acting weakly, allowed them to keep their arms in Palestine.

Towards the end of 1936, a royal commission under Lord Peel arrived in Palestine to inquire into the causes of the 'disturbances'. Haj Amin wanted Jewish immigration suspended while the inquiry was going on. When this demand was refused, he decided that the Arab Higher Committee should boycott the Commission of Inquiry.

The Mufti asked that all the 'promises' of the past, including the Hussein-McMahon correspondence, and contradictions between the Mandate and the League of Nations Covenant be examined again, so that the question of Palestine might be considered in the context of Arab independence. The Nashashibis wanted only Palestinian matters to be dealt with: Jewish immigration, land sales, and the establishment of a national government. They decided against the boycott.

Haj Amin refused to call it off. Again the Arab kings were appealed to, to ask the Mufti to do what his committee wanted him to do, and again Haj Amin obliged them.[6] But he threatened the life of one of the Nashashibis,[7] and the whole family resigned from the Arab Higher Committee, leaving it in the hands of Haj Amin. The old battle-lines were drawn again – Husseinis against Nashashibis – and, with greater fury than had been exerted against the Jews or the British authorities, Arabs went to war against Arabs.

In the middle of 1937 the Peel Commission recommended that Palestine be partitioned between Arabs and Jews: 85 per cent to go to the Arabs, the Holy Places to be placed under a new mandate, and the Galilee with a strip of coast to become a Jewish state.

The Nashashibi faction accepted the proposals, but then many of them were attacked and murdered by the Mufti's followers.[8] They changed their minds and rejected the plan after all.

Haj Amin solicited the support of the Arab states against partition, and Egypt, Iraq, Lebanon, Transjordan, Syria and Saudi Arabia rejected the plan. Under Fawzi al-Qawuqji, preparations for restarting the rebellion were begun at once, this time without the Nashashibis. As the bands had kept their arms and ammunition they were able to start fighting again with little delay.

Jews were killed savagely and indiscriminately in the fields, on the roads and in their houses. The Irgun retaliated. (Contrary to a belief that seems to have become entrenched in British lore, terrorism by Jewish groups was never, either then or later, sanctioned by the Zionist authorities. They condemned it roundly, took active measures against it, and preferred to fight the Arab rebels by co-operating with the British army, especially in the intelligence field. Captain Charles Orde Wingate trained and commanded the Special Night Squads consisting of members of Haganah, which was an illegal but regular Jewish defence force. With the commandos of the Palmach, it was to evolve into the army of Israel.)

This time the government took stronger measures: the Arab Higher Committee was declared illegal and its members were arrested and deported to the Seychelles; the control of the religious trusts was taken away from the Supreme Muslim Council and put into the hands of civil servants; Arab terrorists were arrested by the score, and the leader of the Qassamites was hanged.

Haj Amin eluded the police by retreating into the Haram al-Sharif, the sanctuary area of Jerusalem. Some days later he slipped out disguised as an Arab peasant woman and, for the second time, smuggled himself out of the country. For a while he lived in Damascus and directed the 'Central Committee of the Jihad', which became the rebel headquarters in exile.

His campaign against moderate Arabs intensified. Arab policemen, lesser landowners reported to have sold land to Jews and suspected informers were mercilessly flogged, tortured and executed by slow and agonizing means. Some were thrown into pits with snakes and scorpions. Bodies were left in the streets with shoes stuffed in their mouths as a sign of dishonour. No *imam* (priest) dared to bury them.[9]

The Nashashibi faction, its ranks decimated by terrorist murders, came over almost wholly to the side of the authorities and began to organize against the resistance. They turned to Jewish neighbours to help them with money and advice.[10]

The rebels did not win in the field, and yet the end was a victory for violence and extremism. The Mufti was granted what he wanted: the British bowed to his demands and withdrew the partition plan.

They did even more to satisfy the Arabs. Suddenly, at this late date, Britain saw the Balfour Declaration as a mistake. The only solution for Palestine, the government decided, was for British rule to continue – but with an eye to an eventual settlement that would secure the land as an Arab state. With another world war threatening, the British were again in a mood to placate the Arabs. The old Hussein-McMahon correspondence was taken out and examined. Any justifiable fears they might have had about placing power in the hands of leaders who had treated their own kind with such brutality were suppressed. With an optimism stemming from no discoverable cause, the British put their trust in the Arab states to have a moderating influence on the militant Palestinians. This was to prove a fatal error.

A conference was called in London. The Nashashibi faction – which had given support to the government, had declared that the terror of the last three years proved Palestine could not be self-governing and had asked for the restriction, but not the prohibition, of Jewish immigration and land purchases – did not come to speak for the Palestinian Arabs. Instead, the British negotiated with the Arab Higher Committee, brought from exile in the Seychelles. Of those responsible for the terror, the murders, the tortures, the destructive uprising, the only one not welcome in London was Haj Amin himself (who was in Lebanon at the time). Nevertheless, the Arab Higher Committee, insisting that its members were 'the sole representatives of the Palestinian Arabs' (against any claims by the Nashashibi faction), elected Haj Amin its nominal head. Again face had to be saved, so it was announced that the elected leader was remaining 'voluntarily' in Beirut.

A Palestinian Jewish representation attended the conference too, but the Arabs insisted on sitting separately, so two parallel conferences took place. Yet it was called the 'Round Table Conference'.

Britain conceded almost everything the Arab representatives demanded.

After all those years and all the fever and the fret, they agreed to stop Jewish immigration and land buying. In that year of all years, the very year when war broke out, 1939, when the Jews had the most desperate need they had ever had for a place of refuge, the British government brought out a White Paper which restricted Jewish immigration to Palestine to a total number of 75,000 for five years, after which Arab consent would be necessary for any more immigrants – a restriction tantamount to a total ban.

The Jews were incredulous and appalled. Of necessity, they were staunch allies of the British, but their national home was about to be closed to them by the same power which had opened its doors in the first place. They determined to fight the White Paper by every means, even while they fought with the British forces against the Nazis. There was strong opposition to the White Paper within Parliament (Winston Churchill, for one, opposed it), but the authorities took all measures to implement it zealously. So much so that the first people killed by British soldiers after the declaration of war on Germany in September 1939 were not Germans but Jews, on the shores of Palestine.

The Arab Higher Committee, which is to say the Husseini faction under Haj Amin, had gained everything by terrorism, except their greatest wish. They now also wanted the guarantee of an independent Palestinian state. If this were not promised, Haj Amin would have his Committee accept none of the proposals. It was to be all or nothing.

But on that supremely important point the British, at that time, were not ready to give in. Because the guarantee was not given, the exiled Mufti and the armed rebels rejected all the hard-won concessions which the British were now prepared to pour into their laps and declared that the revolt would go on. Not unreasonably, they concluded that if they had won so much with violence, more of it would surely win more.

When Haj Amin rejected the proposals, so did all the Arab states, except Transjordan.

5
Palestine Lost

If Britain's purpose in retreating from the national home policy was to gain the goodwill of the Arabs, it failed. This was made plain enough as soon as the White Paper was rejected by the Arab Higher Committee and the Arab states. Yet the rejection changed nothing; the White Paper stood. And although, in the following years, evidence mounted that the Arab world as a whole heartily loathed the British and longed for a German victory, still the British turned ships full of Jewish refugees away, sending many Jews back to Europe and into the hands of their killers – as if this human sacrifice would eventually make the Arabs love Britain.

The British could not give up their own Middle Eastern dream. Between 1941 and 1945 the Foreign Office and the office in Cairo promoted the idea of a united Arab nation. Britain would be its patron in its youth, and its friend ever after. It was taking time to achieve, and no one could say that much progress had been made either in unifying the Arabs or befriending them, but a start had been made. That had been at the end of the last war, and at least it was still there when the next one began. The start consisted of one Hashemite ruler on a throne in Baghdad, and another in Amman, both put there by Britain.

Haj Amin al-Husseini did his best to overthrow the Hashemite dynasty in Baghdad. He went to Iraq soon after the war broke out and was received with honour by the Prime Minister, Nuri al-Sa'id. Although the Regent, Abd al-Ilah, and the Prime Minister were pro-British, they let the Mufti have whatever facilities he needed to carry on his struggle for an independent Arab Palestinian state.[1]

A 'Palestine Defence Society' in Baghdad raised money for 'the victims of the Palestine revolt'.[2] Its members were either very cynical indeed, or did not know that the majority of the victims of the revolt in Palestine were the snake-bitten, scorpion-stung, flogged, widowed, orphaned, dispossessed victims of Haj Amin al-Husseini, to whom they gave the money. Haj Amin spent it on continuing his intimidation of Palestinian Arabs and damaging Britain and the Jews by devious means.

The Iraqi government gave him a generous grant of money for the running of his office. He got five times as much again from Hitler and Mussolini.[3]

After he had taken enough from the funds to provide himself with his personal needs, he put the remainder to work for the cause of the Nazis. He planned to undermine the British and encourage support for Hitler.

With this aim, he plotted the destruction of his hosts. He conspired with the German legation and anti-British factions in the government and the army to bring about a *coup d'état* in 1940. It failed, but in 1941 the rebels tried again; this time the Regent was forced to flee the country and the new government declared war on Britain. The British sent troops from India and Palestine, and units of the Arab Legion from Transjordan. They crushed the revolt, and the Regent returned. The British attached importance to keeping their man in power, representing as he did half the total result in twenty years of striving to win the affiliation of the Arabs. While they were in charge, a mob descended on Jews and perpetrated a massacre. In June 1941, 400 members of the Jewish community in Baghdad were murdered, and their property looted and destroyed.[4]

Haj Amin had flown again, this time to Iran, where he sheltered first in the German, then the Bulgarian and then the Japanese embassies. In October 1941 he went to Italy, and Mussolini housed him in a grand villa near Rome. Before 1941 was out he had moved on to Germany.

The Third Reich provided him with everything he needed to make anti-British and pro-German propaganda in the Middle East. He organized a spy service for the Nazis that extended through the Arab countries and North Africa. He had sabotage groups working behind British lines. His agents smuggled information in and out of Lebanon, Syria, Iraq, Palestine, Transjordan and Egypt, making daily reports to Berlin through secret radio transmitters. As Mufti of Jerusalem he was able to help the creation of Muslim SS units in Yugoslavia.[5]

The Mufti expected two rewards. The first was the extermination of the Jews. Fervently he encouraged the Nazi policy of genocide. He became a close friend of Adolf Eichmann, chief executor of the policy. He went to Auschwitz to see for himself the work in progress and literally gloated over the mass murder of the Jews.[6]

The second reward was not plainly promised, but not likely to be kept from him. One day, when Hitler won the war, Haj Amin would be the head of a *judenrein* Arab state, not necessarily only in Palestine: the victorious Germans could, and should, make him head of a vast unified Arab state covering the whole of the Middle East.

With Hitler's defeat that dream was lost. As the allied armies advanced to final victory in May 1945, Haj Amin tried to escape to Switzerland. He was caught by the French, who requested him to confine himself to the pleasant house in a Paris suburb which they made available to him. He should have been tried for war crimes, but he was an enemy of Britain, the power which had encouraged the independence of Syria and Lebanon from France. So the French authorities looked the other way while he slipped out of the country.

In Cairo Haj Amin was warmly welcomed again, this time by King Farouq. From there he resumed control of his Arab resistance movement in Palestine, the 'Army of Salvation' and a paramilitary youth organization, ostensibly a scout movement, called Futuwwah.

After the war, in 1947, Britain handed over responsibility for Palestine to the United Nations. In November of that year a partition plan was proposed for the territory. There was to be a Jewish state and, for the first time ever, an Arab Palestinian state. The Jews accepted the offer; Haj Amin rejected it. He wanted all the territory. He would not accept the existence of a Jewish state in Palestine.

It was a disastrous decision. If ever one man brought ruin to millions, it was Haj Amin al-Husseini. Unlike Hitler and Stalin, he managed it without the apparatus of state and army.

But states and armies bowed to his extremism. He rejected partition, and the Arab states rejected it. They too wanted all or nothing. They did not want the territory in question necessarily for an independent state of Palestine, but it had to remain Arab, so that it could be included in the one great united Arab and Islamic state they dreamt of. And if they were not to be given all, they would take it by force.

The majority of the people were not asked whether they would accept something rather than nothing, or whether they would care to fight to the death to get rid of the Jews. It was not for them that every last piece of land was to be wrested into Arab hands. Their overlords never had and did not now show the least concern for their wants or welfare. When the Arab people started to flee by the tens of thousands five months before the British left, they were forsaking not 'Palestine', not a political entity at all, but their homes, their fields and orchards, their villages and the life they were used to. It was to these they hoped to return. And among the several hundred thousand Arabs who were displaced by the war, many were no more deeply rooted in Palestine than the Jews from Europe.[7] They went out of the way of the war to other parts of the same Arab world. The political issues over which Haj Amin and the Arab rulers were prepared to go to war were not issues that moved them deeply. They saw no need to take up arms. Palestinian nationality did not exist where its only existence could have been, in their own claim to it.

It needs to be emphasized that at the time the territorial dispensations were made, when new states were being created with arbitrary boundaries where none had been before, the contenders were, not the Jews and the 'Palestinians', but *the Jews and the 'Arabs'*. One minority living in the region,

the Jews, were allotted a minute portion of the territory; the vast remainder
went to the Arabs. (In 1984, the size of the Jewish State is less than a
quarter of 1 per cent of Arab territory, and the Arabs have some two dozen
states.)

Not even among the traditional leadership was there any effective opposition to Haj Amin left by 1948. The years of terrorism had broken the will
to resist in rich and poor alike. Hundreds of the rich and influential left
before the fighting started, abandoning the uneducated to whatever
pressures might be brought to bear on them, and setting an example of
flight as the best solution. Whether or not the Arab leaders told their
people to flee has been debated ever since. There is much evidence that
they did, and that the voice they obeyed was the Mufti's.[8]

The Arab armies were waiting to invade as soon as the British withdrew. They had even begun to advance from Syria before the British had
departed, and the British had not tried to stop them.

In the north of the country, the Jewish forces deliberately emptied the
Arab villages of Beit Jiz and Beit Susin[9] to establish a 'belt of security'.
This, they said, was a military necessity. The Irgun justified their attack on
the friendly village of Dir Yasin, in the second week of April 1948, on the
same grounds. Warning was given, but at Dir Yasin many villagers of all
ages stayed in their houses and died in the onslaught when it came.[10] This
act contradicted the pleas of the Haganah, put out in leaflets in December
1947 and distributed in the Arab villages, asking the people 'to choose
peace', and promising that if they acted peacefully they would not be
harmed 'in the course of our self-defence'. While the Jewish authorities
condemned the Dir Yasin killings, the Arab leaders were to hold up Dir
Yasin as a proof that 'the Zionists' had driven the Palestinian Arabs from
the land by a deliberate policy of terror. No such intention can be proved.
The act was done, but it was not decisive in its effect on the Arab people. It
was the war as a whole that they fled from.

On 15 April the Haganah engaged and drove back the main Arab forces
under Fawzi al-Qawuqji; in the following few days took Tiberias and
Haifa, and on 14 May, the day the last British High Commissioner left
Palestine, captured Acre. By this time thousands of Arabs were pouring
out of the country.

David Ben-Gurion proclaimed the establishment of the State of Israel on
14 May 1948, appealing to the Arab population to stay and 'play their part
in the development of the state, with full and equal citizenship'.[11] The
armies of Egypt, Lebanon, Syria, Iraq, Transjordan and Saudi Arabia
invaded, certain of victory.

The process begun by the British shortly before the Second World War,
by which the Arab states had become involved in the affairs of Palestine in

pursuit of a well-established, yet wholly fantastic, British dream of 'a great Arab confederation',[12] had become an inescapable factor. Oddly enough, in retrospect, one of the main protagonists of the policy was Sir Herbert Samuel.[13] He believed the involvement of the Arab states would help a peaceful acceptance of a Zionist state in the region. As a result of this policy, the Arab League had come into existence, encouraged by Britain and sponsored by Egypt and Iraq.[14] Palestine had been made the business of the Arab rulers. They were to use it as it suited them, in pursuit of their own ambitions, which took no account of the people of Palestine.

Mortifyingly, the Arab armies were defeated by the Jews, who fought desperately for their small piece of the earth. Very small it was in the vast expanses of the Arab territories and growing multitude of Arab states.

When the ceasefire came, those parts of Palestine which were not yet lost should have been formed into a state of Palestine. But three neighbouring countries took them: Syria annexed the small town of al-Hamma in the north of Galilee; Egypt brought the Gaza Strip under its own military administration, and Abdullah of Transjordan annexed the ancient biblical lands of Judaea and Samaria lying on the opposite side of the river from his emirate, which, with the Old City of Jerusalem, came to be known as 'the West Bank'.

Abdullah was formally invited to annex the territories by the anti-Husseini factions at a conference in Jericho on 1 December 1948. Two years later the joining of the two banks of the river under Abdullah to create the Hashemite Kingdom of Jordan was completed. Only two governments, Great Britain and Pakistan, recognized the new kingdom. The Arab states, jealous of the aggrandizement of any rival, opposed the annexation. Haj Amin bitterly attacked Abdullah, who compounded the offence by showing a willingness to make peace with Israel.

In September 1948 Haj Amin set up a 'government of All Palestine' under Egyptian auspices. By 'All Palestine' was meant the whole of the area which had been under the British Mandate. The 'government' adopted for 'Palestine' the flag of the Hashemite Sharif of Mecca, although the Sharifians were among the most hated enemies of Haj Amin and his followers. It was designed by another despised enemy, Sir Mark Sykes, co-author of the Sykes-Picot agreement, and it has remained the Palestinian flag.

In July 1951 King Abdullah was assassinated in Jerusalem by an agent of Haj Amin, inside the al-Aqsa Mosque when the King was coming from prayer, his grandson Hussein walking beside him.

Haj Amin himself suffered a political demise. The Egyptian government dissolved his ineffectual 'government', which, in any case, had only been a fiction with little to rule over and few powers granted to it by its Egyptian overlords to rule with.

So at last Haj Amin al-Husseini lost even the shadow of power. Blamed and discredited, he retired to Lebanon, where he lived out his days in obscurity and luxury. He died in his villa near Beirut on 5 July 1974. He never recovered his influence, and his name was execrated by the younger generation of Palestinian intellectuals. His, they said, was the 'generation of disaster'.[15]

Yet, moved by the same ambitions, the new generation was to strive for the same absolutist ends with the same extremist methods.

Part Two

1964 to 1967

Arab states create the PLO and *fedayeen* groups to use in their rivalry with each other for prestige and power. The Palestinian refugee problem is made worse.

6
The Founding of the PLO

The Palestine Liberation Organization was invented by Egypt's President Jamal Abd al-Nasser, and founded in 1964 by the Arab League under his auspices. It was in the line of policy begun by the British to make Palestine the business of the Arab states, and of the dream of a united Arab world which the British had fostered. In its first four years, only its rhetoric was militant. After that it was to undergo a transformation into a match and a successor of the earlier extremist, terrorist movement of the Mufti, and become a power in the Middle East.

Nasser's dream was of a united Arab world under the hegemony of Egypt. Israel impeded Arab unity by occupying 'Arab land'. To avenge the 1948 defeat and destroy Israel was a sacred goal, but Nasser had reason to postpone making a direct attempt to achieve this.

He had become Prime Minister in 1954 and President two years later. At once, in a revolt against Western domination of Egypt, he had turned away from the West and looked for friendship with the Soviet Union, first for the financing of the Aswan Dam, then for military aid. Summarily, he nationalized the Suez Canal. Britain and France, joint shareholders in the Canal, after battling and intriguing for so many years to secure their interests in the Middle East, lost their ownership at a stroke.

Nasser proceeded to close the Canal to Israeli ships, and to blockade the Gulf of Aqaba and the Straits of Tiran. To Israel, this was cause for war.

Both Britain and France wanted to recover the Canal. France found extra provocation in the open assistance Nasser was giving to the rebels fighting French rule in Algeria. These were reasons for them to invade Egypt, but it seems that the two governments wanted a more morally impressive cause. So they entered into an arrangement with Israel whereby Israel struck into Sinai on 29 October 1956 to start a war, and on 5 November Britain and France invaded Egypt on the pretext of restoring peace between the belligerents.

The United States intervened and persuaded the British and French to withdraw, and Israel to relinquish Sinai which she had conquered. The Soviet Union looked up from its preoccupation with crushing a revolt in Hungary to complain about British and French imperialist, neo-colonialist interference in the internal affairs of another country. A United Nations force was interposed between Egypt and Israel. Long-standing and long-ignored guarantees to Israel of freedom of navigation were confirmed by Britain, France and the United States.

Nasser had suffered a total military defeat, yet the resolution of the war was a personal triumph for him. America had turned his defeat into a kind of victory and given a tremendous boost to his prestige and therefore to his power in the Arab world. Had he not successfully defied the might of France and Britain, taken the Canal under his own control and got back the territory seized by Israel? The enhancement of Nasser's image as the strong man of the Middle East enabled him to pursue his pan-Arab dream, but with a change of tactics.

Egypt's second defeat by Israel on the battlefield convinced Nasser that the destruction of the Jewish State by force as a first step towards creating a vast Arab republic was not a practicable plan. Instead, Arab unity would be achieved first,[1] and then a strong Arab world would wipe Israel off the map.

He set about the business of bringing other Arab states under his domination, by persuasion or force.

On 1 February 1958 Nasser took a stride towards his goal when he united Egypt and Syria. The United Arab Republic (UAR) was proclaimed. Cairo was its capital and Nasser was its president. For the Syrians, the 'unification' was more like an occupation of their country by Egypt, with Nasser as dictator ruling through his representative Field-Marshal Abd al-Hakim Amer. The following month the UAR and the Yemen formed a confederation called the United Arab States.

Among the Muslims of Lebanon, smouldering pan-Arabism and a sense of Islamic solidarity, and a burning passion among some factions for Nasser's combination of nationalism and socialism, were fanned into flames by the creation of the UAR. A pro-Nasserite faction so aroused Muslims against Christians that a civil war erupted in 1958. The United States helped the Lebanese government to restore order.

Nasser's agents and sympathizers were everywhere. In Baghdad officers sympathetic to 'Nasserism' were plotting the destruction of the monarchy and the death of the young King of Iraq. In the thirty-seven years since the British had created the Hashemite Kingdom of Iraq, there had been fifty-seven ministries, a history of instability with numerous uprisings, massacres and barbaric assassinations.

The Regent, Abd al-Ilah, uncle of the young King Faisal II, had ambitions of his own for Iraq to dominate an Arab unity embracing Syria, Jordan, Lebanon and Kuwait. In February 1958 he achieved a union between Iraq and Jordan, the two remaining Hashemite kingdoms. This was as intolerable to Nasser as the union of Egypt and Syria in the same month was unbearable to Abd al-Ilah.

Under pro-Nasserite leadership, a contingent of Iraqi troops despatched by the Regent to help quell the pro-Nasser uprising in Lebanon turned instead on their own ruling house. At dawn on 14 July 1958, Faisal was murdered, along with his grandmother, his aunt and others in the palace, including an orphan boy. His uncle, Abd al-Ilah, was dragged through the streets of Baghdad tied with ropes to the back of a truck, then his body was dismembered with axes and his limbs and head tossed about by the hysterical mob. The trunk was hung from a balcony and chunks of its flesh were sliced off and thrown to the crowd below.[2] The Prime Minister, Nuri al-Sa'id, disguised himself as a woman and tried to escape, but he was found and instantly killed, and his body was left lying on the road to be driven over and squashed and broken by the cars of exulting motorists.[3] He was succeeded for a brief period by General Abd al-Karim Qasim, who led the revolt and the massacre and who favoured friendship with the Soviet Union. After five years Qasim too was murdered and his body devoured by dogs.

In one of many attempts to destroy the other Hashemite kingdom, Nasser's agents killed the Prime Minister of Jordan in September 1960, with a bomb which exploded in his office at a time the King was expected to be there.

By these means Nasser hoped to unite the Arab world. But even such unity as he achieved, intended as a great beginning, did not last long. In 1961, after a *coup d'état* in Damascus, Syria revolted against Egypt's domination and reasserted her independence. This meant that the United Arab States was also dissolved, so the Yemen was theoretically set free again. But in 1962, when Ahmad, King of the Yemen, died, a group of army officers, supported militarily by Nasser, seized power and proclaimed a republic. This *coup* brought Egypt into conflict with Saudi Arabia. Five years of war followed, during which Nasser's forces, aiding the republicans, engaged the monarchists, who were aided by the Saudis.

Manifestly, the desire for Arab unity was the chief cause of Arab disunity.

By 1963 Nasser was seeking new means of bringing the Arab states together under his leadership. Verbally at least, the Palestinian cause, which was also of course the anti-Israel cause, was a unifying factor. The humiliation of the conquest of Palestine by the Jews was shared by all the Arab states, and the potency of that common emotion was what Nasser hoped to draw into his hands by creating a 'representative' Palestinian organization.

To be of the greatest utility, it needed to be legitimized by the Arab

League. Nasser called a meeting in Cairo of Arab heads of state, the kings and the revolutionaries, to discuss the one question which could bring them together: Israel and the Palestinians.

In January 1964, at this first Arab summit conference, President Nasser of Egypt proposed the establishment of the Palestine Liberation Organization (Munazzamat al-Tahrir al-Filastiniyya). The proposal was approved, and money was voted for it.

Nasser had chosen its president, and the conference duly appointed him. He was Ahmad Shuqairy, a lawyer[4] whose family came from the Acre region of Palestine. His father, Assad Shuqairy, had played an important part in the resistance movement in Palestine before the war of 1948, and was known as 'the leader of the North'. He was one of the leaders who had complained about Arabs selling land to the Jews, yet at the same time had done it himself.[5]

Ahmad Shuqairy had represented Saudi Arabia at the United Nations, where he had gained the reputation of being a windbag (in that great orchestra of wind!). He lost his post when he made statements not approved by the government he represented.

In the September before the Arab summit, Shuqairy had been invited to 'represent Palestine' at the Arab League, in disregard of objections raised by King Hussein of Jordan. The King had sound reasons for objecting both to Shuqairy's position in the League, and to the creation of the PLO.

Most Palestinians lived in Jordan, so the granting of separate represent-ation to the Palestinians in the League was a threat to the Jordanian government's authority. King Hussein could hardly fail to see the PLO for what it was. He and his kingdom would be the first target of Nasser's new instrument designed to bring every Arab state into Egypt's dominion. Because his approval was necessary to Nasser, the King was promised at Cairo that the freedom of action of the PLO would be 'limited', a word which left much room for suspicion.

Between January and May 1964, Shuqairy set about touring the capitals of the Arab states 'to select members to serve as representatives of the Palestinian community', as an official PLO account has explained the method of forming the Palestinian National Council.[6] The official account goes on:

> Preparatory committees and subcommittes set up by him were entrusted with the task of nominating and preparing the final list of members. When the Council met in May, its members were mainly Palestinian notables – usually elected Pales-tinian public officials and middle-class professionals and businessmen. The elected officials included members of the Jordanian Parliament and that of the Gaza Strip, and mayors and presidents of urban and rural councils. The profes-sionals consisted of categories as varied as clergymen, pharmacists, professors,

lawyers, doctors, engineers, businessmen, bankers, and industrialists. To round out the Council, farmers, labour leaders, and representatives of refugee camps and women's and students' organizations were included. In all, 422 members sat in the Palestine National Council. If, like most parliaments, they were not equally representative of all social classes or categories (there were only twelve trade unionists and ten representatives of women's organizations), they did reflect the geographical distribution of Palestinians rather precisely.

This is clearly an attempt to show that the Council could reasonably be described as 'representative'. But even if the so-called 'elected' public officials had ever been voted into their posts (as some were to the Jordanian Parliament), they were not elected to the Palestinian National Council. The idea that 'all social classes and categories' needed to be represented was to be regarded as an advance on the traditional view of representation among Palestinian Arabs – 'notables and dignitaries of the country . . . sheikhs of the towns and villages',[7] an aristocracy whose authority was traditional and not subject to any check from a popular electorate. No doubt the authors were aware that there were shortcomings in the system by which the 'representative' Council had been formed, which may have been why they slipped in the phrase 'like most parliaments'.

Even the PLO publicists' claim that 'representation' was a 'rather precise' reflection of the geographical distribution of Palestinians does not stand up to examination. Their own accompanying table indicates that while 15,000 Palestinians in the Gulf States were 'represented' by eight members and 5,000 in Libya had ten, Saudi Arabia with 20,000 members had none. And the Israeli Arabs were not listed at all. The largest contingent was 212 members for the Palestinians of Jordan, numbering over 1.5 million.

The founding conference of the Palestine National Council was held in May and June 1964 in Jerusalem. King Hussein had no choice but to give it his blessing, but he made it clear that he did not want it to operate in his territory. On 1 June 1964 the PLO declared its resolutions. Its goal was the liberation of Palestine. The National Council would be the sovereign body of the Organization, and would meet regularly. A National Charter and Fundamental Law – drawn up by Shuqairy himself – 'were adopted as the basic constitution'.

The National Covenant (or Charter) declared that 'Palestine is an Arab homeland', and that Arab unity and the liberation of Palestine were two complementary aims. This view plainly bore the mark of Nasser. A proclaimed intention was to 'forge a Palestinian consciousness' in the present generation. It condemned Zionism as imperialist, racist and fascist. And the Covenant specifically denied that the PLO had sovereignty over the West Bank of Jordan (annexed by the Hashemite monarchy), Gaza (taken under Egyptian administration) or the al-Hamma region (annexed by Syria). So the territory over which sovereignty was claimed proved to be the territory of the State of Israel, no more and no less.

A fifteen-man Executive Committee was appointed 'with autocratic power in it vested in Shuqairy himself as Chairman of the Committee and Spokesman of the Palestinian National Council'; a Palestine National Fund was to be set up 'to draw contributions from all Palestinians'; and there was to be a Palestinian Liberation Army (PLA) 'under the control of the PLO'.[8] In the event the Arab states would not permit the PLA to be under the control of anyone other than themselves. The units were composed of Palestinians, but were under the command of the military chiefs in the various Arab states where they were formed.

The headquarters of the Organization were to be in Jerusalem and branches were to be opened in other Arab cities. It was planned from the beginning to establish offices all over the world for the purpose of disseminating propaganda.

Shuqairy proclaimed that the time of exile had come to an end. A new phase, of unity and self-organization, was beginning.

But unity was not achieved. Enthusiasm and consent were not unanimous. Opposition to the Council came from some half-dozen Palestinian 'revolutionary' organizations (there were several dozen of them in existence at this time), which formed themselves briefly into the Political Bureau for United Action of the Revolutionary Palestinian Forces. They declared that, although they 'would not stand in the way of the proposed Palestinian entity', they 'doubted that an official entity would succeed in isolation' from themselves.[9]

At the time opposition from such small groups could not have seemed a threat to Nasser and his scheme to institutionalize Palestinian resistance under his own control. He was, however, reckoning without Syria.

7
Fatah

The Syrians would not permit Egypt to steal a march on them by taking charge of the Palestinian cause.

The Ba'thist ('Revival') Party[1] had come to power by *coup d'état* in 1963. Like Nasser, the Ba'thists were nationalist and socialist. Their dream also was of a united Arab nation, but under their own hegemony. The Palestinian issue was as useful to them as it was to Egypt.[2]

So, in the latter half of 1964, after the formation of the PLO under Egyptian auspices, the Syrians began to build up a rival Palestinian organization of their own. Agents of Colonel Ahmad Sweidani, head of the Army Intelligence Department, went to work in the refugee camps in Lebanon, recruiting Palestinians to be trained as *fedayeen*.

One of the agents was approached in Beirut by eight men who had formed a group of their own called the Movement for the Liberation of Palestine.[3] Their names were Yasser Arafat, Salah Khalaf, Khalil al-Wazir, Khalid al-Hassan, Farouq Qaddoumi, Zuhayr al-Alami, Kamal Adwan and Muhammad Yusef. They described themselves as the collective leadership of their movement. But before long Yasser Arafat was to emerge as its leader.

He was born in Cairo or Gaza[4] on 27 August 1929; his full name was Abd al-Rahman Abd al-Rauf Arafat al-Qudwa al-Husseini. His mother, Hamida, was a cousin of Haj Amin al-Husseini. His father, Abd al-Rauf al-Qudwa, was a wealthy businessman of Gaza and a member of the Muslim Brotherhood. This Islamic fundamentalist organization was founded in Egypt at the end of the 1920s by a schoolteacher named Hassan al-Banna. It was a religious movement which used terrorist methods. The Muslim Brothers preached a holy war against the occupying British army. Nasser himself had been a member of the Brotherhood for a brief period before he came to power. Afterwards he found them a nuisance and a danger, and imprisoned many of them.

The al-Qudwa family moved back to Gaza from Cairo in 1939, and lived there during the Second World War. Rahman was given the name 'Yasser' by one of his schoolteachers, Majid Halaby, with whom he had a homosexual relationship. Halaby was a half-Christian Lebanese who served as a secret radio operator for Haj Amin al-Husseini's propaganda organization, assisting the Nazis with information from Palestine. Before the war, he had been a member of a Qassamite group led by one Yasser al-Birah. It was in memory of al-Birah, killed by the British while trying to smuggle German guns into Palestine, that Rahman al-Qudwa was renamed by his friend.[5]

In the later 1940s 'Yasser' belonged to the Husseini faction's Futuwwah group, a youth organization which devoted itself to the blood-feud with its counterpart, the Najjadah of the Nashashibis.

In 1951, when he was twenty-two, he enrolled in a civil engineering course at the King Fuad University in Cairo under the name Yasser Arafat. Four years later, after Nasser had become Prime Minister and was calling for a war of vengeance against Israel, Arafat received some military training along with other young Palestinians. He returned to the University of Cairo (as the King Fuad had been renamed) and helped to form the General Union of Palestinian Students, of which he was elected President.

In Cairo he met Salah Khalaf and Khalil al-Wazir, two Palestinians from Jerusalem who were to become his closest associates in his political career.[6] Salah Khalaf was born in 1933 in Jaffa. He went to school in Gaza, where he became the leader of a Najjadah pack.[7] In 1951 he qualified as a teacher in Cairo, then, with Khalil al-Wazir, underwent commando training in a Gaza brigade of the Egyptian army, which had been created by Nasser to make raids into Israel.

Arafat, Khalaf and al-Wazir went to Europe in August 1956[8] to attend an international student congress under Soviet auspices in Prague. They did not return to Cairo, but went on to Stuttgart with a fellow Palestinian studying at Stuttgart Technical University, Zuhayr al-Alami. He was a nephew of Musa al-Alami, who had been a high official in the Mandate. The al-Alami family was one of those which sold land to the Jews, while playing a leading role in the campaign to stop the sales.[9]

From Stuttgart, Arafat applied for a job in Kuwait, working as a civil engineer for the Kuwaiti government's Department of Water Supply; he was accepted and Zuhayr al-Alami went with him.

Arafat formed a construction company and recruited Palestinians to work for him. Among them was Farouq Qaddoumi, who became one of Arafat's close political collaborators. Work permits were acquired for Khalaf and al-Wazir, and Arafat sent for them to join him. Al-Wazir arrived not with Khalaf, but with another Palestinian student from Stuttgart named Khalid al-Hassan, who had been in Algeria and had made contact with the National Liberation Front (FLN). Al-Hassan did not stay long, but he influenced the others to think in terms of organizing armed resistance to Israel, holding up the FLN as an example of what a popular movement can achieve. They agreed among themselves to form the Movement for the Liberation of Palestine.[10]

Salah Khalaf, looking back in 1978 on the early history of their movement, said[11] that 1961 was the year in which it flowered: that it was unified with 'some thirty groups' which had arisen in Kuwait, and also with the organization of Yusef al-Najjar, Kamal Adwan and Abu Mazin, which had operated from Qatar and Saudi Arabia. The break-up of the Egypt-Syria union had disappointed the hopes of many Palestinians who had believed that the achievement of Arab unity would secure them their national sovereignty. They turned to movements such as theirs, Khalaf suggests, when Nasser's way was seen to have failed.

Arafat has related[12] that in December 1962 the group met Ben Bella, the triumphant first President of newly independent Algeria, who agreed to their opening an office in his capital. All Palestinians would have to register to get permits to work in the country; the permits would be granted only if they agreed to pay a percentage of their wages to the cause. In readiness to receive the funds, Arafat opened a bank account in Beirut, in his own name. The office he and his friends were given was on Victor Hugo Street in Algiers and was called the office of the 'Palestine National Liberation Committee'.

Even more helpful was Ben Bella's offer to train Palestinians in guerrilla warfare. Khalid al-Hassan, through a small committee he had formed in Stuttgart, persuaded some hundreds of Palestinian students in Germany and Austria to go to Algeria for training.

What then became of the sizeable membership of the Palestine Liberation Movement? It was a small enough group, eight people, when it finally emerged into the public eye in 1965.

Apparently, it was the formation of the PLO in 1964, to which the Palestine National Liberation Movement had expressed its opposition along with other 'revolutionary' groups, that reduced its membership and put an end to its promising growth; not only because young Palestinians were attracted away from it to the PLO, but because Algeria diverted the money it collected from its Palestinian workers to the new organization and closed the training camps. The collective leadership of the Movement was at a loss to know how to proceed.[13]

It was then, in late 1964, that Sweidani's agent found them. He gave them their first assignment immediately. They were to write the announcement of a raid on Israel's National Water Carrier, which was to be damaged with explosives on the night of 31 December–1 January. Israel had built it to channel water from the Sea of Galilee after the Arab governments had rejected any regional water scheme which would mean their co-operating with Israel, and it had aroused passionate opposition from Nasser and the Arab states.

Arafat and his comrades wrote about the raid as if it were already accomplished, and a triumphant success. The announcement was headed 'Military Communique No. 1'.

> Depending on God, believing in the right of our people to struggle to regain their usurped homeland, believing in the duty of *Jihad*, believing in the revolutionary Arab from the Atlantic Ocean to the Gulf, and believing in the support of the world's free and honest men, units of our strike forces moved on the night of Friday 31 December 1964 to carry out all their assigned operations inside the occupied land, then returned safely to base. We warn the enemy against taking measures against Arab civilians, wherever they may be, because our forces will reply to their attacks with similar attacks and will consider such actions as war crimes. We also warn all countries against interfering on the side of the enemy in any way, because our forces will riposte by clearing the way to the destruction of the interests of these states, wherever they are. Long live the unity of our people and their struggle to regain their dignity and homeland! Signed: the General Command of al-Asifa Forces.[14]

The announcement was to make the group known to the Arab world. However, the name which very soon became famous was not 'al-Asifa', the Storm (which they kept thereafter for the military wing only of their organization), but 'al-Fatah'.

There had been an earlier 'al-Fatah' in Syria, a pan-Arabist association active at the end of the First World War, and one might suspect that Arafat's Syrian patrons now gave his group this name. However, Arafat and his comrades have maintained that they chose the name for themselves. They arrived at it, they say, by taking the initial letters of Harakat al-Tahrir al-Filastini (or in full Harakat al-Tahrir al-Watani al Filastini), the Movement for the (National) Liberation of Palestine, and reversed them. They did this because the letters H, T, F would carry, in the Arabic roots, a connotation of sudden death. In reverse, F, T, H, they spell *Fath* – or, as it is usually spelt in Roman letters, *Fatah*. They admit that they did not use the name at first,[15] but they insist that they did choose it themselves, perhaps to stress that they are a genuine Palestinian movement which did not come into existence under the sponsorship of any Arab state. 'The founders of Fatah', Salah Khalaf says, 'had sworn to resist any temptation to link the Palestinian movement with any state, whatever the price to pay for its success.'[16]

Whether or not the group had adopted the name before Sweidani's sponsorship, it was only then that 'Fatah' became significant; and the importance of the name lies not in its origins but in its meaning, which is not just 'conquest', but 'conquest by means of *jihad*'.

Copies of the announcement were dropped into the mailboxes of all the larger Beirut newspaper offices. It made headline news the next day. A successful raid on Israel had been carried out by a group called Fatah, the newspapers proclaimed.

But in truth it had not. It is a curious fact that this first elevation of Fatah .9..into public notice, its first step on what was to become a steep climb into world renown and power of a unique kind, was the result of a mistake, a falsehood, news of an event which did not take place.

A raid had been planned by Syrian officers. Six semi-trained recruits were to be sent across the border from Lebanon into Israel. But then, almost at the last moment, one or more of the recruits shirked it and reported the plan to the Lebanese authorities. All six of the raiders were arrested.

The Beirut newspapers were informed that their news had been false, but it made no difference to Fatah. Its 'achievement' had been established. Fatah was praised in newspapers and on radio all over the Arab world, although Egypt, Lebanon and Jordan officially condemned such irresponsible action. On the other hand, and not surprisingly, Syria applauded it. The delight of Yasser Arafat, Khalil al-Wazir, Salah Khalaf, Khalid al-Hassan, Farouq Qaddoumi and Muhammad Yusef took in their new celebrity was too great to be dampened when the Lebanese arrested them and sent them to prison for forty days.

It was then that they all assumed their *noms de guerre*: Yasser Arafat chose the name Abu Ammar; al-Wazir became Abu Jihad; Khalaf became Abu Iyad; al-Hassan, Abu Sa'id; Qaddoumi, Abu Lutf; and Yusef al-Najjar, Abu Yusef.

Meanwhile 'Fatah' carried on with the work it had apparently begun.

On the night following the abortive raid, another was attempted. A reserve team of five had been waiting in Jordan for orders to proceed. When they came, only three of them obeyed. They crossed the river, managed to dodge the Israeli border patrols, found the canal, placed the explosive, set the detonators and fuses and escaped safely back again across the river.

Again, nothing happened. The explosive was found and removed safely by an Israeli guard. A border patrol traced the escape route of the raiders to the river, but pursued them no further. As far as the Israelis were concerned it had been a matter of minor importance, although a warning that greater care was necessary.

The National Water Carrier was eventually damaged by explosive two weeks after the first attempt had failed. But when the raiders returned, they were intercepted by Jordanian border guards and one of them was shot. The first martyr of 'Fatah' was the victim not of Israeli but of Jordanian response.

The Syrians sent more raiders into Israel, but always from Jordanian territory. Any reprisals, they reckoned, would be against Jordan. The undermining of the Hashemite regime was one of the objects of the exercise, as they clung to the belief that Jordan, like Lebanon and Palestine, was a rightful part of Greater Syria. But the main object, and the most important, was to show up the ineffectuality of the PLO and therefore of Nasser.

Some of the raiders did quite serious damage, but often they would get no further than the east bank of the Jordan River, hide their dynamite and return with tales of narrow escape and targets destroyed. Sweidani's men saw to it that graphic tales of these 'successful raids' reached the Arab newspapers.

When Arafat, Khalaf and Qaddoumi were released from prison they went to Damascus, where they were told that raiding parties would continue to be sent into Israel from Jordan and Lebanon in the name of Fatah. What they could do, if they wished, was help recruit fighters for training by the Syrians.

The Israelis listened to Arab broadcasts, the most highly enthusiastic from Syria, which claimed that Fatah had done serious damage when its 'storm troops' attacked targets in Israel. They knew the claims, in terms of number, extent of damage and their own emotional reactions, were very exaggerated. In 1965 there were thirty-five raids in all, twenty-eight of them from Jordan, the remainder from Lebanon and the Gaza Strip. The rare incursions from Syria were against the instructions of the authorities. In 1966 there were forty-four raids. In the first five months of the following year, there were thirty-seven. All were attacks on civilian targets. Eleven Israelis were killed and sixty-two wounded. Although Israel gave warning of reprisals, she chose at the time a policy of restraint. So the Syrians became bolder.

Ignoring all protests from the Jordanian government, they established *fedayeen* camps at Qalqilya and Jenin on the West Bank, very near the Israeli border. Qalqilya lies in what was then the narrow waistline of Israel, only about ten miles from the coast. Israel was unlikely to tolerate the existence of the base for long. King Hussein sent a secret message to the Israeli government disclaiming responsibility for raids originating from his territory, but after Fatah fighters had killed three Israelis on 25 May 1965 at Ramat Hakovesh, and blown up a building in the town of Afula the next day, Israel hit back and destroyed both the Qalqilya and Jenin camps.

In 1966 the regime in Syria was overthrown by an even more radical faction of the Ba'th party in a bloody *coup d'état*, during which hundreds of people were murdered on the streets. The regime that came to power appointed a new secret commander of Fatah, named Yusef 'Urabi, a Palestinian officer in one of the Syrian units of the Palestine Liberation Army (PLA). He announced to the organization that he was dismissing Arafat, whom the members of Fatah still believed to be their chief, and would himself assume the role of leader. He was murdered in the Yarmuk refugee camp. The police tracked down Arafat, who was in hiding in Damascus, and arrested him. Most of his comrades fled to Beirut, but Khalaf, al-Wazir and eight others were also imprisoned by the Syrians. All but one were released 'after long discussions' with one of the strong men of the new government, Hafiz Assad.[17]

Abu Iyad (Salah Khalaf) has denied that they were responsible for 'Urabi's killing. 'Urabi, he says, had infiltrated Fatah in order to control it, and he was shot in mysterious circumstances.

After the departure of Arafat and his comrades for Beirut, Fatah raids organized by the Syrians went on as before. The new regime could not have believed, any more than its forerunner had, that terrorism would scare the Israelis into surrender. But they continued the same policy of trying to provoke Israel into reprisals on a scale which would force Nasser into another war.

8
'Jordan is Palestine, Palestine is Jordan'

While Syria was promoting *fedayeen* raids on Israel from Jordan, Nasser was using the PLO to subvert the Jordanian government. King Hussein was the enemy which the PLO fought from its inception until the war of 1967. It did not win, but Hussein's struggle to keep his kingdom ended with his losing a large part of it.

Shuqairy first stirred up contention with the King and government of Jordan by demanding that the PLO should have the right to station its own army along the border with Israel, to give military training to Palestinians, to have a headquarters in Amman, and to receive revenues from special taxation on the wages of Palestinian civil servants. Had the government allowed the PLO to maintain its own army and raise taxes, it would have admitted a second, separate power into the country.

The majority of Palestinians lived in Jordan. More than half the population of Jordan considered itself to be Palestinian; the rest were mainly Bedouin. Even before the annexation of the West Bank there had been a high proportion of 'Palestinians' in Abdullah's state, and he had acknowledged this by bestowing on the refugees the same democratic rights, such as they were, as all his subjects enjoyed; in other words, universal adult suffrage, for men only in practice. Half the seats in the Jordanian Parliament were allotted to the West Bank. What this meant was that Palestinians under Jordanian government were Jordanians, yet the Palestinian National Covenant asserted that 'the Palestinian personality is an innate, persistent characteristic that does not disappear', and that the PLO was 'responsible for the movement of the Palestinian people in its struggle to restore its homeland'; and the Jordanian government had acquiesced in the PLO's establishment and had accepted its Covenant. In such knots Hussein found himself caught by Nasser.

The King and his government sought a way out. The arguments must be answered with counter-arguments. The Prime Minister, Wasfi al-Tal, tried explaining that 'the Jordanian army is the army of the sons of Palestine'.[1] And the King himself said, in a speech to the nation on 13 May 1965, that 'ever since the union of both banks of the Jordan, the two peoples have integrated; Palestine has become Jordan, and Jordan Palestine.'[2] But neither answer helped. If the inseparability of the two 'nations' proved that the Jordanian government had authority over Palestinians, it also proved that the PLO had authority over Jordanians.

So Shuqairy hastened to agree. He told the Palestinian National Council meeting in Cairo later that same month that 'our Jordanian brothers are actually Palestinians'; but, from his point of view, the joining of the two river banks had not made the West Bank part of the Hashemite realm, rather it had made the East Bank part of Palestine. 'What happened after the 1948 war was the annexation of the East Bank to the Palestinian homeland,' he said.[3]

The point was unmistakable. What Shuqairy wanted was to control all of the Jordanian State. His business for Nasser was to displace the King.

Hussein tried to make some accommodation with the PLO. Wasfi al-Tal made a few concessions. He said in Parliament that the government would welcome more Palestinians joining the Jordanian army, but would not permit a distinct Palestinian force: that all able-bodied citizens would be given military training, but there would not be, as Shuqairy demanded, the establishment of training camps for Palestinian youth (in fact, the programme of training a citizen army was not carried out). Towns on the Israeli border were to be strengthened with volunteers and arms, but the volunteer force was not to be put under PLO command. And although al-Tal did introduce a 'tax for the good of Palestine', it was levied on all civil servants.

In his efforts to prevent the PLO constituting a second government within Jordan, Wasfi al-Tal tried to dissolve the issue in the great solvent of pan-Arabism. 'We see the Palestinian issue as a general Arab one,' he said, 'and it would be a mistake to look at it as an issue which concerns only one Arab state.'[4]

Still the Jordanian government intended that Jordan should swallow the Palestinians. And still Shuqairy intended that 'the Palestinian entity' should swallow Jordan: this would be the first part of Palestine to be liberated. Jordanian territory would then be the base from which Palestinian forces, supported by the Arab states, would fight for the remainder by eliminating the State of Israel.

Shuqairy became increasingly vituperative against the Jordanian government and against the King personally. The PLO's broadcasting station in Cairo, 'Voice of Palestine', attacked Hussein so bitterly that the King complained directly to Nasser.

Nasser despatched Shuqairy to Amman to answer the complaint, as if the PLO leader were entirely responsible for his own words and deeds. The King received him on 19 November 1965. What Shuqairy said to Hussein was more in the nature of an irritant than a balm:

If I wanted to be Prime Minister, I would rent a house in Amman and after one week I would become Prime Minister. Your Majesty naturally knows, [and I say this] without bragging, that your present Prime Minister, Mr Wasfi al-Tal, was a clerk under me at the Arab office in Jerusalem in 1946. But all I want is for the Liberation Organization to co-operate with Your Majesty for the benefit of the country.[5]

The King had no choice but to show willingness to co-operate with the Organization. He tried to appease Shuqairy, and hence Nasser, with more concessions. His government exempted the PLO from customs duties and from having to pay for telephone and postal services, and permitted it to keep an office in Jerusalem. And al-Tal allowed that it had a role to play, which was to 'organize the Palestinian people scattered in other Arab countries and throughout the world', though not in Jordan.

Shuqairy was not to be satisfied. He found further causes for complaint. The government, he said, was putting PLO members under surveillance; it had the Organization preached against in the mosques on Fridays; it required PLO personnel to apply for permits to visit the refugee camps and for permission to distribute pamphlets, and its Jerusalem office telephones were tapped.

The Jordanian government bore with it all. Then Shuqairy went beyond complaint and brought about actual confrontation. He sought the alliance of political parties and factions, groups favourable to the *fedayeen* organizations, which had stood in opposition to the Jordanian government and had been declared illegal in 1957. Chief among them were the (Nasserite) Arab National Movement, the Ba'th Party and the Communist Party. Shuqairy approached their representatives in Beirut. He was bent on conspiracy and subversion.

In April 1966 the government ordered the arrest of about 200 persons in Jordan who were affiliated to the outlawed political parties or were members of trade unions known to be associated with the PLO. The reason the Ministry of the Interior gave for their arrest was that they were suspected of sowing seeds of dissension and planning a *coup d'état*. The Prime Minister accused them of trying to split the Arab camp, an argument which would be hard for Nasser to counter. Although he made no mention of any involvement of the PLO, Wasfi al-Tal's intention was to disable it.

The third Palestine National Congress, held in Gaza at the end of May 1966, was attended by a large number of members of the outlawed groups, invited by Shuqairy. The PNC declared that the PLO would never work in opposition to the governments of the Arab states – unless its autonomy was challenged: and that it so happened that the arrests of Palestinians 'in areas of Palestinian settlement' (which, of course, meant

Jordan) constituted such a challenge. Wasfi al-Tal saw this as an incitement of the illegal groups to attempt to overthrow the Jordanian government.

King Hussein replied with a warning that 'any hand raised against this united and struggling nation will be cut off, and any eye which looks at us with a look of hatred will be gouged out'.[6]

His government acted. More arrests of suspected members of illegal groups were made. Certain prominent people on the West Bank were warned that participation on the PLO committees would be regarded as treason. PLO personnel on the Voice of Palestine broadcasting staff in Amman were replaced; the new Voice of Palestine called for another, different organization to represent the Palestinians.

Shuqairy thundered back, in a public speech delivered in Cairo, that Jordan had no right to exist 'in its present character'. And he went further than ever in denying the legitimacy of the State of Jordan. The people of Jordan, he said, 'are ours', and he went on: 'The first person to separate the West Bank from the East was the Emir Abdullah Ibn Hussein, when the English established for him an Emirate by the name of the Emirate of Transjordan.' This Transjordan, he ranted, had not been founded, as a nation should be, in the will of the people, but had been set up (like Israel) by 'imperialism', and that it was to that very day still 'under colonial control by the Hashemite family'. The people of Jordan must rise in revolt, aided by the Arab world, to overthrow the Jordanian government and liberate their country from colonialism, as the first essential step towards the liberation of Palestine. Palestine was a country, he said, whose proper boundaries were the Mediterranean on the West and the Syrian Desert on the East, for that is where the Palestinian people were.[7] He was making an unambiguous claim to Jordan as part of Palestine; to both banks as the rightful territory of the Palestinians, whose proper leadership was the PLO.

As demagogue and firebrand, doing what he did best, Shuqairy whipped up his Cairo audience to a frenzy of hatred for King Hussein, until they were yelling for the King's blood, and the blood of Wasfi al-Tal, and crying out that the two of them must be dealt with like Nuri al-Sa'id, who had been murdered and mutilated by the mob of Baghdad.

Wasfi al-Tal retaliated as best he could, which was weakly. He called a press conference. He accused the illegal groups Shuqairy was courting of being terrorists who were 'trying to make peace with Israel'. Shuqairy himself, al-Tal said, had been guilty of this same crime when he had been Saudi Arabian ambassador at the United Nations in New York. Jordan stood alone, he would have the world know, in preventing such a thing (as peace with Israel) being accomplished. So it was necessary to stop

Shuqairy working with the Marxist Arab groups. Hinting at Soviet involvement in the Shuqairy plot, he referred to the days in which Arabs
hoped 'for a victory of Mussolini and Hitler in order to return Palestine to
our own hands'. There were, he implied, some kinds of alliances that one
did not seek. Shuqairy must be removed.[8]

Shuqairy's riposte, through the Voice of Palestine in Cairo, was to
remind his audience that al-Tal had long had connections with
'imperialism', having been in the British navy; and that therefore his
attack on the PLO, like attacks by the King, did honour to the Organization, because 'we don't expect praise from the mouths of [foreign] agents
and hired lackeys'. The way to Palestine, Shuqairy cried, was through the
destruction of the 'Jordanian entity'.[9]

The Jordanian government now saw no recourse but to break off
relations with the PLO, which it did in July 1966.

Meanwhile, relations among the other Arab states had worsened, partly
because of the Jordanian quarrel with the PLO, but more importantly
because of the tension between Nasser and the Saudi Arabians over the
failure to resolve the crisis in the Yemen. Jordan's breaking off relations
with the PLO gave Nasser a pretext for overt aggression against Hussein.
As the Arab world lined up with the 'revolutionary' states, notably Egypt,
Syria and Iraq, or the 'conservative states', chiefly the Kingdom of
Saudi Arabia and the Emirates of the Gulf, Jordan had to take the side to
which the Hashemite monarchy belonged. That was the side of Saudi
Arabia, despite the fact that little love was lost between him and the house
of Sa'ud which had deposed his great-grandfather.

The internal instability of Syria did not keep it from adventure in
the international arena. The extreme left wing of the Ba'th Party, which
had come to power in February 1966, had turned towards the Soviet
Union. Once assured of political support from the USSR, the new regime
was even more impatient to force Nasser into war with Israel. When an
attempt at a counter-*coup* failed in Syria on 8 September, Jordan and
Egypt gave asylum to fugitives escaping the government's revenge. The
Syrians accused them both of having backed the attempted *coup*. Mutual
distrust deepened among the Arab states. Unless the dream of Arab unity
was to be abandoned as a mere mockery, danger of war with Israel was
needed now more than ever.

So Syria increased the number and intensity of *fedayeen* raids. And at last
Israel retaliated in strength. On 13 November 1966 the Israeli forces hit
the West Bank village of Samu' in the Mount Hebron area, the source of
much of the terrorist activity instigated by Syria. It was the heaviest punishment meted out by Israel since the Suez War of 1956, but it did not stop
terrorist activity. What it did was to administer a shock to Jordan. The

West Bank was in uproar for weeks as crowds of young men, urged on by the PLO (but against the counsels of restraint by their elders, the businessmen and heads of the communities) rioted against the Jordanian government. The riots were quelled, but the rebels talked of seceding from the East Bank. Some even spoke treasonably of a republic being established on both banks. A less incendiary section of opinion sent a deputation from the West Bank to King Hussein to ask for the Tal government to be deposed.

Still Nasser was not to be drawn into war with Israel. Jordan remained his target, and his agency, the PLO. Shuqairy seized the opportunity to renew demands for a PLO army on the West Bank. A border defence force, he said, would have repelled the attack on Samu'. Egypt, Syria and Iraq insisted that united Arab forces should be stationed on Jordanian soil. Nasser accused Hussein of being 'ready to sell the Arab nation'. And the Syrian President called for the overthrow of the Jordan government and the dethronement of the King, for 'the liberation of Jordan means the liberation of Palestine'.[10]

A stream of anti-Hussein propaganda poured out of Egypt. And Nasser, who would not permit the PLO to mount raids into Israel, now sent terrorists to attack targets in Amman, Jerusalem and other Jordanian cities.

On 3 January 1967 the PLO offices in Jerusalem were closed down and its personnel arrested. From then on the headquarters were in Cairo. Jordan withdrew its official recognition of the PLO 'under its present leadership' on the grounds that its main objective had been the overthrow of the Jordanian government, and that its function was as an arm of the Egyptian secret service. Hussein's relations with Nasser deteriorated even further, and the Jordanian ambassador to Egypt was recalled.

Wasfi al-Tal tried to make the attack on Samu' seem of little importance to Jordan, though disastrous for Israel. His account of the raid greatly exaggerated the size of the Israeli force, and he gave out that thirty-five Israelis had been killed. (The true figure was one.) Compulsory military service was introduced, which, if it served no other purpose, would at least keep a large number of rebellious youths off the streets.

To keep up their side in the propaganda war, the Jordanians struck back at Nasser with counter-accusations: that Egypt was protected by United Nations forces while its own were engaged in the Yemen; and that Egypt and Syria made it easy for Israel, who knew that there was no danger of them having to fight on other fronts while they struck into Jordan. King Hussein reminded Egypt that he and the government of Lebanon had forbidden *fedayeen* action from their territory so as not to provoke war prematurely. Al-Tal, carried away perhaps by his own eloquence, went further yet to prove his courage, his staunchness, his readiness to make sacrifices for the sacred cause of Palestine, and recklessly promised that Jordan would 'face up to every battle forced on us, whether were are ready or not. If it is necessary we shall fight with our teeth and our hands.'[11] So he affirmed a commitment which the King could not evade.

'More anti-Israel than thou' was the implicit slogan of every Arab government confronted by every other Arab government. It was a boast which sometimes had to be proved. The time for King Hussein to honour his commitment was to come in June 1967. It was then that Syria's plans, doggedly pursued by means of *fedayeen* warfare, came to fruition: Egypt at last took action that was sure to provoke Israel into another war. The only call upon the Arab states for which they would let go their grip on each others' throats was sounding again.

The Israeli government sent a secret message to King Hussein that if he were to stay out of the conflict, Israel would not attack Jordan.

But Hussein had no real choice. He would have to go to war to save his kingdom; not from Israel, but from Egypt and Syria.

9
The Six Day War

In his attempt to become the sole patron of the Palestinian cause, Nasser had been outmanoeuvred by Syria. The *fedayeen* actions excited public opinion, while the PLO, as the Arab press pointed out, only talked and did nothing.

Nasser's first answer was to lift the restraints he had imposed on Shuqairy and let him use *fedayeen* methods.

As the Syrian-sponsored attacks from Jordanian soil increased in number and became more destructive in the latter part of 1966, towards the point where they provoked the reprisal on Samu', the PLO sponsored two raids into Israel from Lebanon. Of the first four *fedayeen* who crossed the border on 19 October, one was captured and three were shot: the survivor said that their group was called the 'Heroes of the Return'. On 28 October a few more were captured when they entered Israel carrying explosives. They belonged to the same group. Both incidents were highly coloured by the propaganda media obedient to Nasser, and credit for them was given to the PLO. They were hailed as the PLO's answer to Syrian taunts of its inactivity and ineffectuality.

However, the 'Heroes of the Return' was not a wing or sub-group of the PLO, but served the Arab National Movement (ANM), which was pro-Nasser at the time though not controlled by him. The 'Heroes' had been enlisted into the service of the Organization by Shafiq al-Hout, head of the PLO office in Beirut.

The two raids on behalf of the PLO were followed by more. An explosion on the Israeli railway, set off by the 'Abd al-Qader al-Husseini Unit', and bombs exploded in a residential area were proof, Shuqairy proclaimed in jubilant speeches from the PLO radio station in Cairo, that 'the PLO no longer utters mere verbiage, no longer consists of groundless dreams and hopes, but is now a fighting revolutionary organization.'[1]

Syria's response was to make more raids and strive to do more and greater damage. Israel attacked Samu', but Nasser was still not ready for war.

Syria was being supplied with large quantities of arms by the Soviet Union. When it became apparent to the Syrian regime that the *fedayeen* were not likely to provoke a sufficient reaction on their own, conventional military forces were brought into play. Long-range guns were trained on border villages in the zones which had been demilitarized since the peace-treaties of 1949. On 7 April 1967, after heavy and prolonged shelling, Israel's airforce retaliated. Syria sent up Soviet MiGs to intercept the Israeli Mystères, and six of the Syrian planes were shot down. At once Syria, prompted by the Soviet Union, warned Egypt that Israel was now likely to press a full-scale attack and asked for Egyptian help.

But Nasser, after five years of unavailing military engagement in the Yemen, still hesitated to fight another war with Israel. So the Soviet Union announced that Israel was massing troops on the Syrian border. The Israelis invited the Soviet ambassador to come and inspect the border and see for himself that this was not true. He refused to do so and stuck to his story.[2] If it had been disproved, Syria would have had less need of Soviet support.

Nasser had to act like the leader of the Arab world. He poured troops across the Canal into Sinai, and Arab governments applauded him. On 17 May he ordered the United Nations Emergency Force to be withdrawn, and U Thant, the UN Secretary-General, on his own initiative, obeyed.

Five days later Nasser broke the agreement he had made when peace terms were concluded after the 1956 Sinai campaign, and again closed the Straits of Tiran to Israeli ships and the Gulf of Aqaba to all shipping to and from the port of Eilat. Guarantees which had been given to Israel by the Western powers were not honoured. Kuwait and Algeria sent contingents to help Nasser 'destroy Israel', as he was prophesying he would do. On 30 May King Hussein signed a defence pact with Nasser, and Shuqairy flew back with the King to Amman in a spirit of sudden and close amity. Two days later Iraq signed a similar pact with Egypt.

On 5 June, before eleven o'clock in the morning, the Israeli airforce destroyed the Egyptian airforce on the ground. In six days the war was over, a total victory for Israel. She had taken the whole of the Sinai from Egypt for the second time, the Golan Heights from Syria and the West Bank from Jordan. For the first time since 1948, Jews could enter the Old City of Jerusalem. Hussein's kingdom had now shrunk back to the Transjordanian territory allotted to his grandfather by the British after the First World War.

More refugees (about 130,000 in the first wave[3]) moved to the 'temporary' camps on the East Bank, crossing the river by way of the broken Allenby Bridge.

The government of Israel announced that it was ready to negotiate with Egypt, Syria and Jordan to return the captured territory in exchange for peace. But, with the encouragement of the Soviet Union, the Arab states refused. At their summit conference at Khartoum in August and September, they gave their answer: no peace with Israel, no recognition of Israel, no negotiations with Israel.

Part Three

1968 to 1970

The *fedayeen* groups take over the PLO. Arab states become victims of their own creation. Jordan fights for survival against the PLO. Palestinian refugees are moved on again.

Guerrillas

The Arab states accounted for their defeat by claiming that the United States and Britain had intervened militarily on Israel's side (a total fiction). They demanded that the Western powers press Israel to withdraw to the pre-war frontiers and hand back the conquered territories. King Hussein was considered to be in the best position to persuade America to act on their behalf, but was told by President Johnson that he should enter into direct negotiations with Israel. The King reported to the conference at Khartoum that despite the President's 'hard words',[1] he still hoped to recover the West Bank by diplomatic means. At this, Shuqairy interrupted to object that a solution for the West Bank was for the Palestinian people to decide upon, and the Arab states should be prepared to back that decision whatever it was. He asked the conference to agree. The conference did not, and Nasser ordered him to keep quiet. Shuqairy took offence and walked out.[2]

He was beginning to look too ridiculous to be of use except as one of the scapegoats for the 1967 defeat. Rumours were circulated that he had fled from Jerusalem to escape the fighting, and, even more shameful, had disguised himself as a woman.

Discontent with his leadership had been growing within the PLO for some time; he had dismissed some possible rivals to prevent an internal *coup* six months before the war.[3] In order to carry out Nasser's orders to turn to *fedayeen* activity, he had tried wooing *fedayeen* groups to come into the Organization, but they had turned down the invitation. Unable to face the rejection, Shuqairy invented a 'Revolutionary Council' which, he said, was ready to take over from the Executive Committee, but he refused to reveal the names of the Council members, on the grounds that some of them lived in Jordan. Nobody was deceived.[4] A few months after the war he was finally ousted from the presidency of the PLO. On 14 December 1967 seven members of the Executive Committee demanded his resignation.[5] On 24 December he resigned. He was granted a pension and retired in Lebanon.

His successor was a lawyer from the West Bank, Yahya Hammuda. It seems to have been an instance of those frequent cases where the man elected to a presiding office is not the man anybody wants but the man nobody objects to. His opinions were leftist, but he was not a member of any political party. Lack of conviction seems to have characterized him rather than the dogmatism which was among Shuqairy's faults. One of Hammuda's first public statements suggested that Arab-Jewish coexistence was possible in Palestine. The statement aroused such angry protest that he hastily withdrew it.[6]

His chief task, on Nasser's instructions, was to try to persuade the *fedayeen* organizations to join the PLO. He formed a special committee for the purpose, but had no more success than Shuqairy.

The *fedayeen* groups, as soon as the war was over, tried to base themselves in the occupied territory. According to the doctrine of Mao Tse-tung, Che Guevara and other successful revolutionary leaders, this was the sort of environment which would favour guerrilla forces. The guerrilla could move among his own people 'like a fish in a revolutionary sea'.

Yasser Arafat constantly visited the occupied West Bank during the latter part of 1967 to prepare the people for their role as revolutionaries. Fatah was his again. He had visited Damascus in September 1967, was well received by the Ba'th leader, Salah Jadid, and his faction. They put Fatah, which by now consisted of about 500 men, back in his hands.[7]

Fatah issued instructions, in the name of the General Command of al-Asifa forces, on how to make petrol bombs and commit acts of sabotage; how to spy on the enemy; how to resist the enemy's propaganda by not reading its newspapers or listening to its broadcasts; how to set up committees for the self-management of local affairs and boycott the enemy's legal and economic institutions, and how to create a network of resistance cells which would spread to every village and every street. Fatah pamphlets exhorted 'the heroes of the Arab people in the occupied land', in the name of great Arab conquerors such as Omar or Saladin, and on the analogy of Algerian and Vietcong guerrillas, to 'rise against the foreign occupation', which was 'nothing but a new crusade'.

But no popular resistance movement emerged. The Palestinians gave the *fedayeen* shelter, women knitted and sewed for them, but they did not start a campaign of sabotage. The legal and economic institutions of the Israelis were not boycotted. There was, after all, no sea in which the revolutionary fish might safely swim.

Israel's policy was to deal liberally with the West Bank population[8] and severely with the *fedayeen*. The military administration quickly restored normality to everyday life, and then interfered as little as possible in their local affairs. Travel was permitted over the Jordan River with a minimum of regulation, and teachers and civil servants received salaries from the Jordanian government as well as from Israel. The result was that the residents distanced themselves from the would-be guerrillas.

The *fedayeen* made examples of individuals who co-operated with the Israelis more than they deemed necessary, but this, far from helping them to gain political influence, only made them less popular.

Israeli agents infiltrated the groups, captured about a thousand *fedayeen* before the end of 1967, and broke up their centres of command, including Arafat's at Nablus. To punish terrorists and their collaborators, the Israeli authorities did what the British had done: demolish their houses.

Jealous rivalry characterized relations between the numerous *fedayeen* groups. It expressed itself chiefly in the claiming of victories following raids on the enemy. Two or more would lay claim to the same ambush or explosion. The practice was called 'announcement theft'.

They knew well enough that a united effort would be more effective, and from time to time, they conferred to see if they could work together, but they failed. Then in January 1968, Fatah called a meeting of twelve groups with a view to a merger,[9] and no fewer than eight accepted the invitation. The meeting was held in Cairo. Nasser was coming round to the idea that if the groups would not enter his orbit by joining the PLO, he might yet encompass them separately. The PLO itself was invited to attend the meeting as one among many Palestinian organizations. It refused. But among the eight a certain degree of co-operation was achieved. They formed a (short-lived) 'Permanent Bureau' of their representatives.[10]

The PLO tried to create its own *fedayeen* group, the Popular Liberation Forces. But the Executive Committee went on trying to woo Fatah and the others to unite in the PLO. At last, on 16 March 1968, a meeting was held to discuss ways and means. It was proposed that the Palestine National Congress would be reconstituted. Of 100 members, half would represent the *fedayeen* groups and the Palestine Workers' Union.[11] But the *fedayeen* hesitated to accept.[12] They wanted to control all the PNC votes.

They were not yet in a position to get what they wanted. But very soon, events took a turn which rocketed the *fedayeen*, Fatah in particular, to the heights of prestige – and the power that went with it.

The 'Victory' of Karameh

The single event which raised the *fedayeen* to such heights of popularity that they became a power in the Arab world was a skirmish fought at the Jordanian village of Karameh.

When Fatah was chased from Nablus and then Ramallah on the occupied West Bank, it moved its headquarters to Karameh on the East Bank, about five miles north of the Allenby Bridge, eight south of the Damiya Bridge and two miles from the river which was now the border. King Hussein had no choice after the Six Day War but to allow the *fedayeen* to have bases in Jordan. Karameh was the first independent Palestinian military base established in an Arab state.

Others were set up along the valley of the Jordan. Strikes against Israel – mostly by the laying of land-mines and the planting of explosive charges in civilian centres – elicited counter-strikes, as the Jordanian government had anticipated and feared. Jordanians began to desert the border villages, and the *fedayeen* took over control of them, although the Jordanian army was stationed along the river ready to repel Israeli counter-attacks. Then, as *fedayeen* action increased, so did exchanges of fire between Israel and the regular forces of Jordan. The bombardments became so frequent that most of the townspeople, villagers and even farmers who lived on the good agricultural land near the river fled, abandoning their homes and farms, and becoming refugees in their own country. Karameh was one of these deserted villages. After an Israeli air attack on 15 February 1968, all but 1,000 of the 15,000 villagers left.[1]

King Hussein was afraid to rouse the antagonism of the *fedayeen*. It was not until the Israeli airforce answered terrorist attacks with bombs on 15 February 1968, that he tried seriously to curb the groups. Even then his efforts were weak and had little effect. Some *fedayeen* were arrested, but they were soon released on the organizations' demand.[2] New restrictions on their movements were not enforced.[3]

On 18 March an Israeli school bus full of children was blown up by a mine. Two people were killed and twenty-eight injured. The reprisal was visited on Karameh on 21 March. The Israelis dropped pamphlets giving two hours' warning of the intended raid so that the remaining

Jordanian villagers and Palestinian non-combatants could move out of the way.[4]

The attack was launched with helicopter-borne troops and tanks. Armoured columns crossed the river both north and south of Karameh. The number of men was between 1,000 and 1,500, with 150 armoured vehicles.[5] The figure given by Fatah was 12,000 Israeli soldiers.[6]

The contingent from the south divided, one unit making for Salt to intercept the Jordanian army. But they had underestimated the strength with which the Jordanian army would meet them, and it was this unit which suffered most of the losses and injuries on the Israeli side.

The rest went into Karameh. Many of the *fedayeen* had hidden themselves in tunnels burrowed from the command post, the local school, and they were smoked out with 'smoke grenades'. At the Fatah regional headquarters the Israelis found a large arms depot and a prison. They released a sixteen-year-old boy prisoner, who said he had been locked up for refusing to join Fatah. He and others identified members of the organization.[7] They also revealed that when the warning pamphlets had been dropped, Arafat and other Fatah leaders had distributed arms, told the men to fight and then fled. Arafat had commandeered a motorbike and ridden away without waiting to see the outcome of the encounter.[8]

Abu Iyad, according to his own account,[9] stayed and fought, and twice came close to death. By his tally, 300 *fedayeen* fought off 15,000 Israelis and forced them to retreat. He proves his presence by describing scenes of heroism which he witnessed. One young man, he says, put on a belt of explosives, threw himself under an Israeli tank and blew himself up. (A man might have done such a thing, but it is very unlikely that the tank would have been damaged.)

The battle lasted all day and into the evening. The Israelis admitted that they made 'a number of tactical errors', but they did destroy the base.[10]

By the Israeli account, they themselves lost twenty-eight soldiers,[11] and ninety were wounded; the Jordanian army lost 100 dead and ninety were wounded, and 170 *fedayeen* were killed and 200 captured. (On the same day another twenty *fedayeen* and forty Jordanians died when the Israelis struck at five training camps south of the Dead Sea. There were no Israeli losses.) The figures published by the Jordanians gave a different picture: Israeli dead and wounded numbered 200; Jordanian, only twenty dead.[12] And the figure given by the *fedayeen*, the gratifying figure that raised them to the stature of giants, was 500 Israelis dead or wounded.[13]

The Arab news media uproariously acclaimed the heroic resistance of the *fedayeen* at Karameh. The Arab world went wild with joy. All Arabs could bask in reflected glory. The battle was hailed as a turning-point in the fortunes of the Palestinians and of all the Arabs in the long conflict with

Israel. There were public celebrations in the refugee camps and the Arab cities. The funerals of the martyrs turned into great processions.

More than 5,000 recruits presented themselves to Fatah in the two days following the battle, of whom 900 were selected.[14] Among them were some women, and a special women's training camp was opened.[15]

Those now eager to join the fight were not only Palestinians. Throughout the Arab world a great wave of popular feeling rose to exalt them. Thousands of Egyptians volunteered to join them and some hundreds of Iraqis.[16]

Enthusiasm was not confined to the Arab world. Soon young Europeans came too, so many of them that eventually, in the following year, a European camp had to be set up to train them for their part in a world revolution of which the Palestinian struggle was a part. Its first intake was 150 men and women[17] who saw the *fedayeen* as spearheads of victory, not only against Israel but against 'imperialism', of which (according to the dogma) Zionism was an instrument. The *fedayeen* had been adopted by the international Left.

The word *Karameh* means 'dignity', and this association added to the feeling many Arabs had that the *fedayeen* had done much to redeem them from the shame of past defeats. The thrill of pride that ran through the Arab world had to be taken into account by governments. King Hussein found it politic to let the *fedayeen* take credit, although it was his army which had in fact inflicted almost all the damage on the enemy; on the other hand, he could not insult his own people by pretending that they had had no part in the 'victory'. With subtle ambiguity, he said in a speech which was to be much quoted and misquoted: 'The inhabitants at Karameh put up a courageous resistance. It is difficult for me to distinguish between *fedayeen* and others. We may reach a stage soon when we shall all become *fedayeen*.'[18]

It was King Hussein who was the first to suffer the consequences of the national delusion. After Karameh, Salt became the chief *fedayeen* base, from which most of the incursions into Israeli-held territory were made. In the month of August, Israel struck at Salt from the air. The King went to the town after the raid and offered to visit the *fedayeen* bases nearby which had been badly damaged. But the *fedayeen* refused to let him in.[19]

Their disobedience to the law of the land forced Hussein to send the army to surround three of their bases and order them to leave within forty-eight hours or be removed by force. But the *fedayeen* refused to budge, and the army gave up and withdrew.[20]

The Israeli strikes, however, did move them. Driven back from the border, they took shelter in the mountains, in caves and remote fastnesses, and began to concentrate on the wild south-western slopes of Mount Hermon in Lebanon, soon to become known as 'Fatahland'.

Increasingly, the groups set up training bases and arsenals in civilian centres, in the heart of refugee camps, the thick of houses, where schools and hospitals stood. Feeling the insufficiency of their armament, they began to acquire anti-aircraft guns. They used mortar fire and rockets to attack Israeli settlements. The Israelis spent many hours, and whole nights for months on end, in underground shelters.

The 'open bridge' policy was exploited by the *fedayeen* to send infiltrators through the West Bank into Israel for acts of sabotage. Many of the saboteurs were young women. Some of them were responsible for bombs that exploded in public places in Jerusalem and other Israeli cities. The risks for raiders were high. Deaths from *fedayeen* clashes and attacks in 1968 were given by Israel as 177 (military and civilian) for their own dead, and about 700 wounded; and 681 *fedayeen* casualties (dead and wounded). The *fedayeen* figures for Israeli deaths was 2,618 dead; 915 wounded; 5,818 dead or wounded.[21]

Many Arabs died at the hands of Arabs, either as a result of *fedayeen* raids or as victims of terrorist intimidation.[22] In 1969 and 1970 seventy-six Arab residents died on the West Bank and in Gaza, and 1,122 were injured. Not all of these were random. On many mornings Israeli patrols found the bodies of men hanging on the meat hooks in the market of Gaza, warning others against collaborating with the enemy or expressing views out of tune with those of the organizations.[23]

In Jordan the *fedayeen*, feeling themselves in an unassailable position within the country in their new-found sense of victory, power and importance, created a state-within-a-state. There were thousands of them now, and they patrolled the streets with their arms, often humiliating Jordanian army personnel and policemen. They set up their own checkpoints on the main roads. They ignored the Jordanian law courts and held trials in their own 'revolutionary courts'. Prisoners brought from the West Bank and found guilty of spying or collaborating with the enemy were sentenced to death. They licensed their own vehicles and put their own number-plates on them; collected donations at gunpoint from shopkeepers, businessmen and the foreign community in Amman;[24] fired on Jordanian soldiers and police. But armed attacks on police headquarters in Amman were blamed, by the PLO, on 'Zionist elements'.[25]

The King did not dare to attack the larger organizations. Instead, the military police enlisted the aid of Fatah, the PLO and other of the more powerful groups to arrest 'bogus guerrillas'. A mass rally in Amman on the June anniversary of the Six Day War was policed by Jordanian troops mixed with Fatah members – and some soldiers from a contingent of Iraqi troops stationed in Jordan.[26] The government of Jordan was coming close to sharing power with the *fedayeen* backed by foreign Arab governments. The King's sovereignty was more than ever under threat.

In October 1968 Hussein's loyal Bedouin units clashed with *fedayeen* in Amman, but failed to expel them from the city. The government could not stop the Palestinians appearing in the towns in uniform and carrying arms, and could not even make them give up their heavy weapons. The organizations broadcast from Cairo that these attempts constituted a plot to 'liquidate the Palestine Revolution'.[27]

Now the *fedayeen* entered into open alliance with those outlawed political groups and parties in Jordan which Shuqairy had sought to conspire with before the 1967 war: the Arab Nationalists, the Ba'th and the Communist Party. Together, they and some smaller factions formed an opposition consortium which called itself the National Union.[28] It was a conspiracy for treason.

The growing hostility between the government and the *fedayeen* leadership exploded in November 1968. During street demonstrations in Amman marking the fifty-first anniversary of the Balfour Declaration, one of the small groups attacked the American embassy with stones. They were dispersed by the Jordanian police, and some *fedayeen* leaders were arrested. But when the government sent a contingent of Bedouin to take control of the refugee camp headquarters of the group which had attacked the embassy, the *fedayeen* resisted and called on the refugees to take up arms and fight with them. Some dozens of people were killed.[29]

At this point King Hussein appealed to Nasser to intervene. An agreement between Jordan and the *fedayeen* was signed. On the surface, the agreement brought the *fedayeen* under the law of the land. It forbade the wearing of uniforms and the carrying of arms in the towns; the setting up of their own roadblocks and searching of cars. It stipulated that they would have to co-operate with the state security forces and stand trial in the state law courts. But the agreement, nevertheless, served to sanction the existence of an independent *fedayeen* state: for it also stipulated that the identity cards the *fedayeen* must carry were to be issued by their own groups, and that they could make arrests and investigate persons 'in co-operation with the state authorities'; and it provided for the setting up of a co-ordinating committee to settle disputes between the 'sabotage organizations' and the state, which would include, as well as state representatives, members from all the organizations, and it would sit in the PLO offices in Amman. Secret clauses in the same agreement set out certain conditions for the 'sabotage organizations' to carry out their operations against Israel with due notification to the Jordanian authorities.[30]

All this gave the Palestinian groups considerable power, and they took even more, not abiding by the few restrictions to which they had pledged themselves. They continued to fire into Israeli-held territory regardless of the restraints laid on them in the secret clauses. The co-ordinating committee did not last long. And the danger to the King was not diminished but enhanced.

The *Fedayeen* Capture the PLO

After his demoralizing defeat in the Six Day War, Nasser revised his view of the *fedayeen*. He put his faith in the effectiveness of a 'guerrilla war'; not only would it wear Israel down, but it would display the efforts of a 'weak people' against an 'oppressive state' and gain sympathy, the *fedayeen* demonstrated the unconquerable spirit of the Arab people, their proud determination never to accept defeat or the loss of their lands.[1] Nasser's own star had declined. After Karameh, Fatah's rose higher.

'We recognize the resistance movement,' Nasser told a rally about one month after Karameh. 'In no circumstances will we tolerate defeat or surrender.'[2] And, in a speech on Revolution Day, 23 July 1968, he added that 'not only we, but the entire world senses ... that the Palestinian people have risen to champion their own cause by themselves and to defend their rights by themselves'.[3]

Now the hugely augmented importance of Fatah made its leaders feel they could dictate better terms to the PLO Executive Committee than they had been offered before their 'victory'. They began the process by which they were to take over the PLO. On 15 April 1968 the Central Committee of Fatah appointed Yasser Arafat its 'official spokesman and representative'. A week later Arafat informed Hammuda that Fatah rejected the offer of only fifty seats in the Palestine National Congress for the *fedayeen* organizations. At the end of May they were offered almost all of them.[4]

Of the 100 seats, thirty-eight would go to the *fedayeen* groups that had formed the Permanent Bureau, ten to the strongest one among the groups that had remained outside,[5] and two were still to be chosen by the Preparatory Committee. The remaining fifty would be divided mostly among various organizations of Palestinian students and workers, all affiliated with the *fedayeen* groups, and a few could be filled by the existing PLO. The *fedayeen* had captured the Organization.

When the fourth PNC met in Cairo in July 1968, the constitution of the Palestine Liberation Organization was changed fundamentally. Its membership no longer consisted of individuals, notables and dignitaries, the traditional leadership, but was now composed of the delegates of various groups. And its own leadership was now collective. In Shuqairy's

PLO, the Executive Committee had been appointed by the chairman: now it was elected by the PNC, and the chairman would be appointed by the Executive Committee.

The Palestinian National Covenant was revised. The new version still dedicated the PLO to the total annihilation of Israel. But now, in accordance with the principle that Fatah had adopted, the Covenant declared that this end was to be attained by armed struggle, and armed struggle alone, unaided by political solutions. Only through battle, the spilling of blood, only with fire, death and physical destruction, could total victory be won. The conflict with Israel, which the Arab states had made into their own supreme political issue, and in which they were deeply involved, was now to be managed by the armed bands. Nasser had given up direct control of the sacred cause. He could rely on nothing but the PLO's need for patronage and money to keep them from going too far against his interests.

Seven months later, in February 1969, the fifth PNC met in Cairo. In Nasser's presence, Yasser Arafat was elected chairman of the PLO. Arafat wept with pleasure.[6]

Within a year all the other significant *fedayeen* groups had come in under the PLO roof. By the beginning of 1970 most of those which were to remain (though with some coming and going) the constituent member-groups of the new PLO had joined together. The smaller groups of the Permanent Bureau melted into the newer formations, and shared legitimacy, money, arms and political power with Fatah, which remained the largest of the groups. The others were of three kinds.

The Marxist Popular Front organizations numbered three: two branches and the parent stem. Another three groups were created and controlled by Arab states, one by Syria and two by Iraq, with additional support for one of them from Libya. The last organization was a very small one of under 100 members, called the Palestine Popular Struggle Front (PPSF). What makes it of special interest is that it was formed by Palestinians of the West Bank. It attached itself to Fatah in 1971, but remained a separate organization. It did not become a member group of the PLO in its own right until the fourteenth PNC of January 1979. There had been another West Bank group, the Palestine National Front, formed by the Communist Party but it did not last long. Some of its members were to be elected to the PLO Executive Committee as independents.

With its mixture of Marxist, Ba'thist and nationalist groups, the PLO was in many respects a working-model of the larger Arab polity: the same rifts appeared in it: the same antagonisms were fought out within it.

The Marxist groups and those which represented Arab governments in the PLO need to be looked at more closely.

13
Ideologies

Until it had to make adaptations to its collaborators, Arafat's Fatah was simply nationalist. The other groups were formed by ideologues of the Left.

Where there is ideology, there shall be schism.

The Popular Front for the Liberation of Palestine (PFLP) was a Marxist group. Its leader was George Habash. He was born in Lydda in 1926 to a Greek Orthodox family.[1] His father was a successful merchant, dealing in corn. Much of Habash's childhood was spent in Jerusalem. He entered the American University of Beirut in 1944 and qualified as a doctor of medicine in 1951. While at the university he founded the Arab National Movement (ANM) with some like-minded students. Its guiding light was Nasser, who gave it financial support. With a central doctrine of pan-Arabism, and, vital to that end, the elimination of Israel by violent means, the movement gathered strength and spread rapidly as an underground organization throughout the Middle East, on both sides of the Red Sea. It attracted intellectuals and members of the military in several Arab states, where stress had shifted away from the Palestinian aspect to internal political issues. Habash himself believed so unswervingly in the need for revenge (against the British and the Arab leaders who had been responsible for the 1948 defeat, as well as against the Jews), in the annihilation of Israel and in the Nasserite aim of Arab unity, that he sometimes quarrelled with Nasser himself when the Egyptian leader adjusted his own policies. But Habash continued to function as one of Nasser's agents of subversion. He worked for Nasser against the Syrian Ba'thists.

Then Habash's left-wing tendency became more extreme. He began to think of himself as a 'Marxist-Leninist', but scorned the ineffectual Communist parties of the Middle East, and favoured China over the Soviet Union. He no longer saw the issue of Palestine as part of a merely Arab revolution, but both as necessary to world revolution. By Marxist analytic prophecy world revolution was inevitable, yet had to be fought for. The arch-enemy was 'imperialism' of which 'the Zionist entity' was only one aggressive spearhead. The defeat of 1967 persuaded Habash that the immediate and primary goal must be the liberation of Palestine.

Although only a means to an end, it was the first step. And so Habash, along with a number of others in the ANM who had moved along the same ideological route, founded the Popular Front for the Liberation of Palestine on 7 December 1967. Its membership was made up of three small groups: the Heroes of the Return, the Youth of Revenge (another branch of the ANM), and an already active group called the Palestinian Liberation Front (not to be confused with another organization of the same name formed subsequently and supported by Iraq and Libya), which was led by a Syrian army officer named Ahmad Jibril. He was Syrian by birth and not a Palestinian, even by descent.[2]

Jibril had formed his PLF with about twenty other Syrian officers. It carried out over ninety raids on Israel between 1965 and the Six Day War. Through Jibril, it had contacts with the KGB, East Germany and Bulgaria.

With the coming together of Jibril, the professional soldier with support from the Communist bloc and Syria, and Habash, the experienced underground leader with wide influence throughout the Arab National Movement, the PFLP soon became a significant *fedayeen* organization. Habash retained Nasser's patronage, and Popular Front recruits were trained in Egypt.

It soon split. The break came where it might be expected in an organization which attempted to make Syrian interests adhere to Egyptian interests. Habash and Jibril had different loyalties, and they quarrelled. Habash and his friends in the ANM criticized Syria for not permitting *fedayeen* to cross into Israel from Syrian soil. The Syrians arrested and imprisoned Habash early in 1968. When that happened, Jibril found himself in sole command, and he tried to force the PFLP to break with the ANM. But the Heroes of the Return and the Youth of Revenge would not betray their origins. In October 1968 Jibril announced the expulsion of both factions from the PFLP.

Habash was snatched by some of his followers while he was being transferred from one prison to another, and smuggled from Syria into Jordan. Once they had him back, the two small groups expelled by Jibril declared that they were the PFLP and it was Jibril's group that was expelled.

Thereupon Jibril announced the formation of a new organization, the Popular Front for the Liberation of Palestine – General Command (PFLP–GC).

Then Habash discovered that another of his former comrades, Nayef Hawatmeh, had also been working against him in his absence, and there was another split. Hawatmeh and his faction went into hiding in one of the refugee camps pursued by Habash's avengers, and some of Hawatmeh's men were caught and killed.

Hawatmeh was also not a Palestinian. He was born a Jordanian Bedouin Christian, in the town of Salt in 1935. He joined the ANM while he was student at the Arab University of Beirut. Sentenced to death for pro-Nasserite subversive activities in Jordan in 1957, he escaped to Baghdad, where he led the Iraqi branch of the ANM. There he took part in an attempted *coup d'état* in 1959, and was imprisoned until 1963 when the Ba'th Party overthrew the Qasim regime. He changed his views from Nasserism to an extreme leftist revolutionary ideology.

After working underground for a 'radicalized' ANM in Yemen, he joined Habash in Jordan. Soon their ideological differences began to weaken their union. Hawatmeh accused Habash of being a fascist. Their views on Marxism and the USSR were not the same. And while both he and Habash were the declared enemies of the 'conservative' Arab states – Saudi Arabia, Jordan, Kuwait and the emirates of the Gulf – Hawatmeh was also against 'progressive' Iraq, Egypt and Algeria. His ties were with subversive factions of the extreme left, the Communist Party of Iraq and revolutionary movements in the Gulf and Lebanon. He made contact with groups in the wider world which were also working for the 'inevitable' world revolution, notably Trotskyites and New Leftists in Europe.

Hawatmeh and four others formed the Popular Democratic Front for the Liberation of Palestine (PDFLP) after breaking away from the PFLP. Its slogan was 'All Power to the Resistance'. Unusually among the *fedayeen* organizations, the PDFLP did not pay its fighters, which was probably why it attracted fewer recruits.

When fighting broke out between members of the PFLP and PDFLP in Amman, it was Arafat who stepped in to make the peace, although Habash's group was the most fiercely and persistently competitive with Fatah. (Many actions were claimed in public announcements by both the PFLP and Fatah. Fatah called the PFLP the worst 'announcement thief'.)

The Syrian Ba'th regime was not willing to relinquish its role in promoting Palestinian violence. In April 1968 a new large Syrian *fedayeen* organization, called the Vanguards of the Popular Liberation War, was formed out of smaller existing groups. It soon became the second biggest after Fatah. Its military arm was named al-Sa'iqa (Thunderbolt). Its declared aim was a Palestinian state, but essentially as a part of a united Arab world under Syrian leadership.

Palestinian officers were transferred from the regular army to Sa'iqa, but soon after its inception the organization came directly under the Ba'th Party and not the military, although it continued to be supported by the PLA regiments in the Syrian army. The Party used it in its intrigues against King Hussein in Jordan and in the violent cut and thrust of internal Syrian politics. It was given an hour a day to broadcast on Damascus radio. In its early days its members were all Palestinian refugees sympathetic to the Ba'th Party, recruited from the camps of Syria, Jordan and Lebanon; but it was always so tightly tied to the Syrian regime that it could be used against other Palestinians. For the first few months its leader was Colonel Taher Dablan, but he was replaced by Zuhayr Muhsin before the end of 1968. Zuhayr Muhsin was born in Tulkarm in 1936. He joined the Ba'th Party when he was seventeen. Later he became a teacher in Jordan, where he was accused of assisting the pro-Nasser subversives in 1957; he left the country for Qatar, which deported him for subversive activity a year later. He then went to Kuwait and after that Syria. He was among the first members of Sa'iqa.

Muhsin was one of the leaders within the Palestine Liberation Organization who denied the existence of a separate Palestinian people. ('We speak about a Palestinian identity only for political reasons,' he explained, 'because it is in the Arabs' national interest to encourage a separate Palestinian existence.'[3]) The Palestinian revolution, he believed, was part of the Arab revolution, and it was for the Arab states of the Middle East to decide the destiny of Palestine.

Once the Syrian Ba'thists had Sa'iqa, the Iraqi Ba'thists had to have their own *fedayeen* group too. In April 1969 they created the Arab Liberation Front (ALF). Only some of its members were Palestinians. The size of its membership fluctuated at the will of the regime, sometimes reaching a few hundred. *The ALF insisted that no state of Palestine should be brought into existence*, because it would constitute yet another division within the Arab world.[4] The Iraqis later supported another very small group, numbering perhaps 100, called the Palestine Liberation Front (PLF), which was also partly financed by Libya. It was formed by a faction which split off from the PFLP–GC in April 1977. It did not become a member-group of the PLO until 1979.

14
Black September

It was the PFLP's defiance of King Hussein which brought retribution at last to the *fedayeen* in Jordan.

George Habash's second-in-command, Wadi' Haddad, was also a doctor of Greek Orthodox extraction; the two men had been students together at the American University of Beirut. In 1968 Haddad had taken charge of what he called 'special operations', which meant acts of terrorism outside the Middle East, chiefly in Europe. They were intended to draw the world's attention to the Palestinian cause, and therefore had to be what the PFLP called 'spectacular'. The hijacking of aircraft was favoured to take many hostages of many nationalities, all at once. Haddad planned and directed a series of hijackings on international flights between July 1968 and September 1970. In 1969 the PPSF and the PFLP–GC followed the example of the PFLP. Some fifty innocent people, including a child, were killed. Those of the hijackers who were caught and brought to trial in European countries were released when other planes were hijacked and more hostages taken to be exchanged for the convicted terrorists.

On 6 September 1970 the PFLP hijacked four airliners. Two of them, one American plane and one Swiss, were forced to land on a neglected airfield near Zarka in Jordan, named Dawson's Field by the RAF during the Second World War, but now renamed 'Revolutionary Field' by Wadi' Haddad. There the crew and passengers were held hostage in the planes in the heat of the desert for four days and four nights. Meanwhile another hijacked American airliner was flown to Cairo airport, where the crew and passengers were let out and the plane blown up. The fourth was an Israeli airliner on its way to London. The Arab terrorist on board was a young woman named Laila Khaled. Her helper was a man from San Francisco named Patrick Arguello. Their hijacking attempt failed. The Israeli guard on board killed Arguello and arrested Khaled. Before he died Arguello wounded one of the crew. In an attempt to save the injured man, the captain flew on to London, a shorter distance away than Israel, where according to standing instructions he should have returned in such circumstances. The injured man died. Laila Khaled was detained by the British police, but not for long.

On 9 September a British plane on a home flight from Bahrain was hijacked and the pilot forced to fly to join the other two on Dawson's Field. The PFLP demanded that three of their terrorists imprisoned in West Germany, three in Switzerland who had killed an Israeli pilot, and Khaled should all be released, otherwise the planes would be blown up at three the next morning. The release of *fedayeen* from Israeli prisons was also demanded. The Israelis refused to bargain with the terrorists, but the governments of Great Britain, West Germany and Switzerland complied, and so provided complete proof that hijacking, terrorism and blackmail paid. It was a signal that started a decade of such crimes.

Although Israel had not given in, most of the passengers were then set free, and the remaining forty were taken to a refugee camp and imprisoned. Then, as the Jordanian army stood watching helplessly, the aircraft were blown up.

The *fedayeen* had defied King Hussein's authority beyond a point that was politically tolerable. For several reasons the King judged the time to be right to crush the organizations. Peace negotiations between Egypt and Israel were under way, initiated by the American Secretary of State, William Rogers. (Acts of terrorism committed by Arabs were not in Egypt's interest, and so Egypt was unlikely to interfere.) The Rogers Plan proposed that Israel withdraw behind her pre-1967 boundaries, and that the United Nations Security Council Resolution 242 of November 1967 be implemented. But the PLO rejected Resolution 242 on the grounds that it referred to Palestinian 'refugees' and not to the 'right of Palestinians to return to their homeland', and because it required the recognition of Israel; and so the Rogers Plan was also rejected. But Egypt and Israel did sign a ceasefire agreement. Hussein wanted peace too. The impediment was the PLO.

Within Jordan the *fedayeen* groups had been encroaching even further on the state's prerogatives. They had formed their own police force. They had initiated armed clashes with the army. They had started their own radio station. They had organized mass demonstrations and a strike to stop the King receiving an envoy from the United States: on that day, every driver on the roads of Amman, even army drivers, had stopped their vehicles for an hour when the *fedayeen* had asked them to.[1] The *fedayeen* were appealing to the people over the head of the government, with alarming success. They even interfered successfully to prevent the King dismissing two officers and sending two others into exile.[2] Hussein had reason to fear that his power was being usurped and his government destroyed. It seemed plain enough that the intention of the *fedayeen* was to take over the country. Iraq, Abu Iyad has testified, urged them to do so.

Early in September 1970, two attempts had been made on Hussein's life by the PFLP. Yet even then the King hesitated to crush the heroes of the Palestinian resistance, the victors of Karameh, the self-sacrificing warriors who had become the torch-bearers of Arab pride.

His mind was made up for him after the Dawson's Field episode. He was carrying out a formal inspection of his Bedouin troops when he noticed, as he was intended to, that one of the soldiers was flying a brassière from the antenna of his radio.[3] The hint was not to be mistaken. The Bedouin were telling the King that he had turned them into women, keeping them passive in the face of Palestinian provocation. On 17 September the King let his Bedouin soldiers loose on the organizations. They attacked the camps, the bases and the headquarters.

According to Abu Iyad,[4] the leaders of the groups were taken by surprise when the attack was launched. They had thought that Hussein would not dare to crush the *fedayeen*. They formed a unified command only hours before the onslaught began.

The first battle raged for eleven days. According to the organizations, 30,000 people were killed (it seems, however, that for them figures are not precise records of measurement, but rather qualitative terms for evoking emotional reaction); the figure given by the Jordanian army was 1,500.

Syria intervened to support the *fedayeen*, sending tanks into northern Jordan, but the unit – calling itself the 'Fatah Unit' – was repelled. When the Syrians prepared for another advance, Israel massed troops on the northern Jordanian border. It was a warning the Syrians could not mistake, and they made no further attempt to assist the organizations by entering Jordan.

Most of the survivors fled to Syria, followed by their families. Others chose a different course. For a whole week *fedayeen* made their way to the banks of the river and called to Israeli patrols to let them cross. They preferred to give themselves up to the Israelis rather than face Hussein's army.[5]

Sudan, Tunisia, Kuwait and Egypt made representations to Hussein, and gained a respite for the *fedayeen*. The deputation found where Arafat was hiding and smuggled him out of Jordan in disguise. Hussein went to Cairo for talks, and Nasser persuaded him to sign a ceasefire with Arafat on 27 September 1970. It was Nasser's last achievement. He died the next day.

The agreement required the King to tolerate PLO militia in the cities of Jordan. It is not surprising that he balked at allowing the PLO such power again. He repudiated the agreement, and entrusted Wasfi al-Tal with the task of ridding him finally of the menace of the *fedayeen* organizations. First, they were expelled from the cities. Then they were driven into their last strongholds at Jarash and Ajloun. Abu Iyad reports that he then said to the King ('without bothering about protocol'): 'If you strike the *fedayeen* in their last corner of Jarash and Ajloun, I swear I shall pursue you to the ends of the earth, for as long as I have breath left in my body, to inflict upon you the punishment you deserve.'[6]

If the threat was made, the King ignored it. First, Wasfi al-Tal announced that 'trespassers on archaeological sites in the kingdom will be evacuated', and then he sent the army to carry out the order at the archaeological sites of Jarash and Ajloun.[7] The army surrounded the last of the *fedayeen* bases, and called on 'the Resistance' to 'expel from its ranks the supporters of the class war and the world revolution'. It was a last chance offered to Fatah to stay in Jordan if it would repudiate the organizations of the extreme left. But the answer came back: 'We would rather die in dignity than succumb and fall apart for ever.'[8] So, in the summer of 1971, the *fedayeen* were driven clean out of the kingdom.

Bitterly, the organizations blamed the Arab states for failing to come to their aid. The PFLP was condemned by the other groups for its 'extremism', which had brought Hussein's fury down on all their heads.[9] Yet extremist methods were to be used by all the others too.

The Fatah leaders, beaten, humiliated and thirsting for revenge, resolved to create a secret organization to overthrow the Jordanian regime. They named it 'Black September'.[10]

Its first act was to murder Wasfi al-Tal in the entrance of the Sheraton Hotel in Cairo. He was climbing the steps with his bodyguards when two young men moved towards him and shot him at close range. 'Had they failed,' Abu Iyad has said, 'two more were waiting just inside the lobby. The four men had waited two days before acting, so that police vigilance would relax.'[11]

As he lay dying al-Tal moaned, 'I've been murdered . . . murderers! They believe only in fire and destruction.' His wife, Sa'diyya, came running to him. 'Are you satisfied now, Arabs,' she sobbed and shouted, 'you sons of dogs?'[12] A Jordanian officer knelt and kissed the dying man's forehead. And one of the assassins also knelt down and licked the blood that was flowing on to the marble floor.[13]

King Hussein wept for Wasfi al-Tal at his funeral, which took place the next day, with full military honours, in the royal burial place near the palace in Amman.[14]

There was talk in the palace that the assassins had been in the pay of Libya, and that the powers in Egypt had given their silent consent to the crime. Certainly, the trial of the assassins was turned instead into a trial of the Hashemite regime; the murderers were acquitted and acclaimed as heroes.

Part Four

15
The Covenant

The Palestine National Covenant lays down that the aim of the PLO is the total annihilation of the State of Israel. 'The liberation of Palestine . . . aims at the elimination of Zionism in Palestine' (Article 15), and 'Israel is the instrument of the Zionist movement' (Article 22); 'Palestine, with the boundaries it had during the British Mandate, is an *indivisible* territorial unit' (Article 2) and 'an indivisible part of the Arab homeland' (Article 1); 'The partition of Palestine . . . and the establishment of the State of Israel are entirely illegal' (Article 19). In all, twenty-nine of its thirty-three articles call explicitly or implicitly for the elimination of Israel[1] (see Appendix 1).

It is a declaration of destructive intent, unconditional, absolute.

It was drafted by Ahmad Shuqairy[2] in the three months before the May–June 1964 gathering of Palestinian notables that launched the Organization. They made some changes to the draft, and then approved the whole of it. It was formally revised only once, in 1968, when the *fedayeen* groups took over and reconstituted the Organization. It is alterable only by a two-thirds majority of all members of the Palestine National Congress (which have varied in number from 100 to 500).

Zionism, according to the Covenant, is an unmitigated evil. It is 'racist', 'fanatic', 'aggressive, expansionist and colonial in its aims, and fascist in its methods'. It is 'a political movement organically associated with international imperialism and antagonistic to all action for liberation and to progressive movements in the world', Article 22 declares. This is one of the plainest statements in the Covenant of ideological affiliation to those powers which use the word 'imperialism' to mean the West, 'liberation' to describe their severe curtailment of freedom, and 'progressive' to cover a retreat from the ideas of tolerance, pluralism and the open society: in other words, it displays the PLO's ideological affiliation to the Communist powers. The huge quantities of armament supplied by the Soviet Union to the PLO in the later 1970s proved no more about the nature of the Palestine Liberation Organization's intended role in world politics than did its own declarations in its National Covenant. The goal of eliminating the State of Israel is to be achieved by 'armed struggle' *only* (Article 9). Agreement on that point enabled the disparate groups to come together under the PLO roof in 1968.[3]

Yet whether or not 'armed struggle' was to be the only way was one of the most persistent and important of the internal arguments among the various *fedayeen* groups and their sponsoring regimes.

The prospect of a Palestinian state, with which a mooted peace conference at Geneva tantalized at least some of the *fedayeen* organizations, raised the question of whether such a state on only part of the territory claimed by the PLO would be acceptable to it, and whether any territory at all that was gained by political negotiation and not armed struggle could be accepted. These questions threatened to break the groups apart. The PDFLP, Fatah and Sa'iqa (the 'mainstream' of the *fedayeen*) wanted political negotiation and territory for Palestinian self-determination wherever it could be won. The other groups rejected both proposals. By doing so they constituted the 'Rejection Front'.

It was not until after the 1973 war, when it looked as if the Arab side could negotiate from a position of strength, that a PNC (the twelfth, sitting in Cairo from 1 to 9 June 1974) resolved to set up a Palestinian 'authority' (a *sulta*, not a state) on 'every part of Palestinian territory that is liberated'. Still the PNC did not say whether 'liberation' could be effected by negotiation, because that would blatantly contradict its declaration (Article 9) that 'armed struggle is the only way to liberate Palestine'.

Three years later, at the next PNC in 1977, a majority of the *fedayeen* were to agree in principle that political negotiation may be used along with armed struggle as a means of gaining all Palestinian territory for the Palestinian state. In a separate resolution it was implied – though in such a way as to make it possible for it to be denied if necessary[4] – that a state (*dawla*) might be set up on a part only of the claimed territory.

The gaining of a part of the Palestinian homeland was visualized and could only be proposed by the 'mainstream' organizations as a stage in the gaining of the whole. There would be three stages: first, the Israelis would withdraw behind their pre-1967 war lines; second, they would withdraw behind their pre-1948 war lines; third, the Palestinian state would be established.

The third stage, the all-Palestine state, would be 'the democratic state' of Palestine. Since 'the democratic state' would be established on the whole of Mandate Palestine, and could therefore only exist if Israel did not exist, the phrase always implies, and is used as a euphemism for, the total destruction of Israel.

The word 'democratic' could suggest to foreign governments a condition of equal rights for minorities, and Western governments could think of the proposed state as a representative democracy. The Marxist groups, for whom the struggle to establish a Palestinian state was part of a wider revolution, saw it as one to be attained by a victory of a working class (which might embrace anti-Zionist, 'progressive' Jews) and constituted as a 'people's democracy' on the Eastern European model, with rule by a single party, the Communist Party.[5]

By choosing a term which could convey as many possible meanings, and yet as little, as 'democratic', the PLO shelved the need to answer the questions which would otherwise arise about what would be done with those Jews who might survive a victorious PLO armed struggle. The Covenant gave an answer of a sort, that (only) the 'Jews who had normally resided in Palestine until the beginning of the Zionist invasion will be considered Palestinian' (Article 6). But when was the beginning of the 'Zionist invasion'? Was it in 1881 (as Arafat said at the United Nations in 1974), or 1917, when the Balfour Declaration was issued? To say that none at all could stay would contradict the PLO's claim to religious tolerance (Article 16), since it insisted that the Jews were a religious group and not a nation. Some of the planners of the 'democratic state' comforted themselves with the conviction that most Jews would 'return to the countries of their origin'.[6]

The 'democratic state' (or the 'secular, democratic state' as Western journalists have often phrased it[7]) might have the ring of good promise to many; but to know what a PLO state would really be like we cannot examine some unrealized ideal; we can only look at how the PLO actually ruled, in southern Lebanon.

Part Five

1968 to 1976

The PLO destroys Lebanon and becomes the world's central terrorist organization. The Arab states endow it with yet more power, and the greater part of the world glorifies it.

16
A State of Precarious Order

From 1968, the *fedayeen* organizations threatened Lebanon, just as they threatened Jordan, to establish their own independent power within the country.

But Lebanon, unlike Jordan, could not withstand the onslaught. Although a more open and democratic state than Jordan, it was much less stable, and so even more vulnerable. Its instability derived from the unalterable fact that 'Arabs' are not a single people with a single religion, but a large number of peoples with different origins, cultures, creeds, traditions and aspirations, and the creation of a nation-state on the European model failed to join the peoples of Lebanon together in political accord.

When the Ottoman Empire was broken up by the victorious European powers after the First World War, the League of Nations gave France a mandate over Syria and Lebanon.

Lebanon was declared a state in 1920, and became a republic in 1926 with a constitution that provided for a parliamentary system of government. To create the State of Lebanon – still under France – new regions were added to the Mountain: Tripoli, the southern coastal region, and the anti-Lebanon, with the valley that lay between the two ranges, the Beqaa. The idea was that the additional territory would make a satisfactory economic package, with fishing, agriculture, manufacture and service industries. It also meant that a significant number of Muslims was added to a largely Christian population, the Maronites, long settled in Mount Lebanon, and a smaller number of long-settled Druze. The Maronites were a Westward-looking Mediterranean people. But most of the Muslims, while wanting an independent Lebanon, nevertheless felt themselves naturally to belong to the Arab world.

Syria regarded Lebanon as an inseparable part of Greater Syria, and continued to covet not only the territory she had been forced to yield to the new state, but the whole of the country. Successive Syrian governments refused to recognize Lebanon's independent existence, an attitude which from the beginning posed a threat. And within the little country itself traditional religious and political differences, old enmities and mistrusts persisted, not susceptible to cure by document and signature. They were, however, taken into account when the constitution was drafted.

In 1932 a census was taken (not fully trusted but not so misleading as to distort the broad facts) which showed that the Christians were still a majority, with the Maronites preponderating (30 per cent of the total), the Greek Orthodox next in number (10 per cent), the Greek Catholics – or Melkites – next (6 per cent), then the Armenians (Orthodox, Catholics and Protestants taken together, 4 per cent). The Sunni Muslims were reckoned at 21 per cent, the Shiʻites at 18 per cent, the Druze at 6.5 per cent while other smaller Christian sects and Jews made up the remainder.[1] Power was to be distributed in all public institutions according to the numerical proportions of the population. The president was to be a Christian; the prime minister a Sunni Muslim; the speaker of the Assembly a Shiʻa Muslim.

When France fell to German conquest in June 1940, Lebanon came under the Vichy regime. In June 1941 Britain and the Free French reconquered Lebanon and Syria. Lebanon became an independent country in 1943, the only pluralistic democratic Arab state with a representative assembly elected by universal suffrage.[2] The President, Bishara al-Khoury, on behalf of the Christians, and the Prime Minister, Riad al-Solh, for the Muslims and Druze, came to a verbal agreement called the 'National Pact'. They agreed that the Christians would not call on France to interfere on their side against the Muslims, and the Muslims would not seek amalgamation with Syria. And they would preserve the balance of power as it then was between the religious groups.

The constitution was an attempt at pacification by treaty – as if treaties did not record peace already arrived at rather than generate a mysterious power to bestow it. Its authors must have had an almost mystical faith in the power of paper: to bind ancestral enemies together in amity; to soothe feelings of burning injustice; heal deep wounds to tender pride, and calm the seething hatreds.

No census has been taken in recent decades. Muslims believe that their numbers have increased faster than those of the Christians, and express resentment of the fact that they are still held by the constitution to a position of power one notch below that of the Christians.

The Christians deeply fear a change in the *status quo*. They alone among the Christian communities of the Arab world are not a subordinate *dhimmi* community. Their constitution and the National Pact protect them. Other Arab countries, including the 'progressive' – that is, socialist – states, declare themselves in their constitutions to be Islamic,[3] and as religion and politics are indivisible in Islam, non-Muslims under its rule are inevitably subordinate.

The Arab nationalist movements would, in any case, be inimical to the

Christian Lebanese. They could sever Lebanon's traditional links with Mediterranean and Christian Europe, and would dilute its European and Christian character. More disastrously, the socialist movements would seek to change the system from a market to a controlled economy, and its free, democratic, pluralistic polity into a totalitarian dictatorship or oligarchy.

Although the democracy of Lebanon was qualified by a persistent feudalism, democracy it was, and as such it afforded the Christians their only safe haven in the Arab world. To prevent even the possibility of its destruction, they clung tenaciously to the power which the constitution gave them and by means of which they could preserve it. To defend the constitution was their sacred cause.

Yet the seeds of civil war lay in the constitution itself. It was not only that the sizes of the populations were likely to alter in relation to each other so that actual numerical power might outstrip prescriptions. It was also that old, deep, irreconcilable differences could not favour a coalescence of the patched-together state. Peace between the diverse peoples, in the light of their history and character, was improbable, and, in the event, it was not achieved. The dangerous cracks remained in the confessional divisions of the population. When the rivalries and rifts and conflicts in the Arab world as a whole were brought to bear inevitably on Lebanon, the cracks widened. Numerous factions arose, then they themselves split internally as well, the fissures running in all directions.

One of the old and deep antagonisms lies between the Maronite Christians[4] and the Druze[5], the two communities who have lived longest in the Mountain. In the seventh century, the Maronites were the first refugees to seek and find safety and independence in that natural fortress. Between the eighth and eleventh centuries, various dissenters from Muslim orthodoxy, who together were to form the Druze community, found refuge and made their home at the southern end of the Mountain.

The two communities, the Druze and the Maronite, at times feuded, and at times lived in peace with each other. There were periods during which they were in alliance against the Muslims – Shi'a Muslims for the most part, who were also fleeing from the jealousy of an orthodoxy, and who constituted a third sect in the region of the Mountain; and then periods when they made war on each other with the utmost fury.

In 1842 a rebellion of the lower orders among the Christians against their feudal overlords spread when the Druze peasants also took up arms. The uprising turned into a civil war between the Druze and the Christians. The Druze had been persecuted by the Christians and now struck back in fury. The British supported the Druze, who were allied with the Greek Church; and the French supported the Maronites. The authoritative and moderate

Druze leader, Na'man Bey Jumblatt, tried to pacify his own followers and the Christians, exhorting them both to 'cease from their fratricidal war'. But the Druze pressed on to gain conquest and revenge. The villainous Sa'id Bey Jumblatt, supported by the British, pursued a campaign of terrorism against the Christians. The Christian town of Zahle came under siege and fire. The Turks looked on as the country fell into anarchy and disorder. There were massacres and appalling slaughters. Sa'id Bey Jumblatt's sister, Sitt Na'ifa, asked to be taken to view the mangled and mutilated corpses of Christians so that she could gloat over them.[6] After fighting ended in 1860, the peace terms finally agreed included an amnesty, so none of those who had committed atrocities were tried or punished for their crimes. Muslims of Sidon who had slaughtered Christian men and violated the women when they sought refuge in the city were also let off without trial.

After a commission of British, French, Austrians, Prussians, Russians and Turks had pondered over the Lebanese problem and arrived at an agreed solution, the Mountain was granted a form of autonomy: rule, under Turkey, by a Christian governor (*mutasarrif*), assisted by a council (*majlis*) of twelve representatives, elected by the religious groups. The balance in that political area, which lasted into this century, was held by a wary watching of each other by the religious communities of the area.

The independent 'Greater Lebanon' with its additional regions, including the ports of Tyre, Sidon and Beirut, also acquired more people, of more religions, with more mutual antipathies and contradictory desires. Lebanon remained a state of precarious order. While political discontent simmered within it, disruption threatened it from outside.

Syria never stopped regarding Lebanon as a part of her own territory, and so never opened an embassy in Beirut. Successive Syrian governments have only recognized a government of Lebanon in the Arab League and the United Nations.

More dangerously, the political fragility of the young state offered a temptation to Egypt in the late 1950s, when President Nasser had his agents working in Lebanon, as everywhere else; his unification of Egypt and Syria in 1958 infected the whole Arab Middle East with a nationalist fever that spread to Lebanese Muslims and Leftists. The Maronites dreaded then that Lebanon would be turned into an Islamic Arab state. Their enemies accused them of wanting to preserve their 'privileges', but they saw it differently: that in defending their own freedom they were also defending the freedom of their compatriots of all confessions. They were willing to share the land, but only in a spirit of tolerance. Arab nationalism, Islamic fundamentalism, socialist collectivism, all dogmatic and despotic, threatened them, they believed, with an overwhelming darkness.

When the union of Egypt and Syria was proclaimed on 1 February 1958, the Muslims of Lebanon made the day a public holiday. A pan-Arabist group called the United National Front, representing an alliance of Lebanese parties and factions, went to Damascus to help celebrate the great day, and through them the President of Syria issued an invitation to Lebanon to join the union.[7] Lebanon trembled with joy and abhorrence. The abhorrence was the Christians', who faced imminent disaster.

For a while it looked as if Nasser's disruptive endeavours, brought to bear in a country where disruption was only too easy, would succeed. Leaders of various Nasserite factions, Muslim and Druze, called a general strike, and started preparations for war, in their own regions. The Muslim Prime Minister, Sami al-Solh, refused to join them. He continued to stand for Lebanese independence, and was punished by having his house set on fire.[8] Incidents of violence – the burning of the Lebanese flag, attacks with explosives on the homes of leading Maronites, the unexplained murder of a newspaper owner opposed to the Maronite President Camille Chamoun[9] – shook the rickety structure of Lebanese order, and it shattered. The country broke into civil war.

Armed pro-Nasserite rebels started the killing, but met determined resistance from an alliance of Maronites, Greek Catholics and (then, but not later) the Syrian Social Nationalist Party. Most of the SSNP members were Greek Orthodox Christians. It was anti-Nasser, and had been suppressed in Syria because its extreme Syrian nationalist ideology challenged the newly founded United Arab Republic.

The fighting went on for four months, intermittently. An estimated 3,000 people were killed or injured.

Then, on 14 July 1958 the very bloody revolution in Iraq, started by Nasserites, overthrew the monarchy. The new regime turned its eyes on Lebanon. Its open ambition to unite Palestine, Lebanon, Syria and Jordan into a unified Fertile Crescent under Iraq's hegemony provided an added threat to Lebanese independence and parliamentary democracy.

It was then that President Camille Chamoun urgently summoned help from the West. He called upon the United States to come to his rescue. Lebanon alone among Arab states had accepted the Eisenhower Doctrine, which bound America to provide aid and military support. The call upon foreign interference was in breach of the National Pact, but no more so than the Muslim and Druze parties turning to Syria, Nasser and their United Arab Republic.

The United States acted to put an end to the upheaval and provide a protective presence, but not simply in order to honour an undertaking. The American government saw its own interests threatened by the revolution in Iraq and felt compelled to act in a determined fashion because the new regime was pro-Soviet. So the Sixth US Fleet landed marines in Lebanon, and to the huge relief of the President of Lebanon and many of his people that was enough to save them. After some negotiation among the political parties, peace and order, all the more precious for being no less precarious, were restored.

For nearly ten years after that an uneasy peace prevailed, and the country prospered. Then came the PLO.

17
Brothers and Fratricides

As soon as the PLO came to Lebanon, the violence that was to destroy the country began.

On 20 October 1968 large numbers of *fedayeen* began to concentrate on the western slopes of Mount Hermon in the Arqub region of Lebanon, soon to be named 'Fatahland' by news reporters. A few days later, on the 29th, they fired on a Lebanese army patrol. Three soldiers and one of the *fedayeen* were killed.[1] The Voice of Palestine broadcasts from Cairo warned the Lebanese not to interfere with *fedayeen* raids on Israel from their country.[2]

The *fedayeen*'s supply route was a rough road leading to Damascus which they called the 'Yasser Arafat Trail', reminiscent of the 'Ho Chi Minh Trail'. (The *fedayeen* saw themselves as closely comparable to the Vietcong; Amman, when 'liberated' from Hashemite rule, was to be the 'Hanoi' from which Palestine would be 'liberated'.) In the 1970s, the 'trail' was to become a wide highway fit to bear tanks and the heavy transport vehicles of war.

The PLO insisted that it had no desire to interfere in the internal affairs of Lebanon or any Arab state.[3] Events proved this untrue; besides, its presence as an alien militant organization constituted an interference. The sturdiest liberal democracy depends, for the effectiveness of its government and the maintenance of its system, on the state's holding a monopoly of force, with governmental control of obedient security forces. Here, in divided Lebanon, where the army with its Christian command could not be called out except by the consent of the Muslim Prime Minister, where civil war had lately raged and old rifts were barely papered over by the flimsiest of suspicious agreements, a second and formidable armed power was now rising.

Since Lebanon had concluded an armistice with Israel after the 1948 war, she had not been involved in direct hostilities with her southern neighbour. She had stayed out of the Six Day War, and had lost not an inch of territory. Furthermore, she received money and arms from the United States and could not wish to alienate American good-will. Clearly it was in Lebanon's interest to keep the peace, but after their 'victory' at Karameh the *fedayeen* could not be restrained from acting against Israel from Lebanese territory.

The *fedayeen* had no choice but to go on fighting. Their claim to that famous

Karameh 'victory' had cast them in a role in the Arab world which they could not change even if they wanted to. They were obliged to be the wagers of the *jihad* against Israel for all the Arabs. They had trapped themselves in their own boast.

As their actions brought Israeli reprisals, what to do about the *fedayeen* and their activity became the supremely important political issue in Lebanon. Over it the divided country divided further.

When Israeli commandos retaliated for PFLP hijackings of her aircraft by blowing up thirteen planes on the ground at Beirut airport on 28 December 1968, the failure of the Lebanese authorities to act during the incident, the government's impotence to do anything about it except to protest to the United Nations, roused criticism and anger throughout the country.

Various opposition groups, pan-Arab, pan-Syrian and left-wing, acting together under the socialist Druze leader Kamal Jumblatt, demonstrated in support of the *fedayeen* groups, with workers' strikes and students' gatherings to voice demands and protests. On the other side, wanting the *fedayeen* curbed, three Christian leaders, ex-President Camille Chamoun, Pierre Gemayel and Raymond Eddé, formed a 'Triple Alliance' to challenge the government's inaction.

The Lebanese government was faced with a choice between permitting *fedayeen* raids across the border and so risking invasion by Israel, or preventing them and so risking civil war. The choice was paralysing, because war with Israel would not preclude civil war; and civil war could bring intervention, both by economic sanctions and by armed force, from her 'progressive' Arab neighbours, Syria and Iraq.

The Muslim Prime Minister, Abdullah al-Yafi, was sympathetic to the *fedayeen*, but announced that Lebanon would not bear the responsibility for all they did.[4] He could not explain how Lebanon was to avoid being held responsible or taking the consequences, since the government was unable to control the *fedayeen* on the one hand, and unwilling to negotiate with the Israelis on the other.

The Christian President, Charles Helou, made some efforts to have the army strengthened, but they were not and could not be effective. For one thing, as al-Yafi pointed out, the cost of an adequate defence force was beyond Lebanon's means.[5] For another, because the same group enmities existed within the army as within the country, the army could not be relied on to act impartially and in unity.

Christian leaders wanted the *fedayeen* restrained from taking any action that endangered Lebanon; and they protested against any foreign power (the Palestinians and their active sponsors, Syria and Iraq, were implied) attempting to trespass on the sovereignty of the State. A member of

Chamoun's National Liberal Party dared to call the *fedayeen* 'bands of armed foreigners, sent by the Ba'th and the Communists to commit sabotage and to sow dissension among the Lebanese'. And he warned that if they were not removed by force, there would be civil war. But he was quick to add that he recognized the 'sacred nature of *fida'i* activity'.[6]

In April 1969 the army attempted to compel the *fedayeen* to restrict their military activity to 'Fatahland'. The *fedayeen* fought back. A demonstration by *fedayeen* and Leftists honouring a PLO 'martyr' in Sidon on the 23rd became violent. The security forces acted against the demonstrators, and more than twenty people were killed.[7] President Helou declared a state of emergency, and said in a speech broadcast on 6 May, 'Martyr's Day', that PLO raids on Israel from Lebanon should be stopped. The new Muslim Prime Minister, Rashid Karameh, strongly disagreed.[8]

Traditional religious leaders of the Sunni community within Lebanon reacted by asking for the punishment of those (leftists) responsible for the violent demonstration; but also for the legalizing of the *fedayeen* activity in Lebanon.[9]

The Prime Minister gave up. One side, he said, wanted the *fedayeen* to carry on no matter what the consequences were, while the other believed that their doing so was dangerous for Lebanon; whichever side the government took the country would be split.[10] He tendered his resignation, which was accepted by the President, but he carried on with the duties of the premiership.

The Ba'th Party of Iraq, watching as the rickety state began to totter, and reaching out to help shake it, strongly condemned the Lebanese government's action against the 'struggling masses'.[11] The rival Ba'th Party of Syria did the same, its message coming from a mass demonstration organized by the government in Damascus.[12] The Syrians poured more Sa'iqa men into the country. In July 1969, President Helou estimated that there were 3,400 *fedayeen* in Lebanon; and still their numbers grew as Iraq sent further reinforcements.[13]

For six months after the April eruption, clashes between the army and the *fedayeen* continued. The violence spread to Beirut as the Left, under Jumblatt's leadership, incited mass protests against army action. The government saw calamity approaching. Inflammatory publications were banned, press censorship was imposed, and a curfew enforced in the cities. In less than a year, the *fedayeen* had changed the nature of Lebanese democracy.

In October 1969 heavy and sustained fighting broke out between Fatah and the Lebanese army. Jumblatt, who was soon to become Minister of the Interior (on 25 November, when a new cabinet formally took office), found how duty to his country and sympathy with the *fedayeen* were proving irreconcilable. He explained paradoxically that the government's continued use of the army was not to oppose the 'legal Palestinian struggle' but only to 'safeguard the State'; and that his own view was that all measures against the *fedayeen* should be abandoned. Yasser Arafat explained, also paradoxically, that the *fedayeen* did not want to fight other Arabs, but were forced to do so to achieve 'the victory of the revolution and national liberation'; and he reaffirmed that the PLO had no wish to interfere in the internal affairs of any Arab state.[14] Despite the wishes of both of them to coexist in peace and harmony, the fighting went on.

A protest strike and demonstration in Tripoli resulted in the deaths of two soldiers and five *fedayeen*. The airforce was called in and PLO bases in the region were bombed.[15] Elsewhere in the country the *fedayeen* were hit equally hard. In the south, twenty-four of them died in the fighting, and many more were wounded. Lebanese villagers captured three and promptly 'executed' them.[16]

In the capital, leftist students of the American University of Beirut, Communists, Ba'thists, members of the ANM and others 'went on strike' in sympathy with the *fedayeen*, and clashed violently with fellow students who opposed the action they were taking. Under Syrian orders, Sa'iqa entered three of the 'camps' of the city, Burj al-Barajneh, Chatila and Tall al-Za'tar, and in all three the Lebanese police withdrew after their station in Burj al-Barajneh was attacked. Sa'iqa would not let the residents out or the security forces in. Bombs were exploded, one of them near the American embassy. When it looked as if the *fedayeen* were gaining the upper hand in Beirut, the militia of Pierre Gemayel's party, the Kataeb, took up defensive positions around their own headquarters, and offered to assist the army 'to defend the homeland and its sovereignty'.[17]

Arafat was alarmed, and called on the Arab heads of state to 'foil the base plot against the Palestine revolution'.[18] They were quick to respond, most of them angrily rebuking Lebanon for the 'repression' and the 'horrible massacres' of the *fedayeen*. As Palestine was the business of them all, each exercised his right to criticize, advise and interfere with his Arab neighbour.

Iraq warned that measures against the *fedayeen* 'could not be considered an internal affair'.[19]

Syria closed its border with Lebanon on 22 October in order to bring pressure to bear on the government on behalf of the *fedayeen*, and accused the Lebanese army of being involved in an 'imperialist Zionist plot' to 'liquidate *fida'i* action'.[20]

Algeria's President Boumedienne reaffirmed his country's support for the *fedayeen*.[21]

Mu'ammar al-Qadhafi of Libya, recently come to power, sent a delegation to Beirut to try to 'halt the terrible massacre', and it proceeded to Damascus for talks with Arafat.[22]

President Nasser of Egypt asked President Helou to intervene personally to end 'what is taking place'. It grieved him, he said, to see 'Arab fire directed against the wrong target'. He made sure that Arafat knew of his message to Helou, and he proclaimed: 'The position of any Arab state in the national struggle is defined according to its relations with the Palestine Resistance – which we consider the truest and most honourable manifestation of the contemporary Arab struggle.'[23]

Sudan told the Lebanese government to stop the 'massacre', and to 'accept the responsibilities imposed on them by their geographical position', which were to allow the *fedayeen* to attack Israel from their territory, regardless of consequences.[24]

As might be expected, only Jordan did not criticize the Lebanese government, but instead sent a message expressing 'concern' in 'fraternal regard'. It was rather in a message to Arafat that a hint of rebuke came from King Hussein, that he 'viewed with bitterness and pain reports of bloody clashes'.[25]

Helplessly caught between intolerable alternatives, and suffering the economic consequences of the closing of the Syrian border, the Lebanese government appealed to the Arab League for a meeting to discuss what could be done.[26] The Secretary-General of the League refused to propose it, and suggested instead a formal agreement between the Lebanese government, the *fedayeen* and Syria.[27]

President Helou turned to Nasser, pleading that the heads of the 'fraternal states' could not be aware of all the facts. Nasser's response was not discouraging, so the Lebanese government formally requested him to mediate between them and the PLO; this move was intended to force the Egyptian President, the strongest of the Arab leaders, to consider their dilemma and shoulder some responsibility for any proposed solutions. Nasser wanted to be sure in advance that he would not lose face if he agreed, so he asked Yasser Arafat if he would accept his mediation. Arafat consented.[28]

So the Lebanese Chief of Staff, General Emile al-Bustani, met Arafat with the Egyptian Foreign Minister, Mahmud Riyad, in Cairo, and they hammered out terms for peace which were to prove a recipe for war. From the meeting there emerged the 'top secret' Cairo Agreement of 3 November 1969, whose clauses were never officially published, but whose general contents were soon known.[29]

The Agreement was similar to the one which King Hussein made with the PLO, and in Lebanon's case it was to prove fatal. It reveals how little backing the Lebanese could expect in their altercation with the PLO. There was almost nothing in it for their comfort.

It did stipulate that the 'Lebanese authorities – civilian and military –

will continue to exercise their full authority and responsibility in all parts of Lebanon, and under all circumstances': an understressed statement that Lebanese sovereignty was to be recognized and respected. And 'non-interference in Lebanese internal affairs' was 'guaranteed'. But what the Agreement provided above all was the legalizing of a second power in the state, a power with the right to bear arms, the right to use Lebanese territory to attack another country, and the right of direct rule in the camps. Certain checks on these powers were provided for in a loose way – joint units of the Lebanese army and the PLO were to agree upon *fedayeen* raids, and the rule in the camps was to be in co-operation with local authorities and 'within the framework of Lebanese sovereignty' – but they were quite insufficient; nothing now could save Lebanon from the violent disintegration which threatened her.

What it amounted to was that the Lebanese government had agreed to abdicate the little control it had retained over Palestinian-occupied portions of its own territory, and to lay itself open in all its vulnerability to the guns of an alien force, backed by its fraternal enemies.

Despite the clauses providing for Lebanese checks and ultimate authority, PLO control of the Palestinian camps now became total: despite the clauses forbidding the amassing of heavy weapons, they now became arsenals of all kinds of weaponry, including tanks and artillery.

The Cairo Agreement did not even stop the fighting between the *fedayeen* and the army. It went on for months. In March 1970 events took a more dangerous turn when the Kataeb militia carried out its threat to assist the security forces, and clashed directly with the *fedayeen*. Prime Minister Karamih, who had formally resumed office since the signing of the Agreement, negotiated a truce. Kamal Jumblatt, Minister of the Interior, blamed the CIA and the Lebanese intelligence agency, the Deuxième Bureau, which he said had conspired to make the public fear the *fedayeen* and their activity.[30]

Jumblatt tried to fulfil his ministerial responsibilities by requesting the PLO's voluntary restraint. After talks with Arafat, he announced that an agreement had been reached to allow Lebanese policing of the camps, but at once Sa'iqa and the PDFLP angrily denounced it, and other groups denied that it had been reached at all. Jumblatt insisted that the promises had been made, and went so far as to state that he had even persuaded the Organization to stop firing across the Israeli border; but at that all the *fedayeen* groups contradicted him fiercely, expressing outrage at the very idea, accusing the government of breaking the Cairo Agreement, and threatening the authorities with more fire and bloodshed.[31] As leftists and students continued to demonstrate and strike in sympathy with the *fedayeen*, Jumblatt cast about for face-saving excuses for his own failure to exercise authority and for PLO insubordination. He blamed small *fedayeen* groups acting on their own initiative for the disturbances (a recourse which did not serve King Hussein when he tried it), and diffidently maintained that the large ones, especially Fatah, were co-operative, even helpful to the Lebanese army, giving valuable assistance in 'border defence'.[32]

Certainly the *fedayeen* were active on the border. They fired over it and they crossed it in raiding parties. Their targets were almost exclusively civilian. (In the whole of 1969 and 1970, the number of attacks on Israeli military positions totalled two, one per year, out of a total of 560 incidents initiated from the Lebanese side of the border.[33]) All forms of attack provoked retaliation. Most often the counter-attacks took the form of return-fire, and shelling of emplacements from which Israeli towns and *kibbutzim* were fired upon. But from time to time Israel's reprisals took the form of armed incursions in considerable strength, as on 12 May 1970, when her forces hit 'Fatahland'.

According to Israeli accounts, nineteen *fedayeen* bases were 'cleared', about 100 *fedayeen* killed and seventeen captured, many Lebanese soldiers were hit, Israeli casualties were eleven wounded and none killed, and *fedayeen* forces did not attempt to attack them.[34] Lebanese accounts tallied closely enough with Israeli accounts. Both declared six Lebanese tanks to have been damaged or destroyed. Six of their soldiers, the Lebanese reported, were killed and sixteen wounded, and two civilians were killed and one abducted.[35]

Fedayeen reports gave quite a different picture. They said that their strong opposition checked the Israeli advance, that fifty Israeli aircraft had dropped napalm bombs on a number of targets, and *fedayeen* guns had brought one plane down; that engagement of Israelis on the ground at close quarters forced the enemy to retreat, and the Israeli forces suffered heavy losses. The jealousies which usually influenced *fedayeen* announcements showed themselves in differences between the reports of the various groups, chiefly in their claims to courage and self-sacrifice. Fatah claimed that of twenty-five *fedayeen* killed, twenty wounded and three missing, all but seven were Fatah members, the rest members of the ALF. Other reports by other groups claimed many more 'martyrs' from among their own ranks.[36] Exaggeration had seemed to serve them well, especially in reporting the engagement at Karameh, and so they went on exaggerating. The tales were told to excite Arab public opinion and to maintain its emotional support, and apparently they also deceived themselves.

A few days later, on 22 May, an Israeli school bus was attacked by the PFLP–GC. Eight children and four adults were killed, and twenty others were wounded. In retaliation, the Israelis shelled four Lebanese villages: twenty people, including children, were killed, and forty were wounded; some eighty houses were destroyed or damaged.[37]

The government of Israel announced that it placed 'full responsibility' on the government of Lebanon. Prime Minister Golda Meir demanded that it 'halt the acts of aggression from its territory and fulfil its obligations in returning quiet to the area', and Defence Minister Moshe Dayan warned that if the Lebanese government would not curb the terrorists, Israel would.[38]

The Lebanese government complained to the United Nations Security Council about the attacks on the villages, and blamed Israel entirely for the incidents, because, they reasoned, responsibility for the presence and activities of 'part of the Palestinian people' rested 'in the first instance with Israel', which 'would not obey UN resolutions' (of which there were many condemning her for retaliations and requiring her to desist, while offering no censure of the acts which provoked them). However, there were those within the Lebanese government who took quite a different view. Pierre Gemayel threatened to resign if the government did not act to deal with the 'unbearable situation' which the *fedayeen* had created. It did not act. The pattern of raid and reprisal continued. More than 20,000 Lebanese villagers, most of them Shi'a Muslims, fled from the border, and many of them crowded into the shanty towns and Palestinian 'camps' round Beirut.

On 16 September 1972, after undertaking heavy retaliatory raids in reprisal for the Munich massacre, Israel briefly occupied a part of South Lebanon. The government declared a state of emergency. The President, Suleiman Franjiyyeh, and the Prime Minister, Sa'ib Salam, implored the PLO to withdraw from the area. The various PLO groups disagreed among themselves as to whether or not they should comply with the Lebanese government's 'orders', and in the end refused. So the PLO stayed where it was, and continued to draw fire on the south.

After the rout of the PLO in Jordan, thousands more *fedayeen* were passed through Syria to Lebanon, into the Arqub region and the camps in the south.

The Syrians' intention was plainly to use them to undermine the Lebanese State.[39] Hafiz Assad, Deputy Defence Minister and chief of the airforce since 1966, emerged as the strong man of the Syrian Ba'th Party in 1970, and enthusiastically carried on the policy towards Lebanon which both factions of the Party, each in its turn, had aggressively pursued since 1963: to subvert the Lebanese State with a view to embracing it in 'Greater Syria'.[40] Now, ignoring the Cairo Agreement which had been concluded under the auspices of his Egyptian rival, Assad sent ever-increasing quantities of armament rolling along the Yasser Arafat Trail to the *fedayeen*. The source of the arms was the Soviet Union.

Though the PLO factions were not all equally dependent on the Syrians, or necessarily obedient to them, none of them could do without Syrian patronage. The Organization set up its military and administrative headquarters in Beirut, and, with a purposefulness born of humiliation, built up its armed strength. Never again, the leaders resolved, would they be at a military disadvantage in the face of an Arab enemy. They would appeal to the Lebanese 'masses' to back them against governments. They were 'the Revolution'.

In November 1972 they formalized their alliance with the Lebanese Left under Kamal Jumblatt in a new organization which they called the 'Participating Arab Front'. So Jumblatt, the Lebanese nationalist, who was not pro-Syrian, became, with his left-wing revolutionary adherents, a part of Syria's subversive force in his own country.

In the spring of 1973 the PLO struck again at the Lebanese with a campaign of sabotage. They blew up oil-storage tanks, tried (but failed) to set explosives in the American embassy and Beirut airport, and kidnapped Lebanese soldiers.

Again the Kataeb attacked PLO militias. This time the government ordered the army to intervene; it hit the PLO hard, using not only heavy artillery but also air power. The fighting went on for a fortnight. On 4 May a PLA brigade crossed the Syrian border. President Franjiyyeh, coming under pressures and threats from all sides, dared to protest to his friend and relation-by-marriage, Hafiz Assad. He said that 'no Lebanese will accept an army of occupation in Lebanon'.[41]

Assad, now President of Syria, responded by suggesting more talks between the Lebanese government and the PLO. So later that month another treaty was concluded, this time under Syrian auspices, and again in secret. It was called the Melkart Agreement (after the hotel where the talks took place). It noted certain agreed restrictions on the number of armed Palestinian *fedayeen* to be permitted in various parts of the country (no restriction in 'Fatahland') and the quantity and type of arms (light only) to be stored in the camps, and forbade *fedayeen* to carry arms in the towns, or to set up roadblocks. All it really did was to endorse the Cairo Agreement. The fact that such residue of authority which the Cairo Agreement had left with the Lebanese government had been flouted with impunity by the PLO hitherto, did not apparently extinguish all hope among the Lebanese that this time it would be different.

On paper all was fair, since what the PLO wanted was granted, and what the Lebanese wanted was also granted. But the two wants were mutually exclusive: Lebanese sovereignty *and* PLO licence to act as it would on Lebanese territory. It could not be, and did not prove to be, a useful agreement. The Organization did not even keep a promise to reduce the number of offices it had in Beirut; before long, it had many more. And Syria continued to augment its store of heavy weapons in the camps.

18
Power and Glory

While the PLO was shaking Lebanon apart, the Arab League, which included Lebanon, greatly increased the Organization's power and prestige. They officially recognized the PLO as the 'sole representative of the Palestinian people'.

The decision to do so came just at a time when a negotiated settlement with Israel over the territorial question seemed possible, and instantly rendered it impossible.

Yet at least some of the Arab states by now sincerely wished for peace talks, and the chance that they might be held and succeed seemed strong immediately after the 1973 October War. The Christian Lebanese hoped that a Palestinian state would be established on the West Bank of the Jordan, so that their country might be rid of the refugees and the *fedayeen*. King Hussein of Jordan did not want the West Bank to become a Palestinian state, preferring it to be a self-governing Palestinian province in union with the East Bank under his crown. He had announced this plan in March 1972, and had warned then that 'every attempt to cast doubt on any of this [proposed new constitution] or discredit it is treason against the unity of the kingdom, the cause, the people and the homeland'.[1] President Sadat hoped for any settlement which would bring peace with honour to Egypt and allow him to concentrate attention and resources on solving the dire economic problems of his country.

Peace talks were proposed. A conference was convened at Geneva on 21 December 1973, co-chaired by Henry Kissinger for the United States and Andrei Gromyko for the Soviet Union, but it could make no progress since there was instant disagreement on who should be party to the talks. Israel wanted to talk to an Arab delegation, even if it included PLO personnel. But the PLO gave no consent.

The PLO took an ambiguous stand, demanding the right to confer at Geneva, but forbidden by its own resolution embodied in its Covenant to recognize Israel and therefore unable to negotiate with her. As always, there were at least as many opinions within the PLO on whether they should join the talks if invited to do so, as there were groups. George Habash's PFLP declared, in March 1974, that it would 'resolutely and seriously struggle to bring about the failure of the Geneva conference' or any other conference 'convened on the basis of UN Resolution 242'.[2] (This resolution, passed in November 1967, was objectionable to all factions of the PLO because it required the recognition of secure boundaries for 'every state in the area', implying Israel's right to exist, and a 'just settlement of the refugee problem', rather than a return of the Palestinians to their homeland.) Habash was rebuked for taking this stand by his Soviet friends.[3] The Soviet government wanted talks to resume because it wanted to take part in the peace-making process as a means to enhance its own influence in the Middle East.

However, no invitation came to the PLO.

If the Palestinian people themselves hoped that the opportunity had come at last for their status as refugees to be changed to citizenship of their own self-governing territory, and wished that it might be seized, they had no way of making their hopes and wishes known. And if they could have made them known, no power in the Arab world could have done anything to help their realization: because from November 1973 the Palestinians were permitted to be represented only by the PLO.

At the Arab Summit at Algiers the month after the war, from 26 to 28 November 1973, a secret agreement was concluded by which all the Arab states *except Jordan* agreed that 'the national rights of the Palestinian people' would be 'restored' only 'in the manner decided by the Palestine Liberation Organization in its capacity as the sole representative of the Palestinian people'.[4] They consented to the tying of their hands by the PLO. No negotiations whatsoever should from then on be undertaken in relation to Israel by any of them unless by the express permission of the Organization. They gave it control over this aspect of their foreign policy regardless of their own respective interests. The Beirut newspaper *Al-Nahar* leaked the agreement on 4 December, and it provided a thorough discouragement to Israel to attempt any negotiation with any Arab state, since they were now all committed to following the lead of a coalition of uncontrolled armed groups dedicated uncompromisingly to her total destruction. This made it pointless for anyone to try to negotiate a peace settlement, although the USSR urged persistently that the Geneva conference be reconvened. The decision was also invidious for King Hussein, denying him any claim over the West Bank, and questioning the legitimacy of his position in his East Bank kingdom where half or more of his subjects were (Western) Palestinians.

Eleven months later, at the summit held at Rabat from 26 to 29 October 1974, King Hussein endorsed the PLO's claim to the unique right to represent the Palestinians, and therefore formally abandoned his own claim to the West Bank of the Jordan. At that conference another set of secret resolutions confirmed the Algiers decision, and were accepted as binding by *all* the Arab states.

King Hussein's change of mind was sudden and dramatic. Only five months earlier, in March 1974, he and President Sadat had issued a joint statement asserting that 'the PLO is the legitimate representative of the Palestinians except those residing in the Hashemite kingdom of Jordan'.[5]

When he arrived at Rabat, King Hussein clearly had no intention of changing his policy. Early in the conference, he pointed out to the heads of the Arab states, as Henry Kissinger had pointed out to him, that Israel would not be able to reach an agreement with 'the Resistance' (a term for the PLO which he understandably preferred to 'the Revolution').[6]

For a few moments after he had spelled this out, there was a deep silence in the hall. President Assad of Syria said there was a plot by the United States of which King Hussein should beware, for he would be the victim of it.

When Yasser Arafat's turn came to address the gathering, he ominously and truculently recalled the crushing of the *fedayeen* organizations by King Hussein. The atmosphere of the summit became threatening.

But with an eye to the supreme ideal of Arab unity, peacemakers stepped in. Their theme was that the past should not be dragged up. On this theme the most original contribution came from President Boumedienne, who said that the Algerian schools had been asked to cut down on the use of the word 'was': 'We demand the use of the future tense always.' And he declared that the Palestinian flag must be raised 'even if only on five square centimetres of land'.

President Bourguiba of Tunisia, who had been the first to propose a policy of 'stages' in 1965 and had been so berated for it that he was now an enthusiastic supporter of the Organization's official line, declared staunchly that they must all choose between King Hussein and the PLO, and that he chose the PLO.[7]

The atmosphere was not lightened until Arafat rose again to ask for co-operation between the Arab states, admitted that the Resistance had made mistakes, and asked that it be excused on the grounds that the Palestinians faced 'such harsh conditions'. It was not the first nor the last time that Arafat was to attain his ends by appealing for compassion in the name of the people whose wishes he did not consult and whose happiness and very lives he sacrificed to political expediency.

President Sadat appealed for Arab solidarity. The only unreconciled conflict among the Arabs themselves at present lay between Jordan and the PLO, he said, disregarding not only the deep animosities which persisted between the Arab states, but also what was happening in Lebanon. Israel, he said, insisted on 'exploiting the Jordanian-PLO differences' (by pointing out that there was no one with whom they could negotiate over the West Bank).

But still they could not make King Hussein change his mind. A committee was formed to explore ways and means to resolve the difficulty over the King's and the PLO's rival claims to govern the West Bank.

The committee had hardly begun to grapple with its daunting task when a message came from Hussein: *he would undertake in advance to accept and abide by any decision that they reached.* He had been persuaded not by words but by terror. There had been another attempt on his life.

Abu Iyad, while denying that Fatah had anything to do with it, was able to give details of how the plot had been laid, and to state with certainty that the 'young militants' who laid it had been betrayed. Fourteen of them were arrested, and Abu Iyad himself was accused of being their leader. Arafat defended him, and said that of the fourteen he recognized only two. This, Abu Iyad suggested, proved that it was not a Fatah plot. In any case, in his opinion, the King would only have got his just deserts.[8]

The day after the Rabat conference ended, on 30 October 1974, King Hussein addressed his subjects on television and spoke of the 'historical unanimous resolution' which, he said, had been arrived at in a 'sincere and harmonious atmosphere in which maturity and harmony prevailed'.[9]

It was a great triumph for the PLO. Unanimous Arab policy was that a Palestinian national government could only be established under the PLO. And it could set up its government on any part of Palestine that became available. King Hussein no longer had a claim to the West Bank.

That was not all. Even greater power was given to the PLO at Rabat. The group which at first had been a tool in the hands of the Nasser-dominated Arab League was now empowered by the Arab states to rule and overrule them on the central issue of their international relations.

Lebanon too had endorsed the Rabat decision. Yet inevitably Rabat strengthened the position of the PLO in Lebanon even more than the Cairo Agreement had. From now on, whatever the Organization did to 'protect' the Palestinians was legitimate. No Arab state could support the Lebanese government in its conflict with the PLO without defying the Rabat consensus.

19
An Example to the World

'In today's world', George Habash said in 1970, 'no one is innocent, no one a neutral. A man is either with the oppressed or he is with the oppressors. He who takes no interest in politics gives his blessing to the prevailing order, that of the ruling classes and exploiting forces.'[1] His words expose the philosophy of terrorism. It is that the individual has no value whatsoever in himself, but only in so far as he can be made to serve the terrorist's end.

Habash was responsible for the death or injury of multitudes of strangers. He was behind the massacre in the arrival hall of Lod airport, called 'Operation Patrick Arguello'. It was carried out by three members of the Japanese Red Army (Rengo Sekigun) with automatic rifles and grenades on 30 May 1972. In less than a minute twenty-four people were killed, shot and blown literally to pieces, and seventy-eight others lay injured. Among the dead, most of whom were pilgrims from Puerto Rica, lay two of the Japanese terrorists, one shot unintentionally by one of his comrades, the other with his head blown off by one of his own grenades. The surviving killer was a young man named Kozo Okamoto.[2]

The group to which Okamoto belonged had tortured a number of its own members to death in Japan. (One, for instance, was a young woman. They had buried her alive under the floorboards of the room in which the gang lived. Her crime had been to ask one of the comrades to pass her a paper handkerchief. The leader of the group, Fusako Shigenobu, had seen this as proof that she was 'too bourgeois', for which she deserved to die. The murdered woman was pregnant at the time.) After the Lod massacre, Shigenobu explained that her group had done it on behalf of the Palestinians 'to consolidate the international revolutionary alliance against the imperialists of the world'.[3] They had first come to know the PLO when the Japanese Red Army had made a film with a member of the PFLP in 1970, a man who later married Laila Khaled. Kozo Okamoto and the other two terrorists of the Lod massacre had been sent to train for the assignment with the PFLP at Ba'albek in Lebanon.[4]

He was sentenced to life imprisonment, although, as the judge said, no conceivable penalty would fit the crime he had perpetrated. After he had spent some time in jail, he converted to Islam. Later he asked to be converted to Judaism. He tried to circumcise himself with a pair of nail clippers. Slowly he became a 'plant', hardly speaking at all, even to visitors from Japan.[5]

Black September, Fatah's terrorist organization, blew up oil and gas installations in West Germany, Italy and Holland, hijacked planes, shot American and Belgian diplomats in the Sudan, a Jordanian in London. In September 1972, a group of them murdered eleven athletes of the Israeli team at the Olympic Games in Munich. The plot was laid by Abu Iyad, Hassan Salamah, Yusef al-Najjar, Kamal Adwan and Kamal Nasser, encouraged by the Bulgarian Intelligence Service, which, for the next decade, acted as a sub-agency of the KGB for promoting acts of international terrorism.[6] The connection between the Bulgarians and the PLO had first come about through Ahmad Jibril, leader of the PFLP–GC, who kept an apartment in Sofia.[7] Abu Iyad and his right-hand man in the plot, Fakhri al-Umari, plus a third man, Abu Daoud, met their Bulgarian mentors in Sofia in August 1972, a month before the massacre was carried out. (Abu Daoud was arrested with arms and explosives in Amman in February 1973, and confessed in a radio broadcast to his part in the Munich massacre, revealing that it had been planned in Sofia. He said that he himself had gone on from Bulgaria to West Germany to be commander in the field. 'Black September', he said, 'is merely another name for Fatah.')[8]

Abu Iyad has given an explanation for the Munich massacre along these lines: two letters had been addressed to the Olympics Committee asking that a team of Palestinian athletes be allowed to enter for the 1972 Games to be held at Munich. They were not answered. So Black September decided to play a part in the event which would prove the existence of the Palestinian people, as Abu Iyad put it.[9] They would take advantage of the world-wide media coverage of the Games. In addition, they believed they could force the release of 200 Palestinian prisoners, Kozo Okamoto, and two leaders of the 'Red Army Faction' in West Germany – Andreas Baader, a 'drop-out' with a criminal record, and Ulrike Meinhof, a fanatical member of the New Left pacifist movement. (They and their group had killed and maimed Germans and Americans with guns and bombs, and had been arrested three months earlier, after some years of terrorist activities. Both of them had been trained for 'urban guerrilla warfare' in a camp in Jordan in 1970.)[10]

Mainly because the Israelis stuck to their policy of not giving in to terrorist blackmail, the West German authorities decided to use force to rescue the hostages. But their plan was carried out badly. They promised to let the Arabs fly to an Arab country with the captives, and took them in two helicopters to an airport where a plane awaited them. When only four of the Arabs had come out of the helicopters, marksmen shot at them, killing two and injuring one; at this, Black September men, who were still inside the machines with their hostages bound and at their mercy, shot them all. Some of them might still have been alive in one of the helicopters when an Arab, after he and his comrades had alighted, threw a handgrenade into it and set the machine on fire. The German police shot three more of the terrorists, and the Arabs killed one of the policemen.

The Games went on.

'Glory to you, men of September,' the Voice of Palestine radio in Damascus cried. 'Glory, pride and victory.' Colonel Qadhafi of Libya gave the dead terrorists a state funeral. The three surviving Black September men were set free by the West German authorities when a Lufthansa plane was hijacked and eleven people held hostage a few weeks later. The United Nations General Assembly would not condemn the massacre of the athletes at Munich.

Israel fought back. The Israeli Institute for Intelligence and Special Operations (Mossad) began to seek out PLO terrorists in the Middle East and wherever else they might be found. On 10 April 1973, while the headquarters of the PDFLP in Beirut was heavily guarded (they were expecting an attack by the PFLP), a couple of dozen men dressed in *fedayeen* battledress fired mortars at the building, then stormed it. They were Israeli commandos. They removed three filing cabinets housing part of the Black September archive, and killed Yusef al-Najjar, Kamal Adwan and Kamal Nasser. Yasser Arafat was in a neighbouring building at the time, and Abu Iyad was not far away, visiting the terrorists who had carried out the Munich massacre. They were telling him stories of how they had been 'tortured by the West German police' while they had been held, briefly, in custody.[11]

The October War of 1973 boosted morale in the Arab world, and, in a spirit of self-confidence, Arab states began to use the power they had as the major oil-producers for the industrialized West. To warn the United States and West European countries what to expect if they continued to support Israel, Saudi Arabia cut oil production on 18 November 1973; others soon did the same. They embargoed oil supplies to Holland completely, and threatened the United States with total stoppage. Other Western European countries and Japan had their supplies cut by 25 per cent. Arab attempts to cut off supplies of oil to Israel had been included in the economic war planned against her since the 1948 War of Independence, and Egypt's attempt to close the sea routes of the region to Israeli trade had been largely to achieve this aim. Now the economic war was to be extended not only to those nations friendly to Israel but to the whole world.

At the end of 1973, the Organization of Petroleum Exporting Countries (OPEC) raised the price of crude oil steeply, the increase bringing peak prices up by over 300 per cent in just two months (to over $17 a barrel). A part of the increased revenues was to be used directly to promote the *fedayeen* war against Israel, but the chief aim was to bring pressure to bear on the West to force Israel to come to the peace terms the Arab states wanted.[12] Those terms would be dictated by the PLO. They could be nothing less than Israel agreeing to her own demise.

The shock of the 'oil hype' was to make itself felt throughout the world economy. The 'oil-weapon' was effective against the West to some degree, especially in Europe where there was a distinct shift in government policies to tolerance of, and in some cases enthusiasm for, the PLO. However, countries most hurt by the steep rise in the price of crude oil were not the developed countries, nor Israel, but Third World states. If the economies of the industrialized countries were damaged by the OPEC strategy, as the rise in the price of oil increased the rate of inflation where governments were already pursuing inflationary policies, Third World economies were wrecked. Still a majority of them backed the Arab bloc with their United Nations General Assembly votes in the vain hope of advantages which never materialized, or the fear of worse to come.

Fifty-six states asked the Secretary-General to include in the agenda of the twenty-ninth (1974) session of the General Assembly an item entitled 'Question of Palestine'. Another seven states later supported the proposal. (Ninety states had by this time recognized the PLO as the 'legitimate representative of the Palestinian people'.) The proposers were Arab, Muslim, Communist and African states, and Malta. Seventy-two member states – they included India, Indonesia and Jamaica – proposed that the PLO, 'the representative of the Palestinian people', be invited 'to participate in its deliberations on the question in plenary meetings'.

Austria, France, Ireland, Italy, New Zealand, Norway and Sweden supported the resolution.

Britain did not, maintaining that only the representatives of states should participate in the plenary assembly. Australia, Belgium, Canada, Denmark and the Netherlands echoed that view. So did the United States, which also raised other objections, including the opinion that the resolution 'could be interpreted as prejudging the negotiating process'.

With a large majority in its favour, the resolution was carried. So the day came, 13 November 1974, when the United Nations Organization, which had been founded to help the cause of peace between nations, received Yasser Arafat as chairman of the PLO, with due ceremony, and he mounted the rostrum in the hall of the Assembly to address the world. Outside the building there was a demonstration against the PLO, against Arafat and against his being allowed to address the UN General Assembly.

The meeting was presided over by the Algerian representative. The introduction of the guest speaker was made by President Franjiyyeh of Lebanon, whose country had been shaken by violent clashes between the national security forces and the PLO for the past six years.

In the light of the history of the Palestinian Arab resistance and the history of the Jews both in Europe and the Arab countries, Arafat's speech was laden with ironies.

Yasser Arafat condemned oppression, violence, aggression and terror. He expected the United Nations to curb the unlimited acquisition of arms. His appearance there expressed 'our faith in political and diplomatic struggle *as complements, as enhancements of armed struggle*'.

He said that 'the responsibility for fighting inflation' was 'borne most heavily by the developing countries, especially the oil-producing countries'.

Five times in his speech he equated Zionism with 'racism', and he repeatedly affirmed his own aspirations to 'peace, freedom, justice, equality and development'. He was quite certain that the Jews were not a nation. Zionism had 'severed' Jews from their 'various homelands'. Zionism was the other side of the coin of anti-Semitism, because it proposed that Jews should not live 'on an equal footing' with the 'other non-Jewish citizens' of their 'national residence'. He apparently did not notice a contradiction in then referring to 'poor and *oppressed* European Jews' being 'employed on behalf of world imperialism and the Zionist leadership'.

In Muslim Palestine, he said, 'every segment of our population enjoyed the religious tolerance characteristic of our civilization'. And, in those days, Palestine was 'a verdant land'.

Israel, having driven the Palestinian people from their homeland, had got itself accepted as a United Nations member 'with support from imperialist and colonialist Powers', and got the 'Palestinian Question deleted from the agenda of the United Nations'. As a 'base for imperialism' it launched the wars of 1956 and 1967 'to satisfy its ambitions for further expansion'. Egypt and Syria had then to 'expend exhaustive efforts' to 'resist the barbarous armed invasion', to liberate Arab lands and to restore the rights of the Palestinian people, '*after all other peaceful means had failed.*'

The 1973 war 'broke out'. The Arab victory in that war 'brought home to the Zionist enemy the bankruptcy of its policy of occupation, expansion and *its reliance on the concept of military might*'.

'The enemy we face', he said, 'has a long record of hostility even towards the Jews themselves, for there is within the Zionist entity a built-in racism against oriental Jews. *While we were vociferously condemning the massacre of Jews under Nazi rule,* Zionist leadership appeared more interested at that time in exploiting them as best it could in order to realize its goal of immigration into Palestine.'

He declared that 'those who call us terrorists wish to prevent world public opinion from discovering the truth about us and from seeing the justice on our faces'. Nobody is a terrorist who 'stands for a just cause'. A just cause is 'the freedom and liberation' of the fighter's land. The terrorists were those who waged war 'to occupy, colonize and oppress people'.

'If a record of Zionist terrorism in South Lebanon were to be compiled,' he said, 'the enormity of its acts would shock even the most hardened: piracy, bombardments, scorched-earth, destruction of hundreds of homes, eviction of civilians and the kidnapping of Lebanese citizens. This clearly constitutes a violation of Lebanese sovereignty.'

He reminded the Assembly of its resolutions which condemned Israel's 'aggression'. He did not mention Resolution 242.

He assured his audience that 'the Palestinian's allegiance to Palestine' would not wane. Nothing could persuade him to relinquish his Palestinian identity or to forsake his homeland.

He gave his account of the origins of the PLO : 'It is through our popular armed struggle that our political leadership and our national institutions finally crystallized and a national liberation movement, comprising all the Palestinian factions, organizations, and capabilities, materialized in the Palestinian Liberation Organization.' He characterized it as a patron of culture and fount of welfare. It had 'earned its legitimacy because of the sacrifice inherent in its pioneering role, and also because of its dedicated leadership of the struggle. It has also been granted this legitimacy by the Palestinian masses, which in harmony *have chosen it to lead the struggle according to its directives.* The Palestinian Liberation Organization has also gained its legitimacy by representing every faction, union or group as well as every Palestinian talent, either in the National Council or in the people's institutions. This legitimacy was further strengthened by the support of the entire Arab nation, and it was consecrated during the last Arab summit conference which reiterated the right of the Palestine Liberation Organization, in its capacity as the sole representative of the Palestinian people, to establish an independent national state on all liberated Palestinian territory.'

The PLO's 'legitimacy' was 'intensified', he said, 'as a result of fraternal support given by *other liberation movements*', and also by 'friendly, likeminded nations that stood by our side, encouraging and aiding us in our struggle to secure our national rights'.

The Palestinian people had 'borne the burdens of occupation, dispersion, eviction and terror more uninterruptedly than any other people . . .

yet all this had made our people neither vindictive nor vengeful. Nor has it caused us to resort to the racism of our enemies.'

'I am a rebel and freedom is my cause,' he said. He invited those who had converted their dreams into reality by the same sort of struggle now to share his dream 'for a peaceful future in Palestine's sacred land'. There, 'in one democratic State . . . all Jews now living in Palestine who choose to live with us . . . in peace and without discrimination' might do so. The PLO, he asserted, did not want one drop of Jewish or Arab blood to be shed.

He had come there on this day bearing 'an olive branch and a freedom fighter's gun'. Twice he begged or warned his listeners not to let the olive branch fall from his hand.

He received a long, standing ovation. Among the countries enthusiastically cheering him and his declared ideals of 'peace, justice, freedom and independence' were: China, which had seized Tibet in 1959; and the Soviet Union, which had absorbed the nations of Estonia, Latvia and Lithuania, suppressed national liberation movements in Georgia and the Ukraine, suppressed uprisings against the regimes it had imposed on Hungary and Czechoslovakia, and was to invade and seize the Muslim state of Afghanistan in 1980. There were also, among the cheerers, representatives of African and Asian states which had never in their existence held a free election; where people were imprisoned and executed at the whim of their dictators, where torture was an everyday affair, a matter of both custom and policy. There were regimes which survived only by the constant use of force against their own people, the suppression of all freedom of speech, assembly and movement; and which massacred their citizens, dispossessed their minorities, publicly hanged or shot their critics, such as Iraq and Syria. By 1974 only a small minority of countries in the United Nations were liberal, democratic, permitted political and economic freedom, were governed by the rule of impartial law, and sustained a tradition of tolerance. The United States, one of these few, did not cheer Arafat. The Israeli legation was not present.

In the subsequent debate, Israel's right to reply was limited by a vote on a Senegalese proposal supported by Iraq. The Soviet Union dubbed the people of Israel 'cruel and unscrupulous usurpers', and urged that the Geneva peace conference be reconvened. Mauritius said that after hearing Yasser Arafat it was difficult to continue to treat him as a terrorist and not as the leader of his people; his statement had shown that the PLO was not a terrorist organization whose avowed aim was Israel's destruction.

20

The Spark

The Cairo and Melkart Agreements made a legitimate armed force available to those factions within Lebanon which had long desired to overthrow the constitution. They delivered the country into the hands of its destroyers. The revolutionary factions in Lebanon saw their hour approaching. They had not been strong. Even in alliance with each other, they could not have hoped to succeed. It was the PLO which gave them their opportunity, their pretext, their military means; and it was the PLO which gave them their orders.[1]

Their alliance, called the National Movement, was largely leftist and Muslim, and so its component groups are usually referred to as the 'Islamo-Progressives'. That is not, however, a complete description.

Jumblatt's own party was the Progressive Socialist Party. Its membership consisted of some, but only some, of the Druze community. Allied to it in the early 1970s was a faction formed by a part, but again only a part, of the Shi'a Muslim community called the 'Movement of the Dispossessed', under the leadership of the Imam Musa al-Sadr, who declared himself a pacifist; but his followers formed a militia in the south of the Beqaa called al-Amal ('Hope').

Another of Jumblatt's allies was the Lebanese Communist Party. It had been outlawed for its self-proclaimed intention of working against the constitution, but Jumblatt had arbitrarily legalized it when he became Minister of the Interior. Its leader was a Greek Orthodox Christian, George Hawi, and it had many Greek Orthodox members. It was pro-Syrian and pro-Soviet. Other Communists in the alliance were pro-Chinese.

Several Nasserite groups also joined the Nationalists, most notable among them the 'Mourabitoun',[2] who described themselves as 'independent Nasserites', and were led by a man who had been tried for murder, Ibrahim Kleilat.[3]

Groups loyal to the Ba'th parties of both Iraq and Syria were joined together within the National Movement, though fiercely antagonistic to each other.

Jumblatt's alliance included three other political groups: the Movement

of 24 October, named to commemorate one of the days of fighting in
Tripoli in 1969, consisting mostly of Sunni Muslims with some Greek
Orthodox and Armenian Christians; the Arab National Movement, which
had been founded in Lebanon by George Habash and Wadi' Haddad; and
the Syrian Social Nationalist Party, which had fought in 1958 on the side of
the President.

This last, the SSNP, had split, and a part of it under In'am Ra'd now
came on to the same side as the Nasserites in the alliance with the PLO. Its
policies were, by its own definition, 'left wing'. It had been founded in 1932
as a youth movement, deliberately modelled on Hitler's Nazi Party. For its
symbol it invented a curved swastika, called the *Zawbah*. It held that the
Syrians were a superior people destined to lead the rest of the Arab world,
and it was outspokenly anti-Jewish as well as anti-Zionist. It stressed the
importance of discipline, virility, self-sacrifice. It was the only group
among the 'Nationalists' which did not want a state of Lebanon. Its aim
was the establishment of a state of 'Greater Syria', a single political entity
stretching from the Mediterranean to the Gulf, from Turkey to the Red
Sea, embracing all of Lebanon, Palestine (that is, Israel and Jordan), and
also Iraq and even Cyprus. The members were of several denominations,
mostly Greek Orthodox, but in principle it was against religion. Outlawed
in the 1960s as was the Communist Party, it too had been arbitrarily
legalized by Kamal Jumblatt in 1970.

Preparing themselves to oppose Jumblatt's revolutionary parties and
the PLO, literally to the death, were the Kataeb,[4] the Namur (Tigers),[5] the
Tanzim,[6] the Guardians of the Cedars,[7] Maronite churchmen,[8] and other
Christian groups. At first they found it difficult to get sufficient and appro-
priate arms. They bought guns wherever they could. Many had only hunting
rifles. Their only heavy weapons were a very few pieces of old artillery for
which ammunition was almost impossible to find. Their militias consisted
of the leaders' families and close associates. However, as the outbreaks of
fighting continued, arms dealers arrived in Beirut, and the arms market
began to flourish. The Maronites were able to buy whatever they could
afford on the open market. And a very literally open market it was: arms
dealers setting up stalls with guns on display at the kerbside in the streets of
Beirut. Much of the armament was Soviet or Czech made. The Christian
fighters began to carry the Russian Kalashnikovs, 'kleshens', which were the
favourite weapons of the *fedayeen*. (Later still, as arms dealing became very
big business indeed, the PLO entered it as importers and suppliers. Then
the Maronites bought arms *from the PLO itself*.[9] Go-betweens would
arrange a deal, and take the money. Trucks would then appear in the
Christian areas – East Beirut, Jounieh and the Mountain – usually at
night, and quantities of small arms and ammunition would be unloaded.)

Private armies grew. One of those which grew most rapidly was the 'Zghorta Liberation Army', the militia of President Franjiyyeh himself in his 'fiefdom' of the town of Zghorta in the north, which was to be used frequently against fellow Maronites.

A spark was all that was needed to cause a country-wide explosion. It nearly came in February 1975, when a fishermen's demonstration took place in Sidon.

The PLO had formed close ties with the Left-dominated fishermen's unions of both Sidon and Tyre. The unions were stirred to anger against a proposed new fishing company, which included ex-President Camille Chamoun among its directors. The fishermen were instructed that the company would give them 'unfair competition' if and when it started to operate. They marched through Sidon. Shots were fired, nobody knew by whom, and three people were hit, one of them Ma'ruf Sa'd, the local deputy, who was marching in the front rank of the demonstrators. (The bullet ricocheted from another man's body, according to a doctor who tried and failed to save his life, so his death might have been an accident.) When he died tens of thousands turned out for his funeral, itself an occasion for a demonstration that turned into a riot. Car tyres were burned in the streets, and the main road from Beirut was blocked. At least nineteen people were killed (accounts of the number vary) and some dozens were wounded. Prime Minister al-Solh, aware that the Maronites might act if he did not, decided to send the army to clear the road and pacify the rioters. In fact, what the army came up against was not a crowd of poor fishermen but the PLO. It did not succeed in crushing the uprising. But Kamal Jumblatt, still carrying out his duties as a minister under the constitution he wanted to overthrow, and a man who seemed always to be in at least two minds, persuaded the PLO security chief, Hassan Salamah, to have the incipient revolution called off.

There followed a tense pause in active hostilities. Hatred and anger did not abate with the return of the army to its barracks. The various religious communities made ready to protect their neighbourhoods from attack.

On Sunday, 13 April, the leader of the Kataeb Party, Pierre Gemayal, went, with an armed bodyguard, to the Beirut suburb of 'Ayn al-Rummana to attend the consecration of a new church, an event well publicized. There was a barrier across the road to hold back traffic from the crowd.

On that same Sunday there was a procession in another part of Beirut, in the district of Mazra'a, to celebrate the first anniversary of a PLO raid on Kiryat Shmona, the Israeli town near the Lebanese border.

At half past ten in the morning, a small car,[10] with its number-plate obscured, crashed through the barrier at the end of the street. Guns were aimed through its open windows and fired at the people outside the church. Four people were shot dead, one of them a member of the Kataeb.

By noon the news of the shooting had spread all over the city. Yet at one o'clock a bus full of Palestinians, en route from Mazra'a to the refugee 'camp' of Tall al-Za'tar, came past the same spot in 'Ayn al-Rummana where the shooting had occurred. The Maronites were prepared for further attack. They stopped the bus with a storm of bullets.

There is no reliable account of how many were killed in the bus, or who they were. The only point on which all accounts agree is that they were all Palestinians. The dead are numbered variously, from twenty-two to thirty-two. Some say there were women and children in the bus, others that it was full only of armed men. There were certainly some, probably a majority, of armed men. Some reports have it that those who were not killed crouched in the bus until the police came and rescued them. But according to others, there were no survivors. As the Kiryat Shmona raid had been carried out by members of the ALF, it has been assumed by some that the men in the bus were members of that group. But the procession had been a large one, attended by members of all PLO factions and by many Lebanese sympathetic to them.

Perhaps, as some have said, the bus had taken a wrong turn. By whatever route Palestinians rode from Mazra'a to Tall al-Za'tar, they had to pass through Christian territory, but they did not have to pass the very spot where the leader of the Kataeb was attending the consecration of a church, and where his militia had gathered in force in the two and a half hours since the shooting of the four Christians. Some Palestinians and members of the National Front say the bus had been deliberately diverted that way, in order for the Kataeb to have victims for their vengeance. The Kataeb themselves are certain that this vehicle full of armed men had, like the little car, been driven that way with no other mission or purpose but to attack them.

But whether this particular clash on Sunday, 13 April 1975, came about by intention or mishap, it was the spark that ignited war.

In the days after that Sunday, the Palestinians fired heavy artillery on Christian areas of East Beirut from the camp of Tall al-Za'tar. With Shi'a Muslim allies and armed Communist fighters, they overran Christian suburbs in the south-east of the city, killing, destroying and looting. The Christian militias fought back. The Lebanese army did not stir to interfere. Fierce battles raged for three days before the Arab League was able to arrange the first of many brief – and most of them merely token – ceasefire agreements.

What followed were massacres, orgies of rape and mutilation, rampages of looting and wrecking, invasion and partition. The country became a shambles. The State of Lebanon disintegrated in a bloodbath.

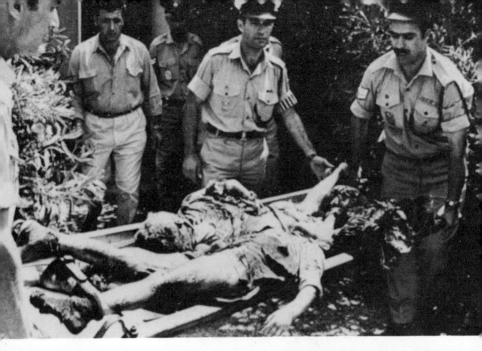

choolchildren killed by the
'FLP-GC, Israel, May 1970

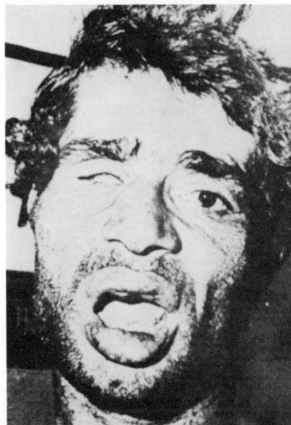

A victim of torture with his right eye
xtracted, Lebanon 1975

Masked fighters during the 'civil war' in Beirut, 1975

Weapons on sale in a Beirut street, 19

Turkish terrorist organization's 'martyr' poster,
[m]nour, after January 1976

The interior wall of an UNRWA school
in Siblin, Lebanon

[ya]ser Arafat and President Hafiz Assad of Syria meet in Damascus

Four photos showing the PLO rounding up a Lebanese who had fled from Beirut to his native city of Damour and murdering him in front of his wife and children, 1976

Elderly Christians a moment before being shot by a Libyan mercenary with the PLO, Damour, January 1976. The photo was taken and sold to *Stern* magazine by another Libyan.

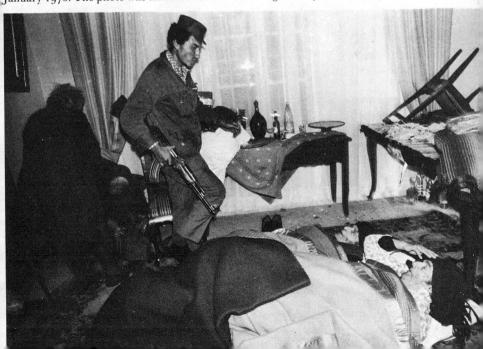

Haj Amin al-Husseini, 1946

George Habash

Abu Iyad

Nayef Hawatmeh

Kamal Jumblatt

Father Mansour Labaky, th
priest of Damour

Major Sa'd Haddad

Bachir Gemayel

Amin Gemayel

A Palestinian woman pleads for her life after Christian forces invade the Moslem quarter of Karantina, January 1976

Bodies bulldozed together on the street, Karantina, January 1976

A tourist bus burnt out by Fatah raiders, Israel, March 1978

A street in Ashrafiyah after being bombed by the Syrians, 1978

Children mutilated and killed by a Syrian atta Beirut, 1981

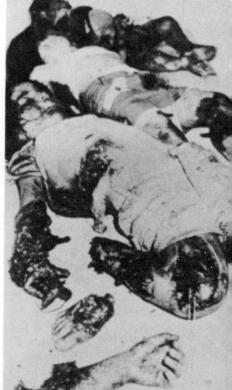

21
Carnival of Death

In the first week of the civil war some hundreds of motorists, halted in a traffic jam in Beirut, witnessed the execution of a man by the PLO. The captors and their victim stood on a piece of open ground at the side of the Avenue Sami al-Solh. Some Lebanese, probably Maronite, were guarded by *fedayeen* armed with 'kleshens'. The captives' hands were tied behind their backs. One was singled out for special attention. Round his neck the PLO militiamen tied sticks of explosives. People in their cars looked and waited uneasily for the arrival of the special police in red berets whose business it was to deal with violent incidents in the streets, but they did not appear. The victim stood still, 'with strange quietness and dignity', as one witness has said,[1] while the *fedayeen* prepared literally to blow his head off. They set a fuse, and ran back from the man, who continued to stand where he was, quite still, until the explosion came. Not only was he decapitated, but the rest of his body was blown to pieces.

Districts of Beirut became 'no go' areas for all but those whose religion let them in. A person's religion was enough to condemn him or her to abduction, humiliation, rape, mutilation or murder. It was not long before a brisk trade in false identity papers was underway. A person moving through the city – and before long anywhere in the country – might depend for his or her life on correctly identifying which roadblock lay ahead, getting the right papers ready to show the militiamen (many of them boys in their early teens), and remembering whether to give a Christian or a Muslim name. Often those who made mistakes were killed on the spot.[2]

While death and torture were suffered in the streets, the political battle went on, most heatedly between Pierre Gemayel and Kamal Jumblatt. Jumblatt drew up a list of fourteen demands. They included one that Lebanon be declared an Arab state, another that the Christians give an undertaking not to indulge in any 'confessional provocation', an example of which he gave as the ringing of a tocsin, another that 'full respect' be paid to the 'Palestinian movement', and a fourth that two Maronite ministers resign.[3] To this last only, Pierre Gemayel agreed. The result was that the government fell. President Franjiyyeh appointed a cabinet of military men, which provoked such an outcry it was soon dissolved, and Rashid Karameh became Prime Minister again.

From June to September a six-man cabinet 'ruled' by emergency powers. Officially a ceasefire prevailed, but there were constant outbreaks of fighting. Hundreds of acts of terrorism were perpetrated against the Christians, kidnappings, murders and mutilations. The Kataeb interpreted the terrorism as part of the plan to keep the hate, the desire for revenge, the sectarian hostilities alive and active. They believed that criminals were hired to do this work: by whom they could only conjecture, but their suspicions fell on Iraq and Libya.[4]

In August there was fighting in the north round Tripoli, between the Muslims who supported Rashid Karameh and Christians of Zghorta who supported Suleiman Franjiyyeh. And Lebanese fought Lebanese in the neighbourhood of Zahle in the Beqaa. Christians began to pour southwards from Tripoli and converge on the Maronite area round Jounieh, which was soon to become the unofficial capital of a Maronite enclave.

In September, after a bus was attacked in Zghorta and its Muslim passengers killed, Islamo-Progressives massacred Maronite villagers at Beit Millat. This time the Lebanese army was sent in, only to be accused by the Islamo-Progressives of giving aid to the Maronites. The Christians, in their turn, struck at the Muslim quarters of Beirut, and Muslims at once retaliated against a Christian quarter of the city.

On 15 September 1975 Kamal Jumblatt called for a general strike. The response he hoped for did not come, but fighting broke out in Beirut between his National Movement and the Christian forces. And so in the autumn the war exploded again.

Now the National Movement was openly joined by Fatah; the carnage was massive. Deaths from the fighting averaged about fifty a day. National Movement fighters and youths from the camps looted and destroyed the stores in the heart of Beirut. Dead and mutilated bodies lay everywhere in public places: corpses of sexually violated women and children, and of men with their genitals cut off and stuffed into their mouths. Shop windows were shattered and their contents looted by a multitude of beggars, many of them small ragged boys out of the camps, who would offer the goods for sale on the streets, wildly setting their own prices on items whose value they could not imagine.[5] Garbage piled up in the streets. Piped water and electric power were cut off more often than not. People were afraid to leave their apartments and seek safety elsewhere, knowing they would lose everything to the looters, who would even tear window frames and plumbing fixtures out of the walls.

To add to the terror and destruction, the Syrian PLO group, Sa'iqa, began its own campaign of bomb explosions in the commercial centre of the city. As this was a mixed area, its targets were indiscriminate. PLO offices and men were hit. It was the covert beginning of a direct Syrian assault on the weakening state. Before the end of 1975, President Assad had started to deploy the Yarmouk and Hittin brigades of the PLA in the Beqaa.

The fighting in the mainly Muslim western side of the city intensified as the Mourabitoun battled against the Kataeb. The commander-in-chief of the Kataeb, Pierre Gemayel's son Bachir, moved his men into the tourists' hotel quarter of the city near the sea front, to try to defend the harbour and the business centre against the Mourabitoun and the PLO.[6] The Mourabitoun took up their positions in the heights of the Murr Tower, an unfinished skyscraper owned by a Christian, and fired on the Kataeb in the Holiday Inn. The Kataeb held out for some weeks but were eventually driven back to their own eastern side of the divided city to try to defend it at all costs.

But here, right in the Maronite heartland, was the Palestinian 'camp' of Tall al-Za'tar. For many months before the outbreak of hostilities, Maronite businessmen driving from their offices in the city to their homes in the mountains had been stopped on the road through the camp by armed Palestinian boys and forced to show their identity papers. And now, from their strongholds in Tall al-Za'tar, the PLO forces were shelling the factories and offices of the eastern Christian suburbs of the city. The Kataeb and their allies marked Tall al-Za'tar for destruction.

In November both France and the Vatican sent envoys to attempt mediation, but predictably they achieved nothing. The Maronites, over whom they might hope to exert some influence, could not simply decide unilaterally to stop fighting and let themselves be overwhelmed and their country and their freedom lost; and neither France nor the Church could have had any sound reason to expect the National Movement, largely Druze and Muslim and partly Greek Orthodox, to accept their advice.

It is instructive to hear from Kamal Jumblatt why he waged the war, or allowed himself to be drawn into it by the PLO. He admitted that there was a kind of wantonness, a touch of terrible frivolity in the conduct of the warfare on the part of the Lebanese revolutionary groups, which was present too in his own motivation: 'True, there is something adventuristic about the whole thing, but then, life itself is a calculated and deliberate adventure.'[7]

The feeling of high 'adventure' was displayed in the streets of Beirut as the numbers of the dead and maimed mounted. Snipers on roofs or at high windows picked off unidentifiable victims in the streets, in their rooms, in shops and offices. A common sight was an open truck bearing a Soviet heavy machine-gun known as a 'Douchka', the gunman holding its grips with both hands to keep his balance as the vehicle hurtled through the streets and careened round corners. (It reminded onlookers of bronco-riding, or water-skiing, and the gunmen came to be known as 'water-skiers'.) Everywhere in the city 'armed elements' sauntered in public places wearing masks, balaclavas, or squares of cloth covering all their features, or carnival papier-mâché faces, comic or grotesque, under cowboy stetsons, helmets, or any kind of headgear. Feather boas were seen draped round necks and shoulders under masked faces, and bits and pieces of all kinds of uniforms were worn: jungle camouflage fatigues, jeans and T-shirts. Guns were carried as an indispensable necessity, even in restaurants and on the beaches, by women as well as men. The masking was done often out of a genuine need for fighters to conceal their identity and so avert possible vengeance. But a certain illicit excitement in the freedom to kill with impunity filled the streets, and the 'adventure' attracted adventurers from far beyond the shores of Lebanon.

Many a *franc tireur* toted his gun in the ranks of the *fedayeen* and the Marxists. Also bourgeois idealists, youths from Europe, most of them die-hards of the New Left's militant 'peace-movements' of the late 1960s and now playing at revolution, and some of them neo-Nazis, were drawn here from the safe societies of the West to revel in the 'real thing'. The parasitic PLO 'state' in Lebanon was a subversives' honeypot. Here they had licence to shoot and kill in an alien world, with no consequence to themselves. Would-be heroes of 'the Revolution', playboys and playgirls of terrorism from West Germany, Italy, Scandinavia and the Netherlands, came to dress up, strut, blow up, gun down.[8] It was a masquerade with a cruelty all too real. The adventure required the suffering and dying of multitudes of helpless people. It was a carnival of death.

To add to the theatricality of the scene, convoys of cars with guns protruding from the windows, armoured vehicles and motorcycles would scream through the streets accompanying Arafat or Abu Iyad on their visits to politicians, foreign envoys, allied commanders of the revolutionary forces. Then, in some office or apartment block or public building, dozens of men armed with 'kleshens' would push down the corridors ahead of the great man: Arafat wearing his *kaffiyah* pinned back from his face, dark glasses, a three-day growth of beard; or Abu Iyad, another short stout man dwarfed by huge bodyguards.

To ideological dreams, Lebanese and Palestinians were sacrificed in their tens of thousands, Christians, Druze and Muslims. There has not been, and probably could not be, a full tally of the massacres, let alone an accurate numbering of the dead. But what is certain and should be known is that there were many massacres, that uncountable atrocities were committed during the seventeen months (April 1975 to November 1976) of what was called the 'civil war' and the years of strife and bloodshed which followed it. News of only some of the mass killings spread beyond the districts and villages where they were perpetrated: in July 1975 Christian villagers were killed at Qaa; in September three monks, blind and old, were butchered at Deir Achache; in October unarmed Christians were massacred at Tall Abbas.

On 6 December 1975 four of Bachir Gemayel's men were killed, just as Pierre Gemayel was about to leave for talks with President Assad of Syria in Damascus, and so, in retaliation, the Kataeb massacred some seventy Muslims. The day was called 'Black Saturday'.

The war continued into the new year, 1976. The Christians concentrated an attack on the crowded slum quarter of Karantina (once used for the isolation of infectious diseases), where Lebanese Shi'a refugees from the southern border villages, Kurds, Syrian migrant labourers and others lived among Palestinians, under the 'protection' of the *fedayeen* groups, which had fortified the camp with heavy armament. In the fierce struggle, the civilian death toll was high, and finally, after much blood was spilt, the Christian forces emptied the 'camp' and bulldozed it to the ground.

In 1976, there were mass killings in Chekka, Taalabaya, Jouar al-Hoz, 'Aintura, 'Ubaydiyya, Araya, Chebanieh, Aichieh[9] and Ma'athir Bayt al-Din. Whole towns were abandoned in ruins. For the Christians, one town in particular came to symbolize their agony: Damour.

Damour

Damour has become legendary, not because its fate was unique, but because its very name has connotations which reinforce its tragic significance for the Christians of Lebanon. It is similar to an Arabic root meaning 'destruction'.

Damour lies, now in ruins, to the east of the Beirut–Sidon road, on the slopes of a foothill of the Lebanon range. On the other side of the road, beyond a flat stretch of coast, is the sea.

It was a town of some 25,000 people, containing five churches, three chapels, seven schools, private and public, and one public hospital where Muslims of the neighbourhood were treated along with the Christians, at the expense of the town.

On 9 January 1976, three days after Epiphany, the priest of Damour, Father Mansour Labaky, was carrying out a Maronite custom of blessing the houses with holy water. As he stood in front of a house on the side of the town next to the Muslim village of Harat Na'ami, a bullet whistled past his ear and hit the house. Then he heard the rattle of machine-guns. He went inside the house, and soon learned that the town was surrounded. Later he found out by whom and how many – the forces of Sa'iqa, consisting of 16,000 Palestinians and Syrians, and units of the Mourabitoun and some fifteen other militias, reinforced by mercenaries from Iran, Afghanistan, Pakistan and a contingent of Libyans.

Father Labaky telephoned the Muslim sheikh of the district and asked him, as a fellow religious leader, what he could do to help the people of the town. 'I can do nothing,' he was told 'They want to harm you. It is the Palestinians. I cannot stop them.'[1]

While the shooting and some shelling went on all day, Father Labaky telephoned a long list of people, politicians of both the Left and the Right, asking for help. They all said with apologies and commiserations that they could do nothing.

Then he telephoned Kamal Jumblatt, in whose parliamentary constituency Damour lay. 'Father,' Jumblatt said, 'I can do nothing for you, because it depends on Yasser Arafat.' He gave Arafat's phone number to the priest.

An aide answered, and when he would not call Arafat himself, Father Labaky told him, 'The Palestinians are shelling and shooting at my town. I can assure you as a religious leader, we do not want the war, we do not believe in violence.' He added that nearly half the people of Damour had voted for Kamal Jumblatt, 'who is backing you,' he reminded the PLO man. The reply was, 'Father, don't worry. We don't want to harm you. If we are destroying you it is for strategical reasons.'[2]

Father Labaky did not feel that there was any less cause for worry because the destruction was for strategical reasons, and he persisted in asking for Arafat to call off his fighters. In the end the aide said that they, PLO headquarters, would 'tell them to stop shooting'.

By then it was eleven o'clock in the evening. As the minutes passed and the shooting still went on, Father Labaky called Jumblatt again on the telephone and told him what Arafat's aide had said. Jumblatt's advice was that the priest should keep trying to make contact with Arafat, and call other friends of his, 'because', he said, 'I do not trust him'.

At about half-past eleven the telephone, water and electricity were all cut off. The first invasion of the town came in the hour after midnight, from the side where the priest had been shot at earlier in the day. The Sa'iqa men stormed into the houses. They massacred some fifty people in the one night. Father Labaky heard screaming and went out into the street. Women came running to him in their nightdresses, 'tearing their hair, and shouting "They are slaughtering us!"'

The survivors, deserting that end of the town, moved into the area round the next church. The invaders then occupied the part of the town they had taken.

In the morning the priest

managed to get to the one house despite the shelling to bring out some of the corpses. And I remember something which still frightens me. An entire family had been killed, the Can'an family, four children all dead, and the mother, the father, and the grandfather. The mother was still hugging one of the children. And she was pregnant. The eyes of the children were gone and their limbs were cut off. No legs and no arms. It was awful. We took them away in a banana truck. And who carried the corpses with me? The only survivor, the brother of the man. His name is Samir Can'an. He carried with me the remains of his brother, his father, his sister-in-law and the poor children. We buried them in the cemetery, under the shells of the PLO. And while I was burying them, more corpses were found in the street.

The town tried to defend itself. Two hundred and twenty-five young men, most of them about sixteen years old, armed with hunting guns and none with military training, held out for twelve days. The citizens huddled in basements, with sandbags piled in front of their doors and ground-floor windows. Father Labaky moved from shelter to shelter to visit the families and take them bread and milk. He went often 'to encourage the young men defending the town'. Only three more townspeople were killed between the first night and the last day, 23 January. But on that day, when the final onslaught came, hundreds of the Christians were killed.

> The attack took place from the mountain behind. It was an apocalypse. They were coming, thousands and thousands, shouting 'Allahu Akbar! God is great! Let us attack them for the Arabs, let us offer a holocaust to Mohammad!' And they were slaughtering everyone in their path, men, women and children.

Whole families were killed in their homes. Many women were gang-raped, and few of them left alive afterwards. One woman saved her adolescent daughter from rape by smearing her face with washing blue to make her look repulsive.

As the atrocities were perpetrated, the invaders themselves took photographs and later offered the pictures for sale to European newspapers.

Survivors testify to what happened. A young girl of sixteen, Soumayya Ghanimeh, witnessed the shooting of her father and brother by two of the invaders, and watched her own home and the other houses in her street being looted and burned.[3]

> As they were bringing me through the street the houses were burning all about me. They had about ten trucks standing in front of the houses and were piling things into them. I remember how frightened I was of the fire. I was screaming. And for months afterwards I couldn't bear anyone to strike a match near me. I couldn't bear the smell of it.

She and her mother Mariam, and a younger sister and infant brother, had been saved from being shot in their house when she ran behind one Palestinian for protection from the pointing gun of the other, and cried out, 'Don't let him kill us!'; and the man accepted the role of protector which the girl had suddenly assigned to him. 'If you kill them you will have to kill me too,' he told his comrade. So the four of them were spared, herded along the streets between the burning houses to be put into a truck, and transported to Sabra camp in Beirut. There they were kept in a crowded prison hut. 'We had to sleep on the ground, and it was bitterly cold.'

When eventually Father Labaky found the charred bodies of the father and brother in the Ghanimeh house 'you could no longer tell whether they were men or women'.

In a frenzy to destroy their enemies utterly, as if even the absolute limits of nature could not stop them, the invaders broke open tombs and flung the bones of the dead into the streets.

Those who escaped from the first attack tried to flee by any means they could, with cars, carts, cycles and motorbikes. Some went on foot to the seashore to try to get away in boats. But the sea was rough and the wait for rescue was long, while they knew their enemies might fall upon them at any moment.

Some 500 gathered in the Church of St Elias. Father Labaky went there at six in the morning when the tumult of the attack awakened him. He preached a sermon on the meaning of the slaughter of innocents. And he told them candidly that he did not know what to tell them to do. 'If I say flee to the sea, you may be killed. If I say stay here, you may be killed.'

An old man suggested that they raise a white flag. 'Perhaps if we surrender they may spare us.'

Father Labaky gave him his surplice. He put it on the processional cross and stood it in front of the church. Ten minutes later there was a knock on the door, three quick raps, then three lots of three.

They were petrified. Father Labaky said that he would go and see who was there. If it was the enemy, they might spare them. 'But if they kill us, at least we shall die all together and we'll have a nice parish in Heaven, 500 persons, and no check points!' They laughed, and the priest went to the door.

It was not the enemy but two men of Damour who had fled the town and had seen the white flag from the seashore. They had come back to warn them that it would not help to raise a flag. 'We raised a flag in front of Our Lady, and they shot at us.'

Again they discussed what could be done. The priest told them that one thing they must do, although it was 'impossible', was to pray for the forgiveness of those who were coming to kill them. As they prayed, two of the young defenders of the town who had also seen the flag walked in and said, 'Run to the seashore now, and we will cover you.'

The two youths stood in front of the church and shot in the direction from which the *fedayeen* were firing. It took ten minutes for all the people in the church to leave the town. But all 500 got away except one old man who said he could not walk and would prefer to die in front of his own house. He was not killed. Father Labaky found him weeks later in a PLO prison, and heard what had happened after they left.

A few minutes after they had gone, 'the PLO came and bombed the church without entering it. They kicked open the door and threw in the grenades.' They would all have been killed had they stayed.

The priest led his flock along the shore to the palace of Camille Chamoun. But when they got there they found it had already been sacked and partly burnt. They found shelter, however, in the palace of a Muslim, who 'did not agree with the Palestinians', and then got into small boats, which took them out to a bigger boat, in which they sailed to Jounieh. 'One poor woman had to give birth to her baby in the little open boat on the rough winter sea.'

In all, 582 people were killed in the storming of Damour. Father Labaky went back with the Red Cross to bury them. Many of the bodies had been dismembered, so they had to count the heads to number the dead. Three of the men they found had had their genitals cut off and stuffed into their mouths.

The ruined town became one of the main PLO centres for the promotion of international terrorism. The Church of St Elias was used as a repair garage for PLO vehicles and a range for shooting-practice with targets painted on the eastern wall of the nave.[4]

The commander of the combined forces which descended on Damour on 23 January 1976 was Zuhayr Muhsin, chief of al-Sa'iqa, known since then throughout Christian Lebanon as 'the Butcher of Damour'. He was assassinated on 15 July 1979 at Cannes in the South of France.

23
Syria Turns

The PLO, in command over its allies of the National Movement, made considerable gains from the Loyalist forces in the early months of 1976. They pressed the Maronites back into their ancient homelands of the Mountain and the coast north of Beirut. When Syria sent PLA units into the Beqaa to assist the PLO's attack on Christian towns in the east of Lebanon, the powerless President Franjiyyeh went to plead with his friend, President Assad of Syria, but acceded to, rather than pressed, demands. Assad extracted a promise from him that he would put forward political reforms in Lebanon which would redress the balance of power to the benefit of the Muslim population. The Christians were to have fewer of the top positions in government, the civil service, and the army, and religion was no longer to be a factor in qualification for civil service jobs.

Franjiyyeh duly announced the constitutional changes in the hope that they would appease the Muslims and the Left. Many Lebanese believed that now the war would be over, but they were wrong. The reforms encouraged the National Movement to fight on. Jumblatt and his fellow revolutionaries regarded the concessions as a victory for them, but only a step towards the far more radical changes they desired, and which the victory encouraged them to fight on for. So alongside the PLO they pressed their attack harder against the Christians and came very close to total victory.

In their desperation, the Christians turned again, as in 1958, to the United States for help. But this time there was to be no landing of the marines. The American Secretary of State, Henry Kissinger,[1] was trying at the time to negotiate a Middle East settlement between the Arab states and Israel. He needed President Assad's co-operation, and President Assad was the ally of the National Movement. Kissinger did send a special envoy, Dean Brown, whose help took the form of advice to the Christians (as many of them testify) to abandon their country to the PLO and the Left, and find homes elsewhere in the West. They refused and fought on.

The defenders of Lebanese independence and constitutional order thought at one point (March 1976) that they might be about to receive moral support from the United Nations, when Secretary-General Kurt Waldheim warned the Security Council that the war in Lebanon was a potential threat to world peace. At once the Christian President of Lebanon sent him a message of gratitude and agreement, but the Muslim Prime Minister sent a protest. The United Nations was dominated by the Communist bloc and its Third World clients, a fact of which Lebanese governments had often enough taken full advantage when they had called upon that institution to censure Israel. Now Christian Lebanon could hardly expect justice and truth to sprout where injustice and mendacity had so assiduously been cultivated. What it reaped was what it had helped to sow. The Secretary-General of the UN apologized to the Prime Minister, agreeing that, after all, the war in Lebanon was an 'internal issue', and he ignored the message from the President.

Pierre Gemayel suggested that the Palestinian refugees should be dispersed throughout the Arab world.[2] But this was declared quite unacceptable by the Muslims, the Left, the pan-Arab parties, the PLO and the Arab states. With no prospect of a change in the conditions that had caused the disintegration, the Maronites could do nothing but fight on for their own survival, which they did in a mood of grim and determined realism. They came to the conclusion that they might have to accept the partitioning of their country, but with great reluctance and only if there were no other way of preserving their freedom.

The forces against them increased in number. In March 1976 one of the commanding officers of the Lebanese army, Brigadier Aziz al-Ahdab, joined with the PLO and the National Movement, and attempted a *coup d'état*. He failed because of the composition of the army, which now broke into pieces along confessional lines. One part of it remained loyal to President Franjiyyeh, but was impotent. When, soon afterwards, the presidential palace at Ba'abdr was attacked, Franjiyyeh had to move to Kfour in the north, and there were yet more breaks in the groupings of the forces until there were no fewer than fifteen little armies.

One of the break-away sections was led by Ahmad al-Khatib, cousin of a socialist deputy named Zahir al-Khatib, who was a friend of Kamal Jumblatt. ('A patriotic young officer with a good sense of politics,' Jumblatt said of Ahmad.[3]) He received arms and money from Iraq and Libya. As a close ally of the PLO, he moved his units southwards, in pursuit of the Christians who had fled that way to join their co-religionists when the war was raging in Beirut and the north; he intended to hunt them to extinction. His men, most of them professional and well-equipped soldiers, emptied or besieged the Christian towns and villages. It cannot be told how many people they killed, only it is certain they amounted to thousands. And as thousands more fled the country, Lieutenant al-Khatib came near to satisfying his ambition to wipe out the entire Christian population in that part of Lebanon.

As his forces surrounded and besieged the town of Zahle in the Beqaa, the National Movement and the PLO advanced on the Maronites in Beirut, and came right to the Metn, the constituency of Pierre Gemayel's elder son Amin, the Maronite heartland. The strenuously fought war was all but over for the Christians.

Again President Franjiyyeh went to Damascus, to plead in the powerhouse of Lebanon's undoing. He issued an invitation to Syria to send its army, openly, into Lebanon. And Assad agreed to come to the aid of the Christians, *against* the National Movement and the instrument of his ambition in Lebanon, the PLO.

It was an apparent reversal of policy which cried out for explanation. The 'reason' Assad gave for sending contingents of the regular Syrian army *against* the PLO explains nothing. It was, he said in a public speech in July 1976, 'in order to protect the Palestinian resistance and the Arab nature of Lebanon'.

Less self-contradictory reasons can be found.

In pursuit of the dream of 'Greater Syria', Assad wanted to dominate Lebanon. But a new Lebanon under the Lebanese Left, far from accepting Syrian hegemony, would have united all the anti-Syrian elements in the Arab world, and threatened his own position. He himself was an Alawite (a religion Muslims despised more than Christianity or Judaism), and kept himself in power with an Alawite military elite under his brother's command. Within the Lebanese Left were many anti-Alawite Druze and Sunni Muslims, as well as pro-Iraqis, pro-Libyans and pan-Arabists. Within the PLO were more pro-Iraqis and pro-Libyans. The Syrian President's personal relations with Arafat were strained.

Assad also had cause to fear that a Lebanon under the PLO would invite invasion by Israel; but if he went in now to stop the revolutionaries, the United States would approve, and Israel would not intervene. The invitation from the Lebanese President was an opportunity for him to seize. It meant that he could claim legitimacy for direct military interference.

So he changed his tactics. But it must still remain a puzzle why Assad had not foreseen the possibility of a victory for his proxy armies; and if he had not foreseen it, why he had wasted resources on them; or if he had foreseen it, why he had not earlier understood these dangers in it; or if he had foreseen the dangers, why he went on sending arms and supplies to Jumblatt[4] and the *fedayeen* until almost the last moment before he switched sides. To look for logic is to find frustration.

He proceeded to take a direct hand in the war. At the end of March 1976 he told Jumblatt to accept a ceasefire. Jumblatt refused, wanting to press home his victory – out of a desire for revenge, Assad believed.[5] The refusal gave Assad the excuse he needed to send Syrian troops, no longer under the guise of Sa'iqa or the PLA, into Lebanon.

Syria's volte-face shocked and infuriated Jumblatt: 'We controlled 82 per cent of the Lebanese territory and nearly all the towns, but when the Isolationists were just about to raise the white flag . . . the Syrians chose to send a regiment with 200 tanks . . . to penetrate our territory, in response to President Franjiyyeh's frantic appeals.'[6]

The Syrian army raised the siege of Zahle, took control of the strategically important town of Chtoura – near the point where the main roads from the Beqaa, the north, Damascus and Beirut meet – and pushed on towards Beirut. When they came close to confronting the combined strength of the PLO and the National Movement, one contingent stopped near Sofar in the mountains, while another curved southwards to Sidon, and turned northwards from there, to take control of the disused Beirut international airport.

As the Syrians rapidly overcame the revolutionaries and the PLO, Arafat appealed to the Arab League for protection. He presented a petition for a meeting of the League to talk about Lebanon, and was at once given support by Syria's strongest rival, Egypt. President Sadat, who had agreed to a disengagement treaty with Israel, seized this opportunity to restore Egyptian prestige by a swift response to the PLO's call. He also sent the PLA's 'Ayn Jaloud brigade, based in Egypt, to fight with Fatah and the smaller factions.

The Syrians pushed the opposing PLO forces back to their southern bases. Israel looked on. When the Syrian army approached Nabatiyyah, about nine miles from the border, Israel drew a 'Red Line', and let Syria know through the United States that she preferred, for the present, to have the PLO on her northern border rather than Syria itself. Assad heeded the warning and stopped short of Nabatiyyah.

So Syria became an occupying power of the greater part of the country, but not of the south.

Meanwhile, the Lebanese politicians had been trying to restore constitutional government and normality. A new president, Elias Sarkis, Governor of the Central Bank, was elected with a respectable majority, gaining the necessary Muslim as well as Christian votes. As he was Syria's preferred candidate, his success was not surprising. His rival candidate, Raymond Eddé, whom he defeated overwhelmingly, was no longer an ally of Gemayel and Chamoun, but of the PLO and the Left. As the election proceeded, the PLO bombarded the temporary parliament building, Villa Mansour, with mortar shells. Not surprisingly, the attack did not make Eddé more popular with the electors. As it did not succeed, Abu Iyad later explained the bombardment by saying that the PLO was 'confused', and did not intend to prevent the elections, but was only making a gesture.[7]

President Sarkis chose Rashid Karameh to be Prime Minister yet again.

Raymond Eddé left the country, after his life had been threatened several times.

In June 1976, as Arafat had requested, the Arab League Secretariat summoned a meeting. Syria, Libya, Saudi Arabia and the Sudan agreed to send troops to 'enforce peace'. Assad sent more Syrian troops in at once, while there were only token forces from the others. The Syrian reinforcements and a few Libyans officially entered Lebanon on 21 June as a vanguard of an 'Arab Peace-Keeping Force'. Under the new name, Syria continued to hammer the PLO. Arafat's enemy had been authorized to protect him.

On 22 June the Maronites' combined 'Lebanese Forces', with the support of Syrian artillery, began a last, long offensive against Tall al-Za'tar.

24
Tall al-Zaʿtar

Tall al-Zaʿtar means 'The Hill of Thyme'. The district had been a Christian one, but had been granted to Palestinians in 1948. They had lived there peacefully enough until the PLO came and turned Tall al-Zaʿtar, like all the other camps, into a military base. The civilians were, as a matter of policy, used as shields for the fighting force. It had permanent buildings, including high-rise apartment houses, alongside the shanties, as did most Palestinian 'camps' in Beirut. People who had come from the same parts of Palestine huddled together in tight communities. Tall al-Zaʿtar was not as mixed as other Beirut camps, where Kurds, Lebanese Shiʿas uprooted from the south by the raids and counter-raids on the Israeli border, and foreigners such as Syrian migrant workers lived among the Palestinians.

One of the larger buildings was a nursery-hospital for abandoned babies. Until the middle of 1975 it had been run by Maronite nuns.[1] In May 1975, about three weeks after the start of the civil war, the PLO broke into the building and set up their Douchka machine-guns on the roof.

They chose hospitals and schools for gun emplacements partly because these were large buildings whose roofs made good vantage points, and partly because they believed that the Christian militias would hesitate to fire back on such targets.

To preserve this form of defence, the PLO kept the nuns and their young charges hostage. In the nuns' care were some eighty babies aged up to fifteen months and a few pregnant mothers, of various religions. Eventually a sister of their order in Italy organized their release through the Red Cross, the Italian branch contacting the Lebanese branch, which negotiated with the PLO. But the *fedayeen* would not let them drive away the larger of their two cars. On its side was the name of the nursery, 'The Good Shepherd', which made it a valuable asset. They used it to transport arms and men through the Christian roadblocks. When the nuns left the nursery-hospital, Tall al-Zaʿtar was an entirely Palestinian encampment, and came under constant fire from the Christian forces.

In January 1976 the Tanzim surrounded the camp with about 300 men. The PLO believed that a very much greater force was threatening them.

The Tanzim left one route open, to Aley, the largely Druze area of the Chouf mountains, but the PLO tried to prevent the people of the camp from leaving. The Fatah count of the number in the camp was 35,000.[2] Only a few found a way out, though many must have wished to go. In June the Christian groups brought their combined strengths to bear on Tall al-Za'tar.

Control of the camp was divided among the militias of various PLO factions. One section was under Fatah, another under the PFLP–GC (Jibril's group), another under the PFLP (Habash's), a fourth under the PDFLP (Hawatmeh's), and a fifth under Sa'iqa, which, unusually for a Sa'iqa group after the open entry of Syria into the war, did not turn to fight against its fellow PLO factions. Among the fighters were boys as young as twelve years old and some women.[3]

When regular Syrian units entered Lebanon on 1 June, they added their fire to the Christians' bombardment of the Beirut camps of Sabra and Chatila. Three weeks later the final onslaught on Tall al-Za'tar was mounted. PLO reinforcements which tried to reach the camp were stopped by a Syrian battalion.

Some 40,000 rounds rained on Tall al-Za'tar in any single day and night. Above ground much of the camp was reduced to rubble. But the *fedayeen* moved about underground through a complicated network of tunnels. The high command was determined that they should hold out.[4] Conditions within the camp became critical, with acute shortage of food and water, as the bombardment continued day after day. The bodies of old women and infants lay in the dust of the streets beside dead fighters. The ideal of self-sacrifice, imposed on the civilians by a leadership which itself took no risks, was never known to be the choice of the unhappy people themselves. And not all of the fighters who fell with their guns in their hands were cut down by the fire of the Christians. Some who tried to surrender or escape from the camp were shot in the back by their own comrades.[5] From time to time, the corpses were collected in an underground chamber to be stowed into plastic bags. Then they were carried out again, to lie in the streets for days on end, rotting to liquefaction in their bags in the heat of summer.[6] The stench from the camp spread for miles.

Soon hunger and disease began to kill more than bullets and shells. Inevitably, dysentery struck and spread. Without medicines or even clean water, the doctors and nurses (Europeans among them) could do almost nothing to alleviate, let alone cure, the sufferings of the sick. To those in 'unbearable agony', mercy came only in the form of a bullet from a friend.[7]

The high command in the PLO headquarters in West Beirut not only refused to let the Palestinians leave the camp, or to let the fighters surrender in order to save them all from hell, but insisted that the entire population, including the children, were to be sacrificed. By late July some of the fighters in the camp were desperate to get out. When the Red Cross managed at last to arrange for a pause in the fighting to allow them to fetch the wounded, at least one PLO field commander tried to smuggle himself out of the camp with the convoy.[8]

The end came on 12 August. On that day the Christian forces – the Namur under Dany Chamoun, the Tanzim under George Adwan, and the Kataeb under the Commander-in-Chief of the combined forces, Bachir Gemayel – stormed Tall al-Za'tar. They advanced from street to street, ready to shoot before they were shot. Families trying to escape met the advancing fighters head-on and fell in the streets. The Lebanese Forces (as the combined Christian militias called themselves) estimated that between 1,000 and 2,000 people were killed on that day.[9]

Some prisoners were taken, and the Christians reported that they delivered them to the Saudi Arabians at the 'Green Line' dividing East and West Beirut, or to the Red Cross. But some prisoners were tortured first.

It was not our policy [a Tanzim commander said], but if a PLO fighter fell into the hands of a man whose family had been killed, or whose sister had been raped, or whose home had been destroyed by them, he would take his revenge. We tried to stop those who wanted to do it, but we didn't always succeed. We admit that some prisoners were tortured. None of us has forgotten Damour.[10]

On that day, not all the Palestinians who fell were killed by the guns of the Christian militiamen, or by the Syrian shells. At the last moment, as the pathetic survivors of the siege, the sickness, the bombardment and the storming of the camp dragged themselves out of it, the PLO turned its own artillery on to them. They wanted as many Palestinian martyrs as possible.[11]

25
The Good Fence

When President Elias Sarkis took office in September 1976, he was persuaded by President Sadat of Egypt to negotiate with the PLO. Talks took place at Chtoura, but nothing came of them. Arafat refused to withdraw the PLO from the Christian villages in the north. In October the combined Syrian and Christian forces drove them out, and they withdrew southwards to the Chouf mountains, a Druze centre where Jumblatt had his headquarters, but also a district where many Christians lived. Once there, Jumblatt's fighters deserted in droves.

Facing defeat, Arafat again appealed to the Arab League to save the PLO. King Khaled of Saudi Arabia called a summit meeting at Riyadh which President Sarkis and Arafat attended. Again the PLO was saved by the intervention of Arab heads of state. An agreement was reached that all forces would return to the *status quo ante*. Syria, Egypt and Kuwait promised to supervise the compliance of the PLO.

Shortly afterwards, on the 25 and 26 October 1976, it was decided that an 'Arab Deterrent Force' should be sent into Lebanon, to replace the Peace-Keeping Force. It was to consist of 30,000 men. The Sudan, Saudi Arabia, North and South Yemen, and the United Arab Emirates were all to send troops, but two-thirds of the force would be Syrian, and the Syrians were already there. Of the others, few came, and those that did soon withdrew. It meant that Assad's army stayed on, but with the official sanction of the League and under a new name. President Sarkis was nominally in supreme charge of the Arab forces, and could, and did, appoint a Lebanese general, but for window-dressing only.

The Riyadh plan was simply not practicable. There was no power that could put the Lebanese army together again, and Christians would not return to territory dominated by their enemies. But the Maronites tried to comply as best they could. They handed over their heavy weapons, as instructed, to the Arab Deterrent Force. The PLO, on the other hand, refused to relinquish its artillery. The governments that had promised to supervise the PLO's compliance now refused to do so, and Kuwait positively encouraged the Organization not to give up its heavy weapons.[1] The Christians were left at a dangerous disadvantage.

The Syrians, with some Sudanese and Libyan contingents, occupied the centre of Beirut. The barricades came down, and roadblocks were removed. So a *pax Syriana* was imposed on the country under military occupation. From November 1976 the 'civil war' was officially over. It was then reckoned that, out of a population of 3.2 millions, some 40,000 people, perhaps more, had been killed, 100,000 wounded, 5,000 permanently maimed, and 500,000 displaced from their homes. About 300,000 Lebanese had fled to other lands.[2]

Lebanon was effectively partitioned into four zones.

The whole of the north and east as far south as Nabatiyyah was under Syrian military occupation. There, the Lebanese people, long used to political and economic freedom, found themselves under the heel of despotism for the first time.

An independent free Lebanon remained as the Maronite enclave between East Beirut and Jounieh with its mountain hinterland.

The south was mostly under the rule of the PLO factions, local chiefs holding sway by the power of the gun over Palestinians and Lebanese alike – a 'gunarchy'. Here too, the Lebanese, most of them Shi'ites, learnt the meaning of tyranny. The lesson was not lost on them. Many of the Shi'a Muslims changed sides, and the Amal militia turned against its erstwhile PLO allies.

Lastly, there was a strip of the south which did not succumb to the PLO, and which constituted a fourth zone. The Christians of the south, outnumbered by the Muslims, were of several denominations, predominantly Maronite and Greek Catholic (Melkite), with some Roman Catholics and Presbyterians. The Druze in the area looked to the leadership of Majid Arslan rather than Kamal Jumblatt.

It was always the poorer, less developed part of the country. The Christian communities of Marja'yun ('The Valley of the Springs') and its neighbourhood are, on the whole, much poorer than those of the north. They found it harder to defend themselves when their small towns and villages came under constant attack from the forces of Lieutenant Ahmad al-Khatib and the PLO. They were unable to reach their fields and orchards. The PLO harvested much of their tobacco and fruit. Under the guns set up on the hills about them, they found themselves virtually under siege. Children could not get to their schools, nor out to play in the open. Parents kept their unmarried daughters indoors for fear of rape by *fedayeen*. Medical supplies and treatment became unavailable. Before long the villagers were short of food.

To the north, east and west they were hemmed in by their enemies. And Israel, the supreme enemy, lay to the south. At night they could see the row of fierce searchlights set along the high fence that Israel had erected along its northern border.

In March 1976 al-Khatib started shelling the Christian town of Qulay'a (pronounced Claire) from the ruined crusader castle of Beaufort, crowning a rocky height which rose sheer from a steep southern escarpment. It afforded an eagle's eye view into Israel and over the country round about. The Lebanese called it 'Arafat's Evil Eye'.

A seventeen-year-old girl was sweeping in front of her parents' house in Qulay'a when she was hit by machine-gun fire from Beaufort, and wounded in the foot. Her parents took her to the hospital at Marja'yun, which had been taken over by the PLO. She was refused treatment on the grounds that she was a Christian. They tried the hospital at Nabatiyyah, also in the hands of the PLO, and were turned away from there too. By this time the foot was so swollen and the girl's temperature so high her parents thought she was dying.

As a last resort, they drove her to the high fence of the national enemy, Israel. When they stood close to the Israeli town of Metulla, they called to the border guards. Through the fence they explained that their daughter needed hospital treatment, and why they had come to Israel to ask for help. They added that they had a relation in Haifa who had been a volunteer in the Haganah in 1947, and if Lebanese money would not be acceptable, the uncle in Haifa would pay.

The Israelis opened a small gap in the fence, and they squeezed through. The girl was treated free of charge in a public hospital, and her limb was saved.

Two months later a small *ad hoc* force of about 150 men converged on the town of Qulay'a to defend it. About thirty of them were Christian refugees from the north, the rest natives of the town. On the first day of the fighting one young fighter, Albert Hasbali, was badly wounded in the chest. After some hesitation (because this time the patient was a soldier), his family took him to the fence at Metulla. Again it was opened, and the patient was passed through.

That was 'the first official link' between the Christians of Southern Lebanon and Israel. 'It was official this time,' the schoolteacher of Qulay'a, Francis Rizek, explained,[3]

> because they had to get permission from the government. The Deputy Prime Minister, Yigal Allon, came to Metulla and gave the order for the fence to be opened between us and our good neighbour. At the beginning there was just a hole, and we had to wriggle through it like foxes. But later they made a gate in the fence, and we called it the Good Fence, and the Good Gate.

On 24 April Qulay'a was bombarded heavily all day from Beaufort, Marja'yun and other positions on the surrounding slopes. Five people were killed. The wounded were taken to Israel. For the next six months there was no respite for the town. Eighty people were killed and as many as 2,000 – half the population – wounded. What they dreaded most was that al-Khatib and the PLO would storm the town, sack it and massacre the people, as they had done at Damour.

Then, in the late spring of 1976, Israel started to supply ammunition to the Christians defending Qulay'a. Some weeks later Israel gave them some artillery and tanks. With the new equipment and very considerable determination, a small Christian unit of thirty-six men liberated Marja'yun, helped by the people of the town, about 3,000 of them, who joined in the battle against the occupying forces as soon as the Christian attack began. The attackers lost none of their own men, and only one was wounded. The number of casualties on the other side, by the Christian account, was high.

It was only after the battle for Marja'yun that Major Sa'd Haddad came to their aid. A former officer in the Lebanese army, he assumed overall command of a small force composed of regular soldiers and recruits, both Christian and Muslim. He himself was a Melkite, a Greek Catholic. By his own account, when the Lebanese army broke apart in 1976, he 'stuck to his post'. Unlike most other officers who took command of pieces of the broken army, he did not promote himself. He set up his headquarters in his own house at the top of Marja'yun.

His militia grew over the next few years, eventually to a strength of between 1,500 and 2,000. Their uniforms, light and heavy armament, ammunition and other supplies all came from Israel. They drove the PLO back from the border and soon controlled a wedge of territory along the southern Lebanese frontier.[4]

Part Six

1976 to 1982

The PLO rules the south of divided Lebanon by means of the gun and provides a world centre for terrorists. Many Palestinians and Lebanese die at the hands of the PLO. Egypt recognizes Israel. The PLO begins to decline and disintegrate. Syria turns again, and, backed by the USSR, rearms the PLO. There is no peace in Lebanon, nor on the border. Israel invades and expels the *fedayeen* from South Lebanon and Beirut.

26
Under PLO Rule

The PLO's authority 'grew from the barrel of a gun', to use the words of Mao Tse-tung. The land it usurped was ruled by fear. Citizens and refugees alike found themselves in the hands of a lawless brigandage.

The southern Lebanese and Palestinians began to suffer a loss of public amenities early in the civil war, when the PLO marched into the post offices of Tyre, Sidon and West Beirut and took them over. From then on there was no postal service. In the hands of the Organization and their allies, the power stations and pumping stations only worked intermittently; so often for many hours, or even days, the towns were without electric power or flowing water. When the water did flow, it was not to be trusted, as established routines of testing it for purity had been interrupted.

There were shortages of certain foods in West Beirut, and of most commodities at one time or another in all the cities.

Roads were not repaired. There was no inspection or licensing of motor vehicles. Children of nine and ten years were to be seen driving cars and trucks. Vehicles of all sorts were taken on the dangerous roads, and, although driving on the right was continued as customary, there was no road-rule enforcement; drivers could and did drive anywhere, park anywhere, and the result was often impassable jams and traffic chaos. With innumerable roadblocks and checkpoints on the roads as well, it could take hours to travel short distances. Number-plates with invented numbers, painted by hand, were hung on the bumpers for purely decorative purposes. Cars without headlamps were driven at night with no lights, except perhaps one signal-light flashing continuously. There were shortages of fuel, but not of cars. New models – many of them Mercedes, smuggled in from Germany – moved among dented and broken heaps of rusty metal, without bonnets, their back ends so buckled that they sometimes obscured the rear windows. And the militia men, the 'armed elements', commandeered whatever cars they fancied. At any of the checkpoints, a PLO man or boy might order the owner and passengers of a car to get out, and simply take the car for himself. (For $1,400 one could usually get it back again.[1])

PLO power was free of all checks and accountability, secular or religious. There were neither written nor custom-established laws to which the rulers had to refer. The PLO was not a government-in-exile, so there was no attempt to legislate, and no mechanism for doing so.

In the stores and markets *fedayeen* could, and often did, help themselves to goods without paying for them. They took charge of the lands, groves and orchards of Lebanese owners, and enjoyed them as they chose.[2]

They gratified all their appetites at whim. The norms of Arab law and morality were constantly violated. Women, girls and boys were dishonoured.

In theory the organizations attached importance to the 'masses' and being 'guided' by them.[3] It was agreed among the top leadership that local committees or councils would be established in the refugee camps, and the members would be elected. The various groups, and only the groups, put up candidates, and each tried to secure a majority on the committees. Each year, as election time approached, excitement in the camps ran high among the rival organizations, and they regularly reached a point of tension when their members would shoot at each other in the streets. Civilian casualties were inevitable. Soon, in every camp, families had their tales to tell of how an old father was shot as he sat in the sun smoking and chatting to a neighbour, a mother was caught in crossfire while walking to or from the market, a little daughter or a son was killed or wounded on the way home from school. The people came to dread election time, and in some camps they drew up petitions to have them stopped, asking that the committee they had last elected be allowed to stay on indefinitely. From their point of view there was nothing to choose between one group and another.[4] The authority of all of them was of a visible kind, in the guns they wore. Now in once-free South Lebanon the gun was government, as in most Arab states. The difference was that here there was no central control.

Although, in theory, there were PLO departments in Beirut to plan and supervise military, political and administrative affairs, in practice their reach was short, and locally each group had its own offices, youth movements and checkpoints on the roads. They feuded with each other over control of territory. Within the groups, the top officers had no restrictions on their power. They were men without experience of government or administration, who had been raised as fighters, dedicated to a mission of violence and destruction, and taught to put a high value on vengeance, hatred and force.

In this 'gunarchy', every individual group-member in possession of his own 'kleshen' was a danger to the civilians. If, in addition, he was intoxicated by drugs – and the *fedayeen* were notorious for their hashish smoking – he was even more likely to shoot and kill for the pleasure of it, as many stories in the camps confirm. Typical of these stories are the following. An illiterate Palestinian hospital porter, Walid A– ,[5] who lived in the Sidon camp of Ein Hilwe, told the story (weeping as he told it) of how his little sister aged ten, was killed.

> 'She came home from school, put her bag in the house, took a sandwich and went out to play one afternoon, and a few hundred metres from the house walked past a little hill where stood a band of PLO people who were completely drugged, and were known to be very dangerous people. They used to break into offices, banks, businesses, and take whatever they wanted, and frighten people, and if anyone tried to stop them they used to shoot him and go away, and nobody dared do anything or complain.'

As the little girl passed them,

> these PLO people just shot all over the place, just as a game, into the camp where people were walking, and one of the bullets hit my little sister. They hit her in the kidney, and she died at once.

A member of Fatah, also from Ein Hilwe, tells a similar story.

> A boy aged twelve, Abdullah Hussein Ayud, went up the hill to play with other boys, and they met a group of PLO people. These people were drugged, and they just shot him dead. They put him in a truck and took him to the [PLO] hospital at Sidon. On the way one of his sandals fell off his foot. The PLO washed the car to remove all traces of what had happened. But his family found his sandal stained with blood, so they knew their son had been hurt. They went to the hospital and found him there dead. There was nothing they could do. None of us could ever do anything. There was no one we could go to. I couldn't go to my superiors in the Organization because they wouldn't listen to me. And we are afraid that if we complain they will shoot us. There is nobody but Allah who is looking after us.

An old woman of the camp said:

> The wife of Ali Abu D–, pregnant in her ninth month, went to the market to buy vegetables. One of the group of Ibn Abd al-Ali al-Haj, of the Iraqi Front, PLF, just raised his weapon and shot her dead, her and the baby she was carrying, just for the fun of it. She was the mother of eleven children.

The *fedayeen* did not have to be drugged to kill at whim, or to avenge some slight, or to make sure that even their most trivial and unreasonable demands were obeyed. A labourer told this story:

> My sister is the mother of five children. She was on her way home from the market in Ein Hilwe one week before this last war started [June 1982], when she was stopped by the people of the Muslim Brotherhood, and with them was Sheikh Ibrahim, who is the representative of the Muslim Brotherhood in Ein Hilwe. They told her that she could not pass. She said she would go anyway and walked on. They threw a hand-grenade after her. Her little boy, Ahmad, two years old, was killed immediately, another boy, Hussein, seven years old, lost a leg, and so did Fatima, a girl aged six.

Two headquarters of the PLO Joint Military Command were established in the south, one at Sidon and one at Tyre. The commander at Tyre was an officer of the 'Kastel' Brigade whose name was Major Azmi Zrayir.

Zrayir was born in Hebron in 1945, was married and had two children. He attended the Military Academy in Jordan, and joined the PLO in 1968. He had become a PLO hero as the chief planner of a terrorist attack in March 1975, on the Savoy Hotel in Tel Aviv, in which seven people were killed and eleven wounded.

Such deeds of violence against Israelis were a source of pride to the PLO. But Zrayir was no less violent with Arabs. He is remembered in Tyre as a drug-addict, a thief, a murderer, a rapist and a torturer. 'The Tyrant of Tyre', they called him. He had all power over the people.

The post he was appointed to carried its own financial reward – as much as he could get out of it. The PLO's income, which came as grants chiefly from the Gulf states, and a tax of between 5 and 8 per cent on Palestinians' wages throughout the Arab world (compulsory, except in Jordan), was not spent on salaries for its local governors. Zrayir was paid, like a medieval warlord, by assignment of power over a city, villages and lands. Actual taxes were not levied. He could extract revenues as he chose, where he chose, and to the level he chose; from bribes and extortions, 'protection' insurance, expropriation of businesses and assets without compensation, seizure of property, drug-trafficking and smuggling.

His smuggling business was mostly in hashish and whisky, run between Tyre and Cyprus. As he controlled the port of Tyre, there was no need for secrecy on his side of the sea. Arms came in as openly as hashish went out.

He formed a football team into which he conscripted teenage children. The players were forced to gratify Zrayir's sexual appetites. He debauched both girls and boys. At least one child who defied him was shot dead.[6]

Apparently Zrayir was not satisfied with what he could gather for himself in Tyre. With a team of picked fighters, he went to Beirut in 1978 to steal gold bullion from the British Bank of the Middle East. On the same expedition they forced their way into the Capuchin Cathedral of St Louis next door, to plunder the church. Another *fedayeen* group came with the same purpose on the same day, and the cathedral became a battlefield. Zrayir's group won after some twenty people had been killed, and drove the others away. Christians in the city say that Zrayir's men then brought prostitutes into the cathedral and copulated with them among the corpses and on the altar.[7] Zrayir took the stolen gold back to Tyre and for safekeeping put it in the public museum. It was restored to its owners only after the Israelis had taken the city in June 1982 and Zrayir had been killed in the fighting.

Under PLO rule, the question of whether a crime had been committed depended first on who commited it. As there was no definition of any crime, or prescription of punishment, such process as there was in the 'people's courts' had to be arbitrary. These courts were set up in December 1969, a month after the signing of the Cairo Agreement, but the 'people' had no voice in them; they were courts in which PLO officials came to arbitary decisions. The PLO could and did imprison or execute anyone without trial, and without having to explain, excuse or account for its decisions and actions to anyone.

In West Beirut the role of the police was taken over by the Palestine Armed Struggle Command (PASC), which had been formed in Jordan in 1969 as a step towards combining the fighters of the various groups. It exercised a higher power over the fifteen or so militias of the organizations that set up roadblocks in the western sector of the capital. It was dominated by Fatah, and Arafat was its supreme commander. Its personnel owed their loyalty directly to him, which meant that in practice it was his own private militia.

Throughout the south, the various organizations had their own 'police', and co-operated in the al-Aman al-Sha'bi, the security police, who constituted the only 'court' of appeal.

The Lebanese police – while they were still to be seen at all – were allotted limited duties and called the 'social police'. They were allowed to inquire into family disputes and neighbourhood quarrels among the Lebanese. But they were afraid to wear uniform, and soon had all but disappeared. (One Lebanese policeman of many years standing, Hassan Samih Jabar, was imprisoned for about a year by the PLO. He has testified that the PLO men put out cigarettes on his body, even on his genitals.[8]) The al-Aman al-Sha'bi took over the Lebanese police force's vehicles and equipment. They divided the city of Tyre into four districts to be controlled by them under Azmi Zrayir, and they closed the ordinary law courts. It was the al-Aman al-Sha'bi which became the chief committer of crime – assault, rape, robbery and murder, the collection of protection money from Lebanese shopkeepers, and the demanding of goods without payment. Protestors were imprisoned. These 'political police' themselves, like the officers of the various groups, were immune from formal accusation by anyone beneath them or outside the Organization.

In Arab society, if a girl is raped it is a disgrace to her family. In some communities the father or brother of the girl is obliged to kill her in order to redeem the family honour. PLO officials and security police knew this perfectly well, but nevertheless commonly committed abduction and rape.

An example is the story of Musa Salih Musa, a Bedouin who lived in a refugee camp near Tyre. He worked as an agricultural labourer, and was a member of Fatah. One of his seven daughters, Wafa', was only fourteen years old when she was abducted by a Fatah commander named Ahmad Ali Numeiry, also known as Abu Yasser. He stopped his car beside her in the street, picked her up bodily, and put her into the car. Three girls who had been with her ran to tell her father what had happened. He went looking for her at the Fatah headquarters in Tyre, and traced her to the offices of the Fatah police, al-Kifah al-Mussallah ('the Armed Struggle'). At first they said they knew nothing about his daughter, but eventually told him that Numeiry, a married man with children, intended to marry Wafa'. He, the father, was to have nothing to do with it. His consent was not to be asked.

Musa then tried sending his wife, his sisters and his sisters-in-law to the Fatah police to ask for Wafa' to be allowed to come home. They were turned away. Musa sent them again with all the money he could get together, but the Fatah police told them they could not get her back even for ransom.

The whole family went to Sidon 'to see the most important sheikhs we could find' and ask them for their help, but none of them could do anything. All that Musa could find out in Sidon was that his daughter had been brought there from Tyre, and had been taken on to Beirut.

Three months after she had been kidnapped, the Fatah police brought her home. She confessed to her mother that Numeiry had raped her, and her mother dutifully broke the bad news to her father. By confessing, the girl had pronounced her own death sentence. Her father took her to the mountain and cut her throat and threw her body into a creek. She was found the next day, and Musa was arrested by the security police of Tyre. A Fatah court sentenced him to seven-and-a-half years' imprisonment. He served four years and five months.

One of the largest PLO prisons was in Sidon, the administrative district of Kastel Brigade Commander Haj Isma'il, in an old stone building with very thick walls, part of a crusader fortress. The lower floors were communal cells, where prisoners awaited interrogation. They were cold and dark, with small barred windows and heavy doors of grey-blue steel. Above them on the third storey was the interrogation room. One of the chief interrogators was a man in his late teens or early twenties named Lutfi Ali, a member of Fatah.

Lutfi Ali had been abandoned by his family. By his own written account,[9] he had 'lived as an orphan': all Palestinian orphans were taken into the care of the PLO to be raised as *fedayeen*. 'Oppressive hands took me in succession,' he wrote, 'and threw me to the pit, with my nearest of kin watching and listening, and they who could have saved me at so small a price, did not, because their selfishness would not let them.' The Organization did not permit orphans to be adopted by strangers,[10] but next of kin might have been allowed to claim him. It is true that children kept in PLO orphanages had little joy in their lives. In the case of this young jailer, the system had apparently raised a would-be poet and a very unhappy man.

The room where he worked contained two desks, a filing cabinet, poster-sized photographs of PLO 'martyrs', and a bed. The mattress was blood-soaked, and Stars of David were drawn on the walls in blood.[11]

Lutfi Ali's poetry[12] is chiefly characterized by self-pity. He felt himself to be a victim. Typical lines are: 'The first thing I wrote, I wrote to you in my own blood'; 'I feel loneliness and pain'; 'My eyes shed hot tears'; 'I gather the strength of this emaciated soul'.

Here is a longer extract (the dots are Ali's, but not all the lines are continuous in the original):

> You can ask about a body that has weakened . . .
> About a face that has paled . . .
> About eyes that have shed all the tears they had . . .
> About a heart that has been torn from grief and
>   anguish . . .
> You can ask about sighs, about wails that
>   pierced through the silence of
>   the night . . .
>
> I tell you I don't own myself any more . . .
>
> I have decided to go on a journey . . .
> I shan't accept a life that has injustice as
>   its law
> And pain all that it contains . . .

Many a prisoner in his charge must have felt the same way.

Spies and traitors were put to death by torture and in public. In Sidon the story is told[13] that a man who was found by the military police to possess a pair of shoes that had been made in Israel and some Israeli money was literally torn apart. It is said that his limbs were tied to four cars which were then driven away in different directions. Nada al-Murr – the daughter of Alfred al-Murr, a well-known Lebanese civil engineer and industrialist, and May al-Murr, a poet and historian – saw a man torn apart by two vehicles.[14]

The bodies of the executed were often put in polythene bags and left in front of the victims' home as a warning to the family. They were usually in pieces. The mutilation of the living and the dead was not done only in the heat of battle. Some people whose eyes were gouged out have lived to tell their own stories, and even small children were punished by the amputation of fingers and hands.[15]

27

PLO Welfare

On paper there was order. As well as administrative and civil affairs, trade unions, 'social affairs', education, medical services, information, Arab and international relations, military affairs and finance[1] were officially the provinces of special PLO departments.

The trade unions were controlled by the Organization as trade unions of the Communist countries are controlled by the state. The 'trades' which were unionized were: students, peasants, teachers, writers and journalists, medical personnel, engineers, artists, lawyers and women.

The General Union of Palestinian Women was made up of the women's organizations of the various PLO member-groups. What a group could do for the woman member was described by the PDFLP as 'widening her contribution in Lebanon to the political and armed struggle of the masses of our people, developing the level of her democratic and national consciousness, defending her interests and rights, and helping to solve her medical, social and personal problems.' The woman's work in her organization was described as 'helping families in need . . . perpetuating the memory of all the martyrs . . . preparing hot meals for the fighters'. Women 'take part in propaganda', 'teach the illiterate and the young', 'help recruit people, and serve as nurses'; they also 'arrange a cleaning campaign in the camps to prevent disease, and clean the shelters'.[2]

PLO money was handed out directly to Palestinians in the camps, but *only to those who joined a fedayeen organization* and their immediate families. Nothing at all was paid to the rest.

Money was an inducement to join the PLO. An adult male member of Fatah was paid between 700 and 1,000 Lebanese pounds monthly (exchange rate to the US dollar – 2.6 in 1975; 3.55 in 1979; 4.25 in 1982), which was about the same as a plantation worker's wage. In addition, his wife would get an allowance of about 650 Lebanese pounds for herself, and a further 25 pounds for every child under the age of twelve.[3]

The PDFLP founded an 'Organization of Social Support' in January 1977 'as a result of the civil war that killed and caused unemployment to many Palestinians. In Tall al-Za'tar alone there were 3,000 martyrs killed. . . . All this forced the Lebanese and Palestinian woman, whether she was a mother, sister or wife, to face many direct responsibilities, social and economic.' To solve them, the PDFLP

> opened centres in seven camps and taught dressmaking, embroidery, typing and foreign languages. They gave courses for the illiterate, and opened kindergartens to clear the way for the working mother to assume her role outside the home on the social and national levels, and also to accustom parents to send their children afterwards to elementary schools. But . . . we have to point to the fact that only 10 per cent of the children aged three to six are in the kindergartens.[4]

How many Palestinian women worked outside the home is not known, but there were certainly very few. More Palestinian women in the camps in Lebanon were literate than in the Arab world as a whole (where 85 per cent are illiterate[5]), but even with free education in the camps provided by an agency of the United Nations, literacy for everyone was not achieved, according to the PDFLP. They did not achieve it even among their own *fedayeen*. 'In spite of the fact that our forces own many advanced weapons that demand high school or sometimes university-level skills . . . the rate of illiteracy continues to be 15 per cent.'[6]

From 1 May 1950 the responsibility for the support and welfare of the needy Palestinian refugees had been undertaken by a specially created sub-organization of the UN, the United Nations Relief and Works Agency for Palestinian Refugees in the Near East, UNRWA. It was established to provide for them and for no other of the millions of refugees in the world. It gave them monthly rations of essential foods, and their schooling. The PLO, although it used every means including intimidation to prevent people from leaving the camps, would only support its own members. All money for the refugees' support came from certain member-nations of the UN, including Israel (although she dispensed with UNRWA on Israeli territory early on, and assumed responsibility for the integration of all Arab citizens). The United States contributed one-third of all UNRWA funds; the Soviet Union contributed nothing.[7]

In time the refugee 'camps' became villages, or almost indistinguishable parts of the cities. Despite numerous petty discriminatory laws designed to maintain their position as temporary settlers,[8] and despite limited opportunity, thousands built up small businesses and, through their own enterprise and industry, achieved a reasonably high standard of living. Many more, however, accepted their state of dependence. As the expected short wait to return to their homes became a very long one, people fell into resentful lassitude. Rather than strive to attain what they wanted for themselves, it became habitual to demand and complain. They bred prolifically in the overcrowded conditions, and while standards of nutrition, health and hygiene were good enough to keep their numbers growing, they were not high. In some of the camps there were cases of leprosy.[9] Generally, camp life was not conducive to happiness.

Even before the advent of the PLO, the UNRWA schools taught hatred of the United States as well as of Israel and Jews in general.[10] From 1968 these schools were taken over in all but name by the PLO. UNRWA accepted the stipulation of the PLO Covenant that it was a 'national duty to bring up individual Palestinians in an Arab revolutionary manner', and that 'all means of information and education' must be used to help forge a national consciousness and prepare the young Palestinian to die in the armed struggle for his homeland.

Students might find themselves refused graduation certificates if they did not join one of the *fedayeen* groups. The vocational training school at Siblin, near Sidon, for instance, awarded qualifications only to members of Fatah. One room in it was reserved as an office for Yasser Arafat. His portrait hung on the wall above a swastika. Teaching material was stacked in the upper storey, including, in 1982, poems praising the assassins of Anwar Sadat. The lower storey of the building was used as an arms store for Katyusha rockets, rocket propelled grenades, hand-grenades, mines, and Kalashnikov sub-machine-guns. Most of them were of Soviet make, but some were from Sweden, and there was also some NATO equipment. A lecturer from Norway visited the Siblin school in July 1982 and reported that 'they were filled with hand-grenades, weapons, uniforms, military manuals, PLO propaganda and posters showing [on the map] the final solution of the Palestinian problem – the abolition of Israel.'[11]

For the most part, the education of the young was an education in active aggression. It formed fighters for the Palestinian Revolution. This was the case even in the ordinary UNRWA school, where general school curricula were followed, but all subjects were used as vehicles of propaganda. The chief aim of education was, as the Covenant declared, to build up a sense of a Palestinian identity. As the identity was defined as that of a displaced people struggling to regain its homeland, the pupil was taught to hate the 'usurpers' of that homeland.

Although almost all the UNRWA personnel came to be drawn from the PLO,[12] and subjects and method were dictated by the PLO, and although the Organization itself contributed nothing to the cost of the schools, it expressed severe dissatisfaction with them. The various factions formed their own students' groups to demand changes in the conditions and teaching material. They complained of 'crowded classes, lack of equipment and shortage of teachers', and that the 'educational programmes do not respond to the minimum of our people's aspirations for education'.[13]

Despite the money paid to *fedayeen* members, and despite indoctrination in the UNRWA schools, the Palestinians were not eager recruits to the *fedayeen* groups. The PDFLP complained of 'limited success' in recruiting the young, and that 'most of our party instruction and guidance failed'. The groups had to resort to methods of compulsion to gain members. Once a year Fatah turned out in force at Rachadiyyah camp, south of Tyre, for a membership drive. They set up roadblocks, and parties of armed men went from house to house collecting UNRWA ration books. The owners had to go to the Fatah offices to get them back, but they were only returned when the suitable members of the family had joined the organization.

An unknown number of adolescent boys were kidnapped by the *fedayeen* groups. The owner of a motorcycle repair-shop in Ein Hilwe had his house broken into one evening at sunset by a party of PDFLP men who took away his son Sa'id Awad, aged twelve. A month later he heard that Sa'id had been taken to an unnamed military training centre, given fifteen days' training, and then sent into some action in which he had been killed. The father was not told whether he had died in Lebanon or 'elsewhere'.

In the youth movements, which children could join at the age of six, the early education was in sports activities and political indoctrination. Girls as well as boys were recruited. At twelve the 'recruit' underwent a short course of two to three weeks' basic military training, and became the owner of a weapon. The training was in the handling of explosives, digging trenches, hand-to-hand fighting, the use of Russian RPGs (rocket propelled grenades), small arms including Kalashnikovs, and the large Katyusha rocket launchers. To overcome squeamishness, each recruit had to tear live chickens apart with his hands.[14] When the brief period of training was over, some were sent immediately on raids into Israel, and some to man the guns which were trained on the northern towns and *kibbutzim* of Israel.

The youth movement of Fatah was called al-Ashbal, the Lion Cubs. A seventeen-year-old Ashbal veteran, Jamal H –, said that he had found the life 'very hard', and he was 'very afraid of the officers'. In his fifth year he had run away and gone home to his family in a camp in Syria. The security police had come to his father's house, arrested him, and taken him back to Lebanon to his unit. 'They beat me and sent me back to my work, which was to man a gun' with which he 'helped to shell Nahariyyah, Metulla and Tiberias', until he was captured and detained by the Israelis in July 1982.

The Palestinian Democratic Youth Organization, PDYO, was the youth branch of the PDFLP. It was responsible for sports activities, it 'encouraged the arts', and it published a magazine called *The New Dawn*. Boys between nine and twelve were Lion Cubs, and between thirteen and fifteen, Scouts (*Ruwwad*). Girls were Flowers (*Zahrat*), and then Instructors (*Murshidat*).[15]

Orphans, unskilled men and some women were given sheltered employment in workshops run by the PLO itself, with two main purposes: to keep the camp-dwellers from leaving the camps, and to 'raise national consciousness'. The enterprise was called 'Samid' (Steadfast). There were forty-five Samid factories and workshops in Lebanon, each one named after a PLO 'martyr'. They made blankets, military uniforms, boots and shoes, school furniture, lace tablecloths, *kaffiyahs*, jam, pots and pans, soft toys, plastic ornaments in shells, and feature films, some of which won prizes at international festivals. The Organization saw Samid as 'the nucleus of the public sector for the Palestinian state-to-be'.[16] About 60 per cent of its workers were children orphaned by the 'armed struggle' against Israel, the war in Lebanon, or internecine fighting. The children were given two hours of political instruction on Saturday afternoons.[17]

The *fedayeen* were clothed and shod by Samid. Libya, Iraq, Kuwait and the Yemens bought its army uniforms and boots. Its films were exported. But it was not a profit-making company. In the year 1980 to 1981 its turnover was said to be US$26 million,[18] and it then employed 3,500 industrial workers and 3,000 women working at home,[19] so the business must either have paid extremely low wages (even by the standards of South Lebanon at that time), or it must have made heavy losses.

The PDFLP offered medical services, of a skeletal kind, to their own *fedayeen* and their families. They started with one doctor in 1971, and by 1979 had four clinics and one 'medical centre'. They also claimed to educate the people in the camps in 'preventive medicine'.[20]

The picture magazines published by the various PLO organizations for family reading, featured illustrated stories about health care and medical treatment. The photographs showed such scenes as white-coated doctors, nurses and auxiliary therapists using up-to-date machinery and electronic aids in neat hospital wards. They often included pictures of the head of the Palestinian Red Crescent, Dr Fathi Arafat, younger brother of Yasser Arafat. Official publications of the PLO give this information:

> In 1969 the Palestinian Red Crescent [founded by the PLO] was given responsibility . . . to provide medical facilities for all Palestinians, civilians and combatants alike. The free facilities offered by the PRCS for Palestinians were quickly in demand from other Arabs. The Palestinian Red Crescent responded by opening its doors to any person in need of medical treatment.[21]

Hospitals and clinics, the leaflet reports, were established in refugee camps of 20,000 inhabitants or more. In Lebanon, it says, 'the Palestinian Red Crescent has been under severe strain during recent years dealing with Lebanese and Palestinian injuries'. The Al-Quds (Jerusalem) Hospital in Beirut was

> operated jointly by the PRCS and the Lebanese Red Crescent. During the 1975 clashes the hospital was shelled by the Phalangist [Kataeb] forces. Within eight

hours of the hospital's destruction an underground hospital of 100 beds was established – with room for a further 400 beds. The PRCS opened training centres . . . operate[d] five major hospitals and four emergency centres, and a number of small clinics [in Lebanon].

The hospitals specialized severally in the treatment of various diseases. The PRCS also ran 'two mobile field hospitals, 70 clinics, 10 dental clinics, 5 recuperation centres, one physiotherapy centre, a graduate first aid school, a social public health school . . . a nursing school . . . a convalescent home'. It was planning a 'frozen blood bank', because, it is explained, 'serious problems arose because of the lack of storage facilities for donated blood'.

The Palestine Red Crescent Society represented 'the Ministry of Health and the Ministry of Public Affairs within the Palestinians' exile administrations'.

PLO hospitals did exist. But the picture of the PLO as an institution devoted to the art of healing is misleading.

In 1982, after the PLO had been expelled from Lebanon by the Israelis, the staff of a hospital in Sidon[22] wanted 'an international investigating committee to look into the crimes against humanity' of the PLO. They said that the PLO had taken over their hospital and converted it into a fortress. The PLO fighters had fired from the patients' rooms, caused the death of patients and damage to the hospital.

Dr Khalil Torbey, a distinguished Lebanese surgeon, told an American journalist that he was 'frequently called in the middle of the night to attend victims of PLO torture. I treated men whose testicles had been cut off in the torture sessions. The victims, more often than not, were not Christians but Muslims. I saw men – live men – dragged through the streets by fast-moving cars to which they were tied by their feet.'[23]

There is a rumour constantly repeated in the cities of the south that when the PRCS found itself short of blood, it took it by direct transfer from the bodies of live Lebanese patients.[24] No hard evidence has been published that this was ever done. It is true, however, that bodies were found drained of blood. (Father Labaky, the priest of Damour, saw some of the bodies of about 250 young people, all of them about eighteen years old, who had been hanged by the PLO in the churches. Those he saw were 'all drained of blood', he said.)

Some of the severely disabled victims are cared for at Beit Chebab, where a seminary in the Christian enclave north of Beirut has been specially converted into a hospital for this purpose, caring for patients of many nationalities and religions. On its terraces the wheelchairs of the limbless and the paralysed are placed in the sun, and among them are the stretchers on which young men lie who cannot sit in a chair. The hospital has its own workshop for the making of artificial limbs. Father Kerbage, who was in charge of the hospital in 1982, said that some of the patients were the casualties of war and accidents, but most of them were the victims of deliberately inflicted violence.

A young Christian girl, Susan S – ,[25] who had returned home to Beirut from her university studies in the United States soon after the 'civil war', is one of the most mutilated survivors of PLO violence. Extreme as her injuries are, her case is not unique.

She was at home with her parents when a number of PLO officers broke in. It remains a mystery why they chose that house, that family, on that night. It may have been a random choice, an act of revenge to be perpetrated on any Christians. The PLO men killed Susan's father and her brother, and raped her mother, who suffered a haemorrhage and died. They raped Susan 'many times'. They cut off her breasts and shot her. Hours later she was found alive, but with all four of her limbs so badly broken and torn with gunshot that they had to be surgically amputated. She now has only the upper part of one arm. Nuns take care of her in a hospital north of Beirut, high in the mountains. She has asked them to let her die, but they have consistently replied that they cannot do that. After the expulsion of the PLO from Beirut in 1982, some Christian women conceived the idea of having Susan's picture on a Lebanese stamp, because, they said, her fate symbolizes what has happened to their country, – 'rape and dismemberment by the PLO'. But they were persuaded to abandon the idea. Susan has chosen obscurity and her friends protect her from intrusion.

28
Information and Propaganda

An official information and propaganda bureau, the PLO Research Centre, was founded in Beirut by Professor Fayez Sayegh in February 1965. Professor Sayegh was a writer, an adviser to the government of Kuwait, and a member of the PLO Executive Committee. On his death his brother, Dr Anis Sayegh, succeeded him as chief of the Research Centre. A third brother, Dr Yusef Sayegh, who taught economics at the American University of Beirut, was director of the PLO Planning Committee, established in 1969. A radio service, the Voice of Palestine, began broadcasting from Cairo in 1965. Time was also allotted to the Palestinians on Amman radio after the 1967 war until the PLO expulsion from Jordan in 1970, and on both Syrian and Iraqi stations. Overall administration of information and popular propaganda services for all the PLO groups was brought under the PLO Central Information Council in Beirut. The Council's 'Palestine News Agency', WAFA, published a weekly journal called *Filastin al-Thawra* (*Palestine – the Revolution*).

Another information centre, the Institute for Palestine Studies, was founded to produce publications with academic respectability. It published, with financial aid from the University of Kuwait, the *Journal of Palestine Studies: A Quarterly on Palestinian Affairs and the Arab–Israeli Conflict*.

Money was spent on propaganda against Israel by the Arab states, bypassing the PLO. The Arab perception was that Israel was strong and victorious because of United States support. United States administrations were necessarily sensitive to public opinion. To turn American public sympathy away from Israel and towards the PLO's cause was therefore imperative. Funds from Saudi Arabia were funnelled through four large American oil companies: Exxon, SoCal, Texaco and Mobil, which, together, own the giant oil company Aramco. Its oil wells are owned by Saudi Arabia. By a reckoning made in 1982,[1] some US$4 million had been distributed to individuals, public relations firms, church organizations and universities.[2]

Universities which receive money from Aramco and other US companies doing business with the Arab states teach courses on the Arab point of view, which sounds fair and innocuous enough – unless it is remembered that the 'Arab point of view' officially includes endorsement of the PLO

National Covenant, and that document makes it plain that the State of Israel should be wiped off the face of the earth: a policy that American governments have not considered to be in the interests of America, and which is not the sort of idea that universities traditionally undertake to communicate as part of their proper intellectual business. But to what extent this dogmatism is propounded would, of course, depend on the opinions and aims of the individual teacher. In Western universities there is likely to be a wide range of prejudices on display, and students will choose from among them according to their own.

More effective have been the threats brought to bear on businesses and governments by the Arab oil states against Jewish business interests. But even this has not proved a devastating weapon (despite co-operation from some governments, including the British). Many Jewish and Israeli firms do business with Arab companies by resorting to devices which allow the Arabs to save face – such as the use of front-organizations; or by a Jewish firm making as merely token a concession as the conducting of all negotiations through a gentile partner.[3]

Extremist neo-Nazi groups also received funds to propagate their habitual anti-Semitism. Anti-Jewish propaganda from Arab and Muslim sources was disseminated in Britain in the early 1980s. Members of Parliament, trade unionists, industrialists and other people in public life received parcels of anti-Jewish publications through the post in the summer of 1981. The source was 'The World Islamic League',[4] with headquarters in Beirut. The organization's president was an adviser to King Khaled of Saudi Arabia. Its director-general was a Pakistani, and the parcels were mailed from Pakistan. It included books arguing that the Nazi killing of six million Jews never happened. One was by an American registered with the US Department of Justice as an agent for the Saudi Arabian government.

Arab connections with leftist groups which publish anti-Zionist propaganda are numerous. Two among many in Britain are: the Workers' Revolutionary Party which publishes News Line,[5] and the Labour Movement Campaign for Palestine, whose attacks on Israel have been published in London Labour Briefing.[6] The General Union of Palestinian Writers and Journalists publish the Palestine Post in Dundee, a periodical which is 'engaged in winning support for the Palestinian people, and combating the lies of the Zionists and imperialists'.[7]

The most impressive propaganda successes have been worked through the United Nations: the passing in 1975 of the resolution by the General Assembly that 'Zionism is a form of racism', for example. Neither semantics nor science could support the motion, but the Soviet Union sponsored it, along with twenty-five other countries, twenty-one of them Muslim, and nineteen of them Arab (others being Cuba, and the partly-Muslim states of Mali and Guinea). The United States representative, Leonard Garment, opposed it in strong terms,[8] saying that the resolution 'asks us to commit one of the most grievous errors in the thirty-year life of this organization'; it was 'a supreme act of deceit', and 'a massive attack on the moral realities of the world', for 'under the guise of a program to eliminate racism the United Nations is at the point of officially endorsing anti-Semitism, one of the oldest and most virulent forms of racism known to human history'; it was 'an obscene act' which placed the work of the United Nations in jeopardy. So it was; but it was passed, with seventy in favour, twenty-nine against, and twenty-seven abstentions.[9]

Courses in political propaganda were taught by the PLO to their own elite. A chief concern of the Organization was the need to impress its will on its own 'masses'. As a sample of PLO theory and method, here are some extracts from a lecture given by Dr Farid Sa'd, in a course of educational studies organized by the planning centre of the PLO, on 27 December 1977.[10] He had given careful thought to Nazi propaganda techniques, and had arrived at some original views:

The basic premise from which non-intellectual propaganda springs is that the vast majority of the masses is in a state of passivity which renders it incapable of fully understanding any doctrine, and Hitler used to compare it with a female, meaning by this comparison of his that it is paralyzed in its will, and easily succumbs. Therefore very rarely does non-intellectual political propaganda resort to a detailed explanation. It is content to use stimulations in a systematic way to create the desired response.

The first of these 'stimulants' is 'the Illustrated Symbol':

In the two [given] examples [of the cross and the hammer-and-sickle] we see a tangible connection between the symbol . . . and the main idea or concept in the doctrine or ideology of that movement. But there are political movements that adopt an illustrated symbol which does not have a tangible connection with the adopted doctrine. Perhaps the best instance of such a sort of symbol is the Nazi symbol, i.e. the swastika. [A swastika is then drawn. In the printed lecture it is the wrong way round.]

There is no tangible connection between that symbol and the Nazi doctrine, which is based on racial discrimination . . .

The question therefore remains, why did Hitler choose that symbol? In regard to its shape it arouses a feeling of disgust, since, as we can see, it resembles a spider to a certain extent, but on the other hand it is very easy to draw. This was, according to our view, the main characteristic that made Hitler adopt that symbol. . . .

The PLO does not seem to have regarded it as a virtue in a symbol that it was easy to draw. The symbol of the Organization itself and those of its constituent groups are complicated.

فليس هناك اى علاقة ملموسة بين هذا الرمز الحفيدة النازية القائمة اساسا على التمايز العنصرى
وقد حاول البعض اعطاء دلالة محددة لهذا الرمز . فمنهم من قال انه متعلق بالحضـــارة
البرهمانيـــة او الديانة الهندوسية وانه كان يرمز الى الشمس رمز القوة والحياة والخصوبة
غير ان هذه الفرضية ، ولو صحت ، لا تكشف لماذا لجأ هتلر الى الحضارة البرهمانيـــة
لاختيار هذا الرمز ولا العلاقة الموجودة بينه والحفيدة الهتلرية .

'There is no tangible connection between that symbol and the Nazi doctrine, which is based on racial discrimination. There have been some attempts to give a clearly defined meaning to that symbol. Some said that it has to do with the Brahman civilization, or the Hindu religion, and was used to indicate the sun: symbol of power, life and fertility. But this assumption, even if true, does not reveal why Hitler resorted to the Brahman civilization for picking up that symbol, nor does it explain the connection between that symbol and the Hitlerian doctrine.'

The second 'basic' of non-intellectual political propaganda is 'Public Celebrations'.

The Nazi celebrations were marked by the following characteristics:

Firstly – Goebbels preferred to organize the celebrations in the evenings, thinking that the participants would be quite tired at that time, and consequently more receptive to impressions and conditioning.

Secondly – The Nazi celebrations were held in wide open places, since Goebbels believed that staying inside four walls or within distinct boundaries creates a kind of self-reliance and a feeling of security in the individual and group, a feeling that can strengthen the willpower and immunity. But if the crowd meets in the open, then the person feels a certain fear, anxiety and lack of confidence, being exposed to dangers from the outside. Thus the will is paralyzed and the person is more receptive to impressions.

Thirdly – Goebbels very often used an assortment of conditioning stimulants in the public celebrations he organized: illustrated symbols (the big Nazi flags everywhere); vocal symbolism ([the singing of] military marches): bodily symbols (the fascist salute constantly repeated). . . . The repetition of the conditioning stimulant in an organized way creates a kind of hypnotic sleep in the individual, and that in turn renders him more receptive to impressions.

In line with the example of Dr Goebbels, both the PLO and the Syrians controlled the newspapers and broadcasting, the content of news reports, and all published comment; and both exercised censorship on the Lebanese and foreign press. This obviously meant that news sent out of Lebanon was unlikely to be reliable, but the Western news media kept this information from their audiences.

Journalists were intimidated. Bombs were exploded in the offices of Beirut newspapers. A number of Lebanese newspapermen were killed, including Edouard Sa'ab, editor of *L'Orient Le Jour*.[11] Salim al-Lawzi, owner and editor of an independent weekly, *al-Hawadith*, which warned in the early 1970s that the PLO was destructive to Lebanese unity, was seized by Sa'iqa, carried off to the PLO-occupied mountain village of 'Armun, and tortured to death. His body was found with the fingers cut off, apparently joint by joint, the eyes gouged out, and the limbs hacked off (this last having probably been done after his death).[12] Western correspondents were also victimized. Among them were four abducted and threatened in 1981 by the PFLP: two from the *New York Times*, one from the *Washington Post* (Jonathan Randal, whose writing on the PLO is noted for its sympathy with the Organization), and one from *Newsweek*. The three papers all heeded a PDFLP warning not to make the fact of the abduction public.[13] In July 1981 a correspondent of the *Observer* was murdered,[14] and an ABC television journalist, Sean Toolan, who had made a film on PLO terrorism, was shot dead in the street in Beirut where he lived. A West German writer, Robert Pfeffer, who had published information on the subject of the training of West German terrorists in PLO camps, was killed. Bernard Debussman, head of the Beirut bureau of Reuters, was shot, but survived.[15]

In 1982 the PLO, totally defeated in battle, won an astonishing propaganda victory. While many, probably a majority, of the people of Lebanon welcomed the Israeli intervention as liberation,[16] the world press commiserated with the PLO and poured execrations on Israel. Among the many reasons advanced[17] for this treatment of the defeat of the Organization was one offered by a practising journalist, Kenneth R. Timmerman, from his own experience.

He was held in an underground PLO prison for twenty-four days during the siege of Beirut in 1982. When he gave the story of his imprisonment to one of the press agencies, he was 'coldly received and dismissed with the assurance that they would report nothing. They still had people in West Beirut and could not put them in jeopardy.' As he has pointed out, this was terrorism, and terrorism that succeeded. He sums up the corruption of the press by the PLO in Lebanon in 1982 in these words:

Terror, intimidation, and the law of silence: these are the basic tools used by the Palestine Liberation Organization to manipulate the international press. Most of the sins committed by Western newsmen under PLO constraint were sins of omission: showing bombed buildings but not the arms stockpiled in their basements; describing bombed hospitals but not the PLO fighters whose bases of operation were inside; and so forth. The list is infinite, but the effect unmistakable: the reversal of international opinion on the moral equation of the Middle East conflict.[18]

29
Arafat's Diary

In Beirut, Arafat received foreign deputations as if he were a head of state. By 1981, 117 countries had granted official recognition in some degree to the PLO. Receiving foreigners occupied much of Arafat's time, though he had a 'Foreign Minister' in the person of his old comrade, Farouq Qaddoumi. The Fatah leadership's diary pages in late 1981 and early 1982, published in the English-language paper *Palestine*, list such diplomatic engagements and international connections as these:

3 December: The Secretary of the International Union of Students (IUS) cabled the General Union of Palestinian Students, congratulating it on the twenty-second anniversary of its foundation. The IUS . . . reaffirmed its solidarity with the Palestinian people who are struggling to establish their independent state under the leadership of the PLO.

19 December: Chairman Yasser Arafat sent a telegram of congratulations to Comrade Leonid Brezhnev, General Secretary of the Central Committee of the Soviet Communist Party and President of the Supreme Soviet, on the occasion of his seventy-fifth birthday.

Arafat met with Enrique de la Mata, President of the International Red Cross and Red Crescent Societies. They discussed the latest developments of the Palestinian cause, the Israeli military concentrations in South Lebanon, the international situation and the US role in escalating world tension. [The International Red Cross has refused affiliation to the Israeli counterpart, Mogen David Adom, on the grounds that it does not use the cross as its symbol. The Palestinian Red Crescent Societies of the Muslim states do not use the cross but a crescent as their symbol. They are affiliated to the International Red Cross. The Palestinian Red Crescent is not affiliated, but the IRC does 'co-operate' with it.[1]]

25 January: Yasser Arafat, Chairman of the PLO Executive Committee and Commander-in-Chief of the forces of the Palestinian Revolution, received a cable from Babrak Karmal, President of Afghanistan, General Secretary of the Central Committee of the Democratic People's Party and President of the revolutionary Council of Afghanistan, on the occasion of the Palestinian Revolution's seventeenth anniversary.

27 January: Yasser Arafat received a message from the Soviet leadership dealing with the latest developments in the Middle East. The message was delivered by the Soviet chargé d'affaires in Beirut.

28 January: The Greek Minister of Foreign Affairs, Mr Ionnis Haralambopoulos, received the PLO representative in Athens . . . who presented his credentials as diplomatic representative of the PLO in Greece. [The PLO's *diplomatic* relations with Greece had recently been established – in December 1981.]

7 February: Chairman Arafat received a delegation of the Council of Churches for North-West America. Also present . . . [was] Father Ibrahim Ayyad, member of the Palestinian National Council [who later arranged Arafat's meeting with the Pope in September 1982].

8 February: Yasser Arafat received the Soviet chargé d'affaires of the Soviet embassy in Beirut and handed him an urgent letter to be delivered to the Soviet leadership. The letter dealt with the dangers of the current situation, and repeated Israeli threats against the Palestinian Revolution and the Joint Forces in South Lebanon and Beirut.

10 February: Farouq Qaddoumi, Head of the PLO Political Department, received the ambassador of the East German Democratic Republic to Lebanon.

Chairman Arafat received a cable from Pope John Paul II in answer to Arafat's message on the New Year. The Pope wished Arafat good health and happiness. [The 'Grey Wolves', the Turkish terrorist group to which the Pope's would-be assassin, Mehmet Ali Agca, belonged, was openly keeping an office among the PLO *fedayeen* and their mercenaries in the ruined city of Damour.]

13 February: Yasser Arafat received the Cuban ambassador to Lebanon and handed him an urgent letter to Fidel Castro, in his capacity as both President of Cuba and current head of the Non-Aligned movement.

15 February: Yasser Arafat received the British ambassador to Lebanon, Mr David Roberts. During the meeting, the ambassador handed Arafat an urgent letter from the British government dealing with the current situation in Lebanon. [Terrorists from Northern Ireland, members of the Provisional IRA, were being trained in PLO camps in Lebanon.?]

16 February: Chairman Yasser Arafat met with Buyan Traikov, member of the Bulgarian Party Central Committee and Director-General of the

Bulgarian News Agency. He was accompanied by the Bulgarian Ambassador to Lebanon. [Bulgaria had a hand in the plotting of the Munich massacre and the attempt on the life of Pope John Paul II in 1981.]

17 February: Chairman Arafat received an invitation to visit the German Democratic Republic.

19 February: Yasser Arafat held a reception in honour of a visiting delegation headed by Dr Jalal al-Din al-Farisi, of the Iranian Islamic Shura Council. During the reception, Arafat briefed the delegation on the latest developments in South Lebanon, in light of the Israeli military escalation and continuing attacks against the Palestinian and Lebanese people.

20 February: Arafat received the Cuban Ambassador to Lebanon.

Yasser Arafat . . . received a Romanian delegation headed by the Foreign Minister, in the presence of PLO Executive Committee member Ahmad Sidqi al-Dajani, Fatah Central Committee member Hani al-Hassan, and Abu Ja'far, the Director of the PLO Political Department.

22 February: Farouq Qaddoumi . . . met with a Norwegian parliamentary delegation.

24 February: Arafat received the socialist delegation of the European Parliament, including nine parliamentarians from Belgium, Holland, Britain, Germany, France and Italy. [Red Army Faction terrorists from West Germany and Holland were trained in PLO camps in Jordan and Lebanon.]

27 February: Yasser Arafat . . . instructed the PLO representative in Madrid to express his congratulations to King Juan Carlos and the Speaker of the Spanish Parliament on the failure of the *coup* attempt, and the victory of constitutional legitimacy and democracy in Spain, which is linked to the Arab world through historic ties of friendship and culture. [In October 1979 Spain was guaranteed oil supplies by Iraq, Libya and Algeria after a visit to Madrid by Yasser Arafat. Recognition of the PLO was offered to Arafat at the same meeting in return for a promise that the PLO would stop helping the Basque terrorist organization.[3] Whatever promises Arafat might have given, he could not have felt himself bound by them.]

5 March: Abu Jihad met Lord William Molloy [sic], member of the British House of Lords, who participated in the rally held by the Syrian Social Nationalist Party . . . [the Lebanese party modelled on Hitler's Nazi Party, ally of the PLO].

6 March: Chairman Arafat received a large Italian parliamentary delegation comprising thirteen members of all major political parties. The delegation was visiting the area on a fact-finding mission, at the time when the barbaric Zionist aggression against the people in South Lebanon continues unabated. During the meeting, the head of the delegation declared: 'We are aware of the delay in our government's recognition of the PLO, but we, the representatives of the three major political parties in Italy, the Christian Democratic Party, the Socialist Party and the Communist Party, are urging for this goal being achieved, something in which we believe.' Chairman Arafat briefed the delegation on the present situation in the area, saying: 'Your visit happens at a time when the whole area is facing a great danger. For the first time since the Vietnam war the American military presence is expanding in this area.' During their stay in Lebanon, the delegation also visited several Palestinian camps and institutions. [The PLO supplied weapons and training to the Italian Red Brigades, the terrorist group which violently seized, imprisoned and murdered the Christian Democrat Aldo Moro, a former Prime Minister, in 1978.[4]]

8 March: Chairman Arafat met in Beirut with the Soviet Deputy Minister of Culture Yuri Barabash, with whom he discussed regional developments in general and the situation in South Lebanon in particular. The meeting was attended by the Soviet ambassador to Lebanon, Aleksander Soldatov, a number of Soviet officials, and Fatah Revolutionary Council Secretary Sakhr (Abu Nizar). Earlier, Yuri Barabash and the delegation accompanying him visited South Lebanon, and the Palestinian-Lebanese Joint Forces positions there. At the Joint Forces headquarters in Sidon, the delegation met with al-Haj Ismail, the Joint Forces Commander in South Lebanon who briefed them on the military and social situation there. Yuri Barabash, in turn, expressed his admiration and appreciation for the steadfastness of the Palestinian and Lebanese fighters in their confrontation of the imperialist enemy.

11 March: Farouq Qaddoumi ... after meeting with France's External Relations Minister Claude Cheysson told pressmen that he regretted the position France has adopted towards the rights of the Palestinian people. He said that France gives the existence and security of Israel priority over the realization of the legitimate rights of the Palestinian people, the victims of Israeli aggression.

14 March: Yasser Arafat received a cable of support and solidarity from Muhammad Ali al-Harkan, General Secretary of the World Islamic League [the same organization which mailed neo-Nazi, anti-Jewish literature to public personages in Britain].

15 March: Yasser Arafat received a delegation from the Socialist International . . . [including] members from Sweden, Cyprus, Italy, Spain and Austria. The meeting dealt with the latest developments in the Middle East, in view of the Israeli threats against Lebanon. Arafat called on the Socialist International to shoulder its responsibilities towards the national rights of the Palestinian people, especially since its stands have so far been below the level required.

Yasser Arafat met with the Assistant Secretary-General of the Arab League for Economic Affairs . . . to discuss the economic situation in the occupied territories and means of supporting the Palestinian people as well as proposed plans for an Arab economic strategy. The meeting was attended by PLO Executive Committee member Dr Muhammad Zuhdi al-Nashashibi [of the family which had opposed the extremist and militant leadership of the Mufti, Haj Amin al-Husseini].

Farouq Qaddoumi . . . met with Italian Foreign Minister Emilio Colombo for three hours in Rome. . . . An Italian statement said the talks were part of the periodic contacts between the PLO and the Italian government, begun in 1977.

30
Foreign Affairs

Libya

Arafat's personal relations with Colonel Mua'mmar al-Qadhafi of Libya were strained and at times broken off, though Qadhafi kept on good terms with the Marxist groups, the PFLP, PDFLP and PFLP–GC. In general, his support for the Organization was erratic, and he often held back money he had promised. But he supplied weapons to the PLO and the National Movement in Lebanon during the civil war. His chief contribution to the upheavals in Lebanon was to kidnap the Shi'a leader, the Imam Musa Sad'r, and imprison him in the fortress of Sebha in the Libyan Desert.[1]

Qadhafi boasted that Libyan soldiers fell in the battles of Damour, Nabatiyyah, Tyre and Sidon when Israel intervened in Lebanon in 1982. But the PLO leadership bitterly denied that he had helped them in their hour of direst peril, any more than had any other Arab state. Arafat called him 'The Knight of the Revolutionary Phrases'.[2]

It is rumoured that Qadhafi paid some millions of dollars (5, 6, and 10 million are the numbers often quoted) to Fatah for the 'Black September' murder of Israeli athletes at the Munich Olympics in September 1972. If he did, he must have changed his opinions soon afterwards. Disliking the attitudes and performance of the PLO under Arafat's leadership, he consequently created his own Palestine liberation organizations: the National Arab Youth for the Liberation of Palestine and the Arab Organization for National Liberation. In 1973 and 1974 Libyan terrorists under Qadhafi's directions made a series of attacks on aircraft in Cyprus and at Rome and Athens: they hijacked and blew up a British plane in March 1974, and six months later blew up a TWA plane over Athens, killing all of its eighty-one passengers. It was at Qadhafi's whim that Joseph Edward Sieff, president of Marks and Spencer, was shot and wounded in his London house on 30 December 1973 by the Soviet-trained South American millionaire mercenary, 'Carlos' (Ilich Ramirez Sanches), apparently as a warning to high-placed Zionists. Another of Qadhafi's schemes was the kidnapping of Sheikh Ahmad Zaki Yamani of Saudi Arabia and other delegates from the OPEC conference in Vienna in December 1975. This was also carried out by 'Carlos' with two associates from West Germany. It was an entirely pointless escapade. It warned of nothing and in no way enhanced Libya's or Qadhafi's reputation.

When the PLO was about to be expelled from Beirut by the Israelis in August 1982, the Colonel advised Arafat that the Palestinians should commit mass suicide.

Iran

Iranian revolutionaries against the Shah were trained in Lebanon by Fatah, which also gave them money and arms. Arafat, though a Sunni Muslim himself and once a member of the Sunni fundamentalist Muslim Brotherhood, maintained good relations with the Ayatollah Khomeini, the fanatical Shi'a fundamentalist who became the ruler of Iran when the revolution succeeded. The Ayatollah granted the offices of the erstwhile Israeli legation in Tehran to the PLO. To win recognition by the United States for the Organization, Arafat offered to act as intermediary in negotiations for the release of American diplomats and staff captured in their embassy and held hostage, but the Ayatollah objected, and the offer was quickly withdrawn.[3] Unlike Fatah and Sa'iqa, the Iraqi factions in the PLO were opposed to the Ayatollah's regime,[4] and the issue was one of many over which the Organization was internally divided.

Central and South America

The PLO attended the first conference of the Organization of Solidarity of the Peoples of Asia, Africa and Latin America, held in Cuba in 1966. After a meeting between Arafat and Fidel Castro in Algiers in May 1972, the PLO co-operated with Cuba in the training of Latin American guerrillas. In 1973 Cuba withdrew recognition of the State of Israel, and in 1974 the PLO opened an office in Havana. After that, the Organization opened offices in Nicaragua, Panama, Jamaica, Guyana, Mexico, Brazil, Colombia and Venezuela. Revolutionary organizations in Brazil, Argentina, Chile, Uruguay, Panama, Peru, Ecuador, Venezuela, Mexico and El Salvador have been given aid by the PLO, or through it by Cuba and the Soviet Union. President Luis Alberto Monge of Costa Rica, a country which has excellent diplomatic relations with Israel, has complained of Libyan and PLO subversion in his peaceful country.[5] The PFLP formed close relations with the Marxist government of Grenada.

The PLO supplied arms to the Sandinistas in Nicaragua, and opened an embassy in the capital, Managua, after they seized power. 'Chairman Arafat' attended the anniversary of the Sandinistas' victory in Managua on 27 July 1981, and in his address he said: 'The way to Jerusalem leads through Managua' – a variation on earlier PLO themes of the road leading through Amman, Beirut and Damascus, but in this case stressing the role of the PLO in the world Marxist revolution.

One effect the PLO may expect to have on countries in this region was realized in Nicaragua, where the small Jewish community, consisting of about fifty families, was driven out of the country by the Sandanistas. Jewish property was confiscated. A few months before his expulsion, the distinguished leader of the community, Abraham Gorn, was kept a prisoner for two weeks and during that time was forced to clean the streets.[6]

Afghanistan

It seems that the desire to please the USSR took precedence over Arafat's Muslim loyalty. The PLO opened an embassy in Kabul in 1980, in support of the Soviet Union's occupation of Afghanistan. A PLO observer attended the Islamic conference at Islamabad which condemned the USSR invasion of Afghanistan, but he did not vote. When later the Organization's representative in Saudi Arabia found it necessary to say that the PLO's position on Afghanistan was 'identical' with that of the other Islamic countries which had attended the conference, Abu Iyad hastened to express the hope that the Soviet Union was 'fully appreciative of all our circumstances', which were such that sometimes they found themselves 'walking a tightrope'.[7]

China

The first government to recognize the PLO as the legitimate representative of the Palestinian people and to give it diplomatic recognition, with ambassadorial status, was the Communist People's Republic of China. Soon after the establishment of the PLO, Shuqairy had visited China. A PLO office was opened in Peking in 1965. China supplied the Organization with small arms, and gave guerrilla training and schooling in the thoughts of Mao Tse-tung to some dozens of Palestinians. However, the Chinese government told the Organization that they would not give it substantial aid; that while it could rely on ideological support, the struggle must be their own, they must fight for themselves. The bond between the PLO and China was not strong at that time, and weakened further when the Soviet Union pressed the Arab states to break the PLO–China connection.

When Arafat took over the chairmanship of the Organization in February 1969 the bond became firmer again. A month after a visit to Moscow in February 1970 had proved unsatisfactory, he went to China. On that occasion, and on all those that followed, PLO leaders were received with the elaborate ceremony usually reserved for honouring the heads of states important to the People's Republic. China began to sell arms in quantity to the PLO, the PFLP and the PDFLP. In the early years of the 1970s, 75 per cent of the PLO's arms came from China.[8]

The Chinese strongly criticized the Soviet Union for advocating peace between Israel and the Arab states. It seems that they looked to the *fedayeen* organizations to keep the conflict alive. When, in the latter half of the 1970s, the Organization began to get large quantities of arms from China's foremost enemy the Soviet Union, China restored good relations with the PLO's enemy Egypt, and her support for the PLO was reduced and became political rather than material.

USSR

The Soviet Union was slower to give official recognition to the PLO. When President Nasser visited Moscow in 1968, he took Arafat, who raised the question of a supply of arms to Fatah.[9] On Arafat's next visit, in February 1970, he went in his capacity as head of the PLO, but not as a guest of the government, only of the Soviet Committee for Solidarity with Asian and African Countries. The visit was little publicized in the USSR, but was made much of in the Arab news media. No large promises were made by the Russians, no official recognition was given. All Arafat got at the time were some small arms and two undertakings: that his arms losses would be replaced, and that, as from the last quarter of 1970, his men could receive some military training for officers and ideological instruction.

Arafat returned to Moscow from 20 to 29 July 1972, again as the guest of the Afro-Asian Committee. His reception, however, was a little warmer, as this was the time when President Sadat was ridding Egypt of Soviet military advisers. Soviet aid to the PLO was increased.

After the Munich massacre two months later, some Soviet disapproval of Black September was publicly expressed, but its wrath was reserved for the Israeli retaliations. All connection between PLO terrorist acts and Israel's reprisals was denied by the Soviet government.[10] Its official attitude to Israel was that she had the right to exist, but should withdraw to her pre-1967 borders and vacate the occupied territories. Again aid to the PLO was increased.

As late as November 1973, after the October War, at a time when the USSR was anxious to participate in the Geneva peace conference, Arafat and his delegation were still received in Moscow only unofficially by the Afro-Asian Committee. Although the Soviet government began to refer to the PLO as the 'sole legitimate representative of the Palestinian people' at that time, it did not give it official recognition as such until late July 1974, when at last Arafat and his fellow PLO delegates were invited to the USSR by the government itself and the Communist Party of the Soviet Union. They were received on 4 August. From that year, the USSR began to supply the PLO with fairly new models of heavy weapons, though never the most up-to-date. It was agreed then that the PLO should keep permanent representation in Moscow, but the PLO office was not opened in the Soviet capital until 22 June 1976.

Through the Moscow office, Soviet financial aid was 'processed', ostensibly for the Palestinian refugees. In fact the money went directly to the *fedayeen* groups in Lebanon.[11] The support for the PLO had three purposes: to influence the Arab states through the representatives of the sacred cause; to channel Soviet aid to leftist revolutionary groups, and to make sure that if the Soviet Union itself could not have a hand in a Middle East settlement, there would not be a settlement at all.

As Soviet aid to the PLO intensified, so did its anti-Israel propaganda. The victimization of Jews in Russia was an easy gift to grant the Arab states, with no dangerous political consequences in the world at large. Anti-Jewish propaganda within Russia went so far as to assert that Jews in the Third Reich had *conspired* with Hitler (with whom, the USSR chooses to forget, it signed a pact to dismember Poland). In its renewed persecution of Jews, Soviet Russia took over the role that Nazi Germany had played in its relations with the Arabs. Soviet-influenced groups throughout the world adopted the same extreme language of hate for Israel and Zionism, and served to disconnect the loyalty of Jewish leftists from Israel even within Israel itself. This, along with the 'Zionism is racism' resolution of the UN General Assembly, served to disguise the anti-Semitism of the Soviet Union (expressed in discriminatory laws against Jews as Jews, and playing on traditional anti-Semitic attitudes) as 'anti-racism'.

USA

United States law forbids public money to be given to the PLO. But large sums are given to United Nations projects which fund the PLO either directly or indirectly. (In 1983 this anomaly was pointed out by the Deputy Assistant Secretary of State for International Organizations, and he called for a more careful application of the law.)

The United States government refused official recognition to the PLO. Americans did, however, make authorized contacts with Organization personnel.[12]

Henry Kissinger records that a representative of the PLO approached the US ambassador to Iran in 1973, to try to arrange a discussion with the

US government 'on two premises: that "Israel is here to stay"; and that Jordan should be the home for a Palestinian state (in other words, that Hussein must be overthrown)'. Kissinger sent back a 'nothing message'. After the October War, a US representative, General Walters, met a PLO official at Rabat. The PLO wanted Jordan, without Hussein, and 'the dismantling of the Jewish state'. There was a second meeting in 1974, but that was all. 'The beginning of our dialogue with the PLO was also its end.'[13]

On 16 June 1976 Francis Meloy, the newly appointed ambassador for the United States to Lebanon, was kidnapped, along with his economics attaché, Robert Waring, and his Lebanese driver, as they were crossing the 'Green Line' between West and East Beirut to call on Elias Sarkis. All three were murdered. The United States' reaction was a decision to evacuate its citizens from Lebanon. To do so, it turned for protection – unofficially – to the strongest force in West Beirut at that time: the PLO. On 20 June 1976 the American Sixth Fleet lay anchored in the port of Beirut, not to land the marines, but to take Americans away. Many other foreigners took the opportunity of a safe departure on the American ships. *Fedayeen* guarded the embassy and the docks as the passengers boarded the ships.

In October 1977 a joint American–Soviet statement was issued calling for a comprehensive settlement in the Middle East, to be arrived at in a reconvened Geneva conference, which would include 'representatives of the Palestinian people'. It was to meet not later than December 1977. Its aims were to be the withdrawal of Israel from the territories captured in 1967; an end to the state of war between Israel and the Arab states; and the resolution of the Palestinian problem ensuring 'the legitimate rights of the Palestinian people'. President Sadat of Egypt pre-empted the conference when he went to Jerusalem in November 1977, and so transformed the political alignments of the region.

Negotiations which were to culminate in the Camp David accords between Egypt and Israel were then conducted under the auspices of the United States. America was enabled greatly to increase its influence in the Middle East. The result was to be an intensification of Soviet disruptive policies, partly through the agency of the PLO, but chiefly through Syria.

On 26 July 1979 the United States ambassador to the United Nations, Andrew Young, met the PLO 'observer', Labib Terazi, in the apartment of the ambassador of Kuwait. Mr Young made the contact on his personal and unauthorized initiative. Although he was censured for doing so and he resigned, the meeting still helped to enhance the international standing of the PLO.

Europe

'Our activity in Europe is based on Europe's need for Arab oil,' Arafat explained to Gromyko and Ponamarev during a friendly, wide-ranging discussion in Moscow on 13 November 1979.[14]

A few months earlier, on 8 July, Arafat had been received in Vienna by Chancellor Bruno Kreisky, who was accompanied by Willy Brandt, erstwhile Chancellor of West Germany. This was the first official visit by a PLO representative to a West European nation. The implication of the event was that the ruling Socialist Party, and therefore the Austrian State, as well as the Socialist International of which Brandt was chairman, recognized the PLO. At a press conference in Vienna, Arafat was asked whether a Palestinian state could exist alongside an Israeli state. Arafat answered by referring to the PNC resolution that the PLO would establish an independent Palestinian state on any part of Palestine. Chancellor Kreisky made comments subsequently which suggested that he interpreted this answer as meaning that the PLO had no desire to destroy Israel. The whole conduct of the discussion, in which meanings were chosen by the Europeans rather than expressed by Arafat, delighted the PLO leadership. For them, it proved that the Organization could establish contacts in Western Europe without having to change any of its principles. Arafat reported back that he had not denied that the National Covenant called for Israel's destruction. He said that when Brandt had asked him if it did, he had replied by asking Brandt whether he had read the Covenant. Brandt said that he had not. Arafat said, 'Read the Covenant first and then ask.'[15]

Soon after his visit to Austria, Arafat was invited to Spain for talks with the Prime Minister. In November he attended the International Conference of Solidarity with the Arab People, in Portugal, and was received by the President, the Prime Minister, the Foreign Minister and large enthusiastic crowds. Meanwhile, Farouq Qaddoumi was received by the Belgian and Italian foreign ministers.

President Giscard d'Estaing of France was unwilling to recognize the PLO. Arafat's reaction was to warn that 'Europe should recognize its [own] interests', and to threaten that it would 'pay a very heavy price' for continued support of Israel.[16] It was not until November 1982 that France received a PLO representative (Farouq Qaddoumi) at ministerial level.

At that time, the winter of 1982 and 1983, Britain's Prime Minister, Margaret Thatcher, in contrast to the other European leaders, still refused to recognize the PLO, and would not receive a proposed Arab League delegation which included a representative of the PLO. Even then, after the PLO expulsion from Lebanon had aroused European sympathy for the Organization to an unprecedented height, she took a principled stand and insisted that, until the PLO gave up the use of terrorism and recognized

Israel's right to exist, it would have no official recognition from her govern-ment. Her refusal was against the preference of her own Foreign Office, which was predominantly and even ardently in favour of recognition of the PLO as representative of the Palestinian people.[17] The PLO had representation in London, but only as part of the Arab League delegation.

The view which the member-states of the European Economic Com-munity shared, and which inspired the Venice Declaration of 13 June 1980, was that the Camp David process had failed – despite its huge and manifest achievement in bringing about negotiation, normalization of relations and agreement on a territorial settlement between Egypt and Israel. The truth was that Europe rejected Camp David because most of the Arab states rejected it. The United States administration saw the Venice Declaration as an attempt to undermine its own continuing efforts to bring peace in the Middle East. The Declaration was ineffectual as a peace-making initiative, because it was unrealistic, and commended itself to none of the parties it concerned. It called upon the PLO to 'renounce violence' and negotiate directly with Israel, and on Israel to stop creating settlements on the West Bank and to negotiate directly with the PLO. Neither the PLO nor Israel was likely to take the advice from Venice, and the nine countries of the European Economic Community which put their signatures to the declaration almost certainly knew this to be the case. But it served as a signal to the Arab states that Europe was more on their side than America was.[18]

United Nations

After the 1973 war, the General Assembly and the agencies of the United Nations were used persistently and predominantly by the Arab states, and by the Communist bloc, with its clients in the Third World and among the 'non-aligned' nations, as a diplomatic powerhouse for the PLO to perpetu-ate the Arab-Israeli conflict.[19] The General Assembly condemned the Camp David peace agreement by eighty-eight votes to twenty-two, with forty abstentions. The Economic Committee for Western Asia expelled Israel, and included the PLO. The International Energy Authority refused to accept Israel because her credentials were date-lined 'Jeru-salem', which is not recognized by most states as the country's capital. This prompted the United States to withdraw her own membership, and threaten to leave any other agency which took the same course. The UN itself has not expelled Israel, only because the United States would bring its existence to an end if it did. Short of that, the UN has allowed great victories to the PLO. Not only is the Organization the only 'national-liberation' movement with observer status at the UN; not only was Yasser

Arafat accorded the honour of being invited to address it although he represented no legally constituted state, but hundreds of anti-Israel resolutions have been passed by the General Assembly. The resolution adopted by the General Assembly on 10 November 1975 that 'Zionism is a form of racism' – that is, equating the desire of the Jews for national survival in their own country with the Nazi ideology in the name of which six million Jews had been killed – was a particular triumph for the PLO, the Soviet Union and the Arab States.

In addition to UNRWA, other special organs were created to deal exclusively with Palestinian matters. At the behest of the PLO, two new bodies were formed: the Committee on the Exercise of the Inalienable Rights of the Palestinian People (November 1975) and the Special Unit on Palestinian Rights in the Secretariat (December 1977). In February 1982 the UN Human Rights Commission condemned Israel's annexation of the Golan Heights, territory it had conquered from Syria in the Six Day War. The resolutions were introduced by Cuba. Other countries where 'human rights' were notoriously disregarded, including the Arab states, Communist bloc states and Greece, supported it.

The Arab-Communist campaign against Israel was pursued in every agency, while all criticism unfavourable to the Arab states was successfully suppressed. The United Nations Relief and Works Agency (UNRWA) was brought almost entirely under the control of the PLO in Lebanon. UNESCO, the World Health Organization (WHO) and the International Labour Organization (ILO) have all been turned to the advantage of the Organization in mounting attacks on Israel. Within UNESCO, at its eighteenth, nineteenth and twentieth general conferences, the Arab states attempted to expel Israel, but failed. Its Executive Committee, meeting in Paris in May 1978, condemned the state of education in the Israeli-administered areas (where the literacy rate among Arabs is higher than in any Arab state). In October 1980 Yasser Arafat addressed a UNESCO conference in Belgrade with a fiery attack on Zionism. In July 1982 UNESCO passed a resolution demanding that the history related by the (Jewish) Bible be rewritten so that the Jews were left out of it. In May 1976 the assembly of the World Health Organization refused to accept its own report by its special committee of experts on the health conditions in the territories administered by Israel, because it was not unfavourable to Israel. If an Israeli bid for a UN project was the lowest received, it was nevertheless turned down. In 1981, when the PLO's oppression of both Palestinians and the Lebanese in South Lebanon was in its sixth year, the UN issued postage stamps bearing the legend: 'Inalienable Rights of the Palestinian People'. At the Decade for Women conference in July 1980 in Copenhagen, delegates concentrated almost exclusively on an attack on

Israel. The extreme disabilities under which women labour in countries under Arab government, or such issues as the sexual mutilation of girls in certain African and Arab countries, were not debated. The ILO has not pursued the question of slavery in the Arab countries.[20] At the 1973 ILO conference, an Iraqi and a Libyan (both of whose countries are dictatorships) proposed a condemnation of Israel for 'violation of trade union rights'.

The PLO was proud to boast (in a pamphlet entitled *Do You Know?* published by the London representative of the PLO, undated but still being handed out in 1983) that 'no Arab State has ever been condemned by any organ of the United Nations for military attacks upon Israel (or any other State)'. Even so small a part of the history of the Middle East as this book records is sufficient to indicate what the statement proves: whether the Arab states are pacific, or the United Nations mendacious and corrupt.

Israel

Officially, the only dialogue the PLO was willing to have with Israel was the conversation of guns. Unofficially, direct contacts were made between PLO officials and Israeli military men, journalists and politicians, as private individuals.

Dr Isam Sartawi, a heart specialist and a member of the Palestine National Council, was adviser to Arafat on matters concerning Europe and the United States. In 1976 he began to meet and talk to Israelis, some of them Communists, and in particular the members of the Council for an Israeli-Palestinian Peace. Among the members of this group were the journalist and parliamentarian Uri Avneri, army officer Matitiahu Peled and the left-wing politician, Arieh Eliav. Sartawi and Eliav were awarded a Kreisky prize by the Austrian Institute for the Defence of Human Rights and Liberty, in recognition of their efforts to reconcile the PLO and Israel.

Sartawi had not always been a man of peace. In 1969 he had broken away from Fatah and formed 'the Action Committee for the Liberation of Palestine', with the support of Iraq. One of the actions it took was to attack a bus belonging to the Israeli airline El Al at Munich airport in February 1970. In 1971 he rejoined Fatah when his group merged with it.

Some of the PLO leaders demanded that Sartawi renounce the prize rather than share it with an Israeli. Sartawi refused, and resigned from the PNC in November 1979. The following month, however, the PNC Chairman, Khalid al-Fahoum, denied that he had resigned. Sartawi was bitterly attacked by the PLO hardliners (that is to say, on this issue, all the factions except Fatah), but Arafat defended him. Supported by his political advisers, Hani and Khalid al-Hassan, Arafat urged the others to consider the usefulness of encouraging European alternatives to Camp David – while insisting that no concessions on the final aim (the elimination of Israel) need be made. The good image, Arafat believed, which Sartawi was creating of the PLO in Europe was an asset to the Organization. He said that the PLO had 'political *fedayeen* as well as military *fedayeen*', and Sartawi was one of the former.[21]

In December 1980 Sartawi sent greetings in a telegram to an Israeli left-wing party, Sheli, when it was holding a conference in Jerusalem during which it raised a Palestinian flag. Again he came under attack within the PLO.

He took his seat at the fifteenth Palestine National Congress in 1981, and tried to make a speech about his contacts with 'democratic and progressive forces in Israel', but was stopped. Again he resigned. And again the Chairman did not accept the resignation.

For a third and last time his resignation was to be tendered and refused at the sixteenth PNC at Algiers in February 1983, the first Congress after the PLO was expelled from Beirut. Some weeks later, on 10 April, Isam Sartawi was assassinated during an international Socialist Congress – at which Israel was represented – in a conference hall at Albufeira in Portugal.[22]

Sartawi's function had been to create the impression for Arafat that the PLO was willing to recognize Israel's 'right to exist', in order to win friends in Europe and the United States. Sometimes he suggested that the European and American demand for the PLO to recognize Israel's 'right to exist' had been fulfilled, and, at other times, that it would be fulfilled if the Organization itself was first granted recognition by the United States government.

He had some success when he told the Dutch Parliament, in November 1979, that if a Palestinian state were established, the PLO was ready to recognize Israel. He also told the Dutch newspaper *Trouw* that the 'Palestine programme does not call for any annihilation' of the State of Israel.

On other occasions too he made statements which seemed to indicate an important change of PLO policy, only to have it firmly denied soon afterwards by PLO spokesmen, who feared the consequences of Sartawi being believed by their own allies and followers. Rocked between what is politic in the wider world and what is dogma in their own, Arafat himself and several of his spokesmen – including Khalid al-Hassan; Labib Terazi, the PLO official at the United Nations; Muhammad Abu Maizar, who was in charge of Fatah foreign relations, and Farouq Qaddoumi – have all made statements to the West, through journalists and politicians, which they have soon afterwards denied emphatically. Above all, whatever impression of moderation and flexibility it is necessary to create in the West, the fragile unity of the groups within the PLO has to be preserved; and as the Covenant provides the only tie, nothing in it can be denied without risk of the Organization falling apart.

On the Israeli side, those who talked with Sartawi also tried to smuggle their wishes into public belief, disguised as realities. At a press conference in Tel Aviv on 2 January 1977, Matitiahu Peled stated that a document had been drawn up two days earlier in Paris, which showed that the PLO agreed with the Council for Israeli-Palestinian Peace that the conflict should be resolved by a mutual acceptance of the principles of freedom, sovereignty and security for both peoples, and the establishment of a Palestinian state which would recognize the Zionist State of Israel. The PLO quickly issued an official denial that the meeting in Paris had ever taken place (which does not mean that it did not take place, only that whatever was said had no official PLO sanction).

The Covenant remains an absolute barrier to compromise. A strong conviction prevails in the PLO that the very least concession on principles would constitute a capitulation which must be resisted at all costs. Furthermore, it is believed that intransigence, or 'steadfastness', has worked in the Organization's favour, and will eventually, and inevitably, accomplish for it all that it desires.

The evidence lies in a 'limited circulation' document dated February 1978, entitled 'Educational Lecture for Officers on Ideas and Alliances, Principles and Manoeuvres'. It is issued by 'Fatah's Supreme Command of al-Asifa Forces, Department of Political Guidance', and reveals that Fatah was no more willing to moderate its objectives or its methods than were the Marxist and Ba'thist groups.[23] It is a testament of 'Rejectionism'. The theme of the lecture, given by one Dr Mahjub 'in the course in the memory of the Martyr, The Hero, Muhammad Ali', is that the PLO must stick to its principles unwaveringly. Principles are called 'conceptual weapons'. No pragmatic concessions must be made, he says; no adaptations in the name of realism.

If the PLO aims and reality do not accord with each other, then it is reality, Dr Mahjub insists, which must be changed. The touchstone which can accomplish this miracle is 'revolution':

> Voices will rise from among the revolutionary forces demanding discussion of the propositions of the enemy . . . saying 'politics is the art of the possible'. . . . We can see that these excuses arise out of their disbelief in an ability to change reality. . . . If 'politics is the art of the possible' in everyday practice, then the revolution is the art of making the necessary possible.

As proof that this can be done, he points out that refusal on the part of the PLO to budge an inch from its absolute demands has already made others waver, and has brought new 'alliances' to the PLO:

There is a clear example from our own experience. After the development and victory of the Palestinian revolutionary war, and to be precise after the October War, the range of friendships, alliances and followers has widened. Political powers within the Zionist camp have changed some of their positions to the point of admitting overtly the existence of 'a Palestinian people'. Moreover, some even recognize the right of the Palestinian people to an independent state alongside the continuation of the Zionist entity 'Israel'. Naturally, such a shift from an attitude of completely ignoring the Palestinian problem and people, and at times even an hostility towards them, to another attitude, supportive of . . . the Palestinian revolution, such a shift is slow though growing all the time. We cannot expect it to conform to ours politically and conceptually all of a sudden, but through a long struggle to strengthen that tendency . . . On this road we face 'propositions' from people who are motivated sometimes by the will to solve the problem, and sometimes by the wish to draw us to adopt their positions. They usually cover their propositions with [appeals to] 'pragmatism', realism, 'seizing the opportunity', and 'going by stages', and so on and so forth – temptations and rationalizations.

He reiterates the two supreme, unshakeable resolutions: to annihilate the State of Israel, and to do so by 'armed struggle' alone:

The forces of the Palestinian revolution believe in the liberation of the whole of the Palestinian homeland by means of a people's long-term war. But the concept of liberating all the lands of the Palestinian homeland is an advanced one for many of the allied political forces in the Arab and international arenas. Some of the allied forces think . . . that it is necessary to guarantee the security of the countries and peoples in the area, especially Israel, and at the same time to support the struggle of the Palestinian people to regain its legitimate rights. Such phrases could do as a minimum for political agreements against the Zionist enemy and American imperialism, but obviously they are totally different from what the Arab revolutionaries think and have achieved. . . .

Another example: we believe that the people's long-term war is the way to liberate Palestine. . . . We have to stress the point of the people's war, that it has no limits but complete liberation. . . .

Two principles above all should never be hidden. . . . The principle that the whole of Palestine is for the Arab Palestinian people, it is their right to come back to it, it being their property, i.e. in no way recognizing the Zionist entity called Israel; and the principle of the right of the Arab people to an armed struggle for the liberation of Palestine, i.e. in no way abandoning the armed fight as the only means for the liberation.

He warns against the siren-song of certain Israelis (with whom Isam Sartawi was willing to hold unofficial talks).

Thus David Shaham in a debate [held by *New Outlook*] towards the end of November 1974, with Matitiahu Peled, Uri Avneri, Simha Flapan and others participating: 'In my eyes, the only solution is that each of the parties involved would hold on to its old politics and assumptions, that each would think it had an historical right to existence in this country: the Israelis to Israel, and the Palestinians to Palestine. But, the target being living together, they would have to agree to a pragmatic solution, i.e. the division by which each side would give up realizing some of its rights over the whole land, for a certain period in its history.'

David Shaham's proposed solution is accepted today . . . by many parties that accepted the division of 1947 and afterwards recognized 'the Zionist entity'. Most of these parties are trying now to propose that solution which is, in short, accepting the division of Palestine between the Palestinian people and the invader-settlers that are sometimes called 'the Jewish people' and sometimes 'the new Israeli people'. . . . It is really unthinkable that we accept such a demand to recognize the Zionist entity in one way or another, on the pretext of being practical, or realistic, or pragmatic, or seizing the opportunity. Even a mere tendency towards such a recognition of the 'right' of the Zionist enemy 'to exist' on the Palestinian land means not only giving up the land, but giving up the Palestinian identity. Whoever denies a Palestinian – any Palestinian – the right to return to his house and village and homeland, has no right to represent the Palestinian anywhere. Whoever denies a Palestinian – any Palestinian – the right to continue his armed struggle until the liberation of his land, has no right whatever to represent the Palestinian. Even by their 'pragmatic' standard by which they justify their propositions, how is it possible for a party that consents to the 'Zionist entity' and to stopping the fight to take upon itself to speak in the name of those who insist on liberating their homeland by means of an armed force? . . .

It is inadmissible that Arab powers should slip that way, claiming that 'something is better than nothing' . . . and 'hiding the slogan of annihilating the Zionist entity is liable to gain us more powerful friends'. The logic of 'something is better than nothing' reveals a lack of belief in the victory, i.e. the possibility of liberating the whole of Palestine.

He argues against the idea that the PLO might practise deceptions such as the use of ambiguous language for the sake of immediate gains:

A revolution is a war, and war has its weapons. And the most important weapon in a revolution is principles and public slogans for which the revolutionaries will fight. The right principle is stronger than the strongest weapon and surpasses the enemy force. The right principle expresses the just cause without any doubt. . . .

As to concealing the slogan, if we publicly deny it while promising in secret to keep it, for whom then will this 'secret' slogan exist?

31
The Popular Liberation War

By self-definition, the PLO was more than the representative organization of the Palestinian people; it was also the 'vanguard of the Revolution', the leader of the Arab masses against 'anti-progressive' Arab regimes. This was the wider context of the PLO struggle, the dogma that the nationalist group Fatah had to accept from the radical socialist groups in order for the PLO to exist and function. Without it, the armed struggle for Palestine would have been a merely nationalist cause, contradicting the ideals of Arab unity and international socialism.

The monarchies and other Westward-looking Arab states were, like Israel, forces of 'imperialism'. The 'popular liberation war' was against them too; so it was a euphemism or code-phrase for revolution within the Arab world.[1]

Still Saudi Arabia and the other oil-producing states of the Gulf continued to finance the PLO. Their contributions were paid to Arafat,[2] the nationalist and Muslim brother, who, they seemed to feel, was on their side. Their money talked not only of their steadfastness in the sacred cause, it also pleaded: 'wherever your revolution strikes, let it not be in my kingdom, my emirate.' It seems that they felt safe enough as long as 'the revolution' was preparing and equipping itself at a distance from their own countries, in the fraternal State of Lebanon.

To pursue the popular liberation war, the PLO had to enlist the support of the Arab masses. They could do so only in Lebanon, the place of their fixed abode.

The general theory of how the *fedayeen* groups should go about recruiting and preparing the masses in Lebanon for their popular revolution is explained fully in a secret document issued by Fatah, the Supreme Command of the al-Asifa Forces' Drafting and Political Department, in April 1977: 'The Role of the Political Agent in Regard to the Masses: Educational Lecture for Officers in the Course in Memory of the Martyr, the Political Agent, Gazi Awad Zaidan', by 'Abu Shadi'.[3] The importance of the document lies in the proof it gives that, contrary to repeated assertions by the leadership, the PNC, and even a promise made in Article 27 of their Covenant, the PLO had every intention of interfering in the internal affairs of

حركة التحرير الوطني الفلسطيني
فتــــح
القياده العامه لقوات العاصـفه
دائـرة التعبئـه والتـوجيه السياسي

دور النفوس السياسي
بيـن الجماهيـر

محـاضرة التثقيـف في دورة الشهيد
الغوث السياسي غازي مـــوض
زيـدان
لتثقيـف الضبـاط
نيـسان ١٩٧٧...............

٣بــروشاسي ٥٠

سـرى محدود التداول

The front cover of the 'secret, limited circulation' lecture on the role of the political agent in regard to the masses, April 1977

Lebanon and any other Arab state. Some extracts show how the winning of recruits and the organizing of the secret structure were plotted:

In order to accomplish the task of preparing the masses for the people's long-term war, it is necessary that the four following phases take place:

1. Enlisting the masses.
2. Organizing and grouping the masses.
3. Training the masses.
4. Arming the masses.

First, the meaning of 'enlisting'. In the political sense, it means preparing for the coming battle, military or national (*qawmiyya*) [that is Arab, not specifically Palestinian] ... by preparing public opinion for the struggle for a political cause, such as Arab Nationalism, or Socialism, or resistance to Zionism or Imperialism, etc. It is possible to enlist by means of education, or religion, or the drafting might take on an economic character, as economics have a bearing on all political and national phenomena.

After an initial survey, we can divide the masses in the village into three groups:

The first group – against the revolution.
The second group – hesitating.
The third group – for the revolution.

As for the first group, it identifies itself either with political feudalism or with foreign powers, neither of which have any interest in the revolution. [A reference to Christian Lebanese and others loyal to the constitution.]

As for the second group, its positions shift according to the centres of power in the village, i.e. its views are not clear, so that you can draw it in and organize it – and so can your opponent if he is more powerful than you.

As for the third group, it feels its interests lie with you, for social reasons, or local nationalist [*wataniyya* – a reference to the Lebanese 'nationalists' of the Left], or Arab nationalist [*qawmiyya*] reasons ... and it is they who will bring [the revolution] about.

[These will] work together with you to achieve the eternal and permanent goal ... [by helping] to carry out the tasks that will be asked of you, whether in the base [Lebanon] or entering the occupied land. ...

The first group ... has fixed attitudes. ... What you can do [however], by continual, long, painstaking work, is to isolate them and soften them, i.e. prevent them from taking up strong positions against the existence of the revolution in the village. This should be accomplished by personal visits ... to the people who are in leading positions in that group, [such as] the *mukhtar* [village chief] or the mayor, or to the key persons in the electorate ... who usually take the stand of their representatives and politicians. ...

During our visits and afterwards, the weak spots of that group should be found, and all our relations with it should be taken from that angle for this group [is] against the revolution, i.e. against progress.

The second and third groups . . . will form the masses for the revolution.

To proceed with the task, once the opposition to the revolution has been separated from the rest, the political agent and other members of the force in the village will make sure they are seen participating in the various public occasions of the village people – whether it is a mourning or a feast – or by an exchange of visits with the peasants. You will [thus] participate in their everyday problems. . . .

Then comes the sorting out of the right people . . . [and] concentrating on certain persons in whom you find the minimum required characteristics of a Fatah member. . . . You begin working on these people in the first phase by assigning them unofficial tasks . . . such as, investigating people that you have previously gathered information about, exploring places you have already got to know . . . distributing pamphlets . . . (while you watch what they do). . . .

[At these tasks] some of the people in the village will succeed . . . and you will then start a follow-up phase, which will last at least six months. . . . You start working on them, and prepare them for Fatah thinking, on issues that are not a matter of life and death. You explain to them the goals of Fatah, the slogans of Fatah, and the Fatah style, and the issue of the people's war . . . after which the regional committee will decide whether they have succeeded sufficiently in this follow-up phase to be admitted to membership.

Coming to the pyramidal structure, the organizing and grouping will take place next by forming the unit cells. That is the main task in the organizing phase.

The cell is the smallest unit in the organization. The units go by the following order: the cell (*khaliyya*), the link or circle (*halqa*), the wing (*janah*), the branch (*shu'ba*), and the regional committee (*lajnat al-mintaqa*).

The cell has 3–5 members, and the trustee in charge of it will be a secret member of a link.

The link has 3–5, and the trustee in charge will be a secret member of a wing.

The wing has 3–5, and the trustee in charge will be a secret member of a branch committee.

The branch has more than 5 wings, and the trustee in charge will be a secret member of a regional committee.

[This] is the agreed order . . . we'll discover in reality how flexible it can be. Remember, the order is always at the service of the work, and not vice versa, i.e. the order should serve the organizational task, which is the forming of unit cells.

The 'most able and attentive person' will be secretly the trustee in charge of the village. He will maintain relations between the new organization and the masses, on the one hand, and the Fatah base, on the other. The work of enlisting new members will continue. 'But at this stage the [new] organization is not yet trained or armed.' First comes 'building up a consciousness' in regular meetings – weekly or fortnightly is recommended, but the main point is that they must be regular, and 'under no circumstances may be neglected'.

The cells are then named after martyrs from the village, and if there aren't any, then from the masses of the region; and if there aren't any of those either, then after the martyrs of the movement. You give the members their organizational names for reasons of convenience and security, bearing in mind that the hidden orders require secrecy in regard to membership.

In a regular meeting we shall discuss:

1. The recommendations and directives of the previous meeting.
2. The general political situation in the world, among the Arabs, in Palestine, Lebanon, Fatah, and the village.
3. Organizational business.
4. Any other business, such as membership fees, followers, members, etc.
5. Recommendations, directives and decisions.

Even if the meeting is agitated and disturbed, it should be regulated, and a trustee to be (secretly) in charge should be assigned in rotation at each regular meeting.

Clause no. 40 of the hidden law of the organization specifies in relation to the duties of a member, 'attending meetings and paying membership fees regularly'.

It is customary for a working member to pay the sum of two Lebanese pounds in exchange for an official receipt, either individually or collectively. . . . The payment is made at the beginning of each month and not at the end, and in no way can there be any concession in regard to the payment of the fee. Even if a person's conditions are bad, he has to pay, for the sake of the principle.

Every official in charge of the organization in a village should establish a fund box for the service of the organization in that village. This fund box is for expenses in states of emergency, for the members of the organization in the village. For example, when a member cannot afford to pay the membership fee, the payment will come from the fund box. The money for the fund box will come generally from the donations of the members in the village, or from other village people, or from the various projects of the organization.

Now we come to the third task, training the masses. As we are a national (wataniyya) liberation movement, we believe that the main task of the revolution is removing the regime by means of armed force. We raise the slogan of armed struggle, therefore we have to shift our organization from the level of everyday struggle to the level of an armed fight. As a result, we have to be an armed organization, capable of carrying weapons and defending the revolution.

The organization should be adept at fulfilling every military task that will be assigned to it. After organizing we come to training, and this may take various forms.

In the secret phase, the training will be in secret, and will consist of [learning the technique of] dismantling and assembling [weapons], i.e. in a village . . . we take a piece of weaponry to one of the houses secretly, and there a cell will be trained in dismantling and assembling [it], and [learning its] main properties. This is called, abolishing illiteracy in regard to weapons.

After drilling, this cell will take upon itself to train the other cells, until we reach a stage when every member of the organization has had weapon drill. The regional committee will take it upon itself to abolish the illiteracy of all the organization members in regard to weapons, so that everyone will know how to use a gun.

If circumstances allow, shooting practice is recommended, because it is extremely important for a member after training to establish a confidence that he can rely on his weapon, and that confidence will be established by means of shooting.

During the second stage of the training, we shall concentrate on the people who have understood the training more than the others, isolate them, and take them to higher courses, further to abolish their illiteracy by, for instance, increasing their capabilities – i.e. their practical and technical capabilities rather than their theoretical ones. Examples: ambushes, attacks and so on, in a simplified manner.

In the third stage we shall lift them to a higher level of training, and in addition to guns we can teach them how to use RPGs, explosives and mortars (howitzers), etc., until military perfection is reached in the organization.

In the fourth stage we concentrate on further training on a [still] higher level, for leaders of groups. They will be given a chance to become leaders in accordance with our principle of self-reliance.

After completing the four stages of training, we shall distribute weapons, taking into account the principle of not supplying a gun to someone who doesn't know how to use it, so that we shan't be responsible for more errors, or more casualties. It is said that in teaching explosives the first mistake is the last one. Then we select a military official from the unit staying in the village or the region, and he will have military control over the [local] organization, and the political agent will shift responsibility to him, i.e. he'll give him the lists of the members' names, those who are training, and they will then be in his charge. Then [comes the] supplying of the weapons, in agreement with the supreme command and according to the desired plan of arming.

What are the tasks of the armed organization?

Defending the security of the revolution. When that has been assured, we shall move on from the defence stage to attack, i.e. we shall assign to this organization certain tasks in order to strengthen it. A member of the organization is a soldier without a khaki uniform [but] in the traditional sense of the word; which is to say, he is required to fulfil all tasks assigned to him, his special circumstances taken into account to a certain extent, but in times of war – and we are always in such times – he is with us in heart and body. We stay in a certain village: the first task of the organization is guarding the forces staying there . . . the bases, warehouses, depots in the village, in whatever way the organization deems fit. It may decide whether the guard [should or] should not carry weapons, as when watching in front of a house at night, watching people, and in securing the safety of people or the forces staying in the village. All these [tasks] are the responsibility of the organization.

The second task of the organization is selecting groups from among its people to accompany a force moving from one spot to another. This is an important matter. Under this clause comes the selection of guides from among the people of the organization.

The third task of the armed organization is forming emergency groups (reserves) for special jobs, such as participating in some of the patrols in the occupied land. . . . [And also] in the work done to establish an everyday co-operation and intermingling between our [local] armed forces and the organization . . . so that you'll reach the goal of not having any difference between someone from the organization and someone from al-Asifa forces. Both of them do the jobs and duties required of them with the same spirit, vigour and dash.

The fourth task of the organization is selecting people for the activities in the military groups, i.e. no new member will be recruited or admitted to our military forces, unless the organization is consulted, and agrees to it.

These pains were taken to little effect. The groups were not successful in their recruiting. Instead, they alienated most of the people. When the PLO fighters needed the Lebanese to support them in 1982, as the Israelis drove them back into West Beirut and then out of the country, no popular uprising materialized.

32
The Armed Struggle

The armed struggle against Israel took the direct forms of shelling towns and settlements, and terrorist raids. The attacks were made on civilians; the *fedayeen* did not willingly seek engagement with the military. Some examples of the raids are these:[1]

On 11 April 1974 an early morning raid was made on the constantly shelled border town of Kiryat Shmona. The terrorists, having managed to get through the border defences, broke into two apartment buildings, shot everyone they encountered, killing eighteen children and adults, and wounding dozens of others. Then they barricaded themselves in on the top floor. When the Israeli security forces stormed the building, all the terrorists were killed. Israel replied, in accordance with a policy always carried out, with air-raids on six villages in southern Lebanon which Israeli Intelligence identified as PLO bases. The raid on Kiryat Shmona was the one celebrated a year later in Beirut on Sunday, 13 April 1975, when the 'civil war' in Lebanon began.

On 15 May 1974 a midnight raid was made on Ma'alot, in the Galilee, where most of the settlers were new refugees from Muslim countries. They broke into an apartment and shot and killed the father, the pregnant mother and their four-year-old child, and gravely wounded a five-year-old daughter in the stomach. She survived, and remembered that 'as the man pointed the gun at me and shot, he was laughing'. The three – they were Nayef Hawatmeh's men of the PDFLP – went on to a local school, and there they found over 100 teenagers with their teachers, who were on a school outing from Safed and were staying in the school overnight. They forced one of the teachers, whom they met in the school grounds, to let them into the building. There they took 105 hostages and held them in the school for sixteen hours. They wired explosive to the walls, and used their hostages as sandbags at the windows, firing past them occasionally as negotiations went on. Their treatment of the children was harsh and relentless, except inexplicably for a few hours, when they allowed them to move a little. And at one point the terrorists started singing. What they sang were old songs of the Palmach, the commando force of the (pre-1948) Jewish Defence Army, which they had learnt, words and tune. When the building was stormed, they shot and killed twenty-two of the children, wounded fifty-six others, and also killed one of the rescuing soldiers. All three of the terrorists were shot and killed. After this raid, the Israeli airforce bombed Beirut and Nabatiyyah, killing about fifty people, many of them Lebanese, and injuring some 200.

On 25 June 1974 a group of terrorists landed from the sea on the beach at the resort town of Nahariyya. They shot the watchman of an apartment building, and broke into one of the apartments, where the father tried to save his wife and children by letting them down through a window. All the terrorists were killed by the security forces. This town came under such frequent attack that the shelters were turned into small cinemas, gymnasia and games rooms to improve the long hours the residents spent in them.

On 19 November 1974, six days after Arafat's speech to the General Assembly of the UN in which he said that he bore an olive branch, another four of Hawatmeh's men broke into an apartment building at Beit She'an, and killed four people. Many of the townspeople, mainly of Asian and North African origin, wild with fury, burnt the bodies of the terrorists – and, accidentally, the body of one of the victims too.

This was the time when the PLO was at the peak of its prestige and self-confidence. The popular belief among Arabs everywhere that Israel had suffered a serious defeat in the 1973 October War, the launching of the oil weapon, the ecstatic acclaim Arafat had enjoyed at the United Nations, all increased the Organization's trust in the inevitability of its victory, the effectiveness of refusing to compromise, and the gains achieved by the 'armed struggle'. And so the number of terrorist raids increased.

On 1 December 1974 a group of *fedayeen* terrorists entered the village of Rechanya at about midnight. This village, only a mile or so from the Lebanese border, was inhabited by Circassian Muslims, whose fore-fathers had migrated from Russia at the turn of the century to escape religious persecution. After the terrorists had broken into a house, killed the husband and wounded the wife, they discovered that their victims were Arabic-speaking Muslims. They apologized, and gave themselves up to the Israeli security forces. Subsequently the villagers rejected the apology, expressed their 'solidarity' with Israel, and asked to be allowed weapons for self-defence in the future.

On 6 December 1974 a group landed from the sea and raided the home of a family on Kibbutz Rosh Hanikra. The other residents dealt with the incident themselves. One terrorist was shot, the others forced to escape. Then the daily work was resumed. The people of the *kibbutz* refused to let the security forces in, or news reporters. This terrorist incident was unique in that no Israeli civilian lives were lost.[1]

Five days later a bomb explosion in a Tel Aviv cinema – the eleventh – brought Israeli airforce planes over Beirut, bombing PLO military bases.

At dawn on 15 June 1975, terrorists attacked the small co-operative farming district of Kfar Yuval on the Lebanese border. Most of the farmers were from Morocco and India. The terrorists shot the watchman, forced their way into a house, and took a woman and her sons hostage. The father of the family fought with the rescuing forces, and was shot dead by the terrorists. The wife and children survived.

In 1975 Israel made sixty reprisal raids, including twelve naval bombardments of border villages. About 150 people were killed, and some 400 were injured.

The 'civil war' changed the pattern of attacks on Israel. Because Major Haddad's militia helped to keep the PLO back from the border, the *fedayeen* used sea-routes more often.

In April 1979 another attack was made in the town of Nahariyya by terrorists from the sea. They captured a man and his four-year-old daughter, took them to the beach, and made the father watch while they dashed the little girl's brains out on the rocks.

Children were often chosen as targets. In April 1980 a nursery was attacked in Kibbutz Misgav Am, where a baby lying in a cot was shot dead. Two other people were killed, and sixteen were wounded.

All attacks brought heavy reprisals. The Israelis bombed the refugee-camp military bases in Lebanon, so on that side of the border too, the innocent died. Multitudes suffered, thousands of young Arabs became killers and 'martyrs', but the 'armed struggle' did not achieve, or begin to achieve, the annihilation of Israel.

The dearth of popular support for the PLO and the lack of victory in the 'armed struggle' against Israel were not discouraging to the theorists of the Revolution, because they saw them as nothing worse than temporary failures in a war that was ultimately, necessarily, victorious. Their optimism was inspired by the success of other left-wing 'anti-imperialist' movements in recent times, such as those in Algeria, Vietnam, Cuba, Ethiopia, the Congo, Angola, Mozambique and Iran. Furthermore, the revolutionaries of the world were far from powerless. The Soviet Union provided them with political backing and arms. The PLO was the chief intermediary and channel of aid between the USSR and most of the world's 'national liberation movements'.

33
World Revolution

In its political programme of January 1973, the PLO openly published its intention of actively aiding and seeking aid from 'national liberation' movements, and 'all world revolutionary forces':

> The Palestinian national struggle and the Arab national democratic struggle are an integral part of the militant movement against imperialism and racism and for national liberation throughout the world. Mutual solidarity and support between the Arab national struggle and the world revolutionary struggle are a necessity and an objective condition for the success of our Arab struggle . . . . The Arab Palestinian national struggle is decisively and firmly on the side of the unity of all world revolutionary forces.[1]

The thirteenth Palestine National Congress, meeting in Cairo from 12 to 20 March 1977, stressed the policy in Clause 12 of its Declaration:

> The PNC affirms the significance of co-operation and solidarity with socialist, non-aligned, Islamic and African countries, and with all the national liberation movements in the world.[2]

During the 1970s, as the PLO established itself as a ruling power in Lebanon, it functioned as a centre for the provision of training and weapons to subversive organizations from most of the non-Communist countries on all continents. To the Communist Party of the Soviet Union these groups were the possible nuclei of future mass movements, as well as the disrupters of order in the present. It was largely because of the PLO, its resources, facilities, control of territory (which included a metropolitan capital) and its special position granted by the USSR as a 'national liberation movement' with a mission of leadership among other such movements, that the 1970s was 'the decade of terrorism'. Terrorist groups became strongly enough equipped, well enough instructed and trained, to constitute a real threat to the stability of emergent African and unstable South American states, and to disturb (though they did not change or even seriously damage) the established liberal democracies.

PLO leaders directed terrorist attacks carried out by foreign groups outside the Middle East. They also participated with foreigners in carrying them out. Although they were stateless, Palestinians who were members of the PLO could travel abroad without difficulty. Fatah could, and often did, issue passports in the name of 'certain of the Arab states', grant the visa permits of those states, and use their respective stamps.[3]

On 27 June 1976, while Tall al-Za'tar was coming under heavy fire from the Christians and the Syrians, sympathizers helped the PLO to carry out a plan – formulated by Wadi' Haddad with a Soviet agent, Antonio Dages Bouvier – to hijack a French airbus and force it to fly to Uganda. Two West Germans, Wilfried Böse and Brigitte Kuhlmann (PLO codenamed 'Halimeh'), carried out the assignment. After landing at Entebbe, in the country where Idi Amin, a self-declared admirer of Hitler, was dictator, these self-declared 'anti-Nazis' separated the Jews from the non-Jews with the same motive as the Nazis: to kill the Jews. One elderly Jewish woman who was ill was sent off to a hospital, and murdered by order of President Amin. All but three of the others were saved when Israeli commandos flew into Entebbe, shot dead the two German idealogues and some of their helpers from the Ugandan army, and, a week to the day after their ordeal had begun, rescued the victims. Israel had helped to build that very airport as a form of aid to newly independent Uganda, and her knowledge of it now rewarded her. For saving innocent lives, however, Israel was censured by the United Nations.[4]

On 13 October 1977 a German plane flying from Majorca was hijacked by four Arabs and finally brought down at Mogadishu in Somalia. The hijackers demanded the release of eleven German terrorists from West German jails, two Palestinians jailed in Turkey, and a ransom of some US $15 million. On the night of 17 to 18 October a West German commando group was sent (the government of the Federal Republic taking a leaf out of the Israeli book) to storm the aircraft. They rescued all the passengers and most of the crew. (One of the pilots had earlier been shot by the terrorists.) Three of the Arabs were killed and the fourth, a woman, was wounded. The West German authorities were given active assistance by Britain, and moral support by France and the United States. The Soviet Union and East Germany, according to the official West German government report, 'assured them of a helpful attitude'. But the attitude was not as helpful to the West Germans and the aeroplane passengers as it might have been. At the time, Wadi' Haddad, whose *ad hoc* group the 'Struggle Against World Imperialism Organization' had carried out the hijacking, was lying ill in an East German hospital. As far as is known, no pressure was brought to bear on him, in that country of constitutional coercion, to call off the operation.[5]

Kurdish terrorists, and terrorists from West Germany, Italy, Northern Ireland, Spain, Holland, France, Turkey, Greece, Cyprus, Japan, Argentina, East Timor, Eritrea, the United States, Chile, and southern Africa visited the PLO in their camps in Lebanon.[6] There were three main training camps for foreign terrorists: Chatila, Burj al-Barajneh and Damour.[7] Basque terrorists were trained in Chatila with Germans and Italians. In 1979 over 100 recruits from Spain attended a training course at Burj al-Barajneh in Beirut, and Hamariyah, in Syria.[8] The Turkish 'Grey Wolves', Emegin Birligi, were assigned their offices at Damour. The original Grey Wolves were a Mongol sect, and the contemporary Grey Wolves claim to be descended from the armies of Ghenghis Khan. Originally a self-styled rightist party in the days of Kamal Ataturk, they became Marxist after the First World War, and declared themselves to be fighting for the rights of the proletariat against the 'fascist' government of Turkey. They were the first foreign terrorist organization to go to the PLO in Lebanon for training. A number of them were to be found in the Palestinian camp of Tall al-Za'tar in the 1960s, where later they were joined by Cubans, Somalians and Pakistanis. Mehmet Ali Agca, who attempted to assassinate Pope John Paul II in Rome in 1980, was a member of the Grey Wolves. (Before he made the attempt he spent three months in Bulgaria.)

The ruined city of Damour became the Lebanese headquarters of a number of foreign terrorist groups. Only 200 yards down the road from the Turkish Grey Wolves' office were the offices of the Armenian group, the Secret Army for the Liberation of Armenia, ASALA, whose headquarters were in Beirut, and which was dedicated chiefly to the avenging of the massacres of Armenians by the Turks.[9]

All enemies of Western liberal democracy were friends of the PLO. In October 1980 the West German neo-Nazi organization, Wehrsportsgruppe Hoffman, opened a training camp of their own, starting with twenty-two trainees, in Bir Hassan camp, under the auspices of the PLO. According to the camp commandant, Uwe Berendt, who was wanted in West Germany for the murder of a Jewish publisher in Erlangen, it was Abu Iyad himself who gave the orders. Berendt and a comrade named Klaus Hubl had been sent by Hoffman to establish the camp at Bir Hassan.

It might be supposed that it was something of an embarrassment to the PLO propagandists that their Organization patronized and was allied to Nazi groups such as this one, while they made constant use of the word 'Nazi' as a strong pejorative to apply to Israel (because the enemies of the Jewish State intended to offer the cruellest and the most outrageous insult that could conceivably be directed at the Nazis' chief victims). But the embarrassment only came when their close co-operation with the neo-Nazis became publicized through an unexpected defection from the Hoffman camp.

Conditions were so harsh that two of the trainees, Walter-Ulrich Behle ('Khalid') and Uwe Johannes Mainka ('Abdullah'), escaped and sought asylum with the Kataeb, who summoned foreign news reporters to hear the story. The PLO was embarrassed and invited the reporters to a press conference of their own, at which they produced two other Germans who, they said, had escaped from the 'fascist' Kataeb, and were now converted to 'progressive' views. But questioned by the pressmen, these two Germans were unable to say what the emblem of the Kataeb was (they drew two crossed swords, an emblem unknown in Lebanon, instead of the cedar tree), and though they denied all knowledge of Wehrsportsgruppe Hoffman, they were identified by West Germans as two of Hoffman's men – Uwe Berendt and Klaus Hubl.[10]

The association between the PLO and European groups resulted in a series of terrorist attacks in Europe. In October 1979 a synagogue was attacked in the rue Copernic in Paris by French terrorists in conspiracy with PLO Rejectionists.[11] In 1980 two mass killings were carried out by bomb explosions. One was at the railway station of Bologna on 1 August, when eighty-five people were killed and about 300 were injured; the other in a Munich beer hall during the Oktoberfest on 26 September, when thirteen were killed and again some 300 injured. According to Lebanon Radio, 25 June 1981, Abu Iyad planned both of these mass murders with the Italian and the German terrorists.

If, as seems likely, the German neo-Nazis encountered their compatriots, members of the Communist Red Army Faction (commonly known as the Baader–Meinhof group) and of the Left-anarchist Movement 2nd June, in Beirut, no report has been circulated of any clashes between them, although the leftist group declared themselves to be anti-Nazi.

Twenty-six Germans were trained by the PLO in one year alone, 1979; and thirty-two Italians and twenty-one Japanese in that same year.[12] They sought and found training, arms, asylum, financial aid and contact with the Soviet Union through the PLO.

A constant exchange of information passed between the PLO and the Soviet embassy.[13] The electronic telephone-tapping system of the Organization – called 'Ecoute', meaning 'Listen', which allowed the PLO to tap all internal messages, including those passing within East Beirut – was housed in a building close to the embassy.

Swedes, Norwegians and Danes found their way to the camps, most of them for humanitarian reasons, but not all: two Norwegians captured by Israel in 1982 were active supporters of the PLO. The PFLP counted Swedes and Norwegians among its active members.[14]

Fugitive terrorists were given asylum in Beirut, usually in Chatila. Several members of the German Red Army Faction were given shelter and false documents by the Organization.[15] At least forty-five members of the IRA were known to have found asylum with the PLO, and the IRA received arms and training from the Organization.[16] Thomas MacMahon, convicted for the murder of Lord Mountbatten in 1979, was trained in a PFLP camp.[17] The bomb that killed the sometime Secretary for Northern Ireland, Airey Neave, in the precincts of the British Houses of Parliament was a 'dual-trigger' device, not seen before by the British anti-terrorist security forces, but commonly used by the PLO.[18]

The foreign terrorists entered Lebanon either through Syria (after the reconciliation of Assad and the Organization), or directly by air and through Beirut airport, by arrangement with PLO officials, who were accessible in most countries in the world. From the late 1960s onwards, there was an 'agreement' between the PLO and the Lebanese government, imposed by the PLO, by which foreigners could arrive at Beirut airport and be allowed into Lebanon without having to go through the usual immigration formalities. The daily list was handed to the passport and customs authorities. Some of the visitors went to the camps for training, others were lodged as guests of the Organization in one of their apartment buildings in West Beirut, on or near the fashionable shopping street of Hamra'. These apartments were the sort that cost about half a million Lebanese pounds each to buy. There were also the 'special hotels' for PLO guests and friends: the Commodore – where the foreign correspondents gathered – the Plaza and several others. The open PLO offices were mostly in the district of Mazra'a, but the whole of West Beirut was under PLO control, and any building or excavated tunnel beneath it could be used by the Organization as and when and for what purpose it chose.

'PLO special baggage', containing weapons, explosives and grenades, left Beirut daily on Middle East Airline flights. Again, the Lebanese authorities could not interfere. Among the employees of every airline, including those of Europe and the United States, there were hostesses or stewards bribed with monthly payments by the PLO, who saw to the transporting of letters and documents for the Organization, and made sure that the 'special baggage', disguised as 'diplomatic bags', got through without difficulty at the foreign ports of destination.

On some occasions the PLO brought in delegations against the expressed objections of the Lebanese government, such as a group of Iranians arriving to join the PLO forces in January 1980.

The PLO daily airport list usually had twenty to fifty names on it;[19] this must mean that literally tens of thousands of foreign PLO 'guests' arrived for short or long stays in the country, protected from the Lebanese authorities. They could, as many did, join the PLO and the National Movement in the killing. As they could leave as freely as they had arrived, their names and origins unknown, they can remain forever safe from any legal retribution for the crimes they committed in Lebanon.

34
Shattering Blows

Although the PLO seemed to be strong in Lebanon and still rising in the world throughout the latter half of the 1970s, its decline had started in 1976 when Syria openly entered the Lebanese war against the main forces of the Organization.

The peace imposed by Syria in November 1976 did not hold. Elias Sarkis found it impossible to restore democracy. Christian groups proposed that the political turmoil could best be ended by a new constitution which would cantonize the country on the Swiss model, and that there should be a national army composed of separate Christian and Muslim units. They wanted the new constitution to be worked out by consultation between all the religious communities, on the understanding that the new laws of the state would be binding on all equally, and family law would no longer, as hitherto, vary according to the diverse religious practices. Stern opposition to the idea came from the Sunni *ulama*, the learned religious men, who feared the domination of the Marxists and the PLO in secularized communities. President Sarkis supported their view.[1] The impossibility of ignoring confessional differences was as plain as ever.

Sarkis thought it best to make no changes, but rather to restore the balance as it had been before the war. Camille Chamoun put it to him that the same conditions would then prevail as had given rise to the 'civil war', conditions which included the armed presence of the PLO and the very political differences which it had exploited, but to this Sarkis gave no satisfactory answer. Furthermore, he refused to permit any charge to be brought against the PLO for its part in causing the bloodshed; nor would he allow it to be called upon to answer for the crimes it had committed during the war.[2] So the fears of the Christians were not assuaged.

Early in 1977 Christians started returning to their places of work in what had been, for months, the totally separated district of West Beirut. The 'Green Line' which had divided the city was eliminated, but not for long. Incidents of bombing, shooting and the blowing up of buildings continued, acts of terrorism directed against the Christians; they retaliated against the Palestinians in the camps.

On 16 March 1977 Kamal Jumblatt was assassinated, probably by the

Syrians.[3] The Druze blamed the Christians, and another massacre ensued.[4] Dozens of Christians were murdered in the Chouf mountains, and their houses were looted. About 130 men, women and children were indiscriminately done to death, bludgeoned, stabbed, or cut to pieces with axes. Survivors fled in droves to seek asylum in the Maronite enclave, north of Beirut. Press censorship kept all but the most cursory report of the massacre from reaching the outside world.

The Arab Deterrent Force (ADF) was manifestly failing to deter the warfare. In West Beirut Syria's Sa'iqa battled with Iraq's ALF. The barriers and roadblocks were put up again, the 'Green Line' was restored.

In an attempt to bring the *fedayeen* under Syrian-Lebanese control, Syrian and Lebanese commanders met Abu Iyad at Chtoura. The result was the Chtoura Agreement of July 1977, by which the PLO undertook to keep its forces 15 kilometres from the Israeli border, letting the Lebanese army take up positions in the vacated area, while the ADF would defend the southern coast. The agreement also required the dismissal of all Lebanese belonging to any of the PLO groups, and restricted the size of the PLO militia and the quantity and type of their armament. It permitted them only one training camp. A committee composed of representatives of Syria, Lebanon, the ADF and the PLO, meeting in Sidon, would see that the new plans were carried out.[5]

Within the Maronite enclave normality soon returned, and it became a self-contained 'city-state'. At first, public services were performed by volunteers. The well-off and educated women of the Lower Metn – Amin Gemayel's constituency – formed committees to organize friends and students into working parties to clean the streets, to visit the sick, and so on, until the normal authorities could resume their responsibilities. Then taxes were gathered, telephones worked (even a foreign link-up was achieved through Cyprus), garbage was collected and disposed of, streets were repaired and street lighting kept in working order. Piped water was tested daily for purity. Hospitals and schools were kept open. Performances were given in theatres and concert halls. Law courts functioned, cases were heard, verdicts given, sentences carried out. Food stores, boutiques and department stores were fully stocked with all the variety of goods available in Paris, Rome, London and New York. Restaurants, clubs, casinos and sports arenas were well patronized. Business flourished. Charity was distributed. Forest destroyed by the war was replanted. The Lebanese Forces continued, under Bachir Gemayel's command, to protect the area, supplied with most of their arms and ammunition by Israel.[6]

In September 1977 fighting in the south between the PLO and Major Haddad's militia became fierce and prolonged, and Israeli units went into Lebanon to support Haddad. Under American pressure, a ceasefire was

declared on 25 September. It did not hold. The PLO launched heavy
rocket attacks on Israel. Israel returned the fire. This time the Organization's Muslim Lebanese allies urged it to stop. Assad ordered the PLO to
observe the ceasefire and carry out the provisions of the Chtoura
Agreement.[7]

The PLO Executive Committee met on 14 November. The atmosphere
was acrimonious and pessimistic. Some of the leaders expressed their fore-
bodings that the Organization was doomed to extinction. To some it
seemed that clinging on in South Lebanon was a last hope. They feared
that if they gave up their military positions, their training camps, their
arms, let their Lebanese recruits and allies go, and disbanded their militias
so that the men returned to the refugee camps (some to camps in other
countries), according to the provisions of the Chtoura Agreement, it would
be the end of all *fedayeen* activity. But Assad could not be defied outright. So
the PLO agreed to withdraw, disband and disarm, but only on condition
that the Christian forces also disbanded and disarmed. They relied on a
refusal by the Christians to save them from having to comply with Syria's
demands. The Christians did refuse, and the PLO forces remained as they
were.[8]

Assad still insisted on compliance with the agreement. He warned
Arafat against drawing Syria into a war with Israel that he was not ready
for. Arafat flew off to Saudi Arabia and Egypt to canvass support for the
PLO's stand, and its right to stay near the southern border to pursue the
'armed struggle' against Israel.

This time Egypt gave him not comfort but a shock. In Cairo Arafat
heard President Sadat making a speech in which he announced that he
would go to Jerusalem to make peace with Israel. In an instant, the whole
political picture of the Middle East was transformed.

On 20 November 1977 Sadat made his historic journey to Jerusalem.
There he spoke about the Palestinian people, and the need for a solution to
their problem of homelessness, but he did not mention the PLO. By recognizing Israel as a legitimate state, so abolishing the grounds on which
perpetual war against her was justified and giving up the claim to Israeli
territory as Arab land, and by separating the Palestinian people from the
PLO, sweeping aside the resolutions of Algiers and Rabat, Sadat struck a
second and shattering blow to the Organization.

The Egyptian apostasy brought the feuding factions into brief unity.
They cried with one voice for vengeance and swore that Sadat must die.
They joined a majority of Arab states opposed to Sadat's initiative in a
'Steadfastness and Resistance Front', formed at a conference early in
December in the Libyan city of Tripoli (and therefore referred to as the
'Tripoli bloc'). Iraq did not join the Front.

There were signs, even then, that unity was as unachievable as ever. All the factions signed a declaration calling for a political boycott of Egypt, but Arafat wanted to keep a line open to Sadat, for which he was attacked by Habash, Hawatmeh and others, some of whom went so far as to call for his resignation. In the end it was Abu Iyad, not Arafat, who signed the declaration on behalf of Fatah.[9] Fatah was beginning to tear itself apart.

After the first shock and attempt at forming a strong front to oppose Egypt, the effects of the Sadat initiative were to make the PLO, firstly, more desperate and angry; secondly, more internally chaotic and self-destructive; thirdly, more easily exploited by rival Arab powers; fourthly, weaker and more dependent.

First: the Organization brought pressure to bear on the community leaders of the Palestinians on the West Bank by means of a campaign of terror.

Sadat was cheered by thousands of West Bank and Gaza Arabs when he went to the al-Aqsa Mosque on his visit to Jerusalem. Very soon after that the lives and property of those suspected of favouring the creation of a Palestinian homeland without the PLO were threatened. Two West Bank dignitaries were shot on the West Bank in December 1977. A businessman, Abd al-Nur Janho, who openly supported Sadat, was shot on 8 February 1978. Sheikh Hashim Khuzandar, a highly respected religious leader of Gaza, was assassinated on 1 June 1979. After his killing, Farouq Qaddoumi said in Beirut:

the PLO and the Palestinian people in the occupied territories and outside them know very well how to use such methods to prevent certain personalities from deviating from the revolutionary path. Our people in the interior recognize their responsibilities and are capable of taking the necessary disciplinary measure against those who try to leave the right path.[10]

Other PLO voices called for action to silence those who wanted to start negotiations for autonomy of the Gaza Strip, without waiting for a decision on the future of the West Bank – the 'Gaza First' movement. A spate of murders followed in November and December 1980. Twelve people were shot dead. Abu Iyad commented then that 'people of weak character' might be tempted to 'participate in the conspiracy of autonomy' (proposed in the Camp David accords of September 1978); but he could 'proudly declare that by the end of 1980 these agents were not able to come out of their holes', though 'some reared their heads a bit and then a resolution was issued to carry out a few executions'. There was, he said, 'a decision to liquidate all elements co-operating with the enemy'.[11] Altogether, between Sadat's visit and the summer of 1982, forty-eight political murders were committed by PLO agents.[12]

Second: the Organization's internecine strife intensified.

Arafat was apparently unable to keep control even over Fatah militiamen. On 11 March 1978 fifteen Fatah men set out in a boat for the coast of Israel without his knowledge or consent (if his own account is to be believed).[13] Two were drowned. The remaining thirteen hijacked a tourist bus on the main Tel Aviv–Haifa road, and, before nine more of them were killed and two captured by Israeli security forces, they had murdered thirty-two civilians, including many children, and wounded another eighty-two.[14] This attack provoked the biggest retaliatory operation yet mounted by Israel on Lebanese soil. It was named the 'Litani Operation', and was another heavy blow to the Organization.

The Israelis pushed the PLO forces back beyond the Litani River, and stayed in Lebanon for two months, until guarantees were given that the *fedayeen* would not return to the border; they then took another month to withdraw completely. The Syrians insisted that the PLO leaders agree and adhere to the terms of the ceasefire.[15] The United Nations International Force in Lebanon (UNIFIL) was created to police the area, temporarily giving the southern Christians and their Muslim allies considerable relief. It became more difficult for the *fedayeen* to mount their operations against Israel from Lebanon. To the fury of the PFLP and the PDFLP, other PLO leaders approached King Hussein to ask for bases in Jordan from which to carry on their struggle. The King refused the request. The disintegration of the PLO accelerated, the factions coming near to destroying each other.

On 17 April 1978 a mutiny within Fatah was led by Abu Daoud. Under him, 123 rebels, more than half of them from Iraq, prepared to break the ceasefire and defy both Syria and the United Nations. Abu Jihad (al-Wazir), head of Fatah's military department and still loyal to Arafat, arrested the lot of them and had two executed. When the news of the arrests reached other followers of Abu Daoud, they attacked Abu Jihad's units in two centres; at Ubra, a refugee camp in Beirut, and in the town of Nabatiyyah. Dozens were killed and scores were injured.[16]

Trying to repair the rifts, Arafat proposed that all the groups' militias be integrated, a plan which would have meant increased Fatah domination. A committee of four Fatah representatives was appointed to talk over the Rejectionist case.[17] To demonstrate that Fatah itself was reunited, the leaders all stood together at a passing-out ceremony for *fedayeen* trainees on 27 April. Arafat declared on that occasion that the unity of Fatah was unshakable.[18] And to make sure that it was, he took steps to bring all Fatah's militia and security departments directly under the control of Abu Jihad.[19] His own control of the purse-strings, of which his rivals complained, also helped him to keep his position.

Third: with Egypt removed as a protector of the sacred cause, it fell to Syria and Iraq to vie for control of the splintering Organization. Iraq exerted more influence now on some of the most radical factions, and attempted to weaken Arafat's power in Fatah. In the middle of July factional fighting broke out again, between units of the pro-Iraqis, on the one side, and Arafat's Fatah and the PFLP–GC, on the other. Dozens were killed and wounded. On 13 August 1978 the Beirut offices of Iraq's PLF were blown up. About 200 people were killed in the explosion.[20]

An outsider who joined the Fatah rebels was Naji 'Allush, chairman of the Palestinian Writers' and Journalists' Union, erstwhile deputy head of a group which had broken away from the PLO in 1974. Its chief was Sabri al-Banna, 'Abu Nidal', and it was under the patronage of Iraq.[21]

While the PLO's internecine fighting went on in Lebanon, Abu Nidal ('Father of Struggle') waged the same war on behalf of Iraq in the wider world. He had called his terrorist group 'Black June', after the month in which Syrian troops officially entered Lebanon in 1976. The name of his organization was the Fatah Revolutionary Committee. He insisted that his organization was the 'real Fatah', and his *fedayeen* the 'real al-Asifa'. Iraq provided him with headquarters in Baghdad, training facilities and arms, and a salary said to be US$10 million a year.[22] He had about 200 *fedayeen* under his command, and the group was a most useful instrument of Iraqi revenge against individual Syrians[23] and non-Rejectionists, especially Arafat's Fatah. It attacked his men in Europe and the Middle East. On 4 January 1978 the PLO representative in the London Arab League offices, Sa'id Hammami, one of Arafat's men who was in favour of political negotiation, was shot dead by Abu Nidal's agents. In June a follower and friend of Arafat survived an attempted assassination in Kuwait. Two more of his followers were killed in Paris on 3 August. In retaliation, between June and August, Arafat's men attacked Iraqi embassies in Beirut, London, Paris and Tripoli.

Abu Nidal attended the Baghdad summit of November 1978, when the decision to ostracize Egypt was endorsed. In December 1978 the PFLP, PDFLP, PPSF, PLF, ALF and Abu Nidal's 'Fatah Revolutionary Council' issued a joint statement repudiating any co-operation with Jordan and all attempts to enter into a dialogue with King Hussein over the question of negotiations for the West Bank, should the Camp David accords bring an offer for its return to Arab hands.[24]

On 16 August Fatah leaders met PFLP leaders. The PFLP had distanced itself from Fatah for the last five years. They now agreed that talking was to be preferred to fighting between PLO member groups, especially as the internal clashes weakened the Organization and made it more vulnerable to pressure from Arab states. A new structure for the

Executive Council was discussed, and disagreed upon by the Central Committee (a short-lived body whose position lay between the PNC and the Executive Council).[25]

The PFLP refused to attend meetings of the Central Committee or the Executive Council until the leadership was changed to its liking. The truth was that there was no possibility of the factions uniting. Early in 1979 Fatah units battled with the PDFLP and more blood was spilt.[26]

Fourth: President Assad of Syria regained and increased his control of the PLO military command in Lebanon.

After Sadat's electrifying change of policy, Assad dropped his erstwhile allies, the Maronites, who were also the secret allies of Israel, and turned his guns on them. From January 1978 the Syrians waged open war against all the Maronite militias, except for Franjiyyeh's.[27] (The few remaining non-Syrian contingents of Arab soldiers, which helped barely to disguise the Syrian intervention as an 'Arab Deterrent Force' – the Sudanese, Saudi Arabian and those from the United Arab Emirates – were withdrawn between October 1978 and April 1979.)

Assad warned that he would not tolerate any attempt by the PLO to provoke the UN forces in South Lebanon at that time, and he had to send a part of his army to keep out a contingent of Iraqi troops which tried to enter the country to reinforce the PLO.[28]

To ensure PLO acceptance of the UNIFIL peace mission, yet another agreement was solemnized; Lebanese Prime Minister Selim al-Hoss and Arafat signed it on 24 May 1978. As was to be expected, the Iraqi-backed factions opposed the agreement. It amounted, they said, to the 'abandonment of the objectives of the revolution in the interest of capitulationist policies'.[29] They insisted that the PLO was 'a revolution, not a regime', and therefore could not be bound by agreements.[30] They said that a ceasefire was a contradiction of their *raison d'être*, and that in their opinion the PLO was now in an excellent position to wage a guerrilla war. They demanded that the power structure of the Organization be revised, and Arafat's personal power reduced. They wanted all groups to have an equal say in decision-making, regardless of size. Fatah (which, according to Arafat, had over 90 per cent of the fighting men in the PLO forces, approximately 9,000 out of 10,000[31]) was, they said, 'too dependent' on certain Arab states which favoured a Middle East settlement. It was not Syria that was implied. Assad and Arafat were allies again in Lebanon, though they were not friends. The suspect governments were those of Saudi Arabia and the Gulf states. (The Sultan of Oman openly approved of Sadat's initiative.)

To prevent active rebellion against the agreement, Arafat had to police his own militias in the south with a force of 500 men to make sure that, for the moment at least, there were no violations of the ceasefire.[32] It was a novel and ironic development that Fatah itself had now to restrain its own members from raiding Israel across the Lebanese border.

On 13 June 1978 Franjiyyeh's son Tony was killed, along with his wife and daughter and thirty or more members of his militia. It was an act of revenge by the Kataeb for murders of some of their members, including a bank manager who had been a Kataeb leader in the north.[33] Syrian units under the command of Assad's brother, Rif'at Assad, entered the Beqaa and launched an offensive against the Maronite 'Lebanese Forces'. Syrian units also deliberately bombarded thickly populated areas in the Maronite 'city-state'. It was a major offensive aimed at the destruction of the Maronite community 'as an autonomous military and political force'.[34]

Still no help came for the Maronites from the Western powers. In Jerusalem, however, Prime Minister Menachem Begin announced that Israel was committed to aid and support all the Christians of Lebanon who were in danger, not only those in the south. Israeli jets flew over Beirut, which may have provided a wordless argument for the ceasefire that Syria then accepted. While it was still in force, however, the Syrians went into Christian villages to hunt down 'anti-Syrian elements'. More civilians were killed. Another ceasefire was announced in October 1978, but still no peace prevailed.

In mid-January 1979, during a pause in PLO inter-factional fighting, a PNC convened in Damascus for the first time. Arafat tried to persuade the Council to augment his authority, but failed. For a very short time Syria and Iraq mended their relations, with the result that Sa'iqa, the second largest of the PLO groups, combined with ALF and the others to oppose Arafat. They objected to his 'autocratic rule', although such rule as he was capable of was by grace of Syria. No differences were resolved by the session.[35] When six months later Arafat was received in Vienna by Bruno Kreisky and Willy Brandt, they were talking, though they seem not to have guessed it, to a PLO chairman who could carry none of the groups with him, not even the whole of Fatah, and who was little more than a figurehead.

35
Expulsion and Dispersion

The re-alliance with Syria meant that, from 1979, the PLO revived temporarily as a military power in the region. Slow progress in the Camp David peace process, ever-improving relations between Arafat and European governments (notably his reception by Kreisky and Brandt), and the need to maintain an outward appearance of unity, saved it from complete disintegration. Its significance grew again as its military strength grew. Syria was preparing it for another war with Israel. Through Syria, the Soviet Union was preparing it for one of its proxy wars against the West. Except for the United States, the Western powers seemed unaware of, or unconcerned by, its intended function.

By the early 1980s the PLO forces had a strength of between 15,000 and 18,000, of which some 5,000 to 6,000 were mercenaries.[1] A few hundred were operating, without restraint by Syria or the PLO command in Beirut, within the area where UNIFIL troops had been placed to keep them back from the border.[2] Shelling resumed over the heads of the UNIFIL forces – Fijian, Nigerian, Ghanaian, Senegalese, Dutch, Irish, Norwegian (with French and Italian technical and logistic support) – who were proving ineffectual and vulnerable. They sustained a number of deaths and injuries. On 18 April 1980 two soldiers of the Irish Battalion were murdered by Shi'ite villagers after a young boy had died in an exchange of fire with the UNIFIL forces. Israel was blamed for the UNIFIL deaths on the grounds that she was indirectly responsible, through her support of the Southern Lebanese resistance to the PLO, and she was condemned for it in the strongest terms by the United Nations, Western newspaper editorials, diplomats and European officials, especially those of the European Economic Community. On 19 June 1981 two soldiers of the Fijian contingent were murdered by the PLO (bringing the number of Fijian deaths caused by the PLO to thirteen). Their deaths were reported in foreign newspapers, but with little or no comment, and the EEC Foreign Ministers did not apparently feel the same 'profound revulsion' over these deaths as over the others. The United Nations Security Council condemned the killings, but did not mention the PLO, referring to the culprits only as 'armed elements',

(22)

رقم
التاريخ

حركة التحرير الوطني الفلسطيني
"فتح"
القيادة العامة لقوات العاصفة
قيادة قوات الكرامة

موجز اتفاق بين منظمة التحرير الفلسطينية والكتيبة النرويجية •

١ — الحجم أو مقدار العسكر :ــ
لجنة الشرق مجموعة العمل لا يسمح لها التحرك اقرب من (٤٠٠) متر من مركز كل السفير
ومن الجنوب الافراد يقدرون التحرك الى الشمال ومن الغرب الافراد يتحركون الى (أم ٢١١٢ – ٣٠٧٥)

٢ — خيام :ــ لم تعد مبنية
منظمة التحرير يسمح لها بوضع اربعة خياماً/في المتر ٠ الخيام يمكن ان تستعمل وكزر للافراد او
ستودع ٠ مطبخ ٠ وملجأ للحمار • ومع ذلك الخيام بتصرف النظم ٠ الخيام تخضع صوبه في مناطق وا — حـدود
في المتر حيث يكونهم من مركز المدفعية (ا—هـ) و (ا—١٠) ٠ حوكمة اسلامية اشكل مع الترب

٣ — التموين :ـ
كل اوقات الاتفاقيه حسب التوقيت اللبناني المحلي ٠ ما يمكن ان يجلب يوميا ابتداء من (١٠٣٠)
التاسعه لغاية الحادية عشره والنصف وبين الثانيه والرابعه الماء يجلب بواسطه رجلين على الحمار ٠ الماء يجلب
من النهر الرجال يلبسون لباس عسكري ولكن لا يسمح لهم بحمل سلاح ولا ذخيره وقنابل ومتفجرات وسوف
يكونو بامرة ومراقبه جنود نرويجيون ٠ الجنود النرويجيون يلتقون معهم على موقع (أم ٢١١٢ – ٣٠٨٦) ويرافقوهم
الى (أم ٢١١٠ – ٣٠٨٨) حيث يجلب الماء بعد ذلك الجنود وسوف يرافقوهم راجعين الى ٢١١٢
٣٠٨٦) حيث يرجعون الى المتر يفتيش شخص واحد فقط سوف يتم اذا كان امتناء بحمل سلاح ذخيره قنابل الى
متفجرات •

٥ — طعام : ـ كل يوم الثامنه العاشره سياره تلتقي على مركز تفتيش كوكبا مع التموين اليومي (ما اذا
ضروري) لاجل المتر سياره التموين سوف تراقب من قبل النرويجيون شخصا وتوافق الى (أم ٢١١٢ ٠٥ ٢٠٨)
مراقبة التموين يجب ان يكون بطريقه وقتلك الوقت المتموين ذلك التموين يجبان لا يكون فاسد ٠ والحد الاقصى
ايمة رجال بما فيه السائق يمكن ان يتمموا السياره ضمن منطقة عمليات الكتيبة النرويجيه الرجال لا يحكم حمل سلاح
ذخيره وقنابل متفجرات معهم ويجبان يكونوا بلباس مدني يمني قميص عسكري بنطلون مدني ٠ قميص مدني نسي
بنطلون عسكري ا لباس مدني كامل التموين يجمع على الوقت (أم ٠ ١) الذكور بواسطة رجلين وحمار من العسكر
والتموين يجبان يوافق جلب الماء •

٨ — ٦ — تبديل الافراد في المتر :ـ
المتر يمكن ان يبدل لغاية ثمانية رجال كل يوم الخامس وذلك لا يجبان يكون الرجال اكثر
يد خلون عما يخرجون الرجال الجدد يصلون الى مركز تفتيش الامم التحده في كوكبا الساعه الواحده ا المخـاص
والسياره سوف يكونوا تحت مراقبة الامم التحده ومراقبة سياره الامم التحده في منطقة عمليات الكتيبة النرويجيه
الاعضاء الذين يبدلون سوف يكونوا بلباس مدني وغير مسلحون ولا يسمح لهم بجلب قنابل ذخيره او متفجرات •

23/...

An agreement between the PLO and Norwegians of UNIFIL

which could have meant any of the militias in Southern Lebanon. The UNIFIL command entered into treaties of co-operation with the PLO, by which they agreed to admit PLO officers and men into the area under their control for access to observation posts.[3] Despite this atmosphere of friendly co-operation, there were still some armed clashes between them, in which more UNIFIL soldiers were killed.

The PLO units were massively over-armed with light and heavy weapons. Their Soviet tanks were not the newest or the best, but they were not in short supply. They also had long-range artillery pieces, rocket launchers, anti-aircraft guns, shoulder-fired missiles and anti-tank guns. The artillery pieces were placed in fields and orchards to command the approaches on the main roads. The rocket launchers were both fixed and mounted on trucks; machine-guns and anti-aircraft guns were mounted on, or towed by, trucks and jeeps. PLO bases were defended with trenches and gun emplacements, many on top of schools and hospitals, and in the midst of houses. Underground arms-stores and shelters for the fighters were capacious, well lit and air-conditioned.[4]

In 1980 the citizens of the Christian town of Zahle, in the Beqaa, tried to construct a new road to the Beirut-Damascus highway, in order to avoid the Syrian roadblocks on the existing road. The Syrians launched a heavy mortar attack on the town. They surrounded it with three battalions, and cut it off from the main highway. It was then subjected to total siege. The Christian forces fought back strongly, but the Syrians brought in a further eleven battalions in an attempt to raze the town. There was great loss of life, and again a civilian population suffered extreme distress. Only when Arab governments expressed uneasiness at the Syrian action did Assad change his plan to destroy Zahle. By agreement with the Lebanese government, Lebanese security forces were brought in, and the siege was relieved at last. About 400 civilians had been killed, and about twice that number injured.[5]

While the battle of Zahle was raging, the PLO, lavishly equipped and considerably reinforced, began, again with Assad's consent, to shell Israel with an incessant barrage that kept the populations of thirty-three northern towns and settlements in shelters most of the day and night. Israeli answering fire kept Palestinians and Lebanese in shelters on the other side of the border.

The Syrians gave no respite to the Loyalists. They tried to dislodge the Christians from Mount Sanine, known as 'the French Room', from which they could control both Zahle, on one side of the Lebanon range, and the Christian-held port of Jounieh, the 'capital' of the Christian enclave, on the other.

On 23 April 1981 the Israeli airforce shot down two Syrian Soviet-made helicopters. Syria responded by bringing Soviet surface-to-air missile (SAM) batteries into the Beqaa. By the end of June there were twelve banks of SAM batteries in place in the valley, south of Zahle. They could reach Beirut, Jounieh, the Christian villages in the north, Major Haddad's strip in the south and the edge of Israel itself.

Syria began attacks from the air with assault helicopters on 25 April, and by doing so was deemed by Israel to have crossed the 'Red Line', which the Israeli government had set as the limit of tolerable Syrian advance. When this happened, Israel came openly to the aid of the Loyalist Christians. In July 1981 Israel attacked PLO targets in Lebanon from the air, and the PLO retaliated with a bombardment of settlements in northern Galilee.

To negotiate a disengagement between Israel and Syria, the United States sent a special envoy, Philip Habib, who achieved a ceasefire on 24 July 1981.

By the Israeli account, the ceasefire was not observed. According to their reckoning, 270 terrorist actions were carried out by the PLO in the year following the ceasefire in Israel, the occupied territories, and on the Jordanian and Lebanese borders, and another twenty acts of terrorism were committed against Israeli or Jewish targets. Some 300 people were injured, of which twenty-nine died.

Attacks on Israeli missions abroad continued in the early months of 1982, with a bomb thrown at the embassy in Guatemala, and a letter-bomb in Athens. An embassy attaché was murdered in Paris on 3 April.

Then, on the night of 3 June 1982, the Israeli ambassador to Britain, Shlomo Argov, was attacked on the pavement outside the Dorchester Hotel in London, as he left a reception held by a textile company for eighty-four ambassadors and heads of mission. He was not killed, but badly wounded in the head. Three members of Abu Nidal's group were arrested, tried some months later, and found guilty of committing the crime.[6] One of them, Marwan al-Banna, is a cousin of Abu Nidal.

Israel reacted first with retaliatory bombing raids on PLO bases in Lebanon on 4 June, and the PLO shelled the settlements of northern Galilee. The next day there was an exchange of artillery fire across the border. One day later, on 6 June 1982, the Israeli army struck into Lebanon in a full-scale invasion.

They called the operation 'Peace for Galilee'. They took Tyre both from the south, advancing overland, and the north, with troops landed from the sea at the mouth of the Litani River.

Simultaneously, a task force invaded the central sector, took the Aqiya Bridge over the Litani Gorge, and established themselves in Nabatiyyah. The UNIFIL forces were brushed aside.

The castle of Beaufort, 'Arafat's Evil Eye', high on its escarpment, was taken at about midnight in hand-to-hand fighting. It was later handed over ceremoniously by Prime Minister Begin to Major Sa'd Haddad.

On the eastern side, Israeli forces advanced rapidly on 'Fatahland', but were slowed by narrow ravines and steep gorges. Within five days, however, they conquered it and severed its supply route from Syria.

As the PLO had no airforce, it must have expected direct Syrian assistance. At first, Syrian ground and air forces did engage the Israelis. But Syria lost twenty-two fighter planes in the first three days, and subsequently over fifty more, to the loss of two Israeli planes. The Syrian SAM bases in the Beqaa were destroyed by accurate bombing from an unprecedented height. On the fifth day, when it was obvious that the PLO could not hold out, let alone win, Assad agreed, through United States diplomatic channels, to a ceasefire with Israel. He had to look to Syria's safety. There was no talk now of Arab nationalism, of *jihad*, or the revolution. It was the PLO that was facing extinction, and Syria was not going to fight a hopeless war with Israel merely to save the Organization, or the 'Palestinian entity'. Nor was any other Arab state. Few would regret it if the PLO were destroyed. Strange to tell, the silence from the Arab world came as a surprise, an appalling revelation, to the PLO leadership.

Almost as shocking to the ideologists and the high command was the failure of the Palestinians in the camps to offer resistance to the enemy. In theory, their resistance should have proved unvanquishable and decisive; but though they had been armed by the groups, trained and indoctrinated, the Palestinian 'masses' did not, after all, identify themselves with the Resistance, the 'armed struggle', the Revolution. Nor did the 'Arab masses' – the Lebanese civilians in the south – a majority of whom, on the contrary, positively welcomed the Israeli invaders as liberators.[7]

The *fedayeen* organizations, with their mercenary auxiliaries, had to fight on alone, and had also now to discover how grossly they had overestimated the fighting capacity of their own forces. The Israelis continued to push them back rapidly, taking thousands of prisoners and capturing large quantities of arms and ammunition.[8] The announced intention of the Israelis was to clear a zone about 45 kilometres wide north of the border. In the event they pressed on, ultimately this time to dislodge the PLO leadership and the bulk of its fighting force from its last stand in Beirut. European governments, the world press, the multitude of states which had established official relations with the PLO, censured Israel in strong, in many cases extreme, terms. Yet the PLO had to complain, despairingly, that no outside power came to its aid. In six days the Israelis claimed that 4,500 square kilometres were 'freed from terrorist occupation'.[9]

The PLO leaders continued to hope, well into the August weeks of siege and bombardment, that they would yet be saved from undeniable defeat; that the UN, the Soviet Union, or friendly European nations might still come to their rescue through diplomatic pressures. The United States might again, as so many times before, stop the Israelis from pressing home their victory. The PLO command took measures to prevent the civil population leaving West Beirut; they needed them as hostages.[10] As was their custom, they positioned their heavy artillery on top of, and beside, hospitals and schools. Surely the humanitarian West would intervene?

Their last hopes were disappointed. They had no choice but to leave Beirut. The United States' envoy, Philip Habib, negotiated with the Israelis, the Lebanese government, and with ex-Premier of Lebanon, Sa'ib Salam, for the PLO, and the Organization gave in.

An international force of French, Italian and American troops was introduced to supervise the departure of the PLO, and to help the Lebanese government keep the peace until its own political and military authority could be re-established. But still the bloodshed was not over. Ambushes, laying of mines and bombing continued between faction and faction. The Israelis came under attack from Syrians, Islamo-Progressives and PLO fighters returning through Syria. Christians and Druze continued to fire on each other in the mountains.[11]

In August 1982, just as the PLO forces were about to start their exodus, elections were held for the presidency of Lebanon, and Bachir Gemayel, Commander-in-Chief of the Lebanese Forces, became the President Elect.[12] To obtain the majority he needed, Muslims as well as Christians had to vote for him – and they did.[13] Lebanese of all denominations – though not unanimously – saw a new hope for Lebanon in the thirty-four-year-old Maronite leader. Israel had good reason to expect that, under his presidency, normal diplomatic and trading relations might be established with Lebanon.

On 21 August 1982 the PLO fighters began to leave. First, about 6,000 PLA soldiers set off along the Beirut-Damascus road. Some 600 women and children went too. Another 8,000 PLA members left by sea for the Syrian port of Tartous. Other fighters went by sea from the port of Beirut to more distant destinations. There was no question of the Iraqi factions being allowed to pass through Syria. It took twelve days for all contingents to leave. Their departure was not ignominious. They paraded through West Beirut as if celebrating a victory, bearing their personal arms and using them to 'make fantasia', by shooting wildly in the air.[14]

They dispersed to Tunisia, Iraq (ALF and PLF), Jordan (the few with Jordanian passports), North Yemen, South Yemen, Sudan, Syria and Algeria. Fatah followers of Arafat went to Tunisia. The wounded were taken to Athens for treatment.

Arafat himself went first to Athens, where he was given a grand
reception, then to Tunis, where he was to set up his new headquarters.
President Bourguiba welcomed him in princely style.

Part Seven

1982 and After

More Palestinians die in the conflict. The PLO, broken up geographically and by internal differences, falls largely under the military and political control of President Assad of Syria. The chance of a homeland for the Palestinians arises again, and is forbidden by the PLO.

36
Sabra and Chatila

After the departure of the PLO from Beirut, the international force was hastily withdrawn, although peace was not to be expected in Lebanon.

On 14 September 1982 Bachir Gemayel was assassinated. During the previous night, Habib Chatouni, a member of the SSNP, had entered the room where Gemayel and his colleagues were to confer the next day, and had hidden a Japanese-made electronically triggered bomb behind a panel in the wall. He told the authorities when he was arrested how he had done it. He had persuaded his sister, who lived on the third floor of the Kataeb Centre in the Ashrafiyah district of East Beirut, to go away for a few days. When he had the apartment to himself, he lowered himself on a rope from a window, entered a window of the Kataeb Centre, laid the bomb, and climbed the rope back to the floor above. The device was capable of being triggered from 200 metres away. (It was the same sort of device that was used by the IRA to commit indiscriminate mass murder in two London parks in 1982.) The next day it was exploded during a meeting of Kataeb leaders, killing Bachir Gemayel and twenty-six other people.

The SSNP had switched sides during the war, and become a faithful servant of Syria again. After Bachir's murder, his brother Amin, much preferred by the Syrians, became President.

The day after the assassination, the remains of Bachir Gemayel were buried in a hill-top church in the Mountain. On the same day Pope John Paul II received Yasser Arafat at the Vatican.

There were still thousands of Palestinians in the camps in West Beirut, and a vacuum of government. Some Israelis said that, Lebanon being what it was, a massacre of Palestinians might be expected in revenge for the killing of Bachir Gemayel. Whether or not the Israeli authorities had this possibility in mind, they asked the Lebanese army to move in to West Beirut to keep order. The Lebanese army refused, and Israel went in, against the wishes of the United States.

The camps of Sabra and Chatila, the Israelis maintained, still sheltered some 2,000 to 3,000 terrorists. Several times they asked the Lebanese army to go into the camps and 'clear them out'. The army refused.[1] The Israeli commanders were unwilling to risk more of their own soldiers' lives, and told the Kataeb that it was time they took an active part in ridding their country of the *fedayeen*. They reached an agreement with the Kataeb – the private militia of the Lebanese President's own faction – that their men would enter the camps and round up the PLO men.

The Deputy Prime Minister of Israel, David Levy, gave warning that the Kataeb might use the occasion for revenge; but the Minister of Defence, Ariel Sharon, and the Chief-of-Staff, Rafael Eitan, did not heed it. On Thursday, 16 September 1982, at about six o'clock, Kataeb militia men entered the Sabra and Chatila camps. Firing was coming from Chatila as they entered, and was directed at the roof on which the Kataeb forward command was posted. Within the first hour, two Kataeb men were wounded. Some time during the night two were killed. Between ten and eleven o'clock reports came to the Israeli officers at the forward command post that 300 'terrorists and civilians' had been 'liquidated' in the Chatila camp. By Friday morning, a number of Israeli soldiers knew that there had been killing and maltreatment of civilians. But it was not until the Saturday morning, 18 September, that the last of the Kataeb men obeyed orders to leave the camp. At five o'clock that afternoon, the Lebanese army finally agreed to enter the camps, and did so the next day. On the Saturday the Red Cross and the press went in, and found that yet another massacre had been perpetrated.

The number of the dead remained unknown. Israeli Intelligence reckoned them at between 700 and 800. The Red Cross delegation counted 328 bodies, but by then some families had buried their dead privately, and some corpses were removed by the Kataeb, who may have buried them themselves. It was possible too that some of the bodies which were counted may have fallen in combat before the assassination of Bachir Gemayel. According to the report (published in February 1983) of the Kahan Commission of Inquiry, set up by the Israeli government, the total number of bodies found between 18 September and 30 September was 460, 'including 109 Lebanese, 328 Palestinians, Iranians, Syrians and members of other nationalities'. Of the counted dead, fifteen were women, eight of them Lebanese and seven Palestinian; and twenty were children, twelve of them Lebanese and eight Palestinian. (These deaths came on top of an estimated 95,000 killed in Lebanon between the spring of 1975 and the summer of 1982.)

The Kahan Commission found that the Kataeb was directly responsible for the massacre.

It found the Israelis who had been in charge, including the Prime Minister, Defence Minister and Chief of Staff, indirectly responsible, because they did not give sufficient consideration to the danger of a massacre if they sent the Kataeb into the camps; did not examine means to prevent it; did not take proper heed when reports began to come in about the actions of the Kataeb; did not draw proper conclusions from them; and took no 'energetic and immediate actions' to restrain and stop them.

37
Of Plans and Men

It seemed urgent to the United States administration that the Palestinian problem should now be solved. The US and the USSR were arguing over whether, and how, they each might reduce the level of nuclear armament. In the Middle East the USSR was arming and advising Syria; Israel was receiving billions of dollars in loans and aid from the US, and adding refinements to certain American conventional weapons to make them even more devastating. Syria and Israel faced each other in the Beqaa in Lebanon. It seemed that the Middle East was a likely sparking point of a wider conflagration.

Plans formed at Camp David to normalize relations between Israel and Egypt were carried out well enough. Though President Sadat was assassinated in October 1981, the process continued, and Sinai was returned to Egypt. Proposals for the Palestinians had not been carried out. Sadat had asked for a withdrawal of Israel from the West Bank, 'in accordance with Resolution 242', and 'the achievement of a just settlement' of their problems. The goal in principle was 'self-determination through talks in which Egypt, Jordan, Israel, and *representatives of the Palestinian people* would participate'. The accords proposed a period of transition of five years, during which the form of 'full autonomy' for the Palestinians on the West Bank and in the Gaza Strip would be worked out. They did not propose a Palestinian state. They made no reference to the PLO.

No local leadership arose to negotiate with Israel and Egypt for West Bank autonomy.[1] Of the elected mayors and other men of influence on the West Bank and in Gaza, the majority were PLO-supporting. Although the Palestinians in the Israeli-occupied territories, not having lived under PLO rule, may in any case have trusted the Organization to fulfil their dreams of self-determination, the PLO took measures to secure their allegiance. From nursery-school age to university they were taught PLO doctrine. When municipal elections by secret ballot were held under the Israeli administration, the PLO ran an intensive radio campaign from Lebanon and Syria promoting PLO candidates, who won most of the positions. These provided the PLO with a power-base in the occupied territories. In addition, the PLO used terror to ensure obedience.

King Hussein did not join the Camp David peace talks. He chose to stand with the Tripoli bloc against President Sadat. His government co-operated with Arafat on the 'Joint Committee to Support the Steadfastness of the Occupied Territories'. The Joint Committee distributed 'stead-fastness' payments to West Bank officials and men of influence who remained loyal to Jordan. The money had been voted for the territories by Arab leaders at the Baghdad summit of October 1978, and had to be distributed through Jordan.

Since the King had agreed, at Rabat, that the PLO alone represented the Palestinians, theoretically he had no authority on the West Bank. In practice, its status in relation to the Kingdom of Jordan remained much the same. After the Six Day War, the elected Parliament, in which half the seats had been allotted to the West Bank, had been 'suspended', and a National Consultative Council substituted whose appointed members were from the East Bank only. West Bank civil servants were still paid by Jordan (as well as by Israel), Jordanian law still applied there, West Bank officials still crossed the river to confer with the Jordanian government, West Bank produce still flowed into Jordan and through it to the rest of the Arab world, and Jordanian passports were still issued to travellers. None of this changed after Rabat. To the obvious advantage of the population, the King did not go so far as to implement the resolution he had been forcibly persuaded to endorse.

Prominent men of the West Bank set up the National Guidance Commit-tee (NGC) to resist President Sadat's proposals, and to prevent residents of the West Bank from leaving their homes and crossing the river to live in Jordan. It included members of various PLO groups, and organized active opposition to the Israeli authorities by means of non-co-operation, demon-strations, stone-throwing,[2] and the surreptitious formation of *fedayeen* cells. The communist Palestine Liberation Front, the PFLP, and the PDFLP – all anti-Hashemite – dominated the NGC.[3]

The Joint Committee fought the influence of the Left by giving its grants of money directly to persons and organizations of its own choosing, bypass-ing the mayors and other officials who were hostile to the King. It rewarded trade unions, religious institutions, co-operative industrial and agricul-tural projects, schools and colleges, and founded a new university in East Jerusalem as a rival to the Bir Zeit University, which had become a hot-bed of rejectionism. The mayors were affronted. Demonstrating its independence of them, the Jordanian government took away their right to issue passports, by opening special passport offices on the West Bank.[4]

On 1 September 1982 President Reagan announced his own plan for settling the Palestinian problem. Its proposals were discussed in advance with King Hussein and the government of Saudi Arabia, but not with

Israel. It did not support the idea of an independent Palestinian state, only of 'autonomy' under the Hashemite crown. It prescribed no role for the PLO. Jewish settlement on the West Bank must be halted. This, it was believed, would 'increase the confidence necessary for wider participation in the peace talks'. Jerusalem should remain undivided, its final status 'decided through negotiations'. And for Israel, there was an assurance that America's 'commitment to her security' was 'ironclad'.

Israel rejected the proposals, mainly on the grounds that they prejudged the issue of the final status of the territories, contrary to the agreement reached at Camp David. (The Opposition in the Israeli Parliament did not find the plan wholly unacceptable.)

The Arab perception was that the United States could compel Israel to give way; but the plan also required King Hussein to take a leading role, and what accommodation could, or should, be reached between the 'sole legitimate representative of the Palestinian people' and the King?

A few days after the Reagan Plan had been published, there was an Arab summit conference at Fez, Morocco. An earlier summit meeting at Fez in November 1981 had broken up almost as soon as it convened, because Syria would not take part, and a plan for a settlement of the Palestinian problem, put forward by Prince (soon afterwards King) Fahd of Saudi Arabia, had been thrown out without consideration. Now the Fahd Plan was to be taken out again, and this time looked at with care. It was considered better at least than the Reagan plan; and the willingness to look at it again, on the part of those who had formerly rejected it, showed that the Arab states were no longer sure that the PLO had the only answer to the problem of Israel. The glory won at Karameh was lost in Lebanon.

The Fahd Plan had envisaged an Israeli withdrawal to its pre-1967 boundaries; the removal of all Jewish settlements on the West Bank; freedom of worship in the holy places; repatriation or compensation for Palestinians who had lost their property; United Nations trusteeship over the West Bank and Gaza for a transition period of a few months, and United Nations guarantee of all agreements reached; Jerusalem to be the capital of the Palestinian state; and the right of 'all states in the region' to live in peace. Israel was not mentioned by name. European spokesmen chose to believe that Israel was 'implied'. They did not ask why, in that case, it should not be named. Nor did Europeans who favoured the Fahd Plan choose to remember that the Arabs did not regard Israel as a 'legitimate state', and could therefore always say that this clause did not apply to Israel. Like the Venice Declaration, the Fahd Plan attempted to push the Camp David accords aside. That it offered nothing positive to the power which actually held the territories apparently did not strike experienced European diplomats as a serious fault.

Still, before the expulsion from Beirut, the plan had been too 'moderate', especially for the PLO and the 'Steadfastness and Confrontation Front' states of Libya, Syria, Algeria and South Yemen. Now, the rout in Lebanon and the return of Sinai to Egypt might have been seen as proof that negotiations did bring better results, after all, than armed struggle. But Rejectionists had not been won to that view by the time the second conference opened at Fez.

A mood of gloom hung over the heads of state when the conference convened.

The Egyptians could speak to their brethren again now that Sadat was dead, but the subject his successor Hosni Mubarak had recently spoken of was 'Arab disintegration'.[5]

Saddam Hussein, President of Iraq, had bemoaned the 'collapse of Arab solidarity'.[6]

No one had forgotten, and the PLO would not forget, that the Organization had cried out in its broadcasts two days after the war began in Lebanon, 'We are now alone in an empty Arab world', a world of 'commanders who do not command, of leaders who do not lead'. And Arafat had accused his fellow Arabs: 'An Arab silence envelops the area as if the nation were in a deep sleep.'[7]

Iraq, Jordan, Egypt, Sudan, Morocco, Libya, all had castigated Syria during the war for not coming to the aid of the PLO. Syria had actually given aid to non-Arab Iran to pursue the war with Arab Iraq.

Where was the dream, let alone the substance, of Arab unity now?

The Saudis had stopped talking of Arab solidarity, and bided their time until the war in Lebanon was over and they could call for this meeting at Fez. Now they would make every effort to reach agreement. Even Syria and Iraq were persuaded into another brief rapprochement. Only Qadhafi of Libya kept aloof and would not attend the summit.

To make unanimity easier, Saudi Arabia allowed its plan to be altered. The alterations made 'the Fahd Plan' acceptable to the conference, but even less accessible to political realism.

The statement in the earlier draft about the 'right of all states in the region to live in peace' was reworded into a proposal that the United Nations Security Council should 'guarantee peace among all states in the region'. This meant that Israel, which had been granted no more reality than a miasma in the first Fahd proposals, was now even less visible, screened off behind the United Nations. To smooth the way for the radicals and the PLO, it was proposed that the Soviet Union take part in peace negotiations along with the United States. Most importantly, the PLO was given a leading role. The Organization had not been mentioned in the clauses of the earlier Fahd Plan, but only in the accompanying elaborations, so this was the biggest change of all. It made the plan presented at Fez self-defeating. By confirming the PLO as the sole representative of the Palestinians, it closed the possibility that King Hussein might negotiate for the West Bank. The Fez Plan was, by implication, a rejection of the Reagan Plan. Yet the conference would have it known that the Reagan proposals were 'not rejected'. They were to be discussed further in Washington.

The adoption of the Fez Plan gave rise to new hopes on the Arab side, in what might be called the plan beneath the plan: to isolate Israel by appearing 'flexible' and 'moderate', while Israel appeared obstinate; to weaken American-Israeli relations; and to make it easier for Europe, supposedly the Arabs' lever on the United States, to insist that the PLO should be recognized by President Reagan as representing the Palestinian people.

The Reagan Plan remained all there was on offer from the United States. If the PLO would agree to it, there could be a homeland for the Palestinians. The PLO wanted the relations of the Palestinian state with Jordan to be worked out after the state was established. Yet there could only be progress towards the creation of an autonomous Palestinian region at all, under the Reagan Plan, if representatives of the Palestinians first agreed to accept Hashemite sovereignty.

As far as America was concerned, the first step would have to be Jordan's: the Jordanian government must recognize Israel, and enter talks with her, under American auspices; King Hussein would negotiate for the return of his former territory. The 'autonomous' Palestinian homeland would be dependent on Jordan, and Jordan would have a peace treaty and formal interstate relations with Israel. The Palestinians would gain a little country, smaller than the partition plan of 1947 had offered them. The PLO, the heroic *fedayeen*, would see their dream dwindle to an inglorious reality.

The likelihood that the PLO would accept the Reagan Plan was negligible. Yet Arafat visited Amman several times and talked to the King, which excited hopes among many Western observers. The outcome of the sixteenth Palestinian National Congress, 383 members meeting at Algiers in February 1983, was awaited with high expectation. Here was another opportunity for the self-appointed leaders of the Palestinians to effect momentous change. Perhaps it would be a turning-point in the history of the Middle East. Western eyes were fixed on Arafat: could he win enough support to empower King Hussein to act on the Reagan Plan?

Arafat was in the greatest danger of losing such small power as he had regained in the Organization: it depended almost wholly on the position he had come to occupy in the misapprehensions of Western powers; yet foreign expectations were more likely to hinder than to help him now, since they fed suspicion within the Organization that he wanted to negotiate on the Reagan proposals. He had to look to his own position. The PLO fighting forces which were within striking distance of Israel were in Syria, under the control of President Assad. That was where the real power lay. Arafat still received the Organization's grants of money from the Gulf, but it was running short as the price of oil came down in a glutted market.

When the time came he rose to speak not of territory and salvation for the Palestinian people, but of unity and independence for the PLO.[8] They were themes more wistful than boastful. Unity between the factions and within Fatah was a slogan only, and the dependence of the Organization on funds from the Arab states was underscored by confessions of financial difficulties, arising chiefly from the non-payment of promised sums.

Isam Sartawi wanted to make a speech about *de facto* recognition of Israel, but was prevented, and, as at earlier PNCs, he resigned. Shafiq al-Hout complained that whereas they, the PLO, had recently ruled over 'a state' (in Lebanon), now they had no territory and no office.[9]

The Congress could not evade the question of whether Jordan could speak for the Palestinians. It dealt with it verbosely. While the 'special distinctive relations between the Palestinian and Jordanian peoples' was acknowledged, as also 'the necessity to work on developing them in line with the national interests of the two peoples and the Arab nation as a whole, with a view to realizing the inalienable rights of the Palestinian people, including the rights to repatriation, self-determination and independent statehood', the PNC nevertheless reaffirmed that the PLO was the sole legitimate representative of the Palestinian people inside and outside the occupied territories, and reminded the Arab states that it rejected 'all imperialist, Zionist schemes that seek to undermine this exclusive representation by proposing various formulae such as mandating, authorizing or sharing it with other parties'.[10]

The Reagan Plan itself was unacceptable, because it denied the Palestinians an independent state, self-determination and return to their homes. The Fez proposals were the minimum which the PNC would consider accepting: but it stressed that *its understanding* of them was that they did not conflict with the Congress's commitment to the political programme and any previous PNC resolutions – which was to say, that the PNC did *not* interpret the Fez Plan as implying recognition of Israel, or its right to exist with secure boundaries and in peace with its neighbours. In other words, the PNC adhered to the policy of achieving the Palestinian state on the whole of Palestine by 'stages', which could be won by political negotiation backing up armed struggle. Still, European politicians could yet choose to believe, and many did, that the PLO now accepted a plan with an 'implication' that Israel might be permitted to exist. Europe was, after all, a willing partner in this verbal dance of seven veils.

What did become clear at Algiers was that the power within the Organization had shifted heavily towards the Syrian and radical side. The PNC urged a strengthening of PLO ties with Syria. Despite all that had happened in recent months, it demanded an escalation of the armed struggle against the Zionist enemy from all fronts, in particular 'with the Lebanese masses'. The Congress recorded its appreciation of a plan put forward, in the same month as those of President Reagan and the Fez convention, by Comrade Brezhnev. This plan spoke of independent statehood for the Palestinians and their right to return to their homes, but implicitly required recognition of the State of Israel, at least for the present. Fortunately for the Congress, Brezhnev had died before the meeting, and no one was actively promoting the plan.

The meeting ended without any momentous decisions which would change the course of history. Yet another opportunity had been lost to the Palestinians by their self-appointed leaders.

Yasser Arafat went to Jordan after Algiers, this time to make demands for the PLO. Officially, since any attempt to negotiate for the West Bank along lines considered secretly by the King and Arafat before the Congress meeting must now be given up and the armed struggle resumed, Arafat was there to say only what the PNC and the Executive Council permitted him to say. The PLO had demands to make of the King. It wanted more from Jordan than the office it was allowed in Amman; it wanted Jordan to provide the political headquarters and military base which the *fedayeen* had lost in Lebanon. Not surprisingly, the King refused.

Unofficially, temptation remained in what Reagan offered. If King Hussein could recover the occupied territories for the Arabs, Palestine could come into existence without the PLO itself having to recognize Israel, negotiate with Israel, or promise peace. That little Palestine could then be, true to the 'stages' policy, an irredentist 'ministate', from which the armed struggle could be continued from an advantageous position with help from powerful friends. If enemies in the PLO and Syria were to be defied by Arafat and the King, powerful allies must first be canvassed.

Arafat flew to Riyadh to see King Fahd. King Hussein flew to Moscow. There he was told that the government of the Soviet Union would 'use all its resources to oppose the Reagan Plan'.[11] When all the talking in all the capitals was done, nothing was changed.

At a meeting of the PLO Executive Council in Amman on 4 April, the delegates of the groups in Damascus vetoed whatever agreements Arafat had tentatively reached with the King. Their decision was to adhere to the resolutions arrived at in Algiers, and accept nothing less than the proposals set out in the plan approved at Fez.

On 10 April 1983 Isam Sartawi, who had conducted talks with certain Israelis, was assassinated by a member of Abu Nidal's group. It was a warning to anyone else who might be thinking of compromising the immutable principles of the PLO.

On that day King Hussein announced that discussions between Jordan and the PLO for a joint approach to negotiations over the West Bank and Gaza had broken down, and that Jordan was 'withdrawing from the peace process'. He said that it was now up to the PLO and the Palestinians themselves 'to determine the course of their action to save themselves and their land'; and that the PLO 'had to decide between standing on its declaration as sole representative of the Palestinians *or* the salvation of the land and the people'.[12]

38
A Welter of Blood

President Assad had the PLO fighters disarmed as soon as they reached Damascus after being expelled from Lebanon. Their personal weapons, which the Israelis had allowed them to keep, were taken from them by the Syrians. The men were put into camps outside the city. On the second day after their arrival discontent in one of the camps threatened to become rebellion, but at once Assad sent in a tank or two, and the trouble subsided.

Assad's chief use for the PLO now was to frustrate the United States' peace-making efforts in the region. In the first half of 1983 he added some 5,000 more PLO men to the 10,000 he had sent back into Lebanon before the end of 1982. These were in addition to his army of 60,000 Syrians stationed there.

The United States helped to negotiate an agreement between the Lebanese government and Israel, which was signed on 17 May 1983. Israel undertook to withdraw her armed forces from Lebanon. The two countries recognized each other's sovereignty. Major Haddad's 'local units' were to be integrated into the Lebanese army, and to be accorded proper status under Lebanese law to enable them to continue guarding the villages in a 'Security Region' in the south along Israel's border. A Joint Liaison Committee, on which the United States would be represented, would supervise the implementation of the agreement and 'address itself . . . to the development of mutual relations between Israel and Lebanon, *inter alia* the regulation of the movement of goods, products and persons, communications, etc.' No provision was made for mutual diplomatic representation. The government of Amin Gemayel resisted normalization of relations with Israel out of fear of sanctions by the Arab world. On the other hand, it undertook more than it could deliver in regard to the PLO and Syria.

The PLO was not mentioned by name in the agreement, but it was promised that 'the territory of each party will not be used as a base for hostile or terrorist activity against the other party, its territory or its people'. The existence of 'irregular forces, armed bands, organizations, bases, offices or infrastructure', whose purposes included aggression against the other party, was to be prevented, and all agreements of the past enabling them to exist were declared null and void.

Syria was not mentioned by name, but the Lebanese undertook to 'prevent entry into, deployment in, or passage through its territory, its airspace, and . . . its territorial sea, by military forces, armament, or military equipment of any state hostile to the other party'.

They were promises which the Lebanese government could not keep. As long as they could not, Israel could stay on Lebanese soil.

Both parties agreed to the deployment on Lebanese territory of international forces requested by the Lebanese government. Americans, French and Italians returned. A token British contingent joined them. The Soviet Union, without being mentioned by name, was disqualified from potential participation, since, according to the agreement, 'new contributors to such forces shall be selected from among states having diplomatic relations with both parties to the present agreement'.

The Israeli government became increasingly anxious to withdraw, or at least pull back its army nearer to the border, under pressure of Israeli public opinion, but the United States did not want Israeli forces withdrawn as long as the Syrian army was still occupying the greater part of the country. The Lebanese army could not fill the defence gap they would leave against the Syrians and the regrouped PLO, and the United States could not wish to commit more American troops for an indefinite stay. There was no peace. The PLO harassed the Israelis; Christians and Druze shelled each other night after night; acts of terrorism were frequent. The American embassy was blown up with the loss of many lives on 18 April 1983. In Lebanon and Israel it was said to be 'common knowledge' that the Syrians had done it.[1] The Americans did not say so. They hoped to persuade Syria to withdraw.

The US Secretary of State, George Schultz, was received in Damascus in July 1983. Assad told him that the Israeli-Lebanese agreement 'infringed Lebanese sovereignty'. (Assad himself, it is to be remembered, had never recognized Lebanese sovereignty.) He refused to withdraw from Lebanon, and would agree only to the reconvening of a Middle East peace conference, co-chaired by the Soviet Union. The Geneva mirage had never faded from the Soviet horizon.

Behind Assad stood the USSR. Within a few months the Soviet Union had replenished his arsenal. New surface-to-air missiles replaced those which Israel had destroyed: they could reach into Israel and even to the NATO bases in Turkey.[2] Some 4,700 Soviet advisers were in Damascus by the middle of 1983.[3]

Both Assad and the USSR stood behind the PLO, but they could not be sure of Arafat. He could set up a government-in-exile in Cairo, and promote a peace on the lines of the Reagan Plan. Assad had to try to prevent such a split in the Organization, which could be fatal to it and end its usefulness to him. His relations with Arafat were strained almost to breaking-point, not only because of personal antipathy. Arafat had given him cause for fear.

Yasser Arafat had never lost his sympathy for, or contacts with, the Muslim Brotherhood. When the 'civil war' in Lebanon was supposed to have been brought to an end by Syrian intervention in November 1976, Arafat supplied arms to the Brotherhood in the Syrian city of Hama. They rose in rebellion in February 1982.

Assad was an Alawite, not a Muslim. The Alawites had come to power through the army. When the French ruled Syria, they had sought recruits among the minority religious communities in order to have a force on which they could rely if necessary against the Sunni majority. By the time the country became independent, the Alawites formed the officer class. The source and mainstay of Hafiz Assad's power in Syria was an Alawite military elite, under the command of his brother Rifʿat. Through it, President Assad controlled a hostile population.

He put down the Hama rebellion with the utmost ruthlessness. Rifʿat Assad's storm troopers massacred the people of the town in vast numbers. With rigid press censorship in Syria, such news of the massacre as reached the outside world was paltry. A report issued by Amnesty International, in September 1983, reckoned that the number of citizens killed may have been as high as 25,000: investigators received unverified information that cyanide gas had been piped into buildings through rubber hoses to kill all inhabitants indiscriminately. Other reports tell of people being lined up in the streets and shot, as had happened in April 1981 when hundreds were killed in the same city. Aerial photographs taken by Americans after the 1982 massacre show that many of the mosques, including the ancient Great Mosque, had been destroyed. Part of the city, the fourth biggest in Syria, was razed by tanks and artillery.[4]

Sunni Muslims thereafter called Hafiz Assad 'the Big Butcher', and his brother 'the Little Butcher'.

Yet within Fatah he had adherents. By mid-1983 Fatah rebels against Arafat's leadership had shifted their loyalty to Assad. They would not serve under the commanders appointed by Arafat in the Beqaa. One of them was Haj Ismaʿil, the erstwhile commander of South Lebanon at Sidon. They complained that he had fled from the Israelis. Soon Fatah men were killing Fatah men by the score in eastern Lebanon.

The news that 'the Butcher of Hama' was behind the rebels increased Arafat's support on the West Bank.[5] The Mufti of Jerusalem, Sheikh Saʿad al-Alami, issued a *fatwa*, a divine dispensation, for any true believer who would kill Hafiz Assad.[6]

Conclusion

Conclusion

After August 1982, Arafat's PLO had its existence only on his own lips, in the columns of Western newspapers, in the briefings of European foreign ministers, and in long speeches at the United Nations. Of the member groups, the Popular Front organizations were as firmly under the thumb of President Assad as Sa'iqa was; so was the rebel faction of Fatah; and ALF was retracted into Iraq.

The United Nations, which turns dreams into deficits, sponsored a conference on Palestine at Geneva in the late summer of 1983, at a cost of $6- or 7 million. The United States officially ignored it; some Western European governments sent observers, but not representatives. The 'PLO delegation' was led by Abu Iyad, but soon felt the want of Arafat. Western Europe was Arafat's theatre. Once again on a platform before 'the world', he rose to declare that the armed struggle would go on. The organization which had been formed to aid the keeping of peace on earth greeted his speech with wild applause. At a press conference on 2 September, he denied that there was any hostility between himself and his Syrian brother Hafiz Assad, or that there were breaks and rebellions within Fatah. Hard times, he conceded, were to be expected, for this was 'a revolution, not a picnic'.

The conference over, he made his way back to Lebanon, sailing in a small boat from Cyprus. In defiance of a ban on his re-entering any territory under Syrian control, he rejoined the remnant of his faction in Baddawi camp near Tripoli. With these five or six thousand Fatah men – of whom one or two thousand belonged to the refugee camps of the area – he awaited a *coup de grâce* from the surrounding Syrians. On 3 November the rebels attacked in force, supported by Syrian artillery. Arafat's men were driven out of Baddawi and Nahr al-Bared camps. They sought shelter in the city, where Syrian fire continued to rain down upon them, so that many hundreds of Lebanese were killed.

On 12 November 1983 Assad was taken ill, struck down by a heart attack as newsmen conjectured. So yet again Arafat escaped what had seemed an inevitable end. The rebel command allowed him time to leave, time enough for his friends in the UN and in certain European foreign ministries (conspicuously the Greek and the French), to facilitate an evacuation of his fighters from Tripoli.

On 20 December, a day before the deadline set by his enemies, 4,000 of Arafat's men and teenage boys sailed from Tripoli in five Greek ships, bound for Tunis, Algeria and North Yemen, 'protected' by the Un flag (from Israeli ships patrolling the coast of Lebanon, was the implication). Israeli Ambassador Blum pointed out in the UN Assembly that Arafat had been allowed to leave Lebanon in 1982 'on condition he did not return'; that he had broken that condition, and had ordered further acts of terrorism to be committed in Israel; and therefore the UN affording him its protection for a second departure was 'grotesque'.

Arafat's ship called at Egypt on the way to North Yemen, and he talked to Hosni Mubarak. The other factions of the PLO condemned the meeting. So did Israel. The United States administration approved of it, still hoping that the Reagan Plan might be implemented. Yet even if Arafat were to reach an agreement with Mubarak and King Hussein which would revive that possibility, he would be committing the Organization to nothing whatsoever. Arafat could not speak for the PLO. (And if he were to assume a new role as spokesman for the West Bank and Gaza, he would have to abandon the armed struggle, and recognize Israel, in order to be accepted by the Americans. But he did not seem to have this course in mind. At a celebration of the nineteenth anniversary of Fatah's 'first strike into Israel', held in Tunis at the end of 1983, he swore he would never do either.)

In the closing months of 1983, Western journalists still sought him out. He assured them that the PLO would survive even if he and all his fighters were destroyed, because it was not 'some fighters', but 'the will of the people'.[1]

Was it? Still no Arab power tried to find out.

Professor Sari Nusseibeh, Oxford-trained teacher of Islamic Philosophy at Bir Zeit University, and a member of one of the oldest and most respected Arab families of Jerusalem, said to me as we sat and talked in his beautiful house in the Old City of Jerusalem[2]: 'We do not want to solve the Palestinian problem in terms of "human rights", what we want is a political solution.'

I asked what plan he had in mind to advance such a solution. Had not the PLO let every opportunity for a political settlement slip away by refusing to adapt to political realities?

'I admire my people more for clinging to their dreams', he said, 'than if they were to compromise with what others call political realities.'

So to the Palestinians in the camps there was no message of hope. They had been sacrificed to the incontinent ambitions of Haj Amin al-Husseini, Nasser, Arafat, Assad and the other Arab leaders, and still they were not to be redeemed.

The whole history has a consistent character: from the days of the Mufti and the British White Paper of 1939, to the expulsion from Beirut and the Reagan Plan, more was always asked for by Arab leaders than could be conceded; and rather than make concessions themselves, they chose, time after time, to fight. Each time they lost and new circumstances took away an offer they had rejected, they would demand that it be offered to them again. The tragedy of the Palestinians is that they were led by people who despised or were devoid of political realism; and Palestinian affairs and concerns were made subordinate to those of the Arab states, which were, of course, pursuing their own self-interest.

If hope lay anywhere it was in the very dissolution of the PLO. From its inception the Organization had been nothing but a savage instrument of Arab politics. It had not been designed or used as a means to liberate the Palestinians. Its business was to keep them in misery and to waste their lives, generation after generation. While its demise was not sufficient to guarantee their redemption, it was entirely necessary if they were ever to be saved from ruin and despair.

Appendices
and Reference Notes

Appendix I
The Palestinian National Covenant

The following is the complete and unabridged text of the Palestinian National Covenant, as published officially, in English, by the PLO.

Articles of the Covenant

Article 1: Palestine is the homeland of the Arab Palestinian people; it is an indivisible part of the Arab homeland, and the Palestinian people are an integral part of the Arab nation.

Article 2: Palestine, with the boundaries it had during the British Mandate, is an indivisible territorial unit.

Article 3: The Palestinian people possess the legal right to their homeland and have the right to determine their destiny after achieving the liberation of their country in accordance with their wishes and entirely of their own accord and will.

Article 4: The Palestinian identity is a genuine, essential and inherent characteristic; it is transmitted from parents to children. The Zionist occupation and the dispersal of the Palestinian Arab people, through the disasters which befell them, do not make them lose their Palestinian identity and their membership of the Palestinian community, nor do they negate them.

Article 5: The Palestinians are those Arab nationals who, until 1947, normally resided in Palestine regardless of whether they were evicted from it or have stayed there. Anyone born, after that date, of a Palestinian father – whether inside Palestine or outside it – is also a Palestinian.

Article 6: The Jews who had normally resided in Palestine until the beginning of the Zionist invasion will be considered Palestinians.

Article 7: That there is a Palestinian community and that it has material, spiritual and historical connections with Palestine are indisputable facts. It is a national duty to bring up individual Palestinians in an Arab revolutionary manner. All means of information and education must be adopted in order to acquaint the Palestinian with his country in the most profound manner, both spiritual and material, that is possible. He must be prepared for the armed struggle and ready to sacrifice his wealth and his life in order to win back his homeland and bring about its liberation.

Article 8: The phase in their history, through which the Palestinian people are now living, is that of national (*watani*) struggle for the liberation of Palestine. Thus the conflicts among the Palestinian national forces are secondary, and should be ended for the sake of the basic conflict that exists between the forces of Zionism and of imperialism on the one hand, and the Palestinian Arab people on the other. On this basis the Palestinian masses, regardless of whether they are residing in the national homeland or in diaspora (*mahajir*) constitute – both their organization and the individuals – one national front working for the retrieval of Palestine and its liberation through armed struggle.

Article 9: Armed struggle is the only way to liberate Palestine. Thus it is the overall strategy, not merely a tactical phase. The Palestinian Arab people assert their absolute determination and firm resolution to continue their armed struggle and to work for an armed popular revolution for the liberation of their country and their return to it. They also assert their right to normal life in Palestine and to exercise their right to self-determination and sovereignty over it.

Article 10: Commando action constitutes the nucleus of the Palestinian popular liberation war. This requires its escalation, comprehensiveness and mobilization of all the Palestinian popular and educational efforts and their organization and involvement in the armed Palestinian revolution. It also requires the achieving of unity for the national (*watani*) struggle among the different groupings of the Palestinian people, and between the Palestinian people and the Arab masses so as to secure the continuation of the revolution, its escalation and victory.

Article 11: The Palestinians will have three mottoes: national (*wataniyya*) unity, national (*qawmiyya*) mobilization and liberation.

Article 12: The Palestinian people believe in Arab unity. In order to contribute their share towards the attainment of that objective, however, they must, at the present stage of their struggle, safeguard their Palestinian identity and develop their consciousness of that identity, and oppose any plan that may dissolve or impair it.

Article 13: Arab unity and the liberation of Palestine are two complementary objectives, the attainment of either of which facilitates the attainment of the other. Thus, Arab unity leads to the liberation of Palestine; the liberation of Palestine leads to Arab unity; and work towards the realization of one objective proceeds side by side with work towards the realization of the other.

Article 14: The destiny of the Arab nation, and indeed Arab existence itself, depends upon the destiny of the Palestinian cause. From this inter-dependence springs the Arab nation's pursuit of, and striving for, the liberation of Palestine. The people of Palestine play the role of the vanguard in the realization of this sacred national (*qawmi*) goal.

Article 15: The liberation of Palestine, from an Arab viewpoint, is a national (*qawmi*) duty and it attempts to repel the Zionist and imperialist aggression against the Arab homeland, and aims at the elimination of Zionism in Palestine. Absolute responsibility for this falls upon the Arab nation – peoples and governments – with the Arab people of Palestine in the vanguard.

Accordingly the Arab nation must mobilize all its military, human, and moral and spiritual capabilities to participate actively with the Palestinian people in the liberation of Palestine. It must, particularly in the phase of the armed Palestinian revolution, offer and furnish the Palestinian people with all possible help, and material and human support, and make available to them the means and opportunities that will enable them to continue to carry out their leading role in the armed revolution, until they liberate their homeland.

Article 16: The liberation of Palestine, from a spiritual point of view, will provide the Holy Land with an atmosphere of safety and tranquillity, which in turn will safeguard the country's religious sanctuaries and guarantee freedom of worship and of visit to all, without discrimination of race, colour, language, or religion. Accordingly, the people of Palestine look to all spiritual forces in the world for support.

Article 17: The liberation of Palestine, from a human point of view, will restore to the Palestinian individual his dignity, pride and freedom. Accord-ingly the Palestinian Arab people look forward to the support of all those who believe in the dignity of man and his freedom in the world.

Article 18: The liberation of Palestine, from an international point of view, is a defensive action necessitated by the demands of self-defence. Accordingly, the Palestinian people, desirous as they are of the friendship of all people, look to freedom-loving, justice-loving and peace-loving states for support in order to restore their legitimate rights in Palestine, to re-establish peace and security in the country, and to enable its people to exercise national sovereignty and freedom.

Article 19: The partition of Palestine in 1947 and the establishment of the State of Israel are entirely illegal, regardless of the passage of time, because they were contrary to the will of the Palestinian people and to their natural right in their homeland, and inconsistent with the principles embodied in the Charter of the United Nations, particularly the right to self-determination.

Article 20: The Balfour Declaration, the Mandate for Palestine and everything that has been based upon them, are deemed null and void. Claims of historical or religious ties of Jews with Palestine are incompatible with the facts of history and the true conception of what constitutes statehood. Judaism, being a religion, is not an independent nationality. Nor do Jews constitute a single nation with an identity of its own; they are citizens of the states to which they belong.

Article 21: The Arab Palestinian people, expressing themselves by the armed Palestinian revolution, reject all solutions which are substitutes for the total liberation of Palestine and reject all proposals aiming at the liquidation of the Palestinian problem, or its internationalization.

Article 22: Zionism is a political movement organically associated with international imperialism and antagonistic to all action for liberation and to progressive movements in the world. It is racist and fanatic in its nature, aggressive, expansionist and colonial in its aims, and fascist in its methods. Israel is the instrument of the Zionist movement, and a geographical base for world imperialism placed strategically in the midst of the Arab homeland to combat the hopes of the Arab nation for liberation, unity and progress. Israel is a constant source of threat *vis-à-vis* peace in the Middle East and the whole world. Since the liberation of Palestine will destroy the Zionist and imperialist presence and will contribute to the establishment of peace in the Middle East, the Palestinian people look for the support of all the progressive and peaceful forces and urge them all, irrespective of their affiliations and beliefs, to offer the Palestinian people all aid and support in their just struggle for the liberation of their homeland.

Article 23: The demands of security and peace, as well as the demands of right and justice, require all states to consider Zionism an illegitimate movement, to outlaw its existence, and to ban its operations, in order that friendly relations among peoples may be preserved, and the loyalty of citizens to their respective homelands safeguarded.

Article 24: The Palestinian people believe in the principles of justice, freedom, sovereignty, self-determination, human dignity, and in the right of all peoples to exercise them.

Article 25: For the realization of the goals of this Charter and its principles, the Palestinian Liberation Organization will perform its role in the liberation of Palestine in accordance with the Constitution of this Organization.

Article 26: The Palestine Liberation Organization, representative of the Palestinian revolutionary forces, is responsible for the Palestinian Arab people's movement in its struggle – to retrieve its homeland, liberate and return to it and exercise the right to self-determination in it – in all military, political and financial fields and also for whatever may be required by the Palestinian case on the inter-Arab and international levels.

Article 27: The Palestinian Liberation Organization shall co-operate with all Arab states, each according to its potentialities; and will adopt a neutral policy among them in the light of the requirements of the war of liberation; and on this basis it shall not interfere in the internal affairs of any Arab state.

Article 28: The Palestinian Arab people assert the genuineness and independence of their national (*wataniyya*) revolution and reject all forms of intervention, trusteeship and subordination.

Article 29: The Palestinian people possess the fundamental and genuine legal right to liberate and retrieve their homeland. The Palestinian people determine their attitude towards all states and forces on the basis of the stands they adopt *vis-à-vis* the Palestinian case and the extent of the support they offer to the Palestinian revolution to fulfil the aims of the Palestinian people.

Article 30: Fighters and carriers of arms in the war of liberation are the nucleus of the popular army which will be the protective force for the gains of the Palestinian Arab people.

Article 31: The Organization shall have a flag, an oath of allegiance and an anthem. All this shall be decided upon in accordance with a special regulation.

Article 32: Regulations, which shall be known as the Constitution of the Palestine Liberation Organization, shall be annexed to this Charter. It shall lay down the manner in which the Organization, and its organs and institutions, shall be constituted; the respective competence of each; and the requirements of its obligations under the Charter.

Article 33: This Charter shall not be amended save by (vote of) a majority of two-thirds of the total membership of the National Congress of the Palestine Liberation Organization (taken) at a special session convened for that purpose.

Appendix II
Constitution of the
Palestine Liberation Organization*
Cairo, 17 July 1968

CHAPTER I

General Principles

Article 1: The Palestinians, in accordance with the provisions of this Constitution, form themselves into an organization to be known as the Palestine Liberation Organization.

Article 2: The Palestine Liberation Organization shall exercise its responsibilities in accordance with the principles of the National Charter, the provisions of this Constitution, and such rules, provisions and resolutions as may be issued in conformity with these principles and provisions.

Article 3: Relationships within the Organization shall be based on commitment to struggle and to national action, the different levels of the Organization, from its base up to its collective leadership, being closely linked together on a basis of the following principles: the minority shall defer to the will of the majority, confidence of the people shall be won through persuasion, the movement of Palestinian struggle shall be continued, the armed Palestinian revolution shall be supported, and every possible effort shall be made to ensure that it continues and escalates, so that the impetus of the masses towards liberation may take its course until victory is achieved.

In implementation of this principle, the Executive Committee shall draft constitutions for the Organization's subsidiary bodies, due regard being paid to the circumstances of Palestinians in all places where they are

*Archives of the Institute for Palestine Studies.
The Fourth Palestine National Assembly, held in Cairo from 10 to 17 July, studied the constitution for the Palestine Liberation Organization and the regulations related to its structure, and introduced certain amendments. (This Appendix is taken from *The Palestinian Covenant and its Meaning* by Y.Harkabi and is reproduced by kind permission of Vallentine, Mitchell & Co. Ltd.)

concentrated, to the circumstances of the Palestinian revolution, and to the realization of the objectives of the Charter and the Constitution.

Article 4: All Palestinians are natural members of the Palestine Liberation Organization, performing their duty to liberate their country in accordance with their abilities and qualifications. The Palestinian people is the base of this Organization.

CHAPTER II

The National Assembly

Article 5: The members of the National Assembly shall be elected by the Palestinian people by direct ballot, in accordance with a system to be devised for this purpose by the Executive Committee.

Article 6: (a) Should it be impossible to hold an election to the Assembly, the National Assembly shall continue to sit until circumstances permit of the holding of elections.

(b) If, for some reason, one or more seats in the National Assembly fall vacant, the Assembly shall appoint a member or members to fill the vacant seats.

Article 7: (a) The National Assembly is the supreme authority of the Liberation Organization. It drafts the policy, planning and programmes of the Organization.

(b) Jerusalem is the seat of the Palestine Liberation Organization.

Article 8: The National Assembly is elected for three years, and it shall be convened in regular session once every six months by its President or, should extraordinary sessions be necessary, by the President at the request of the Executive Committee, or of a quarter of its members. It shall meet in Jerusalem, Gaza, or any other place, depending on circumstances. Should the President not call such a session, the session shall convene automatically in such place and at such time as are designated in the request submitted by its members or by the Executive Committee.

Article 9: The National Assembly shall have a President's Office, consisting of the President, two Vice-Presidents, and a Secretary, elected by the National Assembly when it first meets.

Article 10: The National Assembly in ordinary session shall consider:

(a) The annual report submitted by the Executive Committee on the achievements of the Organization and its subsidiary bodies.

(b) The annual report of the National Fund and budget allocations.

(c) Proposals submitted by the Executive Committee and recommendations of Assembly committees.

(d) Any other questions submitted to it.

Article 11: The National Assembly shall form such committees as it deems necessary to assist it in the performance of its duties.

These committees shall submit their reports and recommendations to the National Assembly, which shall debate them and issue its decisions as regards them.

Article 12: Attendance by two-thirds of the members of the Assembly shall constitute a quorum. Decisions shall be taken by a majority vote of those present.

CHAPTER III

The Executive Committee

Article 13: (a) All members of the Executive Committee shall be elected by the National Assembly.

(b) The Chairman of the Executive Committee shall be elected by the Committee itself.

(c) The Executive Committee shall be elected from the National Assembly.

Article 14: The Executive Committee shall consist of eleven members, including the Chairman of the Board of Directors of the Palestine National Fund.

Should vacancies occur on the Executive Committee, for any reason, when the National Assembly is not sitting, they shall be filled as follows:

(a) If the vacancies are less than a third of the total membership, they shall not be filled until the first session of the National Assembly.

(b) If the vacancies amount to a third or more of the total membership of the Executive Committee, the National Assembly shall fill them at a session convened for the purpose in not more than thirty days.

(c) Should it be impossible, for valid reasons, to convene the National Assembly in extraordinary session, vacancies arising in either of the above cases shall be filled by the Executive Committee, the Assembly's Bureau and such members of the Assembly as are able to attend, at a joint assembly formed for this purpose. The new members shall be chosen by majority vote of those present.

Article 15: The Executive Committee is the highest executive authority of the Organization. It shall remain in permanent session, its members devoting themselves exclusively to their work. It shall be responsible for executing the policy, programmes and planning approved by the National Assembly, to which it shall be responsible, collectively and individually.

Article 16: The Executive Committee shall assume responsibility for:

(a) Representing the Palestinian people.

(b) Supervising the Organization's subsidiary bodies.

(c) Issuing regulations and instructions, and taking decisions on the Organization's activities, provided these are not incompatible with the Charter or the Constitution.

(d) Implementing the Organization's financial policy and drafting its budget.

In general, the Executive Committee shall assume all the responsibilities of the Liberation Organization, in accordance with the general policies and resolutions adopted by the National Assembly.

Article 17: The permanent headquarters of the Executive Committee shall be in Jerusalem. It shall also be entitled to hold its meetings in any other place it sees fit.

Article 18: The Executive Committee shall establish the following departments:

(a) A Military Department.

(b) A Department for Political and Information Affairs.

(c) A Palestine National Fund Department.

(d) A Department for Research and Specialized Institutes.

(e) A Department for Administrative Affairs.

(f) Any other department the Committee considers necessary.

Each department shall have a Director-General and the requisite staff. The authority of each department shall be defined by special regulations drawn up by the Executive Committee.

Article 19: The Executive Committee shall establish close relations and co-ordinate activities between the Organization and all Arab and international organizations, federations and institutions which agree with its aims, or which help it in the realization of the Organization's objectives.

Article 20: The Executive Committee shall continue to exercise its prerogatives as long as it enjoys the confidence of the National Assembly. The Executive Committee shall submit its resignation to the new National Assembly at its first session. It is subject to re-election.

Article 21: Attendances of two thirds of its members shall constitute a quorum, and its resolutions shall be adopted by majority vote of those present.

CHAPTER IV

General Rules

Article 22: The Palestine Liberation Organization shall form an army of Palestinians, to be known as the Palestine Liberation Army, with an independent command which shall operate under the supervision of the Executive Committee, and carry out its instructions and decisions, both general and particular. Its national duty is to become the vanguard in the battle for the liberation of Palestine.

Article 23: The Executive Committee shall make every effort to enroll Palestinians in Arab military colleges and institutes for military training, to mobilize the potentials and resources of the Palestinians, and to prepare them for the battle of liberation.

Article 24: A fund, to be known as the Palestine National Fund, shall be established to finance the activities of the Organization, which Fund shall be administered by a board of directors to be formed in accordance with special regulations for the Fund issued by the National Assembly.

Article 25: The Fund's sources of revenue shall be:

(a) An impost on Palestinians imposed and collected in accordance with a special system.

(b) Financial assistance provided by Arab governments and the Arab nation.

(c) The sale of 'liberation stamps' which the Arab states will issue for use in postal and other transactions.

(d) Contributions and donations.

(e) Arab loans and aid from Arab countries and friendly peoples.

(f) Any other sources of revenue approved by the Assembly.

Article 26: Committees to be known as 'Committees for the Support of Palestine' shall be formed in Arab and friendly countries to collect contributions and support the Organization in its national endeavours.

Article 27: The level at which the Palestinian people is represented in Arab organizations and conferences shall be determined by the Executive Committee. The Executive Committee shall appoint a representative for Palestine to the League of Arab States.

Article 28: The Executive Committee shall be entitled to make such regulations as are necessary for the implementation of the provisions of this Constitution.

Article 29: The Organization's National Assembly shall be empowered to amend, alter, or add to this Constitution by a two-thirds majority of its members.

CHAPTER V

Transitional Provisions

Article 30: On 10 July 1968, the National Assembly convened in Cairo shall replace the former Provisional National Assembly of the Palestine Liberation Organization, and exercise all the prerogatives allotted to it by this Constitution.

Article 31: The National Assembly shall sit for two years as from 10 July 1968. Should it prove impossible to hold elections for its successor, it shall meet and decide either to extend its term for another period or to form a new Assembly in such a manner as it may approve.

Article 32: The National Assembly alone is entitled to co-opt new members from time to time, as it sees fit, should this be desirable in view of the requirements of the battle for liberation and the need to strengthen national unity, in conformity with the provisions of the National Charter, in accordance with regulations to be drafted by the Executive Committee in the coming session.

Appendix III

Organizational Chart of the PLO

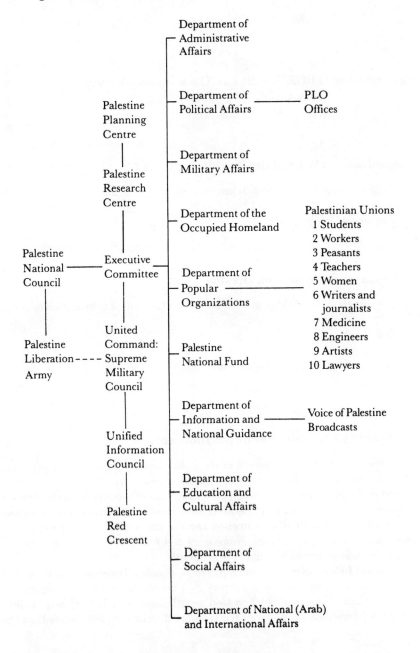

Department of Administrative Affairs

Palestine Planning Centre

Department of Political Affairs — PLO Offices

Palestine Research Centre

Department of Military Affairs

Palestine National Council

Executive Committee

Department of the Occupied Homeland

United Command: Supreme Military Council

Department of Popular Organizations

Palestinian Unions
1 Students
2 Workers
3 Peasants
4 Teachers
5 Women
6 Writers and journalists
7 Medicine
8 Engineers
9 Artists
10 Lawyers

Palestine Liberation Army

Palestine National Fund

Unified Information Council

Department of Information and National Guidance — Voice of Palestine Broadcasts

Palestine Red Crescent

Department of Education and Cultural Affairs

Department of Social Affairs

Department of National (Arab) and International Affairs

Reference Notes

Abbreviations: MECS Middle East Contemporary Survey
MENA Middle East News Agency
MER   Middle East Record

Introduction: Wars of the Worlds

1 35,468 square miles were taken out of 46,339 square miles to become Transjordan.
2 *Merkur*, 28 October 1980.

Chapter 1: Promises and Dreams

1 For the text of the McMahon letter see Walter Laqueur, *The Israel-Arab Reader*, p. 15.
2 *Ibid.*, p. 17.
3 *Ibid.*, p. 12.
4 See Elie Kedourie, *The Chatham House Version and Other Middle Eastern Studies*, pp. 33–51.

Chapter 2: The Slaughter by the Innocents

1 A few instances: in the middle of the eighth century Idris 1 wiped out many Jewish communities; the Jews of Fez were massacred in the eleventh century, and again in the fifteenth century when only eleven out of thousands survived; there were massacres at Basra in 1776, Marrakesh in 1880, Algiers in 1805, 1815 and 1830, Mostaganem in 1897. Extortion and the destruction or seizure of Jewish property – houses, businesses, synagogues and tombs – by Muslims were the common experiences of Jews under Muslim rule.

Bernard Lewis (*Islam in History*, pp. 135–6) quotes a Jewish scholar of the late nineteenth and early twentieth century: "'I do not know any more miserable, helpless, and pitiful individual on God's earth than the Jahudi [Jews] in those [Islamic] countries. . . . The poor Jew is despised, belabored and tortured alike by

Moslem, Christian and Brahmin, he is the poorest of the poor.'"' And yet, Lewis points out, Jewish scholars and writers felt much sympathy for Islam: 'In part this was based on a well-grounded feeling of gratitude', because Jewish creativity in medieval Spain 'owed much to Muslim tolerance'; because Jews had found refuge in Turkey from Christian persecution, and because 'there was nothing in Islam to compare with the specific hatred . . . that was directed against the Jews in Christendom', although there was 'contempt, degradation' and 'occasional repression'.

2 Prompted by a British Intelligence officer, Colonel Brunton. See Y. Porath, *The Emergence of the Palestinian Arab National Movement*, vol. I, 1918–29, p. 32.

3 *Ibid.*, p. 97.

4 Colonel Waters-Taylor. See Porath, *op. cit.*, p. 99. Also Richard Meinertzhagen, *Middle East Diary 1917–1956*, pp. 55–6. Colonel Meinertzhagen was political adviser to General Allenby during the British Military Administration of Palestine. He records his discoveries of the subterfuges which Colonel Waters-Taylor and his wife resorted to in their efforts to assist Haj Amin al-Husseini. Mrs Waters-Taylor visited him frequently disguised as an Arab.

5 Report of Court of Inquiry, FO 371/5121.

Chapter 3: The Mufti

1 On 24 April 1920 Britain was granted a mandate over the Palestine region by the San Remo peace conference. On 1 July 1920 Sir Herbert Samuel took over from the military administration and established a civil administration in Palestine on *both sides of the Jordan* (see Viscount Samuel's *Memoirs*). By the Treaty of Sèvres, 10 August 1920, Turkey resigned her Asian and North African possessions, but the Treaty was not ratified, and was superseded in 1923 by the Treaty of Lausanne. In March 1921 Abdullah was installed as Governor of 'Transjordan'. This decision to treat 'Transjordan' differently from western Palestine was not internationally sanctioned until it was confirmed as part of a text of the Mandate terms by the Council of the League of Nations on 24 July 1922 (Article 25 declared that in the 'territory lying between the Jordan and the eastern boundary of Palestine as ultimately determined' the Mandatory might 'postpone or withhold' application of certain of the provisions of the Mandate). Only on 23 September 1922 did the League approve a memorandum relating to Article 25 which specifically exempted the area of Transjordan from the original Mandate's requirements concerning the establishment of the Jewish national home.

2 Colonel Waters-Taylor.

3 Porath, *op. cit.*, vol. I, p. 129.

4 These were a part of the findings of the Shaw Commission of Inquiry, Cmd 3530.

5 Porath, *op. cit.*, vol. I, p. 270.

6 Y. Porath, *The Emergence of the Palestinian Arab National Movement*, vol. II, 1929–39, p. 76.

7 Arieh L. Avneri, *The Jewish Land Settlement and the Arab Claim of Dispossession (1878–1948)*, e.g. pp. 89, 197–8.

8 *Ibid.*, e.g. pp. 153, 169, 182, 196, 200, 291.

9 A. Granott, *The Land System in Palestine*, pp. 56–9, 61, 89. E.g. 'Frequently they [the *fallahin*] sold their land to rich and influential *effendi* in the town, receiving it back from them as tenants with the obligation to set aside for the owners a fixed portion of the produce' (p. 58). Often they 'used to transfer their lands to mosques. . . . and transfer them into *waqf* (religious trust) property. . . . [But] frequently the representatives of the religious law themselves . . . rose against [the *fallah*] and swallowed his property. . . . In this way landed properties in the whole of Palestine were gradually concentrated in the hands of a few owners, whether wealthy families or *waqf* foundation' (p. 56).

The memorandum presented by the Palestine government to the Royal Commission for Palestine (the Peel Commission) in 1937 records: 'It is generally alleged that the Palestine *fallah* is born in debt, lives in debt, and dies in debt. It is also contended that for many generations, and indeed centuries, his life has been made miserable by the pressure of his creditors, and that his moral and material progress has been severely handicapped by the burden of his debt and by the cruel rate of interest paid by him.' Compensation for the peasants who were uprooted and lost their livelihood when the great landowners sold what was rightfully, if not legally, theirs, was made law only under the British Mandate.

10 Avneri, *op. cit.* Sa'id al-Shawa, a member of the Supreme Muslim Council, sold 1,380 *dunam* near Majdal under a fictitious name; the family of Ahmad al-Shanti, an extremist of the nationalist organization in the 1920s and active in the Great Revolt, sold part of the Taibe; Abdullah Samara, supporter of the Mufti, fought for tenant-farmers' rights in Wadi Hawareth and Wadi Qutani, had poor sandy land which he would not sell during the 1914–17 war to Jews, partly for fear of the revenge of Arab terrorists, but later sold it to Jewish buyers – the settlement of Mikhmoret now stands there; Asim al-Sa'id, Mayor of Jaffa, active in the Muslim-Christian Association, sold a part of the Qubeiba land; Fu'ad Sa'd of Haifa, a Greek Catholic member of the Arab Executive Committee and a signatory to letters of protest over the selling of Arab land to Jews, bought desolate village lands in 1903, and sold them to Jewish buyers; Alfred Rock sold land in Masub, but secretly, for fear of bringing shame on his uncle who was a supporter of the Mufti and a member of the Arab delegation to London; Arthur Rock, brother of Alfred, sold land in Beit Dajan, and another member of the family, Butrus Rock, sold the Duran lands; Zaki Nusseibeh of Jerusalem and Jawdat Nashashibi, members of the Arab Executive Committee, sold the lands on which Kiryat Anavim was founded; Raghib Nashashibi, Mayor of Jerusalem, founder of the National Defence Party, sent a letter of protest to the Turkish Parliament in 1911 against selling land to the Jews, yet tried to sell land in the village of Yalo during the First World War, but he asked too high a price, and failed to sell it; Amin Murad, one of the Committee of the Arab Fund in Safed, co-operated with a Jewish purchaser, Yosef Nahmani, to help him acquire land; the Mufti of Tiberias tried to sell 3,000 *dunam* to Jewish buyers, but a court decision gave the first option on it to the peasants of the village of Kafer Kama; Subhi al-Khadra of Safed, a member of the Arab Executive Committee, led a campaign against selling land to the Jews in Mount Knaan, but sold them his own land in Safed; Abd al-Rahman al-Haj Ibrahim, Mayor of Tulkarm, and his son Salim, a member of the Arab Executive Committee, a prominent leader of the Arab national movement and a leader of the 1921 and 1936 uprisings, and his son Slama, speculated in land buying, concentrated parcels of land and sold them to the Jews, for which Slama was nearly assassinated on 8 November 1946; Ya'qub al-Ghusayn, founder and head of the Arab Youth group, a leader of the 1929 uprising and a member of the Supreme Muslim Council (banished to the Seychelles in 1937), sold the land for Kibbutz Nir Am and orange groves in Beit Hanun. Other leading families who sold land to Jewish buyers were named Faruqi, Dajani, Bushnaq, Baitar, Laban, al-Alami and Shuqairy. The Abd al-Hadi family, some of whom took land by force from Arab tenant-farmers to sell it to Jews, complained, in response to Lord Passfield's White Paper of 1930, that 'the *fallah* cannot free himself from fundamental obligation [to Arab creditors] unless he sells land, that's how the Jews got the land at a very low price'. (In fact, the market was very inflated. Landowners on the east of the Jordan tried to sell land to Jews in order to cash in on the high prices they paid, declaring that salvation from the terrible poverty and underpopulation of the country could come only through the Jews. A majority in the Legislative Assembly tried to legalize the selling of land to Jews in Transjordan, but the British, while maintaining that they had no jurisdiction to prevent such a thing, threatened Abdullah with reducing his subsidy by 25 per cent. See William B. Ziff, *The Rape of Palestine*, pp. 348–9.) Yusuf Fahum, Mayor of Nazareth, sold his land in spite of terrorist threats: 'He was a proud man and hated the hypocrisy of the Arab leaders who sold land in secret and delivered nationalistic proclamations in public. He concluded the transaction without any mediators or fictitious figures and without hiding the fact from the public.' Avneri, *op. cit.*, pp. 70, 77, 85–6, 90, 93, 120–1, 131, 150, 182, 190, 197–200. His sources, in addition to contemporary diaries and other personal records, are chiefly the records of the Jewish land-buying agencies, such as Kerem Kayemeth (Jewish National Fund), and the Israel State Archives. For general confirmation, see George Antonius, *The Arab Awakening*, p. 406.

11 Isma'il Bey al-Husseini sold lands in Nazle near Petah-Tiqva, now Kibbutz Givat Hashlosha. Tawfiq al-Husseini, a founder of the Arab Youth organization, al-Nabi al-Arabi, sold land he owned with Musa al-Alami and Dr Tawfiq Kan'an, and, with his son Yaaqut, sold orange groves in Wadi Hanin, all to Jewish buyers. Jamil al-Husseini, of the Muslim-Christian Association and al-Nabi al-Arabi, sold land to the Jews in Dir Amer. The sons of Musa Kazem al-Husseini, Chairman of the Arab Executive Committee, sold their share of the Miski land. Jamal al-Husseini, of the Gaza branch of the family, sold part of the Idniva land, now the settlement of Kfar Menahem; Fahmi al-Husseini, Mayor of Gaza, sold 5,200 *dunam* of the Nakhabir land, where Kibbutz Beeri was founded. He bought up parcels of land – for example, 3,000 *dunam* near Gaza city – and sold them to the Jewish agencies. (Avneri, *op. cit.*, pp. 189, 190, 197–8. His sources: records of the purchasing agencies and a letter from Jamal al-Husseini of 14 October 1937.)

12 See Bernard Lewis, *The Assassins*, for the history of this branch of a Shi'a sub-sect which established itself in the highlands of northern Persia in the late eleventh century under the Old Man of the Mountain.

13 Porath, *op. cit.*, vol. II, p. 134.

14 *Ibid.*, p. 136.

15 E.g. In the 1979 anniversary issue of *The 22nd February*, an organ of the Popular Democratic Front for the Liberation of Palestine, one of the congratulatory articles (pp. 24–8) connects 'the PLO struggle' with 'the struggle of Izz ed-Din al-Qassam and the revolution of 1936'.

16 According to Simha Flapan (*Zionism and the Palestinians*, pp. 217, 226), they were mainly 'landless peasants unable to find work in the weak Arab sector. . . . People [who] had nothing to lose, and combined the old peasant anti-government, lawless attitudes with religious fervour.'

Chapter 4: The Great Revolt

1 Porath, *op. cit.*, vol. II, p. 162.

2 *Ibid.*, pp. 167–8.

3 *Ibid.*, p. 179.

4 *Ibid.*, p. 173.

5 *Ibid.*, p. 212.

6 *Ibid.*, p. 225.

7 Maurice Pearlman, *The Mufti of Jerusalem*, p. 31.

8 *Ibid.*, pp. 21, 27.

9 Porath, *op. cit.*, vol. II, p. 250.

10 *Ibid.*, p. 251.

Chapter 5: Palestine Lost

1 Pearlman, *op. cit.*, p. 33.

2 Porath, *op. cit.*, vol. II, p. 275.

3 Pearlman, *op. cit.*, p. 35.

4 *Ibid.*, p. 39.

5 *Ibid.*, p. 57.

6 *Ibid.*, p. 73, quoting testimony given at the Nuremburg trials in 1946.

7 'Only some 228,000 descendants of the 1882 Muslim settled population were living in Palestine at the outbreak of World War II. . . . "75 per cent of the Arab population of Palestine are either immigrants themselves or descendants of persons who immigrated into Palestine during the last hundred years, for the most part after 1882."' (Esco Foundation for Palestine, Inc., *Palestine: A Study of Jewish, Arab and British Policies*, vol. I.) The quotation within the quotation is from the German Jewish jurist, Ernst Frankenstein. (All such figures are, however, notoriously unreliable.) From the same study, vol. II, comes this: 'The rapid increase of the Arab population . . . was . . . largely due to better conditions introduced by the Jews.' And from *UNRWA Review*, September 1962: 'A considerable movement of people is known to have occurred, particularly during the Second World War, years when new opportunities of employment opened up in the towns and on military works in Palestine. These wartime prospects and, generally, the higher rate of industrialization in Palestine attracted many new immigrants from the neighbouring countries, and many of them entered Palestine without their presence being officially recorded.' Arab historians attest to there having been no 'Palestinian nation'. For instance, 'A common land and language, a common political fate, and the shock of exile created a Palestinian Arab nation,' Professor Albert Hourani wrote on 3 September 1967 (in the *Observer*). Professor Philip Hitti told the Anglo-American Committee of Inquiry into the Palestine problem in 1946: 'There is no such thing as Palestine in history, absolutely not.'

8 Of seven Palestinian families I talked to in Lebanon in one day, late August 1982, five told me they had left their homes in 1948 because other Arab families were leaving and urged them to go too. One, the Awad family, told me that Fawzi al-Qawuqji himself had come to their house and ordered them to go, 'and return in a week when the war is over'. ('It has been a very long week,' one of them said.) One man told me he had fled with his family because 'the Jews were coming and we were afraid'. The Jordanian daily *al-Urdun* of 9 April 1953 commented: 'For the flight . . . it is our leaders who are responsible because of their dissemination of rumours exaggerating Jewish crimes and describing them as atrocities in order to enflame the Arabs.' Contemporary accounts which support the accusation against the Arab leadership include that of the *Economist* of 2 October 1948, where it is stated that the 'most potent factor' influencing the Arabs to seek safety in flight 'were the announcements by the Higher Arab Executive, urging them to quit'. On 8 June 1951 the Near East Radio blamed 'brotherly advice given to the Arabs of Palestine, urging them to leave their land, homes and property and to stay temporarily in neighbouring, brotherly states, lest the guns of the invading Arab armies mow them down'. An account which has the ring of truth is that given by Atallah Mansour in *Waiting for the Dawn*, p. 30: 'Because of one Israeli Jew, my family has not had to suffer in the refugee camps. But there were [by contrast] cases of Jewish cruelty which contributed to the problem of refugees. . . . However, the leaders of the Arab states and of the Palestinian people are certainly even more blameworthy. . . . The refugee problem was further exacerbated by the British, who, in certain areas, encouraged Palestinians to leave their homes. . . . The Arab and Palestinian leaders, the Israelis and British, all of them helped to create the refugee problem. None of the parties was innocent.' In Haifa the Jews asked the Palestinians to stay, and they agreed, but changed their minds under pressure from an emissary from the Mufti. (See the account in Jon Kimche, *Seven Fallen Pillars*, pp. 220–1.) *Akhbar al-Yawm*, the Cairo daily, ascribed to the Mufti himself an actual order to the Arabs of Palestine to leave: On 'the 15th May 1943 . . . the Mufti of Jerusalem appealed to the Arabs of Palestine to leave the country, because the Arab armies were about to enter'.

9 To break the Arab blockade of Jerusalem, the Palmach 'decided to build a detour . . . from Deir Muheisin to Bab El Wad. . . . This was done secretly; and as a prelude, to clear the path and to maintain secrecy, the Arab villages of Beit Jiz and Beit Susin were taken and the inhabitants ejected.' (E. O'Ballance, *The Arab-Israeli War, 1948*, p. 108.)

10 For Menachem Begin's own account of his organization's attack on Dir Yasin, see Begin, *The Revolt*, pp. 162–4. The village was 'an important link in the chain of Arab positions enclosing Jerusalem from the West'. He records that warning was given to the villagers, which only some of them heeded. Abu Iyad commented some thirty years later (*Palestinien sans Patrie*, chapter 1) that the massacre of Dir Yasin was foremost in the minds of most of the Arabs who fled. He lists atrocities carried out on some of the villagers, but which no independent account corroborates. Allegations of atrocities were made against Arab fighters too: 'When the British removed the tarpaulins from the three trucks [at Kfar Etzion, a Jewish settlement], the men stared in horror' at 'testicles stuffed into eyesockets, penises into mouths' (Demaris, *Brothers in Blood*, p. 93). Such treatment of enemies is common, it appears, in the Arab world. Abu Iyad, for example, indicates this in references to the expectation of torture at the hands of his fellow Arabs in Jordan (*op. cit.*, p. 137).

11 For the full text see Laqueur, *op. cit.*, p. 125.

12 Kedourie, *op. cit.*, p. 80.

13 *Ibid.*, p. 80.

14 The Arab League was founded, with British encouragement, in Cairo on 22 March 1945. Its founding members were: Iraq, Syria, Lebanon, Egypt, Transjordan, Saudi Arabia and the Yemen, with a Palestinian representative.

15 Yasser Arafat and his associates, who later founded the Movement for the Liberation of Palestine (see chapter 7), used this phrase in 1956. Their own, they said, would be 'the generation of revenge'. (Thomas Kiernan, *Yasir Arafat, the Man and the Myth*, p. 168.) The next generation would be 'the generation of victory', Yasser Arafat said in a speech to Palestinian youths in a training camp on 28 November 1969.

Chapter 6: The Founding of the PLO

1 Nasser believed that economic and political changes in the Arab world would also be necessary before the conquest of Israel could be accomplished.

2 Ovid Demaris, *Brothers in Blood: The International Terrorist Network*, p. 121, from Falih Hanzal, *The Secrets of the Assassination of the Royal Family of Iraq*, Beirut, 1971.

3 Kedourie, *op. cit.*, p. 281.

4 Ahmad Shuqairy was one of the founders of the Istiqlal (Independence) Party, founded by a group of pan-Arab nationalists in Palestine in 1931. His father, Sheikh Assad Shuqairy (see also note 5 below) had opposed Arab nationalism in the days of the Ottoman Empire, and later established good relations with the Zionist authorities. (Porath, *op. cit.*, vol. II, p. 332, note 78.)

5 Assad Shuqairy, father of Ahmad, Mufti of Acre and an adherent of the Nashashibi faction, sold 702 *dunam* in Neve-Shaanan, near Haifa, to Hahevra

Lehakhsharat Hayishuv, one of the Jewish agencies, after the First World War. (Avneri, *op. cit.*, p. 152.)

6 *What is the PLO?* published by the London Representative of the PLO.

7 Porath, *op. cit.*, vol. II, p. 286. Kedourie (*op. cit.*, p. 76) writes with reference to the Mandate period: 'The attempt to introduce European representative devices among the Palestinians was hopeless. It is of course perfectly true that the people of Palestine were at one with those who claimed to speak for them in their utter opposition to Zionism. But this was not enough to make those leaders representative, for they were neither properly or periodically elected, nor were they amenable to the checks and controls which representation normally entails.'

8 *What is the PLO?*

9 *Ibid.*

Chapter 7: Fatah

1 The Ba'th Party is socialist and Arab-nationalist. Its two Syrian Christian founders, Michel Aflaq and Salah Bitar, were educated in Paris. During the years of the Second World War they taught at the American University of Beirut, where their ideas prompted the formation of the party.

2 'I believe that Israel is not a state, but serves as a military base for the Imperialist camp. We must not take the line of conventional warfare, using conventional weapons. We must take the line of the Popular Liberation War. . . . Should Israel react to the Popular Liberation War by conventional warfare, the Arab armies must be ready to enter the battle, in order to safeguard the bases of the *fedayeen*, who are the basic element of popular warfare. Arab unity is a necessity. . . . We believe that unity born in battle is the unity we long for. . . . He who liberates Palestine will be the one to lead the Arab nation forward to comprehensive unity. He who ignites the fire of Popular Liberation War can throw all the reactionary regimes into the sea. . . . The sons of Jordan, Saudi Arabia and other reactionary countries will overthrow the Kings and traitors and join the liberation march.' (Syrian Chief of Staff, Major General Ahmad Sweidani, in an interview with al-Musawwar, 28 April 1967; translation, MER, 1967, p. 159.)

3 According to Abu Iyad, who wants to emphasize that the Movement for the Liberation of Palestine was the creation of the Palestinian group which he, Arafat and their close associates formed in Kuwait, and that it is dependent on Arab states only for the provision of places for training and other forms of aid, the Syrian government was, on the whole, hostile to them at this stage, except for Hafiz Assad and Sweidani. (Abu Iyad, *Palestinien sans Patrie*, pp. 77, 78.)

4 Thomas Kiernan, the biographer of Yasser Arafat, 'constructed the events leading up to his birth in Cairo' through two of Arafat's brothers, a sister, an Husseini uncle and 'several cousins on both sides of the family'. Their evidence would seem convincing enough. Kiernan adds, 'to be fair', that 'two other cousins and an uncle . . . insisted that Arafat was born not in Cairo but in Gaza' (Kiernan, *op. cit.*, p. 26). Arafat's own claim, through his publicity agents, is that he was born in Jerusalem (see e.g. Riad el-Rayyes and Dunia Nahas, *Guerrillas for Palestine*, p. 133) in a house, near the Haram al-Sharif (the Holy Mount), which has since been destroyed by the Israelis to clear a space in front of the Wailing Wall. He also denies that he is related to the Husseinis. Abu Iyad stresses that the founders of the movement had their roots 'in the people' and not 'the traditional aristocracy' (Abu Iyad, *op. cit.*, chapter 3).

5 Kiernan, *op. cit.*, pp. 55–61, 65, 90.

6 *Ibid.*, chapters 18, 19, 20; also Abu Iyad, *op. cit.*, p. 43ff.

7 Abu Iyad, *op. cit.*, p. 27.

8 Kiernan (*op. cit.*, pp. 165–6) says that Arafat was in Egypt during the 1956 war, and comported himself bravely, not fleeing from the enemy, and successfully blowing up a munitions store. Abu Iyad endorses this claim (*op. cit.*, chapter 1). However, it is hard to see how the story can be true. Arafat certainly attended a student conference at Prague in August 1956 (see Jillian Becker, *Hitler's Children*, p. 162). Then, according to Kiernan, he went on to Stuttgart, having been warned not to return to Cairo, stayed in West Germany until the spring of 1957 and only then stopped in Egypt, briefly, on the way to Kuwait.

9 The Gaza branch of the al-Alami family, one of those families which were most harsh in their public protests against the selling of land to Jews, offered 6,000 *dunam* in Barbara and Dir Suneid to a Jewish land-buying agency, and the head of the family took it upon himself to get a licence from the High Commissioner for the transaction. In Hirbiya, Hafiz al-Alami sold 1,700 *dunam* to the same agency: 'The agreement with Hafiz al-Alami was signed on Friday afternoon, after a long negotiation lasting the whole day, with his two sons and his brother-in-law helping him. The old man is doubting, and thinking things over, and doubting again, whether to sell his land or not. Doubting the need to sell that land, rather than the selling of it to Jews. He acquired that land by hard work, and it wasn't easy for him to part with it, though he had lots and lots of lands. Before signing the contract, he bore Muhammad's name on his lips and whispered a prayer and a supplication to be forgiven for selling land in general, and to a Jew in particular. But if Fate said it should happen, then this Jew is better than some Muslims.' (Avneri, *op cit*, p. 190, quoting the *Diary* of F. Veitz, vol. II, p. 296.) 'And though he doubted and asked the Prophet for forgiveness, he (Hafiz) offered some more lands in 1947, south of Shoval.' (*Ibid.*, quoting Veitz, p. 153.) Sidqi al-Alami sold 1,600 *dunam* in Hirbet Biza, near Migdal (*ibid.*, p. 200).

10 Kiernan, *op. cit.*, pp. 176, 181; also Abu Iyad, *op. cit.*, chapter 3, who gives a date for the setting up of the movement – 10 October 1959.

11 Abu Iyad, *op. cit.*, chapter 3, p. 67ff.

12 To Kiernan, *op. cit.*, p. 187.

13 *Ibid.*, p. 196.

14 This translation is from el-Rayyes and Nahas, *op. cit.*, p. 27.

15 Kiernan, *op. cit.*, p. 183. Arafat says the organization did not formally become 'Fatah' until 1960, when they decided to 'use that name only from then on'.

16 Abu Iyad, *op. cit.*, pp. 62–3.

17 *Ibid.*, pp. 80–4.

Chapter 8: 'Jordan is Palestine, Palestine is Jordan'

1 *Al-Jihad*, 11 May 1965.
2 Radio Amman, 13 May 1965.
3 Radio Cairo, Voice of Palestine, 15 May 1965.
4 *Al-Difa'*, 22 June 1965.
5 Shuqairy, *From the Summit to Defeat*, p. 115.
6 *Palestine*, 15 June 1966.
7 Radio Cairo, Voice of Palestine, 17 June 1966.
8 *Palestine*, 5 July 1966.
9 Radio Cairo, Voice of Palestine, 5 July 1966.
10 Radio Damascus, 7 December 1966.
11 Radio Amman, 21 November 1966.

Chapter 9: The Six Day War

1 Laffin, *Fedayeen*, p. 20.
2 Chaim Herzog, *The Arab-Israeli Wars*, p. 148.
3 MER, 1967, p. 311. This time Arab leaders, and most insistently the government of Jordan, asked them not to go (Radio Amman, 22 and 24 June 1967). David Pryce-Jones (*The Face of Defeat*, p. 11) writes: 'These refugees were retreating into what they knew . . . choosing a future which would be like the past. . . . By the end of June the Israelis were making them sign a paper that they were leaving of their own free will. If the Israelis permitted the refugees to trek on foot, they were accused of callous indifference; and when they provided transport they were accused of systematic eviction. Had they forbidden departures, they would have been tyrants. In such a position nothing they did could be right; they could neither explain nor apologize.'

Chapter 10: Guerrillas

1 *Jerusalem Post*, 13 October 1967.
2 *Al-Anwar*, 31 August 1967; *al-Hawadith*, 1 and 8 September 1967; *al-Nahar*, 2 and 3 September 1967; *al-Hayat*, 3 September 1967; *al-Jarida*, 4 September 1967; Radio Cairo, Voice of Palestine, 2 and 3 September 1967.
3 Radio Cairo, 26 February 1967.
4 *Al-Anwar*, 11 December 1967.
5 BBC, 23 December 1967.
6 He said that Jews should 'accept living with the Arabs in a Jewish-Arab Palestine state where every faction had its just share'. Radio Beirut, 3 January 1968; BBC, 5 and 6 January 1968.
7 Kiernan, *op. cit.*, pp. 215–16.
8 'No one could pretend that Israeli soldiers are angelic . . . but anyone concerned

with the facts must surely conclude that the Israelis were among the more benevolent of history's occupiers' (Atallah Mansour [a Christian-Arab writer living in Israel], *Waiting for the Dawn*, p. 116).

9 The twelve invited groups were: Fatah, PLO, PFLP, Palestine Liberation Front, Vanguards of the War of Popular Liberation (Sa'iqa, see chapter 13), Palestine Liberation Front, Action Organization for the Support of the Palestinian Revolution, Redemption Vanguards, Palestinian Revolutionaries' Front, Popular Struggle Front, Road of Return, and Palestinian Revolutionary Youth. The Redemption Vanguards merged with Fatah later that year (October 1968), as did a number of other small organizations, such as the Palestine National Liberation Front and the Free Palestinians' Movement (both in September 1968).

10 The eight groups met on 18 January. (*Al-Kitab al-Sanawi* [*Fatah Yearbook*], Beirut, 1968, pp. 127–30.) Those which did not accept the invitation from Fatah were: PLO, PFLP, Popular Struggle Front, and Road of Return.

11 *Al-Nahar*, 17 March 1968; *al-Hayat*, 20 March 1968.

12 *Yawmiyyat Filastiniyya*, 23 April 1968.

Chapter 11: The 'Victory' of Karameh

1 MER, 1968, p. 370.

2 *Economist*, 1 March 1968; *Christian Science Monitor*, 8 March 1968.

3 *Al-Yawm*, 2 May 1968.

4 BBC, 24 March 1968.

5 MER, 1968, p. 367.

6 *Ibid.*, p. 369, from a special edition of *al-Thawra al-Filastiniyya* published in April 1968.

7 BBC, 25 March 1968.

8 'Most [of the guerrillas] fled, including Arafat, who commandeered a motorbike and escaped northeastwards to the town of Salt' (Kiernan, *op. cit.*, p. 218). That he left before the battle was attested (MER, 1968, p. 367, recording a report from Radio Kol Israel, 21 March; also BBC, 25 March 1967) by 'a captive member of Fatah', who 'later told a press conference in Tel Aviv that when the pamphlets were dropped, "Arafat and his deputy in Karameh, Abu Ali al-Maydani, distributed arms, told the men they should fight, and they themselves fled."' Certainly Arafat was not found in the town. The Fatah member's story that he fled before the battle is, however, contradicted by Abu Iyad (see note 9 below), and el-Rayyes and Nahas, *op. cit.*, p. 136: 'Arafat combines undoubted personal courage with the utmost prudence in regard to his personal security. . . . He personally conducted the battle at Karameh.'

9 Abu Iyad, *op. cit.*, pp. 98–9. He says that three others, including Arafat and Qaddoumi, also stayed to fight, while the rest of the leaders retreated for safety. Fatah accused the PFLP (see chapter 13) of 'withdrawing from the battlefield, although it was supposed to defend the northern part of Karameh'. (*What is the PLO?*, citing Fatah, *al-Wahda al-Wataniyya* [*National Unity*], 21 May 1968.)

10 Herzog, *op. cit.*, p. 205.

11 MER, 1968, pp. 367, 368. There were twenty-eight funerals in Israel for soldiers killed in the engagement. Israel is too small, too intimate and too open a society for deaths in action to be concealed.

12 Radio Amman, 21 March 1968; MER, 1968, p. 369.

13 *Al-Thawra al-Filastiniyya* (MER, 1968, p. 369): 'In Karameh itself . . . 400 Israeli troops killed or wounded', and 'another 100' when the 'Israeli forces started their retreat over the Jordan bridges'.

14 Abu Iyad, *op. cit.*, p. 101.

15 *Akhir Sa'a*, 10 April 1968; *al-Anwar*, 11 April 1968; *al-Jumhuriyya*, 25 April 1968. The training of women was an innovation of the PFLP (see chapter 13).

16 *Akhir Sa'a*, 3 July 1968; Radio Baghdad, 30 June 1968.

17 BBC, 30 July 1969.

18 At a press conference on 23 March 1968. King Hussein was replying to a question as to whether *fedayeen* were among the dead at Karameh. His words were often misquoted as 'We are all *fedayeen*.' Abu Iyad relates how a crowd chanted this in response to a speech he made warning them of the King's intention to renew attacks on the *fedayeen* in 1971 (Abu Iyad, *op. cit.*, p. 151).

19 *Ha'aretz, 13 August 1968.*

20 *Al-Hawadith*, 28 June 1968.

21 MER, 1968, p. 352.

22 MER, 1969/70, p. 224.

23 Told to me by an officer of the military administration, and confirmed by others. According to Ehud Yaari (*Strike Terror*, p. 205), by the beginning of 1970, 90 per cent of Arab terrorism in Gaza was directed against Arab men and women employed by Israeli companies. On 2 December 1969 Radio Baghdad, Voice of Palestine, reported: 'Our revolutionaries within the occupied territories are killing all the treacherous agents, in order to eliminate all signs of co-operation with the Zionist occupier.'

24 *Daily Telegraph*, 29 March and 4 April 1968.

25 BBC, 1 June 1968.

26 *The Times*, 14 June 1968.

27 Radio Cairo, 14 and 15 October 1968.

28 MER, 1968, pp. 598–601.

29 *New York Times*, 3 November 1968.

30 Radio Cairo, 23 November 1968.

Chapter 12 : The *Fedayeen* Capture the PLO

1 Radio Cairo, 10 April 1968. Nasser waged a 'War of Attrition' for three years after the Six Day War. On 21 October 1967 the Israeli destroyer *Eilat* was sunk by Egyptian surface-to-air missiles. Artillery and commando attacks on Israeli positions followed. A ceasefire was achieved in August 1970, negotiated by US Secretary of State William Rogers. For the nature of the 'peace' and the 'Rogers Plan' see Herzog, *op. cit.*, pp. 219, 343.

2 Radio Cairo, 18 April 1968.
3 Radio Cairo, 23 July 1968.
4 *Yawmiyyat Filastiniyya*, 23 April and 30 May 1968.
5 The PFLP (see chapter 13). MER, 1968, p. 427.
6 Abu Iyad, *op. cit.*, p. 108.

Chapter 13 : Ideologies

1 These brief biographical details of Habash and the leaders of the other PLO groups, and the accounts of the ideologies of the groups and their formation, have been pieced together from a number of sources, some of which contradict each other. The information given derives from those sources which seem to me the most likely to be reliable. Some information came from personal informants; most came from books and periodicals. The books used were chiefly el-Rayyes and Nahas, *op. cit.*, Yodfat and Arnon-Ohanna, *PLO Strategy and Tactics*; Schiff & Rothstein, *Fedayeen*; Yaari, *op. cit.*; Laffin, *op. cit.*; MER.
2 According to some Arab sources (e.g. el-Rayyes and Nahas, *op. cit.*, p. 143), Jibril was born in Ramleh, in Mandate Palestine.
3 'There is no difference between Jordanians, Syrians and Lebanese. We are all part of one nation. It is only for political reasons that we carefully underline our Palestinian identity, because it is in the interest of the Arabs to encourage a separate Palestinian identity in contrast to Zionism. Yes, the existence of a separate Palestinian identity is there only for tactical reasons. The establishment of a Palestinian state is a new expedient to continue the fight against Zionism and for Arab unity.' (Zuhayr Muhsin, head of Sa'iqa, interview with James Dorsey for *Trouw*, 31 March 1977.)
4 This ALF view was expressed firmly, for instance, at a symposium of representatives of PLO organizations reported in *al-Anwar*, 8 and 15 March 1970.

Chapter 14 : Black September

1 MER, 1969/70, p. 801.
2 Radio Amman, 11 June 1970.
3 Christopher Dobson, *Black September*, p. 42.
4 Abu Iyad, *op. cit.*, p. 134.
5 Abu Iyad, *op. cit.*, p. 121. By his account, some *fedayeen* sought, and were granted, asylum in 'Cisjordan', that is the Israeli-occupied West Bank. Israeli accounts confirm that this happened. Samuel Katz (*Battleground*, p. 157) noted: 'Some of the terrorists now grasped the ironic reality of which they were the victims and swiftly made a choice. They set out westward to seek sanctuary among the only people whose practical compassion and reasonable humanity they could trust. Every day for a week groups of Fatah called out from the East Bank of the Jordan to Israel Army patrols and were enabled to cross the river and surrender. About a hundred

succeeded. Many others were not so fortunate. Alerted Jordanian Arab Legion units intercepted them on their way to the river, and shot them down.'

6 Abu Iyad, *op. cit.*, p. 149.

7 Radio Amman, 2 May 1971.

8 Radio Cairo, Voice of Palestine, 3 July 1971.

9 Abu Iyad, *op. cit.*, p. 152.

10 *Ibid.*, pp. 152, 153.

11 *Ibid.*, p. 155.

12 *The Times*, 29 November 1971.

13 *Ibid.*

14 *New York Times*, 12 December 1971.

Chapter 15: The Covenant

1 Wherever the phrase 'liberation of Palestine' is used, the annihilation of Israel is meant, as the document makes insistently clear. The phrase 'Zionist occupation' implies a temporary and illegitimate presence, which the Covenant condemns to extinction. The 'struggle' is the struggle to destroy Israel. The 'legitimate rights' of the Palestinians are defined as the right to return to their homes, to self-determination and sovereignty, that is in the whole of 'indivisible' Palestine; hence this phrase too implies the annihilation of Israel.

2 Y. Harkabi, in his indispensable exegesis *The Palestinian Covenant and its Meaning* (pp. 9–10), quotes Shuqairy's own words on how he set about writing it: 'Firstly, I started by laying down the Palestinian entity on paper, like the engineer who traces the plan of a building with all its foundations, details and measurements. I wrote, altered, erased and changed the order of the articles until I formulated the "National Covenant" and the "Fundamental Law" [or PLO Constitution, see Appendix II] of the Palestine Liberation Organization. I invested all my experience of the Palestinian problem, both on the Arab and international planes, in their composition, taking into consideration the circumstances under which the Palestinian people were living. More than once I spent two or three nights over one single word or phrase, as I was facing generations of Palestinians who read between the lines more than they read the lines themselves' (Ahmad Shuqairy, *op. cit.*).

3 Only conquest by violence would satisfy the emotional thirst for vengeance. The Covenant, in its 1968 version, attempted to reconcile the irreconcilable aims of diverse factions. It is a programme and a manifesto, but also a description of wishes, hopes and dreams; an attempt to make a new world nearer to the heart's desire by wording it into existence. Against the charge of impracticality stood the determination to use force. The world, the very nature of reality, would be compelled to change by armed struggle, and such a struggle could indeed be nothing less than total revolution, a transformation, a profane miracle.

4 Article 11 of the resolutions of the thirteenth Palestine National Congress 1977 states: 'The PNC has decided to continue to struggle to regain the national rights

of our people, in particular the rights of return, self-determination and establishing an independent state (*dawla*) on their national soil'. This prospective 'state' could be 'the indivisible state' on the whole of the claimed territory, or it could be a state established on a part only. Either meaning could be applied, whichever turned out to be the more useful. The same PNC resolved (Article 15) that the PLO claimed the right to participate independently in all conferences on the Palestinian issue, but only if their terms of reference were those of the UN Resolution 3236, not 242. (Resolution 3236, passed 22 November 1974, soon after Arafat's appearance at the UN, recognized the rights of the Palestinians to self-determination, national independence and sovereignty, and to return to their homes, and the right to gain this 'by all means'.) This PNC also confirmed its policy of 'no peace' with Israel, and 'no recognition' of her.

5 'When we speak of democracy, it must be clear that we do not mean liberal democracy according to the one man-one vote system. Our intention is a popular democracy. . . . Eventually it [the democratic state] will be an Arab state. . . . If the slogan of a Democratic State is only designed to reply to the contention that we aim to throw the Jews into the sea, then it is a successful slogan and an effective political and propaganda tool, but if we wish it as the final strategic aim . . . then I am convinced that it demands continued consideration' (Shafiq al-Hout, speaking at a symposium reported in *al-Anwar*, 8 March 1970; translation, Yodfat and Arnon-Ohanna, *op. cit.*, p. 155).

6 A spokesman for Sa'iqa: 'I was among those who thought five years ago that we must slaughter the Jews. But now I cannot imagine that, if we win one night, it will be possible for us to slaughter them, or even one tenth of them . . . . What do we wish to do with these Jews? . . . I think that many Jews, among those living in Palestine, especially the Arab Jews, there is a great desire to return to their countries of origin, since the Zionist efforts to transform them into a homogeneous, cohesive nation have failed. . . . We cannot imagine how it is possible to solve the problem of these Jews without permitting them to dwell either in Palestine or in another homeland they choose. My estimation is that many of them will choose to live outside Palestine, for Palestine will not be able to absorb all the Palestinians, as well as the Jews living there.' (*Al-Anwar*, 8 March 1970; translation Y. Harkabi, *Palestine and Israel*, p. 91.)

7 'We did not use the slogan for the establishment of a secular state. . . . I am certain . . . that this is a distortion of the expression of democracy we proclaim' (Yasser Arafat, reported in *al-Jumhuriyya*, 6 January 1970). On the other hand, *al-Ahram* had reported earlier, 14 September 1969, that the PNC would debate the proposition that the democratic state of Palestine would be a 'secular and multisociety state'. Arafat remained personally committed to his nationalist (*wataniyya*) and Islamic beliefs, despite the potent socialist-internationalist dogma which emanated from the Marxist groups, whose leaders had Christian backgrounds and non-religious outlooks, and permeated PLO policy. In the light of these differences, trouble could be seen ahead, when the state of Palestine should come into existence. Would it or would it not be an Islamic state? (Even the socialist Arab states, Iraq and Syria, declared themselves in their constitutions to be like all other Arab states, Islamic.) This was one of the points of potential conflict which a present preoccupation with the armed struggle served to obscure or postpone. When the nature of the future state had unavoidably to be considered, different solutions were proposed. The ALF obviated the question by denying that there would ever be a separate Palestinian state; and declaring 'in the unified Arab state, all minorities – confessional or other – will have equal rights' (*al-Anwar*, 8 March 1970). The view of the ALF was that 'Palestine is part of a homeland and not a homeland in itself' (*ibid.*).

An important feature of the Covenant is its attempt to define the relationship between Palestinian and Arab national identity; to take cognizance of such questions as: Are the Palestinians a separate nationality from other Arabs? If they are not, why must they have their own 'homeland'? If they are, what is the geographical territory to which they lay claim? If the Mandate defines Palestine, and Palestine provides the definition of a Palestinian, were not the Jews who lived there during the Mandate also Palestinian? What relationship should exist between the Palestinians and other Arab states? Over half the Articles of the 1968 Covenant grapple with this problem of Palestinian and Arab national identities (1, 4–8, 10–15, 21, 22, 26–29). The answer, however, is not found. For instance: 'The Palestinian identity is a genuine, essential and inherent characteristic . . . transmitted from parents to children' (Article 4); 'Palestine . . . is an indivisible part of the Arab homeland, and the Palestinian people are an integral part of the Arab nation' (Article 1); but Palestine can only be defined by 'the boundaries it had during the British Mandate' (Article 2). It is to be noted that this definition arguably embraces the Hashemite Kingdom of Jordan.

Chapter 16: A State of Precarious Order

1 Vocke, *The Lebanese War*, p. 16.
2 In Lebanon even the women are enfranchised. The only other country in the Middle East where Arab women vote is Israel. In Jordan, which held parliamentary elections before 1967, women never voted in practice, although they had a constitutional right to do so.
3 Algeria, Egypt, Iraq, Jordan, Kuwait, Libya, Morocco, Tunisia and the United Arab Emirates all have articles in their constitutions which declare that Islam is the religion of the State. Article 3 of the Syrian constitution of 12 March 1973 reads: 'Islamic jurisprudence is the chief source for legislation.'
4 The Christian sect of the Maronites derive their name from St Maron, a Syrian hermit who lived at the turn of the fifth century. The Maronites were monothelites: they believed that Jesus, though having two natures, both divine and human, had one will only, which was divine. The sect was persecuted and found shelter in Mount Lebanon. In the late seventh century, under St John Maron, they defended themselves successfully against an invading Byzantine army. In the twelfth century, during the crusades, the sect was affiliated with Rome, although monothelitism was a 'diabolical error', in the words of Jacques de Vitu, then Bishop of Acre. In the sixteenth century the Maronite Church formalized its union with the

Holy Roman Church, retaining its own head, the patriarch of Antioch, under the Pope.

5 The religion of the Druze, or Muwahhidin, is a form of gnosticism. Like the gnostic cults which emerged in Asia Minor early in our common era, it had its roots in the Hermetic cults of ancient Egypt and the Oriental beliefs in hierarchical demi-urges or emanations of the Godhead, one of which, the believers held, created the natural world. The Druze sect itself had its beginnings in the eleventh century, when the Fatimite Caliph Hakim's vizier, Hamza, sent a missionary from Egypt where the Caliph reigned, to Syria to preach that Hakim was an incarnation of God, and Hamza was the creating spirit which emanated from that divinity. The missionary's name was Neshkateen Darazi. He won over a tribe which had come to Mount Lebanon some two centuries earlier, and established himself with a group of disciples at Wadi al-Tim, in the Beqaa. Proud of the esteem in which he was held, he became very grand in his manner, and proclaimed himself head of the sect he had formed. It is rumoured that he attracted converts because the mysteries he preached enjoined practices of physical voluptuousness, lewd and atrocious. (If so, the disciples did only as many other gnostics did. Another point of similarity among many such cults is the division of the faithful into a small enlightened elite and a generality, who remained uninitiated into the most secret rites. This custom prevails among the Druze.) When the news of Darazi's vainglorious self-promotion reached the ears of Hamza, the vizier denounced him, branded him with the name of the 'the Calf', and ordered his assassination by some of Darazi's own followers at Wadi al-Tim. Then, to replace him, Hamza sent Mohtana Baha al-Din, who retaught the proselytes the uncorrupted creed; but the preaching of Darazi's doctrine went on, and the result was a schism. The greater number of the believers followed Baha al-Din, yet curiously the name of both the sects remained the same, and it honours the lustful and licentious Darazi. After the death of Baha al-Din, the preaching of the creed stopped. Since then the religion can only be inherited, and its inner mysteries divulged only to those both born to it and chosen. When the Caliph Hakim died in 1025 CE, Hamza disappeared. Some believe that he will yet reappear, in China, where a hidden multitude of Druze await him; they will advance behind him to Lebanon as a mighty and invincible army which will conquer Mecca and, last of all, Jerusalem.

6 An English author recording these events in 1862 was carried away with indignation at the injustice. His anger was directed at Great Britain, Turkey, the Druze and their allies, and he sought to move the consciences of Christians in his native land: 'Christian readers! is not all this monstrous? is it not incredible? is it not heartless? is it not degrading to our common faith? is it not inhuman?' (Charles Henry Churchill, *The Druzes and the Maronites under Turkish Rule from 1840–1860*, p. 283.) The atrocities (of which no group was innocent), and the indifference with which the Christian powers regarded them, were the same a century later, in our own time. The notion, often expressed by Western politicians, that Lebanon was once, or yet could be, a peaceful land does not seem justified by its history and the enduring causes of its strife. Since 1943 what has been displayed at best is government by mutual suspicion in a country of uneasy truce.

7 David C. Gordon, *Lebanon: The Fragmented Nation*, p. 53.

8 *Ibid.*

9 *Ibid.*

Chapter 17: Brothers and Fratricides

1 Radio Beirut, 30 October 1968.

2 Radio Cairo, Voice of Palestine, 29 October 1968.

3 The National Covenant enshrined such a resolution, and it was often asserted by Arafat, as on Radio Damascus, Voice of Palestine, 28 October 1970: 'We recognize that the existence of a free and independent Lebanon is a necessity.' This was two years after clashing with the state security forces in Lebanon, and a month after the *fedayeen* attempt to take over the State of Jordan had been frustrated by force.

4 Radio Beirut, 29 December 1968.

5 *Al-Nahar*, 30 and 31 December 1968, Radio Beirut, 30 December 1968.

6 Debate on a vote of confidence in the government on 30 January, reported by Radio Beirut, 31 January 1969, and numerous Beirut papers.

7 Accounts of numbers of deaths vary. Israeli sources give the number as ten (MER, 1969/70, p. 905); el-Rayyes and Nahas (*op. cit.*, p. 103) give no precise number but assert that 'scores' were killed.

8 Vocke, *op. cit.*, p. 36; MER, 1969/70, p. 906.

9 Radio Beirut, 24 April 1969.

10 Radio Beirut, 24 April 1969.

11 Radio Baghdad, 25 April 1969; BBC, 28 April 1969.

12 *Ba'th*, 27 and 28 April 1969.

13 *Al-Hayat*, 2 July 1969; *al-Sayyad*, 3 July 1969; *al-Hawadith*, 11 July 1969; *al-Safa*, 13 July 1969.

14 Radio Beirut, 22 October 1969; *al-Difa'*, 22 October 1969; Radio Cairo, Voice of Palestine, 22 October 1969.

15 Radio Beirut, 22–24 October 1969; Radio Cairo, Voice of Palestine, 24 October 1969; Radio Cairo, Voice of Fatah, 25 October 1969; Radio Beirut, 29 and 30 October 1969; *al-Nahar*, 27 October 1969; MENA, 31 October and 2 November 1969.

16 Radio Beirut, 20 and 21 October 1969.

17 *Al-Nahar*, 27 October 1969.

18 Radio Damascus, 30 October 1969; BBC, 1 November 1969.

19 Radio Baghdad, 22 October 1969.

20 Radio Damascus, 21 October 1969.

21 Radio Algiers, 22 October 1969.

22 Radio Cairo, 25 October 1969.

23 Radio Cairo, 22 and 23 October 1969.

24 Radio Omdurman, 22 and 24 October 1969.

25 Radio Amman, 22 and 28 October 1969; Radio Beirut, 28 October 1969.

26 Radio Beirut, 23 October 1969.

27 *Al-Ahram*, 27 October 1969.

28 MENA, 27/28 October 1969.

29 *Al-Ahram* published the Cairo Agreement in part on 6 November 1969, and in full on 20 April 1970. The Lebanese authorities prosecuted the paper for publishing the 'secret' agreement. (MER, 1969/70, p. 919, full text.)

30 Radio Cairo, Voice of Palestine, 27 March 1970. See also Jumblatt, *I Speak for Lebanon*, in which he dilates on this theme.

31 MENA, 11 and 12 January 1970.

32 *Al-Hayat*, 29 March 1970.

33 MER, 1969/70, p. 215.

34 MER, 1969/70, p. 212.

35 Radio Beirut, 12 and 13 May 1970; MENA, 16 May 1970.

36 *Al-Nahar*, 15 May 1970; *al-Hayat*, 22 May 1970.

37 Radio Beirut, 22 May 1970; MENA, 23 May 1970.

38 *Jerusalem Post*, 25 May 1970.

39 In 1969 Lebanese newspapers openly accused Syria of infiltrating Lebanon with *fedayeen* groups aggressive to the Lebanese authorities; both Sa'iqa and Fatah were named (*al-Hawadtih*, 9 May 1969). President Atasi of Syria (in office until 1972) insisted that, although the *fedayeen* were trained in Syria and armed by Syria, Syria 'had no authority over them'. (*Kull Shay'*, 17 May 1969.) President Helou of Lebanon asked Nasser to intervene with Atasi to help solve his problems with Syria (*al-Jarida*, 3 May 1969). In September 1969 Camille Chamoun accused Syria of despatching 60,000 weapons to Kamal Jumblatt (*al-Hawadith*, 26 September 1969). In October President Helou complained directly to Atasi of Syrian support for *fedayeen* attacks on police stations in Lebanon along the Arafat Trail. During the clashes in Tripoli, leaflets carrying the Sa'iqa and Ba'th emblems were found; they called on the Lebanese to revolt (*al-Jarida*, 26 October 1969). An infiltrator arrested in October said that Syria aimed at overthrowing the existing regime in Lebanon (*al-Jarida*, 31 October 1969). A Lebanese official, according to the *New York Times* (14 November 1969), said that 'during the conflict with the *fedayeen*, Syria, in pursuit of more far-reaching goals than mere support of the commandos, tried to foster the leftists and progressives with the ultimate objective of eliminating the present Lebanese regime.' In May 1970 the Lebanese government met urgently to discuss reports of 3,000 to 4,000 Syrian soldiers, dressed as *fedayeen*, entering Lebanon (MENA, 14 May); and the next day the Syrian authorities declared that the armed men were *fedayeen*, and all Syria had done was to provide them with transport (*al-Muharrir*, 16 May 1969).

40 'Why is Syria getting embroiled in the events in Lebanon? . . . Historically, Syria and Lebanon are one people.' (Hafiz Assad, speech to the Council of District Governments, 20 July 1976.)

41 El-Rayyes and Nahas, *op. cit.*, p. 108.

Chapter 18: Power and Glory

1 Radio Amman, 15 March 1972.

2 From the draft programme of the PFLP, published in *al-Nahar*, 10 March 1974.

Another resolution was: 'To fuse our people's struggle with the fraternal Jordanian people's struggle in a Palestinian-Jordanian Liberation Front that will, in addition to its duties in the Palestinian arena, struggle for the establishment of a national [*wataniyya*] rule in Jordan.' The draft programme of the 'mainstream' PLO – Fatah, Sa'iqa and the PDFLP – was even more explicit about its intentions towards Jordan: 'To continue struggling together with the national masses and forces in Jordan to liquidate the agent Hashemite regime and renew Jordanian-Palestinian unity on national democratic bases' (translation, Yodfat and Arnon-Ohanna, *op. cit.*, pp. 168–9). The desire for vengeance against King Hussein was greater than against Israel (see Henry Kissinger, *Years of Upheaval*, p. 627). Colonel Qadhafi told King Faisal of Saudi Arabia in September 1970 that forces should be sent into Jordan from Iraq and Syria to fight King Hussein, because 'what Hussein is doing is worse than the Jews' (Mohamed Heikal. *The Road to Ramadan*, p. 100).

3 *Literaturnaya Gazeta*, 14 August 1974.

4 *Akhbar al-Yawm*, 2 November 1974.

5 Radio Cairo, 18 July 1974.

6 *Akhbar al-Yawm*, 2 November 1974 (translation, Yodfat and Arnon-Ohanna, *op. cit.*, pp. 176–9).

7 *Ibid.* (In 1965 Habib Bourguiba had proposed an acceptance of the 1947 UN partition resolution. He implied that acceptance of a part of the 'Palestinian homeland' could provide a base for attacking Israel and conquering the rest; which is to say, he was proposing political negotiation as a means to the acquisition of territory, and a 'stages' policy. He was taken to task for his proposal by other Arab leaders.)

8 Abu Iyad, *op. cit.*, pp. 224–5.

9 Amman TV, 30 October 1974; *Arab Report and Record*, 16–31 October 1974.

Chapter 19: An Example to the World

1 *The Times*, 29 September 1970.

2 See Dobson, *op. cit.*, pp. 78–84. Kozo Okamoto, the surviving terrorist, spoke of the collaboration of his group with the PFLP.

3 Claire Sterling, *The Terror Network*, pp. 125–6.

4 Dobson, *op. cit.*, pp. 80–1.

5 In 1982 a visitor from Japan sang songs to Okamoto, which, the prisoner roused himself to say, 'brought back his childhood', and apparently stirred a brief vitality in him.

6 Pope John Paul II was shot and wounded by Mehmet Ali Agca, who had come recently from Sofia, and named Bulgarians in Rome as his contacts.

7 Sterling, *op. cit.*, p. 273.

8 Dobson, *op. cit.*, pp. 88–9; *le Monde*, 27 March 1973.

9 Abu Iyad, *op. cit.*, pp. 167–76.

10 See Becker, *op. cit.*, pp. 219–20.

11 Abu Iyad, *op. cit.*, p. 179.

12 See Terence Prittie and W.H. Nelson, *The Economic War Against the Jews*, p. 29ff.

Chapter 20: The Spark

1 Jumblatt, *op. cit.*, pp. 67, 115–16.

2 Al-Mourabitoun means 'the people of the *ribat*'; a *ribat* is a fortified monastery where men were taught religion and the military arts. The name is ancient, and it is the Islamic connotations which make it interesting.

3 Kleilat was tried for the murder of Kamil Muruwwa, owner and publisher of the paper *al-Hayat*, on 16 May 1966, and acquitted. Maronites have told me that in their opinion the court was 'under Nasserite influence' and the verdict unjust.

4 The Kataeb Social Democratic Party is Lebanon's biggest political party. Its membership is almost entirely Maronite. There are even a small number of non-Christian members. *Kataeb* means 'legions'; and in French (the second language of Lebanon) it means *phalange*. To call the party 'Phalangist', as Western journalists do, is misleading, however, since the word has associations with the Spanish Falange Party of General Franco, whose own party is often – not quite accurately – called a fascist party. (It may well be for that very reason that it has been given the name by reporters whose sympathies lie with its opponents.) It is further alleged that its founder, Pierre Gemayel, modelled the original Kataeb, which was a youth movement started in 1936, on the Hitler Youth, after a visit to Germany. He did visit Germany, and other countries with youth and scout groups, in that decade blossoming with youth movements, and then came back and started his own. At no time did he, or any of his followers, adopt the Nazi ideology. (That was adopted by another group, the SSNP, an ally of the PLO.) The Kataeb became a political party in 1943. Its policy was, and is, a pluralistic democracy with universal suffrage, providing equal opportunities for every citizen regardless of religion. It favours a market economy, but has been the chief initiator of such small welfare provision as became statutory in Lebanon.

5 Militia of the National Liberal Party, the second largest party, founded in 1958 by Camille Chamoun. The Namur is commanded by the founder's son, Dany Chamoun. At times the NLP has actively fought against the Kataeb, as in the early months of 1980, but in April 1975 they were allied, and joined with a majority of other Christian political groups to form the 'Lebanese Resistance', and their militias joined under the name of the 'Lebanese Forces', with a united leadership created in August 1976. Bachir Gemayel, Pierre Gemayel's younger son, was President of the Council of Command.

6 The Tanzim ('The Organization') was founded as a secret Christian society in 1968. Its militia, under George Adwan, joined the united Lebanese Forces.

7 A small Christian militia which joined the united Lebanese Forces. Its members are dedicated to ridding Lebanon of all Palestinians, by force if necessary – and they believe it is necessary. They deny that the Maronites are Arab (as many members of the Kataeb also do). The cedar tree is the emblem of Lebanon, and to the Christians it is also a symbol of their particular traditions and ancient establishment in the Mountain.

8 The head of the Permanent Congress of the Lebanese Monastic Orders is one of the leaders who together form the 'Lebanese Front', the organization which controls the Lebanese Forces. Christian religious leaders, patriarchs and bishops, did

not officially ally Church institutions with the Lebanese Resistance, but many individual clerics and members of monastic orders actively assisted the Maronite alliance.

9 'During 1975 we were very short of guns, so we bought from the Palestinians, guns and ammunition, very cheaply. They had so much they didn't know what to do with it all. The chaps in charge of the stocks wanted to make some pocket-money. An RPG which I believe usually costs about $250 in Russia we bought for $25.' ('Maxim', spokesman for the Lebanese Forces, Kataeb).

10 Witnesses whom I spoke to in Beirut told me: the car was a grey Volkswagen; it was a red Renault; two small cars came along, one soon after the other (the intervals varying from account to account), and that these were both Volkswagens/Renaults/some other make of car/two different makes of car. The details are unimportant in themselves, so nobody was trying to mislead me; but the differences in the stories suggest that no testimony can be taken too trustingly. On the main points, however – that there were shootings and deaths, and that they occurred in the way described – all accounts agreed.

Chapter 21 : Carnival of Death

1 One witness among hundreds was Janet Wakim, the American wife of businessman and landowner George Wakim, of Mieh-Mieh near Sidon.

2 Lina M. Tabbara, *Survival in Beirut: A Diary of Civil War*, p. 121.

3 Gordon, *op. cit.*, p. 240.

4 Vocke, *op. cit.*, p. 42.

5 'A Sony tape recorder that used to cost 1,000 pounds is going for 10 pounds, gold Parker pens for 50p apiece, and a kilo can of *foie gras* for 5p. Only mayonnaise is selling for more than its usual price. The sight of the yellowish mixture intrigues those who've never seen the likes before.' (Tabbara, *op. cit.*, p. 76.) 'The prices for staple food and petrol have risen to 3 or 4 times what they were. The prices of "loot" have fallen: you can buy a gold Dunhill lighter, previously priced at $100 for $2, because the looter cannot imagine that something like that can cost $100. Silverware, carpets, chandeliers etc. are all virtually given away.' (*Der Spiegel*, 12 January 1976.)

6 It is often asserted that the PLO did not fight in the 'civil war' during 1975 after the opening round in April and early May. The Fatah leadership in particular claimed that their fighters, the 'mainstream', did not join in. This is untrue. Fatah, as well as the PFLP–GC, ALF and Sa'iqa, were actively engaged on the side of the Lebanese Left. Fatah men detained at Ansar detention camp by the Israelis in 1982 told me that they had fought in summer 1975. See also Vocke, *op cit.*, p. 41, and MECS, 1976/7, p. 504.

7 Jumblatt, *op. cit.*, p. 146. 'I admit, I myself often acted like a dilettante' (*ibid.*, p. 116). 'In Syria . . . the leadership proved incapable of the imaginative effort that a spirit of adventure demands' (*ibid.*, p. 18). 'Our revolutionary pragmatism and our calculated spirit of adventure may have made [the Soviet leaders] a little nervous' (*ibid.*, p. 21). On the other hand, 'we also had reason to regret the chaos created by the Palestinians and nearly all the other parties, the tendency to unbridled self-indulgence and looting. . . . The young people treated the battle as a game. . . . They had been perverted by ideology and the poor education they must have received from their families and school' (*ibid.*, p. 111). Jumblatt remains an enigmatic figure, full of contradictions: at once a millionaire, socialist, feudal lord, capitalist, Marxist, mystic; a pacifist and patriot, yet the adventuristic leader of rebellious factions in a civil war. Some saw him as a buffoon, some as a menace; as psychologically unbalanced, opportunistic, 'a merchant of the fantastic, a catastrophe for the Arabs'; and his own mother considered him abnormal (Gordon, *op. cit.*, pp. 156–7). He was 'sickened by this sewer of daily violence, by the bloody massacres' which he had, at least as much as any other individual, actively brought about. He was capable of taking a very distant and cool look at the cauldron which he heated and stirred: 'I dread the day when the Arabs will be finished (theoretically) with Israel. What bloody games, what internecine wars will they indulge in then?'

8 Later, when the Syrians came, many foreigners were found in the ranks of the PLO and the 'Islamo-Progressives'. *Der Spiegel* of 21 June 1976 records: 'The most fanatical of those still fighting are the foreign extremists caught in Beirut, with no chance of escape. Members of worldwide terrorism: Germans, Japanese, Somalis, Turks and Iranians.'

9 Father John Nasser, a flautist and organist, has given an account of a massacre of Christians in the Chouf village of Aichieh. Sixty-five people were locked in the church by PLO fighters and machine-gunned to death. Their killers then loaded trucks with loot from their houses and drove it away.

Chapter 22: Damour

1 These quotations are in the English words used by Father Labaky, when he told me what had happened in Damour. 'I tell you what I have seen and heard and touched,' he said.

2 Abu Iyad (*op. cit.*, p. 271) says that snipers in Damour had shot and killed innocent Lebanese and Palestinian passers-by. People from Damour emphatically deny that any passer-by was ever shot at. Abu Iyad also says that instructions were given not to harm the civilian population, but he adds: 'However, war is war, and when war is fought in a climate of exasperation, excesses were [sic] committed and innocent people were killed.' I asked the PLO representative in London for the Organization's account of the Damour attack, was promised a reply, but did not get one.

3 Soumayya Ghanimeh, her mother and her sister told me their story.

4 The targets were still to be seen after the Israelis took the ruined town from the PLO in 1982. The vehicles undergoing repair were reduced to burnt-out hulks in the course of the fighting.

Chapter 23: Syria Turns

1 Kissinger (*op. cit.*, p. 789) wrote an eloquent and sympathetic valediction for Lebanon: 'I think with sadness of these civilized men who in a turbulent part of the world had fashioned a democratic society based on genuine mutual respect of the religions. Their achievement did not survive. The passions sweeping the area were too powerful to be contained by subtle constitutional arrangements. As it had attempted in Jordan, the Palestinian movement wrecked the delicate balance of Lebanon's stability. Before the peace process could run its course, Lebanon was torn apart. Over its prostrate body at this writing all the factions and forces of the Middle East still chase their eternal dreams and act out their perennial nightmares.'

2 Radio Beirut, 23 January 1977. The following August the Christians formally asked the Arab League to distribute the Palestinians in member-states.

3 Jumblatt, *op. cit.*, p. 95.

4 Jumblatt, *op. cit.*, p. 113. 'We bought our weapons ourselves. . . . They merely passed through Syria. . . . The Syrians were actually holding up deliveries of the weapons and munitions stockpiled on our behalf in Syria. It was a way of exercising indirect pressure on us, of manipulating us. . . . We had to insist very vehemently to get the blockade lifted' (*ibid.*, p. 81).

5 Gordon, *op. cit.*, p. 252.

6 Jumblatt, *op. cit.*, pp. 113–14. 'We were amazed at the Syrian government's volte-face. It seemed the epitome of illogicality.' (*Ibid.*, p. 109.)

7 Abu Iyad, *op. cit.*, pp. 281–2.

Chapter 24: Tall al-Za'tar

1 One of the nuns, Sister Emilie, described to me in detail how the hospital was seized and occupied by PLO fighters, and how they tried to keep the nuns, the mothers and the babies as hostages. One of the PLO fighters fainted the first time he fired his Kalashnikov at the enemy. Sister Emilie revived him and handed back to him a plastic carrier-bag he had dropped as he fell. Only then she saw, too late to take the bag away, that it was full of hand-grenades.

2 Abu Iyad (*op. cit.*, p. 289) says there were 20,000 Palestinian refugees and 15,000 Lebanese Muslims in Tall al-Za'tar in June 1976.

3 Lebanese Forces Intelligence.

4 Tabbara, *op. cit.*, p. 154. Tabbara asked Abu Iyad why the high command had done nothing for the Palestinians in Tall al-Za'tar when they were being massacred, and he replied: 'You're looking at all this a little romantically. There was no other way we could have acted. If we hadn't remained neutral at that point we would just have speeded up our own defeat.'

5 Tabbara, *op. cit.*, p. 137.

6 *Ibid.*; also John Bulloch, *Death of a Country*, p. 174ff.

7 'They are putting those in unbearable agony out of their misery.' (Tabbara, *op. cit.*, p. 138.)

8 Bulloch, *op. cit.*, p. 177.

9 *Ibid.*, p. 180.

10 Pierre Malychef, officer of the Lebanese Forces, in conversation with me. Some captives were killed in cold blood. 'A group of ten Palestinian nurses was stopped by NLP men [National Liberal Party], lined up and shot.' (Bulloch, *op. cit.*, p. 181.)

11 Bulloch, *op. cit.*, pp. 181–2.

Chapter 25: The Good Fence

1 Vocke, *op. cit.*, pp. 58–60.

2 Joseph G.Chami, *Days of Tragedy: Lebanon 1975–6*. Accounts of numbers vary quite widely: 44,000 dead (Bulloch, *op. cit.*, p. 184); 32,000 dead, 1 million evacuees in Syria alone, of which half were Syrian migrant workers returned home, the others Lebanese with about 150,000 Palestinians (Gordon, *op. cit.*, p. 252).

3 Francis Rizek gave me his account of these events in August 1982.

4 By mid-1980, 7,603 Lebanese were employed in Israel. In the month of July 1980, 3,800 Lebanese came through the Good Fence to visit relatives in Israel, and 3,188 to receive medical attention. They bought US $700,000 worth of goods in Israel. 'The 100,000 residents of "Free Lebanon" (60 per cent Muslims and 40 per cent Christians) enjoyed a measure of economic prosperity. Military aid, including maintenance services, was provided by Israel, which also paid the salaries of Haddad's men. Despite his obvious dependence on Israeli assistance . . . Haddad repeatedly stated that he was not subject to Israeli control – as Israel also frequently affirmed. . . . He was prepared "to take advice, but orders we will take from no state, be it Israel or any other state".' (MECS, 1979/80, p. 150.)

Chapter 26: Under PLO Rule

1 *New York Times*, 15 July 1983. Rima Shabb, wife of Dr Ramsey Shabb of Sidon, in interview with David K.Shipler; confirmed to me by Dr Shabb.

2 This was told to me by numerous shopkeepers, plantation owners and professional men and women. One was Dr Ramsey Shabb (in conversation with me personally, and in an interview with David K.Shipler for the *New York Times*, 15 July 1982). Another was Sharafeddin Ali, a Shi'a plantation owner, businessman and free-marketeer (an admirer of Adam Smith and Milton Friedman). One of the houses on his plantation has been occupied by militiamen of the PLO ally, Ahmad al-Khatib. Mr Ali, who has businesses in Senegal as well as Lebanon, had to stay in Lebanon during the years of war, and visit his plantation constantly, knowing that if he did not his produce would be taken by al-Khatib and the PLO militias. He told me that he welcomed the intervention of the Israelis in 1983; that the PLO had destroyed his country; that what had happened in Lebanon was not a civil war but an invasion by the PLO and Syria. He wanted Lebanon to be modernized and

Westernized, and to have trading relations with Israel. He strongly supported Bachir Gemayel in his bid for the presidency, and had high hopes that Bachir, young as he was, would unite the country.

3 This was particularly stressed by the PDFLP. See, for example, el-Rayyes and Nahas, *op. cit.*, p. 44.

4 These election clashes were in addition to the outright battles fought frequently between the groups, in which many Palestinian civilians died. In *The 22nd of February*, the PDFLP's tenth anniversary publication in 1979, the organization shows concern for this danger: 'The militia' [of the PDFLP] will take care not to shed Palestinian blood, as happens in the revolutionary forces as a result of the armed clashes between their various groups.'

5 I have selected these stories told to me by Palestinians because they are typical. The names of my informants are given only when they have given me permission to do so, and are of an age to understand the risks involved; and, in some cases, when they have already exposed themselves to publicity in a newspaper or on television or radio. I tape-recorded the stories.

6 The West German television company ZDF made a documentary film in 1982 on Azmi Zrayir's regime in Tyre. The film shows an interview with the mother of a boy wanted by Zrayir for his football team. She described how he was marched off from her house by two of Zrayir's men, and said that she never saw him alive again. Others in the same film described how they were robbed and beaten. One man had built a house and four repair garages, all of which were seized by Zrayir, without compensation. Another man, Habib Jarin, who was willing to be named, had both his arms, both his legs and his jaw broken by Zrayir's men, and has remained a cripple.

7 For the battle in the cathedral and the breaking into the bank, reporters found the evidence of bodies, broken walls and missing bullion. The only evidence for the further desecration of the church by copulation with prostitutes was hearsay, which might have been based on the boasts of Zrayir and his men, or the confessions of the prostitutes; there were of course no objective eyewitnesses.

8 *New York Times*, 25 July 1982.

9 This appears on a page of the same book in which the poems were written (see note 12 below). The prose is in the same handwriting as the poems.

10 'The resistance movement wants to take charge of all the orphans of the massacres and to raise them in the spirit of the Palestinian revolution, making *fedayeen* material out of them as early as possible. . . . The thousands of abandoned children we can see playing in front of us [in a PLO orphanage] will have no other future but that of arms – which some of them already know how to use.' (Tabbara, *op. cit.*, pp. 151–2.)

11 I cannot know when the mattress was soaked with blood, or when the Stars of David were drawn on the walls. I cannot even be sure that the Stars were drawn with blood, only that that is how they looked. When I saw the room it was badly damaged after it had been bombed some six weeks earlier. Its walls partly stood; it had no ceiling and was open to the sky; most of the furniture was overturned, though not the bed which stood in one corner with the mattress in place. The stains on the mattress might have come from the body of someone who was lying on the bed when the bomb hit the building.

12 I found the hard-covered exercise book in which Lufti Ali had written his poems in the rubble on the floor of the interrogation room. In the drawer of an overturned desk I found printed interrogation forms and punctiliously-kept account books. Lufti Ali's name is written in books and on documents. On some pages he inscribed 'Fatah' in decorative writing.

13 'While searching a citizen of the town, the PLO found on him Israeli money and a pair of shoes made in Israel. . . . His hands and legs were chained to the fenders of four vehicles. When a Fatah officer signalled with his pistol, the four cars raced away, tearing his body apart while the horrified spectators screamed. The cars raced through the streets with the bloody limbs dangling. People fainted.' (Salah Shafro, Mukhtar of Burj-Bachel near Sidon, quoted in *Maariv*, 16 July 1982.)

14 Frank Gervasi in the *Los Angeles Herald Examiner*, 13 July 1982.

15 Even infants are to be seen with missing fingers and hands. For details about the mutilation of children and their sufferings in the civil war, see *The Issue of Lebanon* (a Lebanese Forces publication), especially pp. 113, 117. Children of all confessional groups suffered severely.

Chapter 27: PLO Welfare

1 From its inception, the PLO was financed chiefly by grants in aid (see Appendix II, The Constitution of the PLO). At the Baghdad summit of 1978, the Arab oil-producing states agreed to provide US$3.5 billion per annum in aid to the 'frontline states' for ten years, of which a total of $300 million per annum was to go to the PLO (*Middle East Economic Survey*, 23 October 1978). Major expenditure was on arms, wages of fighters and their families, and representation abroad. (In June 1982 the Israelis captured 1,320 military vehicles including several hundred tanks; over 33,000 small arms; 1,352 anti-tank weapons; 215 mortars; 62 Katyusha rocket launchers; 82 field artillery pieces; 196 anti-aircraft weapons; and 5,630 tons of ammunition. The price of a Kalashnikov was about US$870; Russian tanks, US$100,000 for the T.34, US$350,000 for the T.55, and $550,000 for the T.62, but the Soviet Union adjusts prices according to who the client is, and the PLO was a favoured client.) The Libyan government 'delayed' paying its contributions of 16 per cent of the total, US$44.7 million, to the PLO. (It is interesting to note that Saudi Arabia's minimum guaranteed contribution, about $85 million, represented a little over half of one day's oil revenues. The Saudis gave more than they guaranteed, but it is unlikely that additional sums brought the total much beyond eighteen-hours' worth of their annual oil production. A very small fraction of the Gulf states' oil revenues could resettle the Palestinian camp-dwellers. Saudi Arabia has a shortage of population for its labour needs.) There was strong resentment among the lower ranks of PLO officials when they discovered how their leaders were enriching themselves. Among others, a Sa'iqa officer, Mohammad Issa Abdul Ghawry, known as Abu Tarek, expressed this view to me in late August 1982. Among the leaders he named were Zuhayr Muhsin and Azmi Zrayir, both dead by that time, and Haj Isma'il, the Fatah commander driven out of Sidon; but he said that the blame lay with Arafat: 'In my opinion the one who betrayed the revolution was the big one. Abu Ammar [Yasser Arafat], because the person who is responsible should know what is right.'

2 *The 22nd of February*, 1979.

3 Dr Zvi Lanir in the *Jerusalem Post*, 13 August 1982. Confirmed to me by Palestinians in Rachadiyyah camp.

4 *The 22nd of February*, 1979.

5 See note 6, chapter 28.

6 *The 22nd of February*, 1979.

7 From 1948 to May 1950, the United States donated half the money for the relief aid of the refugees. In 1981 – a year which indicates fairly the proportion of the burden shared by United Nations members through UNRWA – the USA contributed $462 million, 32 per cent; the European community, 13 per cent; Japan, Sweden and Britain (in addition to her contribution through the European Community), in that order of generosity, gave between $10 and 11 million each, their contributions taken together amounting to 16 per cent of the total budget. West Germany gave over $5 million. Austria, whose (Jewish) Chancellor Kreisky declared much sympathy for the Palestinians, less than $200,000. Greece, whose Prime Minister Papandreou is known to be a PLO sympathizer, $35,000. Turkey and Nigeria gave $20,000 each. Saudi Arabia gave over $6 million; Kuwait, the richest country in the world in per capita income, just over $1 million. By comparison and proportionately, impecunious Israel was far more generous with just under half a million dollars. Libya gave $4.25 million, Iraq $3.5 million. Lebanon gave close to $63,000; Syria $168,000; the United Arab Emirates $800,000; Yemen $2,000. The Holy See gave $12,500. The only Communist countries to give anything at all were Romania, $3,300; Yugoslavia, $25,000; and China, $3,500. (For the complete list see the UNRWA 1982 report issued by the United Nations.)

8 These laws applied to all Palestinians, not just the camp-dwellers, from 1948 until the coming of the PLO in 1968 (after which many changes were brought about by the Organization). For example: they had to carry distinctive black-and-white identity cards; they could not buy houses, land or business premises; they could not put concrete roofs on the houses they built in the camps; they could not be the main shareholders or sole directors of companies; they had to buy special licences in order to practise the various professions; they could not have ordinary passports, and such travel documents as the Lebanese government issued to them had to be renewed annually.

9 I saw a leper in an advanced stage of the disease in Rachadiyyah camp in August 1982.

10 'The camps were hotbeds of hatred for Israel and for the United States as well. Hatred was taught in the UN-sponsored schools; books paid for with American money were filled with anti-Semitism. One such book, a history text for third-year junior high school, contained a line that might have come out of a German textbook in the 1940s: "The Jews in Europe were persecuted and despised because of their corruption, meanness and treachery."' (Demaris, *op. cit.*, p. 117.)

11 Johan I. Holm, of the College of Bryne, in a letter to the *Jerusalem Post*, 18 July 1982.

12 UNRWA employed 9,700 Palestinians in 1977.

13 *The 22nd of February*, 1979.

14 'An instructor gave an order and a boy reached into the basket and pulled out a chicken. Then . . . he wrung its neck and dropped the dead bird. "No, no, no!" Arafat said reprovingly. He too reached into the basket and dragged out a chicken. And without wringing its neck he pulled the thing apart.' (Laffin, *The PLO Connections*, p. 8.) I have seen captured PLO archive film showing the pulling apart of live chickens by trainees.

15 *The 22nd of February*, 1979.

16 *New Outlook*, December 1981.

17 *Ibid.*

18 'PLO Ltd', in *Jerusalem Post*, 6 August 1982. The information supplied by Ibrahim Ghaddar, brother of Muhammad Ghaddar, leader of the Shi'a militia, al-Amal, in South Lebanon.

19 *New Outlook*, December 1981.

20 *The 22nd of February*, 1979.

21 *The Other Face of Palestinian Resistance*, PLO London Office.

22 *Maariv*, 16 July 1982.

23 Frank Gervasi in the *Los Angeles Herald Examiner*, 13 July 1982.

24 I was told about this by Christians in Sidon in August and September 1982, and again in January and February 1983. Israeli journalists – for example Aharon Dolev, who reported in *Maariv*, 16 July 1982 – were told the same thing. As far as I can discover, the accusation has not been proved. A British doctor has informed me that it is not uncommon for blood to be taken from the newly dead for blood banks, especially in time of war, and that the Russian army did so regularly in the Second World War.

25 The friend of Susan S – who told me her story is Janet Wakim, a Baptist from Kentucky married to a Lebanese Presbyterian, George Wakim. His family owns the land on which Mieh-Mieh Palestinian camp was established on the mountain above Sidon. The family was not able to enter their own manor house, or harvest their olives, from 1948 until the Israelis took Sidon from the PLO in 1982. In 1983 the Wakim family sued the Lebanese State for handing their property over to UNRWA without paying them compensation. The court's finding was in their favour and compensation was awarded.

Chapter 28: Information and Propaganda

1 Steven Emerson in the *New Republic*, 19 May 1982.

2 *Ibid.* The universities named are Duke, the University of Colorado (the International Center for Energy and Economic Development), and John Hopkins (School of Advanced International Studies).

3 The would-be visitor to Saudi Arabia has to produce a No Objection Certificate signed by a clergyman to prove that he is a Christian when he applies for a visa. Apparently the Saudis object to dealing with Jews as such, not only with 'Israelis' or 'Zionists'. For a full account of the economic war against the Jews, see Prittie and Nelson, *op. cit.*

4 The World Islamic League was set up in 1939 by the Grand Mufti, Haj Amin al-Husseini, with its headquarters in Beirut. For newspaper accounts of this spate of anti-Semitic communications sent to Britons by the WIL, see *New Life* (British Asian weekly), 7 August 1981; *Jewish Chronicle*, 17 July 1981; *Daily Mirror*, 28 July 1981.

5 'It is generally believed that Col. Gaddafi sponsors the WRP. A rival Trotskyist paper referred to: "the fact that the WRP is widely believed to be in receipt of subsidies from Gaddafi and possibly other Arab governments".' (*The Agitators*, the Economic League Central Council, 1981.)

6 A sample: 'Zionism, Women and Israel', in *London Labour Briefing*, April 1983, which seems to be saying that Jewish women in Israel are oppressed, but carries no convincing evidence for such a thesis. On the subject of the position of women in the Arab world, an interesting short exposition is to be found in Laffin's *The Dagger of Islam*, chapter 13, 'Islam Judged by its Women'. UNESCO figures for 1970 showed that 85 per cent of Arab women in the Arab states were illiterate, as against 65.5 per cent of Arab men. In Israel there is free universal education for girls and boys, Arab and Jewish.

7 *New Worker*, 15 July 1983.

8 See David P. Moynihan, *A Dangerous Place*, pp. 182–3.

9 *Ibid.*, p. 185.

10 I found this document in the rubble of the bombed PLO prison in Sidon, in August 1982.

11 Kenneth R. Timmerman, 'How the PLO Terrorized Journalists in New York', in *Commentary*, January 1983. Also Frank Gervasi, 'Media Coverage; The War in Lebanon'.

12 Frank Gervasi, *op. cit.*, p. 14.

13 *New Republic*, 10 March 1982.

14 *Daily Telegraph*, 15 July 1981.

15 On Toolan, Pfeffer, Debussman; Kenneth R. Timmerman, in *Commentary*, January 1983; also Frank Gervasi, *op. cit.*

16 'For most of us Lebanese, the Israeli invasion has been long overdue. Having failed politically and diplomatically to rid Lebanon of Syrian and Palestinian occupation, we became more and more convinced that Lebanon could only be freed by military action.' (Dany Chamoun, at a press conference in New York, 22 July 1982.) See also article by Robert Fisk in *The Times*, 2 March 1983, a belated discovery that at least some Lebanese saw the Israelis as liberators. I witnessed the welcoming of the Israelis, and was told by Muslims as well as Christians that they had wished the Israelis to come and drive the PLO and Syria out of Lebanon; after which they would want the Israelis to leave too. Citizens of Marja'yun told me they had stood together cheering when the Israelis bombed Beaufort to 'soften up' the target before the infantry took it.

When the Israelis withdrew southwards from the Beirut area early in September

1983, crowds lined their route to throw flowers into their vehicles, and many wept (ITN 10 pm News, 4 September 1983). At that time some 150,000 refugees moved south in order to stay under Israeli protection, as the Syrian-backed militias and PLA units advanced on Beirut against the resistance of the Lebanese army and the multinational force (*The Standard*, 5 September 1983). Many Western news media reported how the Lebanese and the Western powers regretted the Israeli withdrawal, without attempting to reconcile this information with their antagonistic reports of the Israeli intervention a year earlier.

17 For discussion and analysis of the news-reporting of Israel's intervention in Lebanon in the summer of 1982, how the facts were distorted, by whom, and with what probable intentions, see: Norman Podhoretz, 'J'accuse', in *Commentary*, September 1982; Edward Alexander, 'The Journalists' War against Israel, Techniques of Distortion, Disorientation and Disinformation', in *Encounter*, September 1982; Joshua Muvarchik, 'Misreporting Lebanon', in *Policy Review No. 23*, Winter 1983; Frank Gervasi, *op. cit.* Other articles of interest on the subject are: Pearl Sheffey Gefen, 'The Big Lebanese Lie' (interview with Colonel Trevor N. Dupuy), in the *Jerusalem Post International*, 6 November 1982; George F. Will, 'Mideast Truth and Falsehood', in *Newsweek*, 2 August 1982; Edward Luttwak, 'Playing the Numbers Game', in the *New York Times*, 18 July 1982, which is about the PLO exaggerations of numbers killed or displaced by the Israelis, as issued by Dr Fathi Arafat of the Palestinian Red Crescent and published by most leading newspapers, and later retracted by some. Among the small minority of journalists in Britain who opposed the general misreporting were Conor Cruise O'Brien in the *Observer* and Paul Johnson in the *Spectator*. Annie Kriegel, in her book, *Israel, est-il coupable?*, examined the reasons for prevailing attitudes in France. A Dutch journalist, Eva Kellerman, refused her editor's demand that she send despatches confirming what other reporters were saying, and continued to report what she herself saw, though fearing he would dismiss her; instead, he soon came to believe she was telling the truth.

18 *Commentary*, January 1983.

Chapter 29: Arafat's Diary

1 'The Palestinian Red Crescent is an organization which offers medical aid to Palestinians injured in conflicts in the Middle East, especially in Lebanon. The delegates of the ICRC co-operate with it on a practical and purely humanitarian basis' – from a letter to me from the head of National Societies and Principles Division of the International Red Cross Society.

2 See note 16, chapter 33, concerning the IRA and the PLO, and the text referred to.

3 See note 8, chapter 33, concerning the Basque terrorists and the PLO, and the text referred to.

4 See note 12, chapter 33, concerning the Red Brigades and the PLO, and the text referred to.

Chapter 30: Foreign Affairs

1 The Imam flew to Libya in August 1978, and was reported to have left on a flight to Italy, but the plane arrived without him. For a while, according to Lebanese Forces Intelligence, he was guarded in the fortress by Palestinians. Shi'a Muslims of Lebanon petitioned Israeli military authorities in July 1983 to free him from Colonel Qadhafi and return him to Lebanon: they were unconvinced by the Israelis' reply that it was not in their power to do so.

2 Voice of Palestine (Lebanon), 10 December 1979.

3 Yodfat and Arnon-Ohanna, *op. cit.*, p. 120.

4 *Al-Tha'ir al-Arabi* (the official organ of the Arab Liberation Front), e.g. No. 18, 30 April 1982, pp. 36–7: the ALF complains of the Ayatollah Khomeini's executions, and that 'some of the parties which had an interest in change and struggled hard to overthrow the Shah find now that the present regime, after three years, has changed nothing'. The antagonistic attitude of the ALF was to be expected, as Iraq had been at war with Iran since September 1980. Sa'iqa was friendly to the Ayatollah, as Syria supported Iran.

5 Eileen Scully, report for the Heritage Foundation, Washington DC, 2 August 1983.

6 *Jewish Chronicle*, 27 May 1983.

7 Voice of Palestine (Lebanon), 30 January 1980; Radio Riydh, 3 February 1980; *Monday Morning*, 25 February–2 March 1980.

8 Head of the PLO mission in Peking, 1972 (quoted in Yodfat and Arnon-Ohanna, *op. cit.*, p. 79). Arafat himself once said, to stress that he was not aligned ideologically to the Marxists or the anti-Marxists, 'I take money from Saudi Arabia to buy arms from China.' (*Al-Sayyad*, 23 January 1969.)

9 Heikel, *op. cit.*, p. 82. Arafat saw Kyril Mazurov, who was responsible for national liberation movements.

10 Yodfat and Arnon-Ohanna, *op. cit.*, p. 85. For full accounts of the development of relations between the USSR and the PLO, see Galia Golan, *The Soviet Union and the Palestine Liberation Organization: An Uneasy Alliance*; and Roberta Goren, 'The Soviet Attitude and Policy to International Terrorism since 1917'.

11 Yodfat and Arnon-Ohanna, *op. cit.*, p. 95.

12 Moynihan, *op. cit.*, p. 170.

13 David Ignatius (*Wall Street Journal*, 10 February 1983) claims that there *was* a result of the meeting between General Walters and the PLO representative: an intimate and surreptitious association with Ali Hassan Salamah, known as Abu Hassan and also as 'The Red Prince'. He was trained in Moscow, and was a Black September leader. He led a PLO intelligence unit. It is alleged that he gave warning of plots against the lives of American diplomats, including one against Henry Kissinger in December 1973 when he was visiting Lebanon; also that he provided protection for Kissinger and for Dean Brown. (Ignatius suggests that his death was caused by the Israelis on 22 January 1979, when he was caught in the blast from a car explosion as he was passing by.) Evidence for all this is lacking, and I remain sceptical of it, especially in the light of Kissinger's own assertion that the meeting in Rabat had no consequence.

14 The record of this interesting meeting was captured by the Israelis in Sidon, June 1982. See Raphael Israeli, *PLO in Lebanon: Selected Documents*, pp. 34–55.
15 *Al-Safir*, 23 July 1979.
16 *New York Times*, 7 October 1979.
17 In 1982 the lean towards the PLO of the British Foreign Office under Lord Carrington caused US Secretary of State Alexander Haig to call the British Foreign Secretary a 'duplicitous bastard'. Lord Carrington's successor, Francis Pym, blamed Israel for the breakdown of the talks between King Hussein and Arafat after the PNC at Algiers/in 1983, at which the PLO rejected the Reagan Plan and accepted the Fez Plan (see chapter 37). He advocated that the United States come 'closer to the Arab position set out in the Fez summit'; apparently suggesting a compromise between an independent state (as per Fez) and a dependent state (as per Reagan); no direct negotiations between Arab states and Israel (as per Fez) and direct negotiations (as per Reagan); inclusion of the PLO (Fez) and exclusion of the PLO (Reagan). This desire to have it both ways, though impossible, was in the sixty-year tradition of British Middle East policy. On 22 April 1983 a junior minister of the British Foreign Office flew to Tunis to talk to Farouq Qaddoumi, but this was not, according to the Foreign Office, to be interpreted as a sign of official recognition of the PLO.
18 Austria, under Chancellor Bruno Kreisky, was friendly to the PLO long before Arafat's official visit to the Chancellor. In September 1973, two armed Sa'iqa terrorists boarded a train in Czechoslovakia, armed with Kalashnikovs which were not taken from them at the frontier. Once in Austria, they seized three Jews, two of them old, and would not let them go until Kreisky agreed to close down the transit camp at Schonau Castle where emigrant Jews stopped on their journey from Russia to Israel. Kreisky did agree, and abided by the promise he had given to the terrorists. His sense of honour towards blackmailers was matched, or surpassed, by the Turkish government, which kept a promise to PLO terrorists that if they would come out peacefully from the Egyptian embassy, which they seized in August 1979, they would be granted diplomatic recognition and allowed to open a PLO office in Ankara.
19 See Juliana Geran Pilon, 'The United Nations Campaign against Israel', a project study for the Heritage Foundation, Washington DC, 16 June 1983.
20 The British government report on the Palestine Mandate to the League of Nations in 1925 admitted that there were still large numbers of slaves in Transjordan, and declared that any attempt to remedy their condition would be met with resistance from the slaves themselves. On 14 July 1960, Lord Maugham informed the House of Lords that he had heard eyewitness reports of children in fetters in a market-place in Saudi Arabia, and that he himself had bought a slave in North Africa (and then freed him) to prove that people were for sale in Arab states. Slavery was officially abolished in Saudi Arabia on 6 November 1962, but the UN Economic and Social Document on Slavery, 1965, reported that King Ibn Sa'ud still owned many slaves. Rumours of the traffic in slaves in Saudi Arabia were still circulating in 1983, but the ILO did not try to prove publicly whether they were founded or not.
21 BBC, 24 October 1979; *al-Watan al-Arabi*, 22–28 November 1979.

22 He was shot by a member of Abu Nidal's group, for details of which see chapter 34.

23 I found this document in the rubble of the bombed PLO prison in Sidon in August 1982.

Chapter 31 : The Popular Liberation War

1 See note 2, chapter 7.

2 Arafat announced at the fourteenth PNC in Damascus that $67 million had been paid to him personally during 1978 (*The Middle East*, March 1979). He was given an American aeroplane, a 'New Star', as a personal gift by the Saudi Foreign Minister, Sa'ud al-Faisal, in November 1979 (*al-Hawadith*, November 1979).

3 I found this document in the rubble of the bombed PLO prison in Sidon in August 1982.

Chapter 32 : The Armed Struggle

1 Some of the details of the incidents related in this chapter were collected in personal interviews with the victims by Ofra Ayalon (*Coping with Terrorism: The Israeli Case*).

Chapter 33 : World Revolution

1 Translation: Harkabi, *The Palestinian Covenant*, p. 145.

2 MENA, 20 March 1977. Translation: Yodfat and Arnon-Ohanna, *op. cit.*, Appendix Two.

3 Lebanese Forces Intelligence, confirmed to me by senior employees of Middle East Airlines in Sidon and Beirut.

4 For a full account see William Stevenson, *Ninety Minutes at Entebbe*.

5 For a full account see Peter Koch and Kai Hermann, *Assault at Mogadishu*.

6 PLO documents captured in Sidon by the Israelis in June 1981 give ample proof of this. One example, similar to many: a document of 17 March 1981, signed by one Halim Mamnoa, of the Qassam Brigade of Fatah, to 'Administration Affairs', informing that department that '12 guests from Rhodesia (Zimbabwe)' will require that an official 'attend to the matter of their flight from the airport on 19 March at 0700 p.m., and accompany them to the airport'. A final sentence reads: 'This matter is most urgent.' See also *al-Nahar*, 15 January 1981, which reported the arrival in Beirut as guests of the PLO of a group from El Salvador; members of the Chad National Liberation Front; and Basque revolutionaries from Spain. For many more connections between terrorist groups and the PLO, see Sterling, *op. cit.*; Goren, *op. cit.*; Israeli, *op. cit.*

Documents captured by the Israelis give details of the relationships between the foreign groups and the PLO: visits, training courses, lectures in ideology, etc. The PLO was host and trainer, and in addition PLO personnel were themselves received abroad and trained in the USSR, East Germany, Cuba and other Communist countries. See Israeli, *op. cit.*, especially section v.

7 There were two or three others according to Lebanese Forces Intelligence. It was common knowledge in Beirut that Chatila was the main camp for European terrorists. Muslim Lebanese told me they 'often' saw foreigners in Burj al-Barajneh.

8 *Daily Telegraph*, 1 December 1980.

9 The names of these organizations were painted on the walls of half-ruined houses in Damour. The quantity of evidence for the training of Turkish terrorists by the PLO is considerable. One example from the pages of a PLO office diary captured in Tyre in June 1982: '4 June, a group of five persons arrived from Turkey; 8 June, the course started for the comrades from Turkey; 4 July, the course of the comrades from Turkey was completed; 6 July, the Turkish group left.' The same diary recorded for different days, 26 February and 6 July: 'Final exams for the Salvadorean course'; 'The comrades from South Africa left today'; 'The training started for the comrades from Malawi'.

10 See, for example, *Der Spiegel*, 28 June 1982. For other forms of co-operation between both Nazis and neo-Nazis with the PLO, see Sterling, *op. cit.*, e.g. p. 113; *le Monde*, 7 March 1982, for a report on François Genoud, Lausanne banker (Banque Commercial Arabe), heir to the works of Josef Goebbels, and friend of the Grand Mufti, and patron of several members of the PFLP, including Bruno Breguet, a young Swiss who served seven years in Israel for attempted sabotage on behalf of the PFLP. See also chapter 28 above for co-operation between neo-Nazis in Britain and Muslims in anti-Jewish activity.

11 The rabbi of this synagogue, Michael Williams, was given this information by the police.

12 *Daily Telegraph*, 1 December 1980.

13 Goren, *op. cit.*, p. 236. 'Ambassador Soldatov was posted to Beirut from Cuba and is generally regarded as an expert on urban guerrilla warfare' (*ibid.*). All the embassies were in West Beirut, and after October 1978 when the Syrians left the PLO in charge of that part of the city, they were, though still officially accredited to the Lebanese government, unofficial legations to the PLO.

14 Lebanese in Beirut told me that they encountered Swedes and Norwegians among the Palestinians. The Israelis captured the two Norwegians and a Canadian in June 1982, took them back to Israel for interrogation, and soon released them. Captured documents revealed visits of Danish 'study groups' to the PFLP.

15 Beirut was an open refuge for members of European terrorist groups fleeing from the law. Hans Joachim Klein, one of the raiders of the OPEC meeting in Vienna (see chapter 30, the section on Libya) reported, after he had had a change of heart and repudiated terrorism, that he had encountered Juliane Plambeck, a member of the Movement 2nd June terrorist organization (see Becker, *op. cit.*), at a PLO training camp in September and October 1976, shortly before she went to Greece, where she was arrested and returned to West Germany (*Der Spiegel*, 3 November 1980). The close collaboration between West German terrorists and the PLO has frequently been demonstrated, with West Germans taking an active part in PLO-planned operations (e.g. the Entebbe hijacking), and with the demanding of their release from detention as part of the ransom for hostages captured by the PLO. The leaders of the Baader-Meinhof gang (or Red Army Faction) were given guerrilla training by the PFLP (see Becker, *op. cit.*, pp. 219–20). A Dutch woman, Ludwina Jensen, was arrested at Lod airport on 24 September 1977 while, by her own confession, employed on a mission for George Habash (*Die Welt*, 26 September 1977). Jörg Lang, lawyer and member of the Red Army Faction, was trained in a PFLP camp in Beirut (*Der Spiegel*, 28 June 1982). The *Economist's* Foreign Report of 14 February 1980 told how three members of the Italian Red Brigades were caught in Italy with SAM-7 missiles supplied by the PLO and smuggled in a Lebanese vessel. One of many documents captured by the Israelis in 1982 which proved that West Beirut under the PLO was the world headquarters for the terrorist war against the free world was one recording that two meetings had taken place with the Japanese Red Army; in the first 'they apologized for not supplying us [the PLO] with information on the crises and the international situation in Japan ... promised to supply us in the future with information [and] informed us that they will give us addresses of several Asian solidarity organizations *which could be utilized*'; and 'in the second meeting, practical problems were discussed'. I have added the italics because the phrase makes it clear that the PLO actively sought to make contact with subversives in the free world and put them to their uses.

16 In February 1978 a 5-ton load of weaponry bound for the IRA from the PLO stores in Beirut was intercepted at Antwerp (*Sunday Times*, 12 February 1978). The Fatah service card of one Stephen Robert Howe, cover name 'Qasim Muhammad Salim', a construction worker born 1955 in Northern Ireland, was found by the Israelis in 1982 among PLO documents. He had joined Fatah in November 1980.

17 *Daily Telegraph*, 24 November 1979.

18 *Observer*, 1 April 1979.

19 The estimated figures were given to me by senior personnel of Middle East Airlines in Sidon and Beirut.

Chapter 34 : Shattering Blows

1 Vocke, *op. cit.*, p. 54.

2 *Ibid.*, p. 55.

3 Abu Iyad (*op. cit.*, p. 296) says Kamal Jumblatt 'fell under Syrian bullets'. An Israeli academic assured me that Jumblatt was 'definitely' killed by men under the orders of the Syrian military commander, Rif'at Assad, brother of President Hafiz Assad. A Druze member of the Israeli Defence Force said that Lebanese Druze whom he knew – followers of Jumblatt's rival Majid Arslan – 'knew' the Syrians to be the murderers. Jumblatt was a nuisance to the Syrians, and murder is a political expedient which the ruling Ba'th Party of Syria has not shown itself averse to. Against the Christians being guilty, I have heard it argued that they knew only too well what the consequence would be to themselves; but then, risking and exacting vengeance is the whole story. Evidence of anyone's guilt is still missing.

4 Vocke, *op. cit.*, p. 57.

5 *Al-Usbu' al-Arabi*, 1 August 1977. The text of the Chtoura Agreement was not officially published. Its provisions were, however, set out in *Arabia and the Gulf*, 19 and 26 September 1977.

6 That Israel had become the main supplier of weapons to the Maronites from 1976 onwards, was information openly imparted in Israel in 1982, and reluctantly admitted in Mount Lebanon.

7 *New York Times*, 12 November 1977; *al-Safir*, 24 March 1978.

8 *Al-Sayyad*, 1 December 1979; *al-Nahar*, 29 November 1977.

9 MECS, 1977/8, p. 273.

10 *Monday Morning*, 24 June–1 July 1979.

11 *Al-Watan*, 18–19 January 1981.

12 Figures from Department of Information, Israeli Ministry of Foreign Affairs. Between 1967 and 1 January 1982, 346 residents of the West Bank and Gaza were killed by terrorists. Of these thirty-nine were children and fifty-nine were women. In the same period 1,764 were wounded, of whom 245 were children and 120 women.

13 Yodfat and Arnon-Ohanna, *op. cit.*, p. 9.

14 The Soviet Union's news media said that the thirty-two dead and eighty-two wounded (among whom were a number of children) were 'soldiers', and the engagement had been with 'army units' (Goren, *op. cit.*, p. 216).

15 'While the Israeli forces halted their advance and declared that they were preserving the ceasefire, our forces continued their constant shelling of the Israeli forces, because the ceasefire does not interest us at all.' 'The Eight Day War in the South', in *The 22nd of February*, 1979.

16 *Al-Amal*, 21 April 1978; Radio Beirut, 23 April 1978.

17 *Al-Qabas*, 28 May 1978.

18 Voice of Palestine (Lebanon), 25 May 1978.

19 *Arabia and the Gulf*, 15 May 1978.

20 *The Times*, 15 July 1978; *Guardian*, 15 August 1978.

21 Sabri al-Banna had been the Fatah representative in Baghdad. He rebelled against Arafat's authority and was sentenced to death in absentia by Fatah in 1974. He 'stated in an interview . . . in January 1975 that his group . . . had links throughout the Arab world that enabled it to take initiatives in the name of the PLO' (el-Rayyes and Nahas, *op. cit.*, pp. 35–6).

22 *Sunday Times*, 29 August 1982.

23 *Ibid.*

24 The ALF later supported the idea of dialogue (MECS, 1978/9, note 39 on p. 306).

25 The Central Committee was set up in May 1970 when agreement was reached among the main *fedayeen* groups in readiness for their takeover of the PLO. The PFLP and other groups, which had not until then co-operated with Fatah, were represented on it, and sat with three independents, the twelve members of the Executive Committee, the PNC Chairman and the Commander-in-Chief of the PLA. It met intermittently and faded out for a while, but was re-established towards the end of the 1970s.

26 Radio Baghdad, Voice of Palestine, 7 January 1979.
27 MECS, 1977/8, p. 604.
28 BBC, 19 March 1978.
29 *New York Times*, 25 May 1978; BBC, 31 May 1978.
30 Voice of Palestine (Lebanon), 18 April 1978.
31 *Al-Ra'y al-Amm*, 15 June 1978.
32 *Guardian*, 30 May 1978.
33 *Der Spiegel*, 19 June 1978.
34 *Observer*, 30 July 1978.
35 MECS, 1978/9, p. 286.

Chapter 35: Expulsion and Dispersion

1 MECS, 1979/80, p. 262. Most mercenaries came from African and Far Eastern countries: Bangladesh, Sri Lanka, Pakistan, Mauritania, Libya, India, Malaysia, Iran, South and North Yemen, Mozambique, Nigeria, Niger, Chad and Morocco. Some of them were drawn to Lebanon by the promise of work, and found themselves impressed into the PLO forces. This happened to some thousand or more Sri Lankans. Two to three hundred of them were killed in the 1982 war in the south. The survivors were flown back to Sri Lanka free of charge by British Airways.

2 *New York Post*, 8 September 1981. Between 500 and 700 PLO fighters were deployed within the UNIFIL area, according to the Israelis ('Operation Peace for Galilee', issued by the spokesman for the Israeli Defence Force). UNIFIL personnel 'were not permitted to enter terrorist positions within a radius of 500 metres'.

3 A document captured by the Israelis in June 1982 sets out the agreed conditions under which the PLO could man a certain observation post within the UNIFIL area (see p. 203).

4 I saw some of these underground arms stores in August 1982. One of them, at Damour, was dug deep into the mountain. In one of the tunnels there was a hill of Katyusha rockets lying unpacked in their boxes.

5 Lebanese Forces Command, Foreign Relations Department, 'The Issue of Lebanon', pp. 88–9. Also 'Operation Peace for Galilee'.

6 In the latter part of 1980, Abu Nidal moved his headquarters to Damascus, and began to get some assistance from Libya. His terrorists carried on killing Jews in Europe and Arafat's followers. In May 1981 they murdered the Chairman of the Israel-Austria Friendship Society, Heinz Nittel, and the following month the PLO representative in Belgium. The enmity between Iraq and Syria notwithstanding, either country might have used him that night for an act of revenge against an Israeli ambassador. Israel had annexed the Syrian Golan Heights some eighteen months earlier; and had bombed Iraq's French-supplied nuclear reactor on 7 June 1981.

7 See note 16, chapter 28.

8 See note 1, chapter 27.

9 'Operation Peace for Galilee'.

10 'Positions should be taken up in the built-up areas in Sidon, the refugee camps and the villages' (PLO battle order, 28 May 1981 – see Israeli, *op. cit.*, p. 214). On the PLO using civilians as shields, Bill Moyers, CBS network, 23 August 1982, said: 'Arafat led [the Palestinian fighters] into this cul de sac where they made their last stand behind the skirts of women and among the playgrounds of children.' Arthur J. Goldberg, former US Supreme Court Judge, wrote (*Jerusalem Post*, 6 August 1982): 'The hijacking of West Beirut's inhabitants is a most horrendous immorality committed not by Israel, but by the PLO.' He mentions in the same article that 'There is substantial evidence that the Israeli army, at great risk, has sought as best it could to minimize [civilian] casualties.' People in Tyre told me how the civilian population had been not only warned by the Israelis to move out before they entered the city for hand-to-hand fighting with the PLO, but actually evacuated on to the beach. Signs of the recent camping on the sand under the trees were still to be seen in August 1982. A Palestinian, Abbas al-Haj, told a reporter from the Israeli newspaper *Ha'aretz* (20 August 1982) that after the Israeli planes had dropped leaflets on his camp telling the civilians to leave, 'the PLO would not let anybody out. My neighbour, Saleh, tried to escape. They shot him in the back and tied him up in the square until he bled to death. Three hundred people were killed in our camp. Who is to blame for their death? Write it down – the PLO.'

11 While the Israelis remained in the Chouf region, the fighting between Maronites and Druze was intermittent and comparatively restrained. Both sides were willing, up to a point, to be co-operative with the Israelis' peace-keeping efforts. At that time the Maronites were still Israeli allies, though relations between the two were luke-warm. The existence of a Druze population in Israel loyal to the Israeli State was taken into consideration by the Druze of Lebanon, particularly by the followers of Majid Arslan, as also by the Israelis, and so a measure of amity between them was achieved. This meant that the Israelis could mediate between the two Lebanese groups. When the Israelis withdrew southwards from the Chouf, in early September 1983, the fighting between the two became much fiercer. Walid Jumblatt, son of Kamal, led a 'National Salvation Movement', a re-formed coalition of Islamo-Progressives supported by the Syrians. The fighting escalated into a new civil war waged against the Lebanese government which was supported by the International Force (USA, France, Italy and Britain). Massacres were again perpetrated on helpless civilians, thousands of whom, Christian and Muslim, fled south to seek the protection of the Israelis (BBC TV, 13 September 1983.)

12 The timing of the Israeli intervention was probably due at least in part to the approach of the presidential elections in Lebanon. Hopes that Bachir Gemayel could unite the country, and would recognize Israel and normalize relations with her, were obviously tempting. But if the Israeli leaders did pin so much hope on one man in an anarchic country of daily blood-letting, and a country, furthermore, mostly occupied by a Syrian army, their optimism outstripped hard-won knowledge of their region and their neighbours.

13 The votes were: for, 58; against, 3; abstention, 1. The turn-out was over two-thirds.

14 The PLO regarded the battle of Beirut as a political and propaganda victory.

This was true, if strange. The news media of the West, as well as of the Communist bloc, the Arab bloc and most of the Third World, reported the war sympathetically to the PLO, and so made it a victory for them, of a kind. ('What do you suppose the evacuation from Beirut would be like were there no cameras? . . . would there be . . . all those victory signs flashing from a defeated army? Without the cameras, the PLO revelers would be vastly more subdued – and then they would be gone' – R. Emmett Tyrell, 'How the Cameras Lied for the PLO', in *Washington Post*, 30 August 1982.) But also, still less credibly, the Organization represented the outcome as a military victory. 'The war that does not kill me makes me stronger,' Arafat said (*al-Mustaqbal*, 9 January 1982). PLO strategists reasoned as follows: Operation Karameh, 1968, was the 'one-day war'; Operation Qalakhat – the Israeli offensive on 'Fatahland' in 1972 – was the 'four-day war'; Operation Litani was the 'eight-day war', which was when the *fedayeen* surpassed the combined Arab states' performance in resisting Israel in 1967, the Six Day War; and in July 1981, the 'two week-war' was the PLO artillery bombardment of northern Galilee. As each battle in the sequence was 'inevitable', and as their resistance became 'inevitably and progressively stronger', each was a greater 'victory', proving an advance to ultimate 'total victory'.

Chapter 36: Sabra and Chatila

1 This information, and all that follows in this chapter, comes from the English version of the Kahan Report, published in February 1983, by the Kahan Commission, set up by the Government of Israel to inquire into the killings.

Chapter 37: Of Plans and Men

1 In 1978 Mustafa Dudein, formerly a West Bank minister in the Jordanian government, started a 'village league' in Hebron to improve the roads, schools, clinics, and water and electricity supplies in the villages. The idea spread, and seven leagues had been formed by 1983, with a total membership of over 40,000. The leaders are the heads of large families. Despite threats from Jordan to West Bank notables against co-operating with Israel, and the terrorism of the PLO, the village leagues continue to work with the Civil Administration of the occupied West Bank (or Judaea and Samaria, as the Israelis prefer to call the regions). It seems that the Israeli government hoped for a local leadership to arise from the leagues, but if so have been disappointed.

2 *Al-Hadaf*, 30 August 1980.

3 MECS, 1979/80, p. 274.

4 *Al-Quds*, 28 February 1980; *Economist*, 19 January 1980.

5 *Jerusalem Post Magazine*, 17 September 1982.

6 *Ibid.*

7 *Ibid.*

8 *Al-Nahar Arab Report and Memo,* 28 February 1983.

9 *Ibid.*

10 *Ibid.*

11 *Jewish Chronicle,* 22 April 1983, quoting King Hussein, from an interview he gave to *Wall Street Journal.*

12 *Daily Telegraph,* 12 April 1983.

Chapter 38: A Welter of Blood

1 On separate occasions I was told of this 'common knowledge' by an officer of the Kataeb, a member of Lebanese Forces Intelligence and an Israeli academic.

2 Eight batteries of high-altitude, long-range Soviet SAM-5 missiles were installed at four bases. Their range is at least 150 miles. See the *Economist's* Foreign Report, 17 February 1983, p. 4.

3 *Ibid.* 'A special suburb has been built [at Latakia] for the growing colony of Soviet personnel in Syria.'

4 No foreign reporters have been allowed near Hama by the Syrian government, and so all reports remain fragmentary and most uncertain. Neither the Arab League nor the World Islamic League, nor any other Arab or Islamic organization openly protested against the massacre.

5 At the end of June 1983, 500 people met at al-Aqsa Mosque to condemn the anti-Arafat rebellion and the 'Syrian and Libyan' backing of it. Leading institutions and organizations of the West Bank and Gaza issued a statement after the meeting to the same effect, and it was endorsed by a majority of the mayors and other persons in influential positions. To find out the views of the general public, the East Jerusalem Arabic daily, *al-Bayader,* conducted a poll of 777 West Bank residents between 22 and 28 June 1983. 92.1 per cent said they supported Arafat as leader of 'the Palestinian march', a rise of support since February 1983 of 2.3 per cent. (*Jerusalem Post International,* 3–9 July 1983.)

6 *Ibid.*

Conclusion

1 The quotation comes from the *Observer,* 9 October 1983.

2 This conversation took place in the spring of 1983, six months before the Geneva conference. Sari Nuseibeh is the son of Anwar Nuseibeh, who had been Secretary to Haj Amin al-Husseini's 'Government of All Palestine', but later accepted Abdullah's annexation of the West Bank and became Jordanian Defence Minister under King Hussein, and ambassador in London.

Bibliography

Books

Abu Iyad (as recorded by Eric Rouleau), *Palestinien sans Patrie* (French text), Edition Fayolle, Paris, 1978.

Aldington, Richard, *Lawrence of Arabia*, Collins, London, 1955.

Alush, Naji, *Arab Resistance in Palestine 1917–1948* (Arabic text), Dar al-Taliah, Beirut, 1970.

Alush, Naji, *Towards a New Palestinian Revolution* (Arabic text), Dar al-Taliah, Beirut, 1972.

Antonius, George, *The Arab Awakening*, Hamish Hamilton, London, 1955.

Aumann, Moshe, *Land Ownership in Palestine 1880–1948*, Israel Academic Committee on the Middle East, Jerusalem, 1976.

Avneri, Arieh L., *The Jewish Land Settlement and the Arab Claim of Dispossession (1878–1948)* (Hebrew text), Hakibbutz Hameuhad, 1980.

Becker, Jillian, *Hitler's Children: The Story of the Baader-Meinhof Terrorist Gang*, Panther, London, 1978.

Begin, Menachem, *The Revolt*, W. H. Allen, London, 1983.

Bulloch, John, *Death of a Country*, Weidenfeld & Nicolson, London, 1977.

Cattan, Henry, *Palestine, the Arabs and Israel*, Longmans, London, 1969.

Chami, Joseph G., *Days of Tragedy: Lebanon 1975–6*, Arab Printing Press, Beirut, 1983.

Chami, Joseph G., *Days of Wrath: Lebanon 1977–82*, Arab Printing Press, Beirut, 1983.

Churchill, Charles Henry, *The Druzes and the Maronites under Turkish Rule from 1840 to 1860*, Bernard Quaritch, London, 1862.

Demaris, Ovid, *Brothers in Blood: The International Terrorist Network*, Scribners, New York, 1977.

Dishon, Daniel (ed.), *Middle East Record* (vols 3–5), Israel Universities Press, for The Shiloah Center for Middle Eastern and African Studies, Tel Aviv University, 1971, 1973, 1977.

Dobson, Christopher, *Black September*, Robert Hale, London, 1974.

Dobson, Christopher and Payne, Ronald, *The Carlos Complex*, Hodder & Stoughton, London, 1977.

Esco Foundation for Palestine Inc., *Palestine: A Study of Jewish, Arab and British Policies*, Yale University Press, New Haven, 1947.

Flapan, Simha, *Zionism and the Palestinians*, Croom Helm, London, 1979.

Glubb, Sir John B., *A Soldier with the Arabs*, Hodder & Stoughton, London, 1957.

Golan, Galia, *The Soviet Union and the Palestine Liberation Organization: An Uneasy Alliance*, Praeger, New York, 1980.

Gordon, David C., *Lebanon: The Fragmented Nation*, Croom Helm, London, 1980.

Granott, A., *The Land System in Palestine*, Eyre & Spottiswoode, London, 1952.

Hadawi, Sami, *Bitter Harvest: Palestine between 1914–1979*, The New World Press, New York, 1967.

Harkabi, Y., *Arab Attitudes to Israel*, Keter House, Jerusalem, 1972.

Harkabi, Y., *Palestine and Israel*, Keter House, Jerusalem, 1974.

Harkabi, Y., *The Palestinian Covenant and its Meaning*, Vallentine, Mitchell, London, 1979.

Heikal, Mohamed, *The Road to Ramadan*, Collins, London, 1975.

Herzog, Chaim, *The Arab-Israeli Wars*, Arms & Armour Press, London, 1982.

Hirst, David, *The Gun and the Olive Branch*, Faber & Faber, London, 1977.

Hitti, Philip K., *History of the Arabs*, Macmillan, London, 1940.

Israeli, Raphael, *PLO in Lebanon: Selected Documents*, Weidenfeld & Nicolson, London, 1983.

Joumblatt, Kamal (as recorded by Philippe Lapousterle), *I Speak for Lebanon*, Zed Press, London, 1982.

Katz, Samuel, *Days of Fire*, W. H. Allen, London, 1968.

Katz, Samuel, *Battleground*, Bantam Books, New York, 1973.

Kayyali, A. W. (ed.), *Zionism, Imperialism and Racism*, Croom Helm, London, 1979.

Kazziha, Walid W., *Revolutionary Transformation in the Arab World*, C. Knight, London, 1975.

Kedourie, Elie, *England and the Middle East: The Destruction of the Ottoman Empire 1914–1921*, Bowes & Bowes, London, 1956.

Kedourie, Elie, *Nationalism*, Hutchinson, London, 1966.

Kedourie, Elie, *The Chatham House Version and Other Middle Eastern Studies*, Weidenfeld & Nicolson, London, 1970.

Kedourie, Elie, *In the Anglo-Arab Labyrinth: The McMahon-Husayn Correspondence and its Interpretations*, Cambridge University Press, Cambridge, 1976.

Kedourie, Elie, *Islam in the Modern World and Other Studies*, Mansell, London, 1980.

Kelly, John, *Arabia, the Gulf and the West*, Weidenfeld & Nicolson, London, 1980.

Khaled, Leila (ed. G. Hajjar), *My People Shall Live*, Hodder & Stoughton, London, 1973.

Kiernan, Thomas, *Yasir Arafat*, Abacus, London, 1976.

Kissinger, Henry, *Years of Upheaval*, Weidenfeld & Nicolson, London, 1982.

Kimche, Jon, *Seven Fallen Pillars: The Middle East 1915–1950*, Secker & Warburg, London, 1950.

Kimche, Jon, *The Second Arab Awakening*, Thames & Hudson, London, 1970.

Koch, Peter and Kai, Hermann, *Assault at Mogadishu*, Corgi, London, 1977.

Kriegel, Annie, *Israel, est-il coupable?* (French text), Éditions Robert Laffont, Paris, 1982.

Laffin, John, *Fedayeen*, Cassell, London, 1969.

Laffin, John, *The Dagger of Islam*, Sphere, London, 1979.

Laffin, John, *The PLO Connections*, Corgi, London, 1982.

Laqueur, Walter (ed.), *The Israel-Arab Reader*, Weidenfeld & Nicolson, London, 1969.

Lawrence, T. E., *Seven Pillars of Wisdom*, Jonathan Cape, London, 1935.

Legum, Colin, Shaked, Haim and Dishon, Daniel, *Middle East Contemporary Survey* (vols 1–5), Holmes & Meier, New York, for The Shiloah Institute of African and Oriental Studies, Tel Aviv University, 1978–83.

Levins, Hoag, *Arab Reach: The Secret War Against Israel*, Sidgwick & Jackson, London, 1983.

Lewis, Bernard, *The Assassins*, Weidenfeld & Nicolson, London, 1967.

Lewis, Bernard, *Islam in History*, Open Court, New York, 1972.

Lloyd George, David, *The Truth about the Peace Treaties* (2 vols), Victor Gollancz, London, 1938.

Mansour, Atallah, *Waiting for the Dawn*, Secker & Warburg, London, 1975.

Meinertzhagen, R., *Middle East Diary 1917–1956*, The Cresset Press, London, 1959.

Moynihan, David P., *A Dangerous Place*, Secker & Warburg, London, 1979.

Nutting, Anthony, *Nasser*, Constable, London, 1972.

O'Ballance, Edgar, *The Arab-Israeli War*, Faber & Faber, London, 1959.

Parkes, James, *Whose Land?*, Penguin, Harmondsworth, 1970.

Pearlman, Maurice, *The Mufti of Jerusalem*, Victor Gollancz, London, 1947.

Peretz, Don, *Israel and the Palestine Arabs*, The Middle East Institute, Washington DC, 1958.

Perlmutter, Amos, Handel, M. and Bar-Joseph, U., *Two Minutes Over Baghdad*, Corgi, London, 1982.

Polk, W. R., Stamler, D. M. and Asfour, E., *Backdrop to Tragedy: The Struggle for Palestine*, Beacon Press, Beacon Hill, Boston, 1957.

Porath, Y., *The Emergence of the Palestinian Arab National Movement*, vol. I, 1918–29, Frank Cass, London, 1974.

Porath, Y., *The Emergence of the Palestinian Arab National Movement*, vol. II, 1929–39, Frank Cass, London, 1977.

Prittie, Terence and Nelson, W. H., *The Economic War against the Jews*, Corgi, London, 1977.

Pryce-Jones, David, *The Face of Defeat: Palestinian Refugees and Guerrillas*, Weidenfeld & Nicolson, London, 1972.

El-Rayyas, Riad and Nahas, Dunia, *Guerrillas for Palestine*, Croom Helm, London, 1976.

Samuel, (Viscount) Herbert, *Memoirs*, Cresset Press, London, 1945.

Schama, Simon, *Two Rothschilds and the Land of Israel*, Collins, London, 1978.

Schiff, Zeev and Rothstein, Raphael, *Fedayeen*, Vallentine, Mitchell, London, 1972.

Shadid, Mohammed, *The United States and the Palestinians*, Croom Helm, London, 1979.

Sheehan, Eduard R., *The Arabs, Israelis and Kissinger*, Reader's Digest Press, New York, 1976.

Shuqairy, Ahmad, *Liberation – Not Negotiation*, PLO Research Centre, Beirut, 1966.

Sid-Ahmed, Mohamed, *After the Guns Fall Silent*, Croom Helm, London, 1976.

Simson, Hugh J., *British Rule and Rebellion*, Blackwood, Edinburgh & London, 1937.

Smith, Colin, *Carlos: Portrait of a Terrorist*, Sphere, London, 1976.

Sterling, Claire, *The Terror Network*, Weidenfeld & Nicolson, London, 1981.

Stevenson, William, *Ninety Minutes at Entebbe*, Bantam Books, New York, 1976.

Stone, Julius, *Israel and Palestine (Assault on the Law of Nations)*, John Hopkins University Press, Baltimore, 1981.

Tabbara, Lina M., *Survival in Beirut: A Diary of Civil War*, Onyx Press, London, 1977.

Tuma, Elias H. and Darin-Drabkin, H., *The Economic Case for Palestine*, Croom Helm, London, 1978.

Twain, Mark, *The Innocents Abroad*, American Publishing Co., Hartford, 1875.

Vocke, Harald, *The Lebanese War*, St Martin's Press, London, 1978.

Winstone, H. V. F., *The Illicit Adventure*, Jonathan Cape, London, 1982.

Yaari, Ehud, *Strike Terror*, Sabra Books, New York, 1970.

Yodfat, Aryeh Y. and Arnon-Ohanna, Yuval, *PLO Strategy and Tactics*, Croom Helm, London, 1981.

Ziff, William B., *The Rape of Palestine*, Greenwood Press, Westport, Conn., 1975.

Documents

'Abu Shadi', 'The Role of the Political Agent in Regard to the Masses: Educational Lecture for Officers in the Course in Memory of the Martyr, the Political Agent, Gazi Awad Zaidan' (Arabic text), Fatah, Supreme Command of al-Asifa Forces, Department of Drafting and Political Guidance, 1977; marked 'secret, limited circulation'.

Amnesty Report on the massacres at Hama, Syria, February 1982; Tadmur Prison, Syria, 1980; Hama, April 1981, Amnesty International, British Section, September 1983.

Anderson, Dewey *et al.*, 'The Arab Refugee Problem': Proposals submitted to the General Assembly of the United Nations, UN, New York, 1951.

Ayalon, Ofra, 'Coping with Terrorism: the Israeli Case', University of Haifa, 1982.

Bat Ye'or, 'Dhimmi Peoples: Oppressed Nations', Éditions de l'Avenir, Geneva, 1978.

Bat Ye'or and Littman, D., 'Protected Peoples Under Islam', Centre d'Information et de Documentation sur le Moyen-Orient, Geneva, 1976.

'Do You Know? Twenty Basic Facts About the Palestinian Question', The London Representative of the PLO.

Gervasi, Frank, 'Media Coverage: The War in Lebanon', Center for International Security, Washington, DC, 1982.

Goren, Roberta C., 'The Soviet Attitude and Policy to International Terrorism since 1917', unpublished Ph.D. thesis, London School of Economics, London University, November 1982.

Harkabi, Y., 'Fedayeen Action and Arab Strategy', Adelphi Papers No. 53, Institute for Strategic Studies, London, December 1968.

'The Issue of Lebanon: Elements for an Analytical Approach', Lebanese Forces Command, Foreign Relations Department, April 1982.

Kahan, Yitzhak, Barak, Aharon and Efrat, Yona, Final Report, the Commission of Inquiry into the Events at the Refugee Camps in Beirut, Government of Israel, 1983.

Lanir, Zvi, 'Israel's Involvement in Lebanon: A Precedent for an "Open" Game with Syria?', Center for Strategic Studies, Tel Aviv University, 1981.

Mahjub, Dr, 'Educational Lecture for Officers on Ideas and Alliances, Principles and Manoeuvres in the Course in Memory of the Martyr, the Hero Muhammad Ali' (Arabic text), Fatah, Supreme Command of al-Asifa Forces, Department of Drafting and Political Guidance, February 1978; marked 'limited circulation'.

'Operation Peace for Galilee', Spokesman for the Israeli Defence Force, June 1982.

Pilon, Juliana G., 'The United Nations Campaign against Israel', The Heritage Foundation, Washington, DC, 16 June 1983.

Record of the 2,282nd Meeting at the 29th Session of the General Assembly of the United Nations, 13 November 1974, UN, New York, 1974.

Report of the Court of Inquiry into the Disturbances at Jerusalem on the 4th April
and the following days, British Public Record Office, April 1920.
Sa'ad, Farid, 'Some Psychological Aspects of Political Propaganda' (Arabic
text), PLO Planning Centre, Beirut, 1977.
Sasser, Asher, 'A Political Biography of Wasfi al-Tall' (Hebrew text),
unpublished MA thesis, Tel Aviv University, School of History, March 1980.
Scully, Eileen, 'The PLO's Growing Latin American Base', The Heritage
Foundation, Washington, DC, 2 August 1983.
UNRWA 1982: an edited summary of the report of the Commissioner-General of
UNRWA to the UN General Assembly for the period of 1 July 81 to 30 June
82, UNRWA Public Information Division, Vienna, 1982.
'What is the PLO?', The London Representative of the PLO.

Newspapers, Magazines and Periodicals

al-Ahram, Cairo, 14 September 1969; 27 October 1969; 6 November 1969.
Akhbar al-Yawm, Cairo, 2 November 1974.
Akhir Sa'a, Cairo, 10 April 1968; 3 July 1968.
al-Amal, Beirut, 21 April 1978.
al-Anwar, Beirut, 31 August 1967; 11 December 1967; 11 April 1968; 8 March
1970; 15 March 1970.
Arabia and the Gulf, 19 September 1977; 26 September 1977; 15 May 1978.
Ba'th, Damascus, 27 April 1969; 28 April 1969.
al-Bayader, Jerusalem, 29 June 1983.
Christian Science Monitor, Boston, Mass., 8 March 1968.
Commentary, Ann Arbor, Mich., January 1975; May 1981; September 1982;
January 1983.
Daily Mirror, London, 28 July 1981.
Daily Telegraph, London, 29 March 1968; 4 April 1968; 24 November 1979; 1
December 1980; 15 July 1981; 12 April 1983.
al-Difa', Amman, 22 June 1965; 22 October 1969.
Economist, London, 2 October 1948; 1 March 1968; 19 January 1980.
Economist Foreign Report, London, 14 February 1980; 17 February 1983.
Encounter, London, September 1982.
Guardian, London, 30 May 1978; 15 August 1978.
Ha'aretz, Tel Aviv, 13 August 1968; 20 August 1982.
al-Hadaf, Beirut, 30 August 1980.
al-Hawadith, Beirut and London, 1 September 1967; 8 September 1967; 28 June
1968; 9 May 1969; 11 July 1969; 26 September 1969; 11 November 1979.
al-Hayat, Beirut, 20 March 1968; 2 July 1969; 29 March 1970; 22 May 1970.
Herald Examiner, Los Angeles, 13 July 1982.
al-Jarida, Beirut, 4 September 1967; 3 May 1969; 26 October 1969; 31 October
1969.
Jerusalem Post, Jerusalem, 13 October 1967; 25 May 1970; 18 July 1982; 6 August
1982; 13 August 1982; 17 September 1982.
Jerusalem Post International, Jerusalem, 9 July 1983; 6 November 1983.
Jewish Chronicle, London, 17 July 1981; 22 April 1983; 27 May 1983.
al-Jumhuriyya, Cairo, 25 April 1968; 6 January 1970.
Kull Shay', Beirut, 17 May 1969.
Literaturnaya Gazeta, Moscow, 14 August 1974.

London Labour Briefing, London, April 1983.

Maariv, Tel Aviv, 16 July 1982.

Merkur, Munich, 28 October 1980.

The Middle East, London, March 1979.

Monday Morning, Beirut, 24 June–1 July 1979; 25 February–2 March 1980; 27 March 1980.

le Monde, Paris, 27 March 1973; 7 March 1982.

al-Muharrir, Beirut, 16 May 1969.

al-Nahar Arab Report and Memo, 28 February 1983.

al-Nahar, Beirut, 17 March 1968; 30 and 31 December 1968; 27 October 1969; 15 May 1970; 10 March 1974; 29 November 1977; 15 January 1981.

New Life (British Asian Weekly), London, 7 August 1981.

New Outlook, Tel Aviv, 9 December 1981.

Newsweek, New York, 18 July 1982; 2 August 1982.

New Republic, Washington, DC, 10 March 1982; 19 May 1982.

New Worker, London, 15 July 1983.

New York Post, New York, 8 September 1981.

New York Times, New York, 3 November 1968; 14 November 1969; 12 December 1971; 12 November 1977; 25 May 1978; 7 October 1979; 25 July 1982; 15 July 1983.

Observer, London, 3 September 1967; 10 September 1967; 30 July 1978; 1 April 1979; 1 August 1982; 19 September 1982.

Palestine, Jordan, 15 June 1966; 5 July 1966.

al-Ra'y al-Amm, Kuwait, 15 June 1978.

al-Qabas, 28 May 1978.

al-Quds, Jerusalem, 28 February 1980.

al-Safa, Beirut, 13 July 1969.

al-Safir, Beirut, 24 March 1978; 23 July 1979.

al-Sayyad, Beirut, 23 January 1969; 3 July 1969; 1 December 1977.

Der Spiegel, Hamburg, 12 January 1976; 21 June 1976; 19 June 1978; 3 November 1980; 28 June 1982.

The Standard, London, 5 September 1983.

Sunday Times, London, 29 August 1982.

al-Tha'ir al-Arabi, (ALF) Beirut, 30 April 1982.

The Times, London, 4 June 1968; 29 September 1970; 29 November 1971; 15 July 1978; 2 March 1983.

Trouw, Amsterdam, 31 March 1977.

The 22nd February, (PDFLP) Beirut, 10th Anniversary Issue 1979.

UNRWA Review, New York, Information Paper No. 6, September 1962.

al-Usbu' al-Arabi, Beirut, 1 August 1977.

Wall Street Journal, New York, 10 February 1983.

al-Watan, Kuwait, 18–19 January 1981.

al-Yawm, Beirut, 2 May 1968.

Yawmiyyat Filastiniyya, Beirut, 23 April 1968; 30 May 1968.

Index